SWIMMING AND DIVING

SWIMMING

&

DIVING

DAVID A. ARMBRUSTER, Sr., B.A., M.A.

Associate Professor of Physical Education Emeritus
and Head Swimming Coach Emeritus, University of Iowa, Iowa City, Iowa;
elected to Swimming Hall of Fame of Fort Lauderdale, Florida,
December, 1966

ROBERT H. ALLEN, B.S., M.A.

Head Swimming Coach, University of Iowa, Iowa City, Iowa;
President, American College Swimming Coaches Association, 1966

HOBERT SHERWOOD BILLINGSLEY, B.S., M.S.

Diving Coach, Indiana University, Bloomington, Indiana;
U. S. Olympic Diving Coach, 1972

SIXTH EDITION

with 214 illustrations

THE C. V. MOSBY COMPANY

Saint Louis   1973

Cover photograph of Cindy Potter
courtesy Dr. Richard F. Lewis,
Cincinnati, Ohio

Preface

The material in this book has been presented with the idea of aiding beginning instructors and coaches and beginning swimmers and competitors, in addition to improving the techniques, skills, and performances of advanced swimmers and divers. To this end, the technique of each stroke and dive is presented in some detail. Where technique and form are somewhat involved, we have attempted to present each phase and illustration in a clear, logical, and orderly sequence so that both the high school and college athlete can easily understand the discussion. We do not claim that the methods and techniques of swimming and diving and the styles and methods of teaching, learning, and coaching are to be taken as absolute. We merely present them as a means of more nearly approaching the basic fundamental principles of the ideal.

We recognize the differences of opinion as to what constitutes good form in swimming and the different methods of teaching beginners. Kinesiologic and physiologic principles as well as physical laws were the guiding factors in presenting the material. An attempt is made to fit the discussions to practices that are recognized as being correct. Some new studies and techniques have been advanced as a result of experiments carried out at the University of Iowa. Where opinion was the only source material available, practices that are generally considered as being correct are given.

The diagrams presented in this book were drawn almost entirely from an underwater movie study of some of the world's greatest swimmers. These underwater motion picture studies, taken through underwater observation windows, have opened a new technique in the swimming world.

Our readers should bear in mind that this method is most accurate and desirable, since it eliminates distortion of light upon surface refraction. For example, the range action of a swimmer's flutter kick appears to be much smaller when it is viewed above the surface than when it is viewed below the surface.

Comparative records are presented. The work schedules given are designed for summer swimming programs for high school and college men and women. Personalities have been intentionally omitted.

Crawl stroke techniques are evaluated, and information on conditioning, training, and refinements in technique of the back crawl, the dolphin butterfly stroke, and the breast stroke are included. Topics on preparations for a swimming and diving meet, responsibilities of the various officials, and swimming pool design are presented.

The method of teaching beginners to swim presents a logical progression of water skills. The elementary back stroke, the resting back stroke, the inverted breast stroke, the side stroke, the trudgeon, double trudgeon, and trudgeon crawl stroke are discussed. A new stroke, the dolphin crawl, is introduced for the first time.

A new chapter, The Fundamental Techniques of Teaching and Learning Basic Diving, with complete emphasis on teaching the beginner basic dives, has been compiled by Jerry Darda, the University of Wisconsin Diving Coach.

Dr. Laurence Morehouse, Professor of

Physical Education, and Director, Human Performance Laboratory of the University of California at Los Angeles, has presented modern ideas, trends, and practices in the new chapter, Training and Conditioning.

We are indeed grateful for the excellent contribution of another new chapter, Specificity of Training, by one of the outstanding authorities in the field of swimming and research—Dr. Robert Bartels, Professor and Chairman of Graduate Studies, School of Health, Physical Education and Recreation at the Ohio State University. Dr. Bartels, the former Head Swimming Coach at Ohio State, is President of the College Swimming Coaches Association of America.

A suggested procedure for teaching water polo has been recommended by Alan Twietmeyer, Graduate Assistant at the University of Iowa.

We thank Dr. George Q. Rich, Associate Professor at San Fernando Valley State College, and Director of the Human Performance Laboratory, for his contribution of materials in the scuba chapter.

We also wish to express our gratitude to Dr. Leon E. Smith, Head of the University of Iowa Motor Performance Laboratory, and Dennis L. Vokolek, Lincoln, Nebraska, Swimming Coach, NAUI, for their contributions to the scuba chapter.

We wish also to acknowledge the expert advice and consultation of Neil Fisher, M.S. Civil Engineering, Associate Professor of Preventive Medicine and Environmental Health. Professor Fisher filled the role of sanitary consultant on swimming pool water analysis and hygiene.

Unfortunately it is impossible to mention everyone to whom we owe a grateful debt of thanks for advice and encouragement. However, we wish to express additional thanks to the following:

The late Dr. W. W. Tuttle, Professor of Physiology, University of Iowa, and Dr. L. E. Morehouse for their inspiration and guidance throughout the preparation of the book and for their counsel pertaining to matters of a physiologic nature; the late Dr. C. H. McCloy, Professor of Physical Education, University of Iowa, for his inspiration and encouragement; Dr. Arthur Wendler and Assistant Swimming Coach John Fitzpatrick, University of Iowa, for their helpful guidance in pacing plans; Mrs. Paul J. Cilek, former Iowa City AAU Secretary, for her contribution in the chapter pertaining to summer age-group swimming meets. Also, Dr. Donald Casady, Professor of Physical Education and former Diving Coach, University of Iowa, for guidance in diving; Mr. Lee Allen, Medical Illustrator, Department of Ophthalmology, University of Iowa Hospital, for the beautifully executed diagrams; Mr. Lee W. Cochran, Supervisor of Visual Instruction, University of Iowa, and his associate Mr. John Hedges, for their patient and accurate services in filming the motion pictures used; The Dolphin, a national honorary swimming fraternity, for rendering invaluable service in the promotion of swimming studies at the University of Iowa and for supplying moving picture materials for the filming of underwater pictures; those champions who performed before the cameras and the many former and present members of the university swimming teams; and the leading swimming and diving coaches in the United States, for their suggestions and discussions throughout these many pleasant years for the advancement and improvement of swimming and diving.

David A. Armbruster, Sr.
Robert H. Allen
Hobert S. Billingsley

Contents

SWIMMING AND DIVING

Chapter 1

Introduction—historical evolution of swimming and diving

Swimming and diving have been known as long as recorded history. The ancient Egyptian, Hittite, Assyrian, and Minoan civilizations have all left pictorial evidence of their knowledge of swimming and diving. Greek, Roman, and Scandinavian mythology all include mentions of great feats of swimming prowess. Other ancient narratives mention swimming in connection with religious rites, but these practices usually included dousing or bathing and not the art of moving progressively through the water.*

The earliest known book on swimming technique was written by Nicolas Wynman, a German professor of languages, in 1538.† A more scientific treatise was later written by Thevenot, a Frenchman, in a book entitled *The art of swimming*.‡ The method Thevenot described resembles closely that which we now designate as the breast stroke. The arms stroked sideward like the oars in rowing a boat, except that they were recovered under the water. The legs also stroked sideward in unison in an action similar to the kick of a frog. Although the breast stroke was not adapted to speed swimming, it had many

advantages that caused it to remain popular. The stroke gave the swimmer unobstructed forward vision and permitted more freedom for natural breathing. Stroking the arms under the surface prevented splashing the swimmer's face. The stroke thus gave the swimmer a feeling of stability, even in rough water. The pioneers constructed this stroke so well that it established the foundation of all strokes. This method of swimming still retains many of its original characteristics. It is the most seaworthy of all our modern strokes.

Benjamin Franklin was one of the earliest American experimenters in swimming. He realized at least as early as 1768 the importance of convincing learning swimmers of their buoyancy. In a letter to Oliver Neave advising him on how to learn to swim, Franklin suggested that he wade into a river breast deep, turn to face the shore, and then try to retrieve an egg from the bottom. His inability to do so was to convince him of his buoyancy. Similar methods are used today in working with beginning swimmers. Benjamin Franklin was also an early innovator with hand paddles and fins, as the following excerpt from a letter to M. Dubuorg indicates:

When I was a boy I made two oval palettes, each about ten inches long and six broad, with a hole for the thumb, in order to retain it fast in the palm of my hand. They much resembled a painter's palettes. In swimming I pushed the edges

---

*For a more complete account of historical swimming literature see Cureton, T. K.: How to teach swimming and diving, New York, 1934, Association Press, Chapter IV.

†Wynman, Nicolas: Colymbetes, sive de arte natanli dialogus et festivus et incundus lectu (Dutch Copy), Bavana, 1538, Ingolstdt. The title of this book is translated literally as follows: "The diver, or a dialogue, concerning the art of swimming, both pleasant and joyful to read."

‡Thevenot, M.: L'art de nager, Paris, 1696.

1

of these forward, and I struck the water with their flat surfaces as I drew them back. I remember I swam faster by means of these palettes, but they fatigued my wrists. I also fitted to the soles of my feet a kind of sandals; but I was not satisfied with them. . . .*

Franklin was probably swimming with a breast stroke. Using his famous kite, Franklin carried on more experiments in swimming. He flew his kite while floating on his back. The wind in the kite provided the propulsion to move him across a lake.†

SIDE UNDERARM STROKE

With the advance of swimming as a competitive sport, ways to speed up the breast stroke were sought. Some of its utilitarian values had to be sacrificed for the sake of speed. All of the foregoing strokes, that is, from the orthodox breast stroke era, have been originated and refined for speed in competition in less than 100 years. European coaches began practical experiments to devise methods that would reduce the resistance of the arms and legs under water. It was found that if the swimmer swam on his side, he could lift one arm over the water on the recovery of that arm and thereby speed the recovery as well as reduce the water resistance that impeded his forward motion. This shift to the side also necessitated an alteration of the leg action. A leg movement resembling that of the blades of scissors, in which the principles of the frog kick are employed in the horizontal position, was adopted. This stroke was called both the "side overarm" and the "English overarm," the names being descriptive of the arm action rather than the leg action. The best time recorded for swimming 100 yards with the English overarm stroke was 1:15.0, set by W. Cole of England at the first English championships in 1871. In the next 20 years this stroke was refined, and in 1895 J. H.

Tyers of England reduced the time for swimming 100 yards to 1:02.5.

Experimenters in swimming then reasoned that, if by lifting one arm out of the water at the completion of its pull greater speed was obtained, then further speed might be expected from recovering both arms out of the water. The first practical use of this principle was made by J. Trudgeon. Each arm was permitted to recover out of the water by rolling the body from side to side. A kick resembling the action of scissors occurred during each arm cycle. The stroke was named after its originator, Trudgeon, but was sometimes called the "alternating overarm" stroke. The success of this innovation as a speed stroke was proved by further time reductions for swimming 100 yards. In 1901 F. V. C. Lane of England used the trudgeon stroke and achieved the astounding time of one minute flat.

In 30 years the record for swimming the 100-yard crawl had been lowered 25 seconds. The first two eras in the history of speed swimming had produced considerable headway. During the English overarm era of 23 years, from 1871 to 1894, the swimming time for 100 yards improved 12.5 seconds. During the 7-year trudgeon era from 1894 to 1901, there was a further improvement in time of 0:02.5.*

So far, attention had been given only to the arm action. The legs had been only a little more than just trailing members. An analysis of the leg action employed by swimmers using the trudgeon stroke revealed three factors that had to be revised before the leg action could make a contribution to speed. First, the recovery phase of the trudgeon kick involved too much resistance to forward progression. Doubling up the legs and their lateral spread preliminary to the drive of the scissors kick, presented an op-

*Bigelow, John, editor: The works of Benjamin Franklin, vol. 4, New York, 1904, G. P. Putnam's Sons, pp. 447-448.
†Bigelow, John, editor: The works of Benjamin Franklin, vol. 5, pp. 4-6.

*Note: Although other distances were also being swum, the 100-yard event is alluded to, since records are most complete in this event. Also, this distance is excellent for measuring man's speed in water.

posing force that materially discounted the drive of the power phase of the kick. This counterforce had to be reduced. Second, the trudgeon kick had only one single unit of power for each arm cycle. A leg action that provided a continuous series of forward drives to each arm stroke was, therefore, sought. Third, the rhythm of the trudgeon kick did not synchronize with the alternating overarm stroke. The body had to be rolled from side to side in order to deliver a good scissors kick. This rolling movement retarded the action of the arms and had to be eliminated before better timing could be attained.

The delivery of one kick with each arm stroke in the refined, or double, trudgeon technique was an advance over the single kick for each arm cycle as employed by the side overarm swimmers. In order to double the number of leg kicks for each arm cycle, the width of the leg spread in the recovery phase was reduced. With this, the resistance to forward progression was also somewhat reduced.

The pause after each scissors kick in the side overarm stroke was eliminated in the trudgeon stroke. Although the leg action in the latter stroke was slow and each kick was performed in an alternately different position, the kick was somewhat continuous and resembled a fluttering action. The increase in leg kicks from one to two beats for each arm cycle in the change from the side overarm to the trudgeon stroke did not improve the timing, since the leg movement still had to be arrested in order to correspond with the recovery of the arms.

BEGINNING AND DEVELOPMENT OF THE CRAWL STROKE

In Australia a man named Richard Cavill conducted an experiment that demonstrated the ineffectiveness of the trudgeon kick when used with the alternating overarm stroke. Cavill observed a race between his brother, Tum, and a friend named Syd Davis. Both used the alternating overarm stroke, but Tum swam with his legs tied while Syd used the regular trudgeon kick. Tum was able to beat Syd. When Tum's legs were untied and they raced over the same distance again, this time both of them using both arms and legs, Syd beat Tum. Here was a demonstration that the trudgeon kick was a retarding rather than an advancing factor! Richard Cavill recalled a rapid, vertical action of the legs used by Alec Wickham of Colombo, Ceylon. He combined this leg action with the alternating overarm stroke and found that greater speed could thus be attained. This "Australian crawl" stroke was first introduced by Richard Cavill at the international championships in 1902. He lowered the world record for swimming 100 yards to 0:58.4 seconds. This new style immediately gained in popularity among the coaches of all nations, and soon the Australian crawl stroke was being swum in many parts of the world. The new leg action provided solutions to the three recognized drawbacks present in the trudgeon stroke. The kick was called the "flutter" kick, its name being descriptive of the thrashing action of the legs. The recovery phase of this leg action offered only a small resistance to forward progression. It provided a continuous series of four power units for each arm cycle and was easily synchronized with the alternating overarm stroke. The reciprocal succession of acceleration and deceleration had been diminished, and now the forward progression was steady and more economically derived. The increased power from the legs in using the flutter kick permitted the body to maintain a position at the surface of the water, which reduced the resistance of the water to the body considerably. The introduction of the flutter kick in 1902 established a new era in speed swimming.

There were still a few mechanical mysteries pertaining to the flutter kick that remained to be solved. The theory that the straightening of the bent leg at the knee pushed the water backward and provided the main propulsive force that drove the swimmer forward was still held. This propelling force was also thought to be supplemented by squeezing the water from between the legs as they came together. That phase of the leg action in which the legs are thrust vertically apart was considered to be a recovery phase only and, as such, provided no forward propelling force. The emphasis was therefore placed on the extension of the knee and the closing of the legs.

The face was held down in the water, and the arms were moved in a crawling fashion. Because of the peculiar appearance of this stroke, it was first called the "creeping crawl" stroke.

American coaches sought to meet the keen competition by revising this new speed stroke. They increased the leg action from four to six beats to each arm cycle. An eight-beat kick was tried but was found to be too fatiguing and was soon abandoned. The crawl stroke was confined to use in short distances only, since the swimmers were soon out of breath. A system of breath control was developed in which the swimmer raised his head forward for a gasp of air and then slowly bubbled it out under water. This so-called "underwater breathing" contributed to swimming performance over greater distances. Later it was found that breathing could be further improved by turning the face to the side for the inhalation.

A slightly "pigeon-toed" position of the feet was introduced in order to present a greater surface area to the water during the flutter kick. A further refinement by American coaches included a brief relaxation period for the arms. This occurred during the recovery phase while the arm was above the surface of the water. The coaches in the United States termed this revised edition of the Australian crawl stroke the "American crawl" stroke.

The results attained by the American coaches in perfecting the crawl stroke soon became evident. In 1906, Charles M. Daniels became the first United States speed swimming champion of the world. He low-

ered the 100-yard swimming record to 0:55.4 seconds. The crawl became so popular that it was the first stroke taught to beginners. "Duke" Kahanamoku, a Hawaiian, using the American crawl stroke, lowered Daniel's record to 0:54.6 seconds for 100 yards. This record was made in 1913 and remained unbroken until 1923. Kahanamoku's chief asset was a pair of long, broad feet, which provided a large surface for propulsive action. He was tall and powerful and used a tremendous leg action. He was one of the first great swimmers to develop a purely vertical, full-measured, six-beat flutter kick to each arm cycle.

The leg action that was generally used at that time was the "trudgecrawl" kick, developed by Frank Sullivan of Chicago for distance swimmers. Six beats for each arm cycle were used. The first and the fourth beats were wide and scissorslike. These were called the major beats. The second, third, fifth, and sixth were narrow and faster. These were called the minor beats. The popular use of the trudge-crawl kick was gradually replaced by the faster, evenly measured, vertical flutter kick.

In 1923, Johnny Weissmuller, then 17 years old, lowered Kahanamoku's record to 0:52.8 seconds. In 1927, he lowered it again to 0:51.0 seconds. During this same year, Weissmuller, in a 20-yard course, swam 100 yards in 0:49.8 seconds. In 7 years he established over fifty American and world records.

Weissmuller introduced four new and significant developments in the speed crawl stroke*

1. The pull-and-push power arm stroke in which the pull starts from a straight arm action as soon as the arm enters the water. The arm is pressed down and slightly inward until it reaches a point just ahead of the shoulder. Here the arm is bent slightly at the elbow, re-

*Weissmuller, John, and Bush, Clarence: Swimming the American crawl, Boston, 1930, Houghton Mifflin Co.

sembling a boomerang, and from this point continues in a pushing delivery.

2. The turning of the head for breathing, which was independent of the arm action.
3. A deep leg action for the flutter kick in order to obtain greater traction in the water.
4. The deeper leg action, which allowed the chest and shoulders to be carried higher.

In the 1928 Olympic Games, Weissmuller captured nearly all of the sprint swimming championship titles. His style was generally accepted by American swimmers and coaches as the best speed swimming stroke in existence. The youth of this country set about to master this stroke with the aid of a special device that was soon to aid in again revolutionizing the speed swimming stroke. This special device was the slowmotion picture camera.* Many miles of film were distributed, which showed both out-of-the-water and underwater shots of Weissmuller's speed swimming style.

The use of these films was not limited to the Americans, however; Weissmuller and other American and European swimmers were photographed in action from all directions by the Japanese swimming technicians. These films were taken to Japan and were widely exhibited among the Japanese schools. These school children thus observed and were coached in the best styles from early youth, and through intensive training some of them were able to overcome all competition in speed swimming at the 1932 Olympic Games in Los Angeles. Four years before, in the 1928 Olympics, they won only the 200-meter breast stroke event. In 1932 they won every swimming event except the 400-meter freestyle.

The Japanese style contained nothing new

but was essentially a combination of the best speed swimming mechanics used by previous champions. The essential features of the arm action were the quick recovery and long glide of each arm after it entered the water. This style was introduced by Buster Crabbe and his coach, "Dad" Center from Hawaii, at the 1928 United States Olympic tryouts.

A great portion of the success of the Japanese could be ascribed to their superb physical condition. This condition was the result of a careful control of diet, exercise, and rest, as well as a rigorous training regime.

Although overshadowed by Japanese successes, two other styles of the crawl stroke were seen at the 1932 Olympics. Many European swimmers used a peculiar arm action in which the arms recovered with a low, lateral, straight arm sweep above the surface of the water. The arm action of this European crawl stroke resembled the sweep of a scythe. Another crawl style, used by the women's team from Holland, employed a high, straight arm recovery and smashed the arms into the water as the recovery was completed. This method is presently called opposition rhythm; that is, as the arm enters the water, it immediately goes into its press, catch, and pull, thus eliminating the glide of the arm almost entirely.

American swimmers and their coaches returned from the 1932 games with a determination to develop their style and condition in order to recover the swimming crowns lost to the Japanese. Their efforts were rewarded at the 1936 games in Berlin where they were successful in winning the Olympic swimming and diving championships.

Again in Los Angeles in the summer of 1949 at the National Amateur Athletic Association Swimming Championships, the Japanese gained sweeping victories in the crawl stroke events. This time they had something new. Although underwater movies were not taken at this time, Furuhashi, whose performance was most outstanding, was watched very closely by keen-eyed ob-

---

*In 1928 Armbruster introduced underwater movies of swimming strokes before the American College Swimming Coaches Association Forum in Fort Lauderdale, Florida. These movies were taken from the observation underwater windows of the University of Iowa fieldhouse swimming pool.

servers. What was seen was a feature that Jam Handy, a Detroit producer of training films, had suggested at the coaches' meeting in Florida the winter before and what McCloy and Armbruster, working with hydraulics engineers, were learning from tedious research studies at the University of Iowa. It was this. Simply by shortening two of the beats of the six-beat flutter kick, some of the parasitic drag of the legs during the arm pull is reduced. Also, the slide of the supporting arm at the entry is eliminated so that the arm goes deeper for the catch and is thus more effective. This change in arm entry allows the shoulder of the pulling arm to be lowered, thus allowing the water to wash over it. This reduces the resistive bow wave ahead of the swimmer. However, the shoulder must remain on top of the hand and elbow as it goes down for the deeper catch.

Research studies of the arms and legs acting separately in swimming the crawl stroke have shown that the ratio of propulsive force between the arms and legs is approximately 70 to 30 in favor of the arms. At present this ratio is even greater in favor of the arms. It is obvious, then, that in coordinating the arm and leg action, when a compromise must be made, it should be in favor of the arm action.

In the 1956 Olympic Games at Melbourne, Australia, the Australian men's team won five of the nine gold medals, while the United States team won two. The Australian women's team, led by Dawn Frazer, won every freestyle event, including the 400-meter freestyle relay.

The outstanding success of the Australian swimmers became a challenge to the American coaches and swimmers. A study of the Australian swimming program indicated little differences in stroke technique, except for a greater roll of the body along its longitudinal axis. The training method was the big factor. The Australian was swimming more often, the total mileage of each workout was greater, and the stress placed upon the swimmer was more severe.

The desire on the part of the American coaches and swimmers to regain lost prestige led to the adoption of training methods used by track coaches and runners in breaking the 4-minute mile. The emphasis placed on training young swimmers, the popularity of the summer age group competitive program, and the application of new theories and techniques by swimming coaches were instrumental in the great success by the American swimmers in the 1960, 1964, and 1968 Olympic Games.

During the 1964 Olympic games Donald Schollander, an 18-year-old member of the United States Olympic team, was the first swimmer to ever win four gold Olympic medals. He won the 100-meter freestyle, the 400-meter freestyle, setting a new world record, and he anchored the 4 × 100-meter and the 4 × 200-meter relays. He was voted the outstanding athlete of the games and was elected to carry the American flag in the closing ceremonies of the Games.

Five new world records were set in the 1968 Olympic Games held in Mexico City in spite of the altitude. Mike Wenden of Australia set a mark of 52.2 in winning the 100-meter freestyle event. Debbie Meyer, a 16 year old, was the outstanding woman swimmer in the United States. She won three gold Olympic medals and set four world freestyle records during the year.

200 meters in	2:06.7
400 meters in	4:24.5
800 meters in	9:10.4
1500 meters in	17:31.2

Shane Gould the 14-year-old Australian woman swimming champion set four new world records and tied another in 1971.

100 meters	*tie*	0:58.9
200 meters in	2:05
400 meters in	4:21.2
800 meters in	8:51.8
1500 meters in	17:06

American Mark Spitz astounded the swimming world at the 1972 Olympic Games held in Munich, Germany. Spitz won four individual gold medals all in world record times.

He swam on three relay teams that also won the gold medals, setting three more world records.

Champions have always had a large following. Some swimmers have become champions in spite of an arm stroke or leg kick that was mechanically unsound. A great many swimmers and some coaches have sought to copy the style of a champion on the theory that, if it was good for the champion, it was good enough for them. Others believed that certain styles should be adapted to athletes of a certain build. Many coaches contended that Weissmuller's style could be used by tall swimmers but that it was not suitable to those of less height.

The development of the technique of swimming the American crawl stroke has evolved from the trial-and-error method of experimentation, the criterion of the success of certain innovations being the increase in speed in swimming. The constant lowering of records is a good indication that the mechanics of the swimming strokes are still being improved.

ORIGIN AND DEVELOPMENT OF THE DOLPHIN BUTTERFLY STROKE

The underwater recovery of the arms and legs was the retarding factor in the breast stroke. The best time for swimming 100 yards using the breast stroke was 1:07.0 until in 1934 an arm stroke that complied with the rules and yet employed an out-of-the-water recovery was discovered. The recovery was a double overarm stroke in which the arms were simultaneously swung laterally and then forward. The swimmer resembled a butterfly in flight, and the name "butterfly" was given to this stroke.

Using the new butterfly breast stroke, 100 yards was swum in 1:05.0, a new record for the breast stroke. Although this stroke did not violate any of the rules pertaining to the breast stroke, it was a departure from the orthodox method, and it met with disapproval among many coaches and officials. The International Swimming Federation gave it sanction for universal use in 1937.

Later the butterfly breast stroke was permitted only if used throughout the entire race. There was at this stage of development no interchange permitted between the butterfly and orthodox styles in international competition. In fact the FINA* then went on record of dividing the breast stroke into two categories: the orthodox and the butterfly. In the butterfly style either the breast stroke kick or the dolphin fishtail kick may be employed, so long as they are executed in unison. For speed the dolphin butterfly stroke is now in second place to the sprint crawl stroke.

American records for the short course as established up to 1972 are as follows:

	NCAA
100 yards freestyle	0:45.00
100 yards butterfly	0:47.98
100 yards back	0:51.29
100 yards breast	0:56.83

The butterfly breast stroke was faster than the orthodox, but it still had a retarding factor to greater speed, the so-called frog kick, which had to recover under water and against forward progress.

With this new and faster arm action, the retarded recovery action of the legs became a matter of Armbruster's attention. In 1935 Jack Sieg, a University of Iowa swimmer, developed the skill of swimming on his side and beating his legs in unison similar to the action of a fish's tail. He was then asked to try the same leg action while swimming face down. With a little practice Sieg could perform the leg action just as efficiently in this position. Finally Armbruster and Sieg combined the butterfly arm action with this leg action and found that the two could be synchronized. Swimming with two leg beats to each butterfly arm action, Sieg swam 100 yards in 1:00.2. This kick was named the "dolphin fishtail" kick.†

The dolphin fishtail butterfly stroke has at

*Federation Internationale de Natation Amateur.
†Armbruster, David A.: The dolphin breast stroke, Journal of Health and Physical Education 6:23-26 (April), 1935.

present been so well refined that it now is in second place to the crawl stroke in speed.

It has taken the rule makers approximately 20 years, after much debate, to legalize this stroke. It was used for the first time in Olympic competition in 1956 at Melbourne, Australia.

The dolphin kick was ruled illegal because the legs moved in a vertical plane; also the soles of the feet did not engage the water on the downbeat of the kick as was required of the orthodox breast stroke.

Today, the dolphin kick is still the fastest of all kicks used by man in the water.

Originally, the butterfly arm action was combined with the orthodox breast stroke kick in order to give the stroke greater speed. However, later, this same butterfly arm action was combined with the newly discovered dolphin kick, giving the entire stroke surprisingly much greater speed, in fact, so much greater speed that the original butterfly breast stroke has at this writing become obsolete as a competitive stroke. For this reason the butterfly breast stroke is not discussed in this writing.

ORIGIN AND DEVELOPMENT OF THE BACK CRAWL STROKE

The origin and development of the back crawl dates back to 1902, at about the time that Richard Cavill was combining the flutter kick with the trudgeon crawl. The back crawl stroke, in fact, is a by-product of the crawl stroke. In its early form its was also a by-product of the breast stroke, since the breast stroke kick and double overarm action were used. This inverted breast stroke was soon abandoned as a possible competitive stroke, since it was too slow and served only to duplicate the regular breast stroke.

Previous to 1902 the back stroke had been considered to be nothing more than a stunt, combining a sculling action of the hands with a leg action similar to a flutter kick. Following an attempt to make the back stroke a speed swimming event by inverting the breast stroke, it was noticed that an inverted reverse alternating overarm

crawl combined with the inverted flutter kick resulted in a stroke that gave more speed than the breast stroke. Jam Handy, then swimming at the Illinois Athletic Club of Chicago, and his coach did the foundation work in developing this style of swimming. In 1912 the back crawl stroke was established as a competitive swimming event and was gradually improved through the years by many refinements.

In 1935, a Chicago schoolboy, Adolph Kiefer, swam the back crawl stroke for 100 yards in 0:57.6. The technique developed by Kiefer contained three features that distinguished his back crawl stroke from the generally used form. First, the recovery of the arms was made in a very low, lateral fashion, with the arms held straight. Second, the arms entered the water just above a line opposite the shoulders instead of straight up from the shoulders, alongside the head. Third, the arms were drawn through the water just below the surface as contrasted with the deep pull then employed generally and were held straight. At present the current trend in the back crawl stroke is a high recovery of the arms followed by a slightly deeper purchase and pull of the arms. Two styles of pull, the straight arm and the bent elbow pull, are both being used to advantage. However, most champions of today are using the bent elbow pull-and-push drive.

The sensational performances of the American swimming team in the 1960 Olympic Games were largely the result of the increased emphasis on conditioning and training since the 1952 games. The American coaches and swimmers generally followed a program of workouts consisting of a great number of sprint repetitions of distances from 400 meters to 25 yards, with predetermined rest intervals. This type of conditioning has replaced the longer distance, slower type of swimming of each workout. Then, too, champion swimmers work out two and three times a day, the year around. This type of conditioning has given the American swimmers nothing short

ALL-STROKE ARMBRUSTER METHOD

PROGRESSIVE LEARNING PROCEDURE CHART FOR SCHOOL SWIMMING

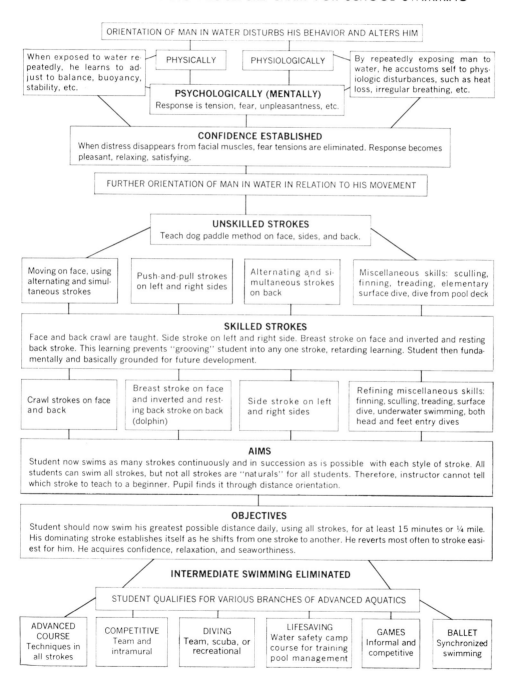

ORIENTATION OF MAN IN WATER DISTURBS HIS BEHAVIOR AND ALTERS HIM

When exposed to water repeatedly, he learns to adjust to balance, buoyancy, stability, etc.

PHYSICALLY

PHYSIOLOGICALLY

By repeatedly exposing man to water, he accustoms self to physiologic disturbances, such as heat loss, irregular breathing, etc.

PSYCHOLOGICALLY (MENTALLY)
Response is tension, fear, unpleasantness, etc.

CONFIDENCE ESTABLISHED
When distress disappears from facial muscles, fear tensions are eliminated. Response becomes pleasant, relaxing, satisfying.

FURTHER ORIENTATION OF MAN IN WATER IN RELATION TO HIS MOVEMENT

UNSKILLED STROKES
Teach dog paddle method on face, sides, and back.

Moving on face, using alternating and simultaneous strokes

Push-and-pull strokes on left and right sides

Alternating and simultaneous strokes on back

Miscellaneous skills: sculling, finning, treading, elementary surface dive, dive from pool deck

SKILLED STROKES
Face and back crawl are taught. Side stroke on left and right side. Breast stroke on face and inverted and resting back stroke. This learning prevents "grooving" student into any one stroke, retarding learning. Student then fundamentally and basically grounded for future development.

Crawl strokes on face and back

Breast stroke on face and inverted and resting back stroke on back (dolphin)

Side stroke on left and right sides

Refining miscellaneous skills: finning, sculling, treading, surface dive, underwater swimming, both head and feet entry dives

AIMS
Student now swims as many strokes continuously and in succession as is possible with each style of stroke. All students can swim all strokes, but not all strokes are "naturals" for all students. Therefore, instructor cannot tell which stroke to teach to a beginner. Pupil finds it through distance orientation.

OBJECTIVES
Student should now swim his greatest possible distance daily, using all strokes, for at least 15 minutes or ¼ mile. His dominating stroke establishes itself as he shifts from one stroke to another. He reverts most often to stroke easiest for him. He acquires confidence, relaxation, and seaworthiness.

INTERMEDIATE SWIMMING ELIMINATED

STUDENT QUALIFIES FOR VARIOUS BRANCHES OF ADVANCED AQUATICS

ADVANCED COURSE
Techniques in all strokes

COMPETITIVE
Team and intramural

DIVING
Team, scuba, or recreational

LIFESAVING
Water safety camp course for training pool management

GAMES
Informal and competitive

BALLET
Synchronized swimming

of phenomenal performances at the 1968 games. At present, the American high school and summer age-group swimmers are also responding to this type of conditioning. One need only look at their sensational performances from year to year. This holds very great promise for future Olympics.

The quest for speed has brought about revolutionary changes in swimming styles in the past two and one half centuries. It is expected that this advancement will be continued. Swimming and diving performance is gradually improving. This improvement is brought about mainly by refinement of techniques, more rigorous training, and better diet habits. The most important single factor that has put the United States out in front in the swimming world today is the great impetus given to this sport by the school, youth age swimming clubs, and groups actively engaged in competitive swimming and diving all over the country. The techniques used by swimmers and divers today are not to be considered an ultimate refinement.

DIVING

Competitive diving is an outgrowth of aerial acrobatics and tumbling. The first recorded diving competition took place in England in 1905. Since that time, diving has been an integral part of the competitive water sports program. Feats of diving have been recorded as early as 1871, when divers were reported to have plunged from London Bridge and other high places.

From the simple head-first and feet-first dives, there have been developed more than one hundred fancy dives. These are combinations of forward dives, backward dives, handstands and twists, somersaults, reverse dives, and jackknives and inward dives. They are performed in either a straight, pike, tuck, or free position. They are executed from either the low or high board or from a high platform.

The construction of new platform diving facilities and the increased interest in tower diving stimulated by the Pan-American and Olympic Games competition has helped to maintain the prestige of the American divers as being the best in the world.

The disciplines of the sciences of physics, physiology, kinesiology, and psychology are continually being applied in attempts to improve swimming and diving to greater performances. The application of the scientific method in testing new techniques is transforming swimming from an art to a science.

ALL-STROKE ARMBRUSTER METHOD FOR TEACHING BEGINNING SWIMMING

The all-stroke Armbruster method not only teaches all of the skilled swimming strokes but is a sound method of teaching beginners to swim. We call this method the all-stroke Armbruster method. Its aim and objective is to teach all of the skilled swimming strokes to the beginning student. He is thoroughly and basically grounded in all levels of aquatics. After completion of the course, should he not desire to enroll for more advanced classes in water training, he most certainly has been well grounded to be safe and able to manage himself adequately and satisfactorily in water.

This method has been used at the University of Iowa by us for the past 20 years with the younger-aged students, at the college age level, and in summer school with adult students to 60 years of age.

This method has produced tremendous results for students as a whole. If taught intensively, it creates tremendous interest. Discipline is no longer a problem because action creates interest.

This type of program speeds up the advancement of the student from the beginning level to the advanced levels. It eliminates the intermediate levels. It absorbs and stimulates the student's interest and is a challenging motivation for him to continue in the advanced areas. He now has acquired an urge to enter lifesaving, ballet, or varsity swimming.

The accompanying plan for an all-around school or college aquatic program is recommended.

Chapter 2

The all-stroke Armbruster method for teaching beginning swimming*

No instructor can truthfully stand in front of a class in beginning swimming and say, "We will teach you the crawl stroke or any other stroke in this course." All members of his class undoubtedly will swim the crawl, but it will not be a natural stroke for all members of the class.

Human beings differ physically in many respects—some have short or long necks, small or large hands or feet, a short or long torso, and short or long arms and legs. All of these physical characteristics may be a physical limitation to some students as they try to swim comfortably the crawl, back, side, breast or dolphin stroke. All persons can swim any one of the fundamental strokes, but not all swimmers can swim all strokes equally well and swim them with comfort and ease. Therefore, if the student is well grounded in the various categories of strokes and is well trained and orientated in a distance swimming program, somewhere within these categories of strokes (as he swims along) he finds one or two strokes that tire him least. He naturally resorts to them more often while learning in order to extend himself in distance swimming. For example, one need only look at any one of the top medley swimmers in the competitive field. Within the four styles that he swims, there will be one or two styles in which he is weaker, even though he swims

the strokes well. One of the styles (usually the one he is least adept in) will be the one he likes least. This only proves that all students can swim all strokes, but not all students can swim all strokes equally well with ease and comfort.

It is then a problem for the student, not the instructor, to find his most pleasurable and satisfying stroke, or strokes, and to make these predominant through his orientation in distance swimming during his class instruction practices.

If the all-stroke method is used, the instructor should have at least two class periods per week for one semester. Three periods are better. At the end of the course these beginners are fundamentally and basically grounded in all strokes. The student should be able to swim each of the fundamental strokes at least 50 yards before attempting distance orientation. He is easily beyond the intermediate level and can now enter an advanced class, a lifesaving class, or try out for the swimming squad.

PREWATER CONDITIONING— MENTAL ATTITUDE

A nonswimmer's mental attitude will influence his progress considerably in the early stages of learning. A favorable mental attitude that depicts the desire to achieve the objective and the courage and willingness to follow instructions is highly desirable. The swimming instructor can establish a sound basis for proper mental attitude before tak-

*Formerly called the all-stroke Iowa method for teaching beginning swimming.

ing a class into the water by means of a group discussion.

The time devoted to prewater conditioning may be determined by the age level of the class. Adults and young adults want to know how and why and derive considerable benefit from the discussion. However the interest span of the very young is limited; they want action and tend to progress faster by imitation and progressive water drills that are associated with fun and games. The beginning swimmer should be aware of what to anticipate as he enters the water. When he enters into water at navel depth, the respiratory center is affected, resulting momentarily in irregular breathing. He may momentarily gasp for breath and have difficulty in exhaling. The muscles tense, and he may shiver as a result of the loss of body heat. This experience is quite comparable to that of standing under a cool shower, and, when it is explained in this manner, it becomes less frightening and more understandable. Standing in chest-deep water, he may experience difficulty in maintaining balance because of buoyancy and loss of body weight. When he bobs up and down and moves about, he quickly learns to establish balance. His body gradually adjusts to unstableness in water, and he experiences a feeling of well-being and vitality.

In extreme cases because of this unstable feeling in water, some individuals may at first be reluctant to move from the end of the pool where they cling tightly to the side of the pool for support. It is advisable to allow these students to maintain this position for a short period, gradually dipping up and down until they develop the courage to move toward deeper water without support. The instructor may hold such a student by the arm and guide him as he bolsters his morale. Encouragement and praise help tremendously at this point.

When a student submerges his face beneath the surface, several new sensations are evident. Water irritates the nose, eyes, and ears. The typical reaction is to recover a standing position and rub the closed eyes. Rubbing the eyes can be eliminated if the eyes are squeezed shut and blinked several times. This procedure will minimize irritation to the eyes. The skill of submerging with the eyes open, which at first seems uncomfortable, becomes a very satisfying experience with repetition. One has only to observe a group of youngsters at play in the water to realize the pleasure they derive from underwater activity. They appear to be under the water more than they are above it. Fears and insecurity generally can be attributed to the unknown. When the pupil is informed as to what to anticipate and what his role must be to overcome the obstacles present, his chance of achieving the desired goal is greatly enhanced.

BUOYANCY

Archimedes' law of buoyancy states that a body is buoyed up by a force equal to the weight of the volume of water displaced.

A swimmer completely submerged in a large container of water filled to the brim would displace a certain quantity of water. The swimmer would float if the actual weight of his body is less than the weight of the water displaced.

Specific gravity is the scientific name for the ratio to determine the buoyancy of a body. Specific gravity equals the true body weight divided by the weight of an equal volume of water. The specific gravity of a human body may range from approximately 0.970 to 1.120. Individuals with a specific gravity of 1.0 tend to sink, whereas those under 1.0 tend to float. Fat has a specific gravity under 1.0, while body substances such as bone and muscle are over 1.0.

BASIC TECHNIQUES AND SKILLS IN ADJUSTING THE BEGINNER TO WATER

After the pupil has been mentally conditioned out of the water, he is now ready to learn elementary water skills designed to develop his confidence and to adjust him to water. It is well at this point to have the class paired so that each student will have a partner. The advantages of using a partner relationship are numerous. From a safety viewpoint each partner is aware of the other's welfare. Psychologically, competition in performance is established. Each student acts as an instructor for his partner. He becomes more attentive to directions and, in the act of his performance as a teacher as well as student, acquires a better understanding of the skill being taught. With a large class, time usually does not permit the instructor to check each student individually on each progressive step. In the paired-pupil method, each swimmer is checked by his partner. The instructor can then survey the group and give his attention where it is most needed.

Most teachers of swimming are in accord in using some form of the Brink* word-picture system for adjusting the nonswimmer to the water. The following progressive procedure utilizes some of the basic steps of the Brink system, with supplementary material found to be of practical application.

Confidence drills

Water orientation. The following instructions are given to the members of the class.
1. Enter the water and wade to waist-deep water.
2. Hold partner for support and bounce up and down.
3. Individually bounce around in circles to establish balance.
4. Cup water into hands and lower face to hands, simulating washing face.
5. Hold partner's hands for support, bend forward and lower face into the water, relax face muscles, repeat.
6. Hold partner for support and submerge entire body; repeat several times, holding breath.
7. Submerge individually; repeat several times, staying submerged longer with each repetition.

*Cureton, Thomas K.: How to teach swimming and diving, New York, 1934, Associated Press.

8. Place hands on knees, lower face into water, and open the eyes; reflex action may cause them to shut; immediately open them again and they soon adjust to the water.
9. Lower entire body, open eyes, and identify objects underwater; count partner's fingers, and so on.
10. Do not rub the eyes; instead squeeze them together momentarily and blink them several times.

Breath control. Poor stroke technique is very often a result of improper breathing habits. Emphasis must be placed upon the importance of breathing correctly in the very early stages of learning. Patience on the part of the instructor is essential. He must be enthusiastic and original in creating interest through action. Action not only creates interest but also eliminates the problem of discipline. Most instructors of swimming advocate breathing through the mouth. The air can be exhaled more rapidly, and pressure needed to exhale through the nose is eliminated. Many skilled swimmers exhale primarily through the mouth, with some air passing through the nasal passages, keeping them clear of water droplets. The following instructions are now given to the members of the class.
1. In waist-deep water, cup hands, together and scoop water from pool; inhale deeply through the mouth and blow the water from the hands by exhaling forcefully through the mouth.
2. Repeat step 1; exhale slowly, with a steady stream through the nose.
3. Repeat step 1, exhaling through the nose and mouth.
4. Place hands on spread knees, lower face into water, and exhale completely through the mouth.
5. Join hands with partner, facing each other; one partner submerges and exhales; as he comes up to inhale, the other partner submerges, and so on; start slowly and increase tempo gradually.

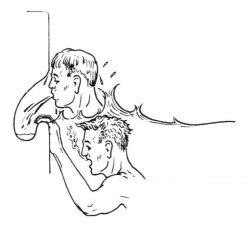

Fig. 2-1. Shipping water.

6. Place hands on spread knees, lower shoulders and head below surface, and exhale; turn head only to the left, look over left shoulder and inhale; repeat 10 times; duplicate procedure, turning head to the right.

7. Line up at sides of pool, facing overflow gutter; take a deep breath, bend knees, and submerge with mouth wide open; retrieve and "ship" water out of mouth into overflow by squeezing mouth from the rear (Fig. 2-1). (This skill teaches student the reflex of "shipping" water rather than swallowing it, which causes one to strangle.)

Back breathing drill. Give the following instructions to the members of the class.

1. Stand on the pool bottom facing the pool side.

2. Hold the scum gutter with both hands.

3. Bend the knees and slowly lower the back of the head until the ears are submerged. The face remains above the surface with the eyes directed toward the ceiling.

4. Air is inhaled through the mouth and exhaled through the nose in a natural relaxed manner.

5. Relax the muscles of the face and neck.

6. Repeat until confidence has been established.

Jackknife float. Give the following instructions to the members of the class.

1. In shoulder-deep water stand with feet spread well apart; inhale deeply, bend forward, slide hands downward along the legs toward the feet; lower the head and shoulders beneath the surface.

2. As the hands reach the ankle area, the feet will gradually rise from the bottom of the pool; hold this free-floating position momentarily (Fig. 2-2, *A*).

3. Slide the hands upward toward the hips, elevate the head, and plant the feet firmly on the bottom of the pool.

Standing up from a horizontal floating position. Give the following instructions to the members of the class (Fig. 2-2, *D* and *E*).

1. Extend arms forward and lower head and upper body beneath the surface; as partner tows you forward, elevate your legs so that the body is in a horizontal position.

2. To recover to a standing position, bend the knees, moving them forward toward the chest; now press downward and backward with the arms and simultaneously elevate the head and shoulders; place the feet firmly on the bottom of the pool.

Jellyfish float. Give the following instructions to the members of the class.

1. In shoulder-deep water, inhale deeply and slowly lower head and upper body beneath the surface.

2. Lift the feet from the bottom, bend the knees, and draw them up to the chest; wrap the arms around the legs and keep the chin lowered to the chest. The body will now resemble a ball floating in the water (Fig. 2-2, *B* and *C*).

3. To recover, release the legs, straighten the knees and back, elevate the head, and stand up.

Front float. Give the following instructions to the members of the class.

1. Assume a jellyfish floating position.

2. From this position extend the arms and

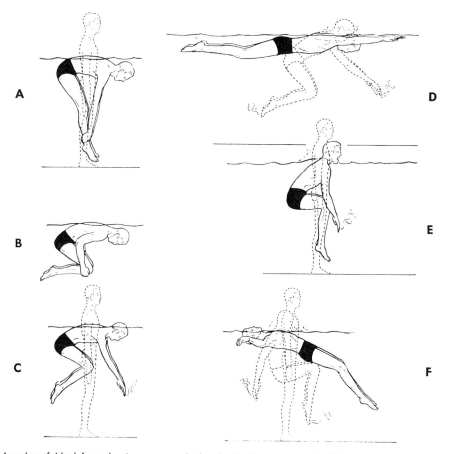

Fig. 2-2. A series of ideal form showing some methods of adjusting to water. **A,** Submerging to jackknife float position and recovery. **B** and **C,** Turtle float and recovery. **D** and **E,** Prone float position and recovery. **F,** Back float position and recovery.

upper portion of the body forward, and simultaneously extend the legs and lower part of the body to the rear (Fig. 2-2, *D*).

3. To maintain this position, press forward and downward on the arms, head, and shoulders, and lift up on the legs.
4. Regain standing position as illustrated in Fig. 2-2, *D* and *E*.

Back float. Give the following instructions to the members of the class.

1. Review back breathing drill.
2. Bend knees and lower the back, shoulders, and head slowly until the body is completely submerged except for the eyes, nose, mouth, and chin.

3. Extend the arms sideward and downward, hands reaching gently upward from the bottom (Fig. 2-2, *F*).
4. Lift the hips toward the surface, and push the feet gently upward from the bottom.
5. Recover standing position by dropping the hips to a sitting position, pressing the arms and hands downward, then forward and upward; lower the chin on the chest, plant the feet on the bottom, and stand up (Fig. 2-2, *F*).

Front glide with kick. Give the following instructions to the members of the class.

1. Start from a standing position in waist-deep water; bend forward and extend

arms together and forward beneath the water surface.

2. Fall forward, submerge the head, and push off the bottom with the feet; lift the legs, and press the feet upward; glide.

3. Move legs up and down, keep the feet extended, and allow the knees to bend for relaxation.

4. Recover standing position as described for standing from a horizontal floating position.

Rear glide with kick. Give the following instructions to the members of the class.

1. Start from a back floating position.

2. Move the arms to the side of the body.

3. Initiate the kick from the hip joint, and emphasize the upbeat.

4. Move legs up and down slowly.

Body spin. The body spin teaches the pupil to appreciate the potentials of the arm action in swimming. It serves as a lead-up drill in teaching the arm action for the elementary and resting back strokes. Give the following instructions to the members of the class.

1. In breast-deep water, hold the feet together and bend the knees until only the head is above the surface; stand on toes, keeping knees together.

2. Position the left arm so that it is pressed across and held closely to the chest. Reach back with the right arm bending and leading with the elbow to a point as far to the rear as possible, without moving the trunk.

3. Pull forward with the right arm held straight and simultaneously twist and spin the body to the right; the resulting action should spin the body completely around.

4. Repeat action with the left arm.

5. Assume position of ball floating; bend right elbow, move well back, extend right arm, and pull forward with a straight elbow; repeat action in a continuous series; resulting action should spin the body in circles.

6. Repeat, using left arm, and spin to the left.

7. Repeat, using both arms simultaneously, and move the body to the rear.

Horizontal submerging. Utilize the pool ladder in the shallow end of the pool.

1. Take a breath of air.

2. Maintain the body in a horizontal or prone position. Use the hands and arms to descend the ladder, step by step, slowly exhaling. Keep the eyes open and the elbows straight to eliminate the possibility of hitting the head against the ladder.

3. Climb the steps with the arms back to the surface before the need for air exists.

4. Repeat until the pupil can relax momentarily in a prone position on the pool bottom.

Sculling. Sculling is a basic skill required in treading water and various water ballet maneuvers. Give the following instructions to the members of the class.

1. Standing in waist-deep water, extend arms forward above surface of the water at shoulder level, with palms facing the water.

2. Elevate the little-finger side of the hands until the palms are at a 45-degree angle to the surface of the water; move the hands outward and slightly downward about 12 inches.

3. Reverse the position of the hands so that the thumb side is elevated, palm still facing downward at a 45-degree angle, and move hands and lower arm inward while pressing downward to original position.

4. Repeat the complete action in steps 2 and 3 several times, increasing the speed each time.

5. Continue action and lower arms and body into the water until water level reaches the chin.

6. As the hands engage the water, the legs are slowly eased off the bottom, and the body is supported by the sculling action of the arms.

7. Lower the head backward into the water until the ears are submerged, and gradually extend the body by lifting the chest and hips while the hands continue the sculling motion.

Motivating skills. The student is now sufficiently advanced in the basic fundamentals in water to proceed with motivating skills. These strokes are a natural or instinctive type and do not require highly skilled techniques. The purpose of this procedure is to condition the pupil so that he can make elementary progress through the water with the body in almost any position. It also teaches the student appreciation of the use of the hands and arms against the resistance of specific gravity, which is the constant upward pressure of the water. Give the following instructions to the members of the class.

1. In breast-deep water swim the elementary crawl stroke (dog paddle), keeping the head beneath the surface and the eyes open and using a slow, deep knee-bend kick.
2. Elevate the head until the mouth is just above the surface, and repeat step 1.
3. Start swimming as described in step 2, and turn over on right side; reach farther foward with the right arm, shorten the action of the left arm, and keep arms recovering under water; turn head to the left, keeping the back of the head in the water.
4. Continue swimming, and turn over on the back; scull with the hands, and continue using deep, slow kick.
5. From the back position lower the left shoulder, bring the right arm across the body, and turn the head to the left (this action places the swimmer on his left side); reach well forward with the left arm, and shorten the right arm stroke; keep the arms under the surface throughout the stroke cycle while swimming on the left side.
6. Swim half the distance across the pool; turn around without touching bottom and return to starting position.

WATER GAMES AND UNDERWATER FUN SKILLS

Water games and fun skills should be introduced periodically throughout the learning period.
1. Submerging and swimming under a partners spread legs—progress from one person to several people in a row.
2. Horse and rider game.
3. Escaping from a circle of swimmers holding hands.
4. Water basketball.
5. Water football.
6. Walking on the hands in shallow water.
7. Forward and backward somersaults.
8. Water polo.

DEEP WATER ORIENTATION

Fear of deep water is natural for a nonswimmer. This fear may be deeply seated if it has been caused by an unfortunate accident or experience in which the nonswimmer may have almost drowned. To overcome this fear, the progression from shallow water work to deep should be slow and well planned. A procedure that has been proved to be effective and is an integral part of the all stroke. Armbruster method is described on the following pages.

After the class has had instruction in the basic skills in adjusting to water and practice in the execution of the elementary and resting back stroke, deep water orientation is the next logical progression. The paired-pupil system is used as an added safety factor. The class is assembled on the deck of the pool at its deep end. The instructor enters the water with one of the class's weakest pupils and demonstrates submersion, bobbing, ball float, elongated float, bobbing float, treading water, and jumping from the deck into deep water.

Submersion. The instructor and the pupil hang onto the scum gutter for support with their outside hand. They hold hands and the pupil is told to squeeze the instructor's hand should he want to be elevated to the surface at any time. The pupil then pulls himself upward, lets go of his support on the scum gutter, and submerges. The pupil squeezes the instructor's hand and is pulled to the surface. In most cases the student will have more difficulty in submerging than in raising to the surface because of his bouyancy. This procedure is repeated slowly until the pupil is acclimated.

Next, the procedure just described is repeated except this time the pupil is instructed to open his eyes, look around, and stay down longer.

Then, the pupil takes a deep breath and submerges alone to the bottom of the pool. The knees bend as the feet contact the bottom and then extend as the pupil pushes from the bottom to the surface. The instructor submerges his body but keeps one hand holding the scum gutter. His eyes are open, and his free arm is extended downward in a position to give assistance if needed. Repeat until the pupil is relaxed and confidence is established.

Bobbing. The pupil takes a deep breath and elevates the body by pressing down on the scum gutter. He then lets go and submerges, exhaling on the way down. Arms are stretched above the head. When he pushes up from the bottom, his body should angle toward the pool edge so that upon arrival at the surface he can grasp the scum gutter. Inhale and submerge again in one up-and-down movement without pause. This bobbing technique is repeated until the student can bob five times without stopping.

The instructor demonstrates the use of the arms in bobbing in deep water without the use of the side of the pool for support. The bobbing action is started by elevating the body as high above the surface as possible. A scissors kick accompanied by a downward sweep of the arms to the sides of the body will accomplish this elevated position. Now as the upward force is spent, the body will start to submerge, and the momentum will carry it downward about 4 feet. At this point the arms, which have been held close to the sides, sweep sideward and upward to an extended position above the head. This action of the arms will carry the body in a vertical position to the bottom of the pool. As the feet reach the bottom, the knees flex, then extend, moving the body upward. Half way to the surface the arms sweep sideward and downward from their extended position above the head to a resting position at the sides of the body. The arm action results in a drive that lifts the head well above the surface and permits adequate time to inhale without destroying the continuous up-and-down movement of the body. The pupil may practice this skill on the deck before executing it in the water. The instructor should stress the complete exhalation while the body is submerged so as to facilitate the timing of the inhalation.

Ball float. The instructor demonstrates the ball float. The pupil executes the ball float close to the side of the pool, always within reach of the instructor or partner.

Elongated float. The instructor demonstrates the elongated float. By taking a deep breath, he lowers the face into the water, keeping the body as relaxed as possible and in a vertical position with the arms extended downward and slightly forward. The pupil practices this within reach of his partner.

Survival float. The survival float is demonstrated by the instructor. A vertical float position is held until the need for air is experienced. At this point the legs kick using a vertical breast or side stroke kick. The arms, which have crossed beneath the face, press sideward and downward in a half sculling action simultaneous with the kick. The resulting upward force permits the head to be elevated to take in air. The exhalation is forceful through the mouth just prior to the inhalation to permit maximum bouyancy during the float phase.

After the air has been taken in, the kick and arm action is repeated to prevent the body from sinking. Once this skill has been acquired, the pupil can continue the action for an hour or more if necessary.

If in an accident the arms are unable to function, the same action as above is executed using the legs only. When the arms have been disabled the same procedure is followed using only the legs for the support. In an extreme case where the arms and legs are no longer able to function, a buoyant individual can still survive by employing a vertical float position, breathing by lowering and elevating the head.

Treading water. The instructor reviews the sculling arm action and then demonstrates the leg action. The gutter is used as a support with one arm extended. The body is in a vertical position with the side of the body facing the pool edge. While one leg moves forward, the other moves to the rear in a scissors kick (Fig. 5-1). The legs do not reach as far forward and to the rear as they do in the side stroke, and the action is continuous, without pause.

When the pupil feels the support of his legs, he can then release his hold on the side of the pool and use his hands for support in the water, sculling as previously taught and reviewed. A breast stroke kick may be used equally well in treading water (see Chapter 11). To learn this kick in a vertical position, use the gutter for support, grasping with both hands, body facing the side of the pool. Bend the knees slightly, bringing the heels upward toward the buttocks. Execute a small breast stroke kick. Keep it moving without pause. When support is felt by the pupil, he releases the hands from the gutter and uses them in a sculling action for added support in the water.

Jumping from deck into deep water. A corner in the deep end of the pool is selected. The instructor stations himself in the water about 4 feet from the side of the pool and supports himself with one hand on the gutter at the end of the pool. The pupils are instructed to elevate both arms over their heads and keep them in that position as they step off the side of the deck, jumping feet first to the bottom of the pool. As the pupil enters the water, the instructor grasps the pupil's wrist with his free hand and maintains this contact as the pupil submerges to the bottom. Assistance in regaining the surface may thus be given by the instructor if he feels it necessary.

For his next jump, the instructor submerges in close proximity to the pupil but makes no contact unless it is needed. The pupil is then taught to jump in the water, bend his knees as the feet reach the bottom, and push off the bottom at an angle, so that it is in a horizontal position rather than a vertical position when he surfaces. This action places the body in a position to go immediately into a stroke and not be required to struggle from a vertical hole.

PROFESSIONAL AID FOR SUCCESSFUL TEACHING

The personality of the swimming instructor can be one of his greatest assets in effective teaching. He should have a thorough knowledge of the material he plans to use. His knowledge in the professional field should include an understanding of anatomy, kinesiology, physiology, psychology, and physics.

PERSONALITY OF INSTRUCTOR:
1. Ability to inspire confidence and motivate
2. Good voice control (low and loud)
3. Natural sense of humor
4. Energy
5. Sympathetic understanding
6. Patience
7. Perseverance
8. Tact
9. Integrity

KNOWLEDGE OF MATERIAL:
1. Ability to detect errors in technique performance and to correct them
2. Invite questions and answer them with substance and meaning

3. Present material in a logical, progressive sequence
4. Take nothing for granted; repeat basic material
5. Remember that a solid foundation in elementary skills is a "must"; provide adequate time for learning; do not rush through basic fundamental skills

ABILITY TO DEMONSTRATE:

1. Learning through imitation is highly recommended, provided the instructor has the ability to demonstrate accurately the skill he is demonstrating; and concurrent with the demonstration, he explains the substance involved. The ability to demonstrate is essential. However, competitive swimmers, highly skilled in performance, do not always make the best instructors because they place too much emphasis on demonstration and often lack the ability to put into words what they are hoping to achieve through demonstration.

UNDERSTANDING OF ANATOMY, KINESIOLOGY, AND BODY MECHANICS:

1. The instructor must be able to speak with authority. He should be a student of kinesiology, of anatomy, and of the mechanics involved in the skills being taught.
2. Technical training should be constantly supplemented by current theories and procedures. The instructor should have an open mind to new methods and evaluation of theories.

THE LESSON PLAN

The lesson plan is an important tool for the instructor. He should list the items he hopes to achieve, with an approximate time allotment for each item. Perhaps the greatest value of the lesson plan is for future teaching. After the class period the instructor would benefit by re-evaluating the lesson plan, noting the time actually taken for each item. Did he achieve what he had planned to do in the given time? and so on. Comments following the lesson period added to the lesson plan will be of great value the next time the same plan is used. Objectives and goals should be included in the plan.

Suggestions for developing a lesson plan are as follows:

1. Discuss and review material covered in the preceding class period.
2. Discuss new material and skills to be learned during the class period.
3. Demonstrate land drills of new skills.
4. Demonstrate lead up drills for new skills, including water bracket drills with stationary support, floating support drills with aides.
5. Review practice of learned skills.
6. Practice new skills.
7. Play games designed to compliment new skills learned in the class period.
8. Hold a final question and answer period following activity.

recovery at the same time that the arms start their recovery. The thrusting drive of the legs takes place while the arms are being extended beyond the head. The glide is held until the legs start to drop. Prior to the loss of momentum, the arms press in unison toward the feet. They come to rest at the outer sides of the thighs just below the hips (Fig. 3-3, *D* to *F*). Air is normally inhaled during the recovery action and is held during the glide to assist buoyancy. Some swimmers block the nasal openings of the nose with their upper lip and slowly exhale during the glide to prevent droplets of water from entering the nasal passages.

Variations of the stroke include a double glide with the second glide taking place following a powerful arm pull. Another variation is to permit the elbows to bend during the propulsive pulling and pushing action similar to the bent elbow action described in the back crawl stroke (see Chapter 10).

TEACHING AND LEARNING PROCEDURES

1. Review and practice the three styles of inverted breast stroke kick using the side of the pool or a partner for support.
2. Each swimmer selects the kick that proves most natural and produces the best results for him. Using the selected style, kick 200 yards with the aid of a floating device.
3. From a standing position on deck or in shallow water the class simulates the arm action only. The instructor leads the class slowly, emphasizing the main points.
4. The kicking action using one leg while standing on the other, is added to the simulation. The instructor stresses timing of the arms and legs.
5. The arm action is practiced in very shallow water. The legs are permitted to sink to the bottom for support.
6. The whole stroke is practiced. The instructor points out faults in technique.

Chapter 4

Introduction to teaching the higher level skilled strokes

The following instructions and procedures are suggested in teaching and learning the higher level skilled strokes, such as:

1. The side stroke on both left and right sides, the overarm side stroke, the trudgeon, the double trudgeon, and the trudgeon crawl
2. The crawl strokes on both back and front sides
3. The breast stroke, the dolphin butterfly stroke, and the dolphin crawl

The instruction may be conducted with or without the aid of floating devices. This procedure will serve as a guide to conform to the all-stroke Armbruster method of teaching beginners in the area of the highly skilled swimming strokes.

We highly recommend the use of floating devices to facilitate the learning of these highly skilled strokes.

PREREQUISITE

A thorough schooling in the area of orientation and conditioning the student to water is necessary. This is accomplished by the learning of all the elementary skills as recommended in the chapter on the all-stroke method of teaching and learning requisites. Having accomplished these prerequisites, the student is then well adjusted to any situation or position in shallow water. He is then conditioned and in readiness to proceed in learning the various skilled strokes.

TEACHING AND LEARNING PROCEDURES FOR ALL SKILLED STROKES

Once the student has learned to motivate himself in the water with the resting and elementary back strokes, the instructor may proceed with any sequence of strokes. All of the skilled strokes can be learned by all pupils—just how well each stroke is mastered by each individual will depend on his distance orientation, which procedure follows after each stroke has been coordinated into the whole stroke.

If there is a best sequence of learning the skilled strokes, we have found, through experimentation, a plan that has proved to be highly successful, and it is hereby strongly recommended. To accomplish this, these strokes are grouped into three categories: (1) the crawl stroke, back and front; (2) the side strokes, both right and left sides; and (3) the breast stroke, dolphin butterfly stroke, and dolphin crawl.

The crawl and back crawl strokes are learned in a combination sequence. Also, the side stroke is learned on both sides in sequence combination. Likewise, the breast stroke and dolphin butterfly are learned in combination sequence. The order of sequence of learning these group combinations is left to the discretion of the individual instructors.

Leg kicks. During the land and water drill practice of any one kick of any one stroke, we recommend that the fundamentals of all kicks of all the skilled strokes be taught and practiced during successive class sessions, until overlearned by the students. This method results in surprising and very rapid learning of the whole stroke in the future sessions. This phase of learning all the kicks of all the strokes is the heart and core of the beginner learning in the all-stroke Armbruster method. The kick is more difficult in different learning situations than are the arm strokes. The arms have smaller muscles and react readily to complex movements, whereas the legs have larger muscles and react more slowly to learning situations. Therefore, the instructor should emphasize and stress the land and especially the water drill exercises. This work may be accomplished either with or without floating devices.

Arm and breathing skills. The arm and breathing skills can be practiced during rest intervals of the kicking exercises. Constant repetition of the various kicks in the water with adequate rest intervals is highly recommended to assure rapid improvement and achievement in learning all strokes in future weeks.

Whole stroke. Once the arm, breathing, and leg techniques have been individually learned during the water drills, the whole stroke is attempted. Here the instructor should emphasize the point of putting in sequence at least four consecutive whole strokes without a stop. Once four strokes are organized by the student, unhurriedly, and without a stop, he has mastered the coordination of that stroke. He can now motivate himself to almost any point or any given distance, providing he breathes regularly. At this point of learning, when the arms and legs have been coordinated, proper and regular breathing determine the distance he can swim the stroke. One must breathe to swim, not swim to breathe.

During the phase of learning the whole stroke, some students may have greater difficulty than others in either the coordinations or breathing or both. Floating supports are recommended for these students. By the use of supports, he is able to concentrate upon the technique of his stroke as well as breathe more freely. As soon as he is able to motivate himself and breathe properly, the support is taken away.

DISTANCE ORIENTATION

Instructors will differ as to where and when to utilize distance orientation in the learning progression. Some will employ it as soon as a single stroke is coordinated. Others will delay its use until all strokes are learned and are swum only for short distances. The advantage to the latter plan is that the student can change from one stroke to another, without stopping when tiring, and thereby can learn to swim the other strokes while resting from the tiring one. This is sound pedagogy in learning; that is, by swimming longer distances without stopping, more strokes are practiced and greater ease of performance is experienced by the student.

As the student increases his distance on each stroke from class session to class session, he begins to unconsciously relax and breathe more freely and naturally. He is learning to give himself over to the water completely and to rely upon the momentum of each stroke and the water to support him while swimming. Distance swimming now becomes a pleasurable and tireless experience. He has now gained water strength and self-assurance in his ability in water.

Chapter 5

Teaching the side stroke

The side stroke, an outgrowth of the breast stroke, was used in early competitive swimming. It was succeeded in the evolution of speed swimming by the overarm side stroke, the trudgeon stroke, and the trudgeon crawl stroke, all of which retained the scissors kick as an integral part of the stroke. All of these strokes in turn gave way to the faster Australian and American crawl strokes, which elminated the scissors kick, replacing it with a variation of the so-called flutter kick.

The side stroke is one of the most seaworthy strokes known to man. It is easy to learn and requires comparatively little effort to swim. It is preferred by women, whose natural buoyancy enables them to carry the head fairly high, keeping the hair and face out of the water. Many men favor the stroke because the head position, with the nose above the surface and directed to the rear, facilitates breathing.

Unless students are taught to use both sides of the body at once when learning the side stroke, the stroke should not be taught.

This stroke is the basis of two methods of rescue in lifesaving techniques. The cross-chest and hair-carry techniques utilize the strong scissors kick and the underarm pull of the side stroke to support and tow a drowning person to safety. The scissors kick may be used in treading water and is a foundation for numerous water ballet maneuvers.

Scissors kick. The scissors kick is so called because it resembles the action of the blades of a house shears. It is one of the most powerful of all kicks in the water. The pelvic girdle must remain in the vertical plane throughout the entire execution of the kick to give it effective, forceful, propulsive power.

The recovery of the legs starts from a side horizontal position of the body. The legs are extended one directly above the other, with the toes pointed. The knees are flexed, and the heels are drawn slowly backward. Both legs are held together and moved simultaneously. Drawing the heels backward gives just the proper amount of flexion at the hip joint.

In this position, if an imaginary line were passed through the midpoint of the shoulder and hip joints, it should project out over the legs at a midpoint between the knees and ankles when the legs are in full recovery position. The scissors are now opened by moving the under leg backward and the upper leg forward, while maintaining the flexed position of the knees. The foot of the top leg cocks itself, or flexes, toward the knee. The under foot remains extended. From this position the legs start the drive, reaching outward then forcefully together simultaneously by extending the knees and the foot of the top leg. The under leg is extended backward as far as anatomically possible, hooking the water and acting in the same manner as kicking a ball, while the top leg has a whip motion similar to the pawing of a horse. The legs meet together, are stretched straight and relaxed, and then pause for the glide.

Arm stroke. During the glide the body is on the right side, with the shoulder girdle in a true vertical plane. The under right arm is extended forward directly under the head, with the palm facing down and hand just beneath the surface (Fig. 5-1, *A*). The upper left arm has completed its pull and is held close to the upper front part of the body, with the palm resting on the front side of the upper leg, never on top or be-

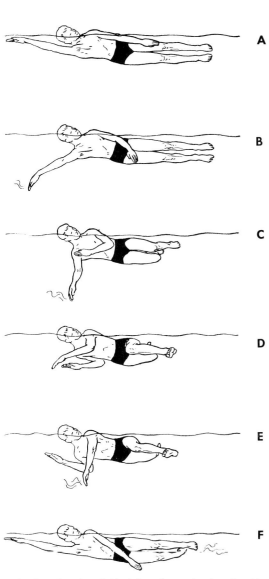

Fig. 5-1. A series of ideal form for performing the side underarm stroke. **A,** The starting position. **B,** The stroke is initiated with the pull of the under arm. **B, C,** and **D,** Full recovery of the upper arm and the legs, while the under arm completes its propulsive phase. **D,** The hands are crossing under the head, while the legs have spread laterally on the horizontal plane, with the top ankle cocked toward the knee. The body is in position for the propulsive drive of the scissors kick and upper arm, while the under arm is in recovery position for the forward thrust. **E** clearly shows the action described in **D. F,** The final closing of the stroke and return to starting position, **A.**

hind. If it is held on top, the body will have a tendency to sink. If it is carried beyond and behind, it will cause the body to roll toward the back.

The student should have a clear mental picture of the pattern of the arm stroke from this starting position. Both arms move simultaneously along the longitudinal plane of the body. They meet just under the head, change direction, and simultaneously extend again to their starting position. The under arm moves forward, the upper arm moves backward. The swimmer can chant to himself "everything drawn in; everything thrust out." Therefore the upper arm moves forward during its recovery and the lower arm pulls diagonally downward and backward to a position directly beneath the head. Here it changes direction and starts its recovery movement, with hand and fingers pointed toward its starting position, while the upper arm pulls downward and backward to its starting position. Even though the hands move in and out together, the under arm is always pulling on the "in" movement, while the upper arm is always pulling on the "out" movement.

The upper arm is held close to the front upper part of the body, with the palm of the hand resting in front of the top thigh. The arm is held straight and submerged in this position. As the hand recovers, it slides away from the thigh, palm facing downward and slightly forward toward the face. The elbow bends but hugs close to the lower chest until the hand is well on its way forward to meet the under hand. There is a very special skilled technique that the beginner should learn at the very start of the upper arm recovery phase. If a slight pressure downward is brought to bear on the hand sliding forward, well under the surface, close in front of chest, and moving on a horizontal plane, it will support the learner's face above the surface. The upper elbow and shoulder must be submerged as much as possible during the recovery phase to prevent the upper arm from pushing a wave over the face, causing choking and difficulty in breathing. The hand recovers about a hand's length beyond the face and passes above and beyond the under hand, just releasing the water and starting on its recovery. (See Fig. 5-1, *D*.) The upper hand now starts its pull by pressing downward and backward to its starting position in front of the thigh.

The planing effect of the upper hand and submergence of its elbow are very definitely factors in quick learning, even though it may be a resisting movement to forward progress.

Whole stroke. In the all-stroke method, the side stroke is taught on both sides. Most men prefer the right side, putting the strong arm underneath. However, if one side is dominant, it should be the left side because the upper arm, not the under arm, is the driving stroke. Then, too, in lifesaving techniques one usually reaches with the right arm in the approach, which results in a carry on the left side in which the right arm holds the person being towed and places the swimmer on his weak under arm in towing.

From a side-gliding position the stroke starts as the lower arm catches and begins its pull. The upper arm and legs recover. As the lower arm moves from its vertical position at the end of its pull directly under the shoulder to a doubled-up position, with the elbow bent and pressed against the chest wall and the hand in position ready to move forward, the legs have doubled-up and simultaneously spread in preparation for the kick. During the power or propulsive phase of the kick, the top arm pulls, and the lower arm extends forward. All movement comes to a halt as the body momentarily glides through the water. (See Fig. 5-1, *A*.) Breathing is not a hazard since the nose and mouth are turned to the rear and the water passes by the side of the face. Breathing should be regular and continuous throughout the stroke. Inhale through the mouth as the under arm pulls, and exhale during the pull of the top arm, again chanting "Everything in, arms, legs, and air; everything out, arms, legs, and air."

TEACHING PROCEDURE

The following instructions and procedures are used to teach the side stroke.

1. Demonstration and explanation of the kick by the instructor. Then the student is instructed to do the following:
a. Practice kick 50 times on each side, holding side of pool for support. (Daily drill strengthens the neuromuscular pattern.)
   (1) Hold shoulder girdle and pelvic girdle in vertical position during the execution of the kick, since this will hold the legs in the correct horizontal plane.
   (2) Prevent under knee from dropping down during recovery; hold it up against the upper leg.
   (3) Emphasize under leg action by reaching as far back as possible at the beginning of the kick.
   (4) Close legs at completion and hold there momentarily, simulating the glide. Do not permit the legs to cross each other.
b. Push from the side of the pool in glide position (face in the water). Repeat several times on each side until balance is established.
c. Learn coordination and timing of the side stroke using a four-step procedure or pattern as follows (learn one step at a time).

Step 1. Scissors kick only (Fig. 5-2, *A*). Take a deep breath and lie on right side floating position, with body straight and right under arm extended in line with body. Holding breath, turn face down into water on top of under arm. The left upper arm is in front of upper thigh. Take at least four kicks in succession, and pause between each stroke for glide. The upper hand is in front of the upper thigh, and remains on it during these kick exercises. This trains the upper arm to work in unison with the kick as it must in the whole stroke.

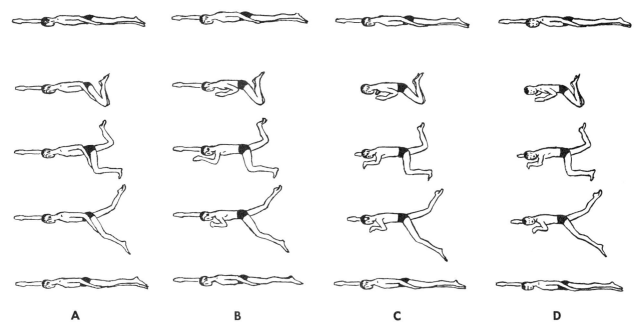

Fig. 5-2. A series of four learning steps of the side stroke, using the "part-whole" method. **A,** Skill 1, scissors kick only, with the face turned under. **B,** Skill 2, scissors kick and use of the upper arm. **C,** Skill 3, kick, upper arm and under arm. **D,** Skill 4, whole stroke, with the face turned out.

Step 2. Kick and upper arm (Fig. 5-2, *B*). The body is still on its extended right side, face under, as in Step 1. To execute Step 2, the upper hand and arm recover at the same time that the legs recover. The hand planes forward beyond the face, with the elbow and hand submerged to a point beyond the face. The arm pull starts at the same time as the kick. Here, again, as in the resting back stroke the upper arm and legs recover at the same time and kick and pull at the same time.

Step 3. Kick, upper arm, and under arm (Fig. 5-2, *C*). The body with face under is still in the same position as in Step 1. To execute Step 3, press, do not pull, the under arm diagonally down and in a backward direction to a point under the face. At the same time that the upper arm starts its press, the legs and upper arm are recovered. The hands meet, cross over, and repass as the hand of the under arm recovers and thrusts forward to guide the glide. At the same time as the under arm recovers, the upper arm

and legs start the kick and pull, pause, and glide. Again chant the same singsong, "Everything in; everything out." Glide. This makes it simple to coordinate the arms and legs into the whole stroke. Take at least four stroke repetitions before stopping for air. If the student can coordinate four strokes in succession correctly, success is assured.

Step 4. Breathing (Fig. 5-2, *D*). Take one or two strokes in the Step 3 position, and then turn the face out of the water and face to the rear, chin in line with the upper shoulder. Breathe in at the same time the arms and legs come in, breath out at the same time the arms and legs go out. "Everything in; everything out." In learning Steps 1, 2, and 3 the face is held under water in this position because the student is not likely to strangle. Once four or five strokes are correctly timed and coordinated, the student has learned the skill of coordinating the whole stroke. Now repeat the same four-step procedure on the right side. The water level should remain constant at the face, leveling at the corner of the lower eye and at the lower corner of the mouth.

As the swimmer develops proficiency in the execution of the stroke, further refinement may be accomplished by delaying the action of the upper arm and legs until the lower arm has completed its pull.

The degree of elbow bend in the lower arm during its propulsive pull varies with the individual. The applied force should be directed to the rear rather than straight downward.

Chapter 6

Teaching the overarm side, the trudgeon, the double trudgeon, and the trudgeon crawl strokes

OVERARM SIDE STROKE

After the side stroke has been mastered, the next logical stroke in a progressive method of teaching is the overarm side stroke. The overarm side stroke differs from the side stroke in the recovery action of the upper arm, the left arm for a swimmer swimming on his right side or the right arm for a swimmer swimming on his left side. From the side stroke glide position in which the palm of the hand of the upper arm is positioned in front of the thigh of the upper leg (see Fig. 5-1), the elbow is elevated well above the surface of the water permitting the arm and hand to recover above the water. The hand enters the water at a point just beyond the eyes, the elbow is extended as the arm pulls downward and backward, the fingers face the botton of the pool as the arm passes close to the body. All other aspects of the stroke are the same as in the basic side stroke. The key to the timing is to have the upper arm recover simultaneously with the recovery of the legs, the upper arm goes through its propulsive action as the legs squeeze together.

Teaching the overarm side stroke. Class instruction consists of the following: (1) a review of the side stroke, (2) an explanation and demonstration of the overarm side stroke, (3) a land drill stressing the eleva-

tion of the upper arm and the proper timing of the upper arm in relation to the lower arm, (4) the same drill repeated standing in waist-deep water, (5) practice of the arm action with a partner or a floating device supporting the legs, (6) swimming the whole stroke without breathing, and (7) swimming the whole stroke with breathing, stressing timing, glide, relaxation, and form.

TRUDGEON STROKE

In the evolution of competitive strokes, swimmers using the side stroke found that they could swim faster recovering the top arm above the surface of the water resulting in the overarm side stroke. They reasoned logically that if speed was gained by recovering one arm above the surface, additional speed might be achieved by recovering both arms above the surface of the water. John Trudgeon of England is credited as being the originator of this stroke, which utilizes an alternating out-of-the-water arm recovery and the side stroke scissors kick. A variation of the trudgeon stroke utilizes a breast stroke kick and is preferred by individuals who find the breast kick action easier than the scissors kick. The trudgeon stroke is ideal for recreation swimming. The scissors kick provides additional support for the body during the breathing phase, allowing for more time and ease in breathing. Champion distance swimmers have been known to swim with a form of trudgeon stroke; however, instead of bending the knees in the recovery of the legs, they merely allow the legs to drift apart with the knee straight. The power kick is then initiated by a bend in the knee and a small powerful scissors kick.

Teaching the trudgeon stroke. The class reviews the side stroke and overarm side stroke. As the student swims with the overarm side stroke, he is instructed to reach a little further forward each time his top arm recovers until the arm reaches a fully extended position well beyond the head. He is then encouraged to roll from the side position to a prone position during the upper arm in its reach forward, and this enables him to recover the lower arm above the surface of the water as well.

Every effort should be made to continue the timing of the upper arm with the legs. If the swimmer turns his head to the left to breathe, the air will be inhaled through the mouth as the left arm recovers. The positive phase of the scissors kick occurs during the propulsive pull and push of the left arm. As the stroke becomes refined and highly skilled the timing is such that the shortened scissors kick is executed during the push phase of the original top arm of the side stroke.

DOUBLE TRUDGEON

The double trudgeon differs from the orthodox trudgeon in two main respects. Two small scissors kicks occur during one complete cycle of the arms. The body rolls to a greater degree away from the breathing side to accommodate the second kick.

Teaching the double trudgeon. In teaching the double trudgeon the student is instructed to review the scissors kick on the right side, gradually shortening the spread of the legs. The same procedure is repeated on the left side. The next step is to use a kick board or floating device for support and, after rotating the hips by lowering the right hip, to execute a small scissors kick. Rotate the hips in the opposite direction, lowering the left hip, and execute the second scissors kick. Continue across the pool alternating the kicks from side to side. When sufficient skill is acquired, the arms are added to the leg action, with emphasis on the timing. Each kick is performed during the pushing action of each arm. Care should be taken not to allow the student to introduce an inverted scissors kick. In the early stages it is well to encourage a short glide on each arm entry. The breathing is then added and the pupil is given sufficient practice time to become skilled in the stroke.

TRUDGEON CRAWL

The trudgeon crawl stroke is similar to the single trudgeon stroke except that three flutter kicks are added to the leg action. From a side stroke glide position on the right side, three flutter kicks are executed as the right or lead arm pulls backward and the left or trailing arm recovers forward. The scissors kick takes place as the left arm pulls backward and the right arm recovers. All other aspects of the stroke are identical to the single trudgeon stroke.

Teaching the trudgeon crawl stroke. Students practice three flutter kicks followed by a scissors kick for several repetitions, using the side of the pool or a partner for support. The same emphasis on the kick pattern is stressed while using a free floating device such as a kick board. Breathing is added to the drill.

The class reviews the single trudgeon stroke, then adds the flutter kick to the kicking pattern. Distance practice is encouraged to gain relaxation and proper timing.

Chapter 7

Coaching the racing start

The competitors with the fastest starting times have a significant advantage over those who are slow in leaving the marks. Likewise, a fast swimmer may see his efforts go for naught if for some reason he fails to leave his mark with precise, forceful, and well-timed movements. The mechanics of the start and the physiologic and psychologic factors entering into its performance are indeed complex.

The swimming start is defined as including the events that take place between the command, "Take your marks," and the beginning of the first swimming stroke.

The description of the start of a race in which the crawl stroke is used is presented in this chapter. The start of all distances of crawl swimming races is essentially the same, but the importance of having a good start is magnified as the swimming distance becomes shorter. The start of the butterfly stroke race is the same as that of the crawl until the body enters the water. The events that take place in the breast stroke race are described in Chapter 11.

Since the start of the back stroke race is altogether different from that of the crawl, dolphin butterfly, or breast stroke, it is discussed in detail in Chapter 10.

The takeoff platform may be sloped toward the pool not more than 10 degrees from the horizontal. The front edge is 30 inches above the water surface and is flush with the end of the pool. At the signal, "Take your marks," the swimmer assumes his starting position with his toes gripped over the edge of the starting block. After he has held a steady balance in this position for an appreciable length of time, a pistol is fired. The swimmer throws his center of gravity in front of his base of support and then supplies the thrust that projects him forward from his mark with as much force as he can generate. He leaves the mark at the angle that will give him the greatest distance from his mark.

The start may be divided into the following components: (1) the preparatory position, (2) assuming the starting position, (3) leaving the mark, (4) the flight, (5) the entry, (6) the glide, and (7) the initial strokes.

Preparatory position. After the contestant is in his proper lane and starting station, adequate warning is given by the official starter that in a few moments the race will be underway. During this brief interval the swimmer can make preparation for the race. Stretching movements, such as lifting the legs, bending the trunk forward, swinging the arms in circles, and twisting the trunk, will improve the condition of the muscles. Loose shaking of the arms and legs is effective in reducing tension caused by the excitement of the competitive situation. He then assumes the preparatory position standing erect, relaxed, and motionless, with both feet on the starting mark in readiness and alert for the starting command, "Take your marks." Two or three deep breaths, with emphasis on the expiration phase, taken just before taking the marks prepare the body for the violent exertion that is to follow and will ensure adequate ventilation at the beginning of the race.

Assuming the starting position. On the command, "Take your marks," the swimmer immediately assumes his starting position. A false start can be charged to a competitor if, in the opinion of the starter, he

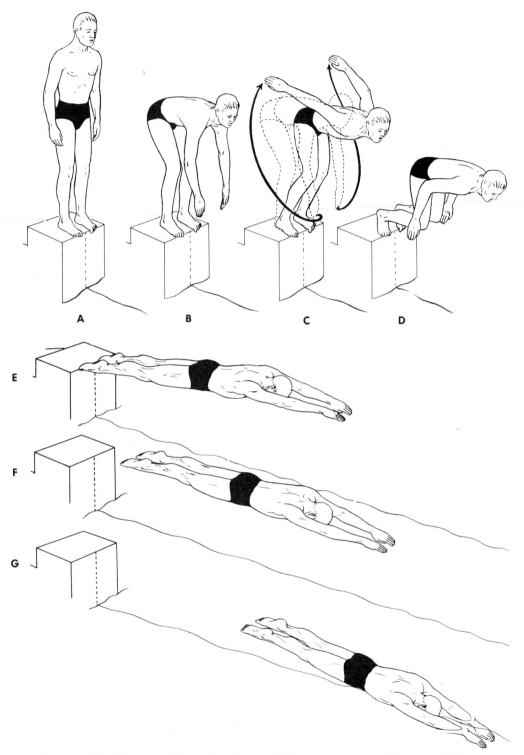

Fig. 7-1. A series of ideal form for performing the circular technique crawl stroke start. **A,** The preliminary stance. **B,** On the mark in a position of momentary steadiness. **C,** Note the short, forward, preliminary movement of the arms after the gun is fired. The arms continue a lateral, upward, and backward sweep while the body continues to drop to the takeoff position. **D,** The position for the drive. **E,** Position of the body as it leaves the mark. **F,** Position of the body in flight. **G,** Position of the body as it enters the water.

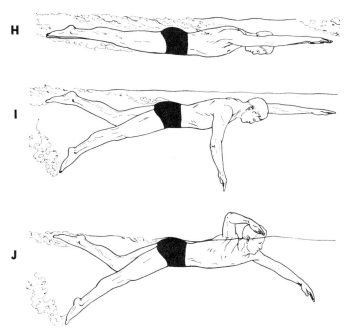

Fig. 7-1, cont'd. H, Position of the body in the glide under the surface. **I,** Position of the body at the start of the stroke at the end of the glide under the surface. **J,** Position of the body as it swims to the surface.

is too slow in moving to his starting position. A false start may also be charged if the swimmer does not come to a definite halt in his body movement before the starting pistol is fired. A study of the starting positions used by competitive swimmers reveals a wide variation in techniques.

Position of the trunk. The trunk in the starting position is bent forward to an angle approximating a right angle with the upright position (Fig. 7-1, *B*).

Position of the feet. The feet are parallel with each other and at right angles to the starting line (Fig. 7-1, *B*). The lateral spacing of the feet depends on the width of the hips and the structure of the bones of the legs. The foot position that seems most natural and presents the most stability is commonly one in which the feet are from 3 to 6 inches apart. This position places the ankle and knee joints directly below the hip joints and places the leg muscles in the optimum position for the drive. The feet are parallel to each other and at right angles

to the starting line. The force of the ankle and leg drive is exerted directly over the toes, which grip the edge of the platform. The mechanical advantage of the straight pull of the muscles in this position is diminished when the legs are overspread and the toes are turned out. The weight of the body rests mainly on the balls of the feet. The heels rest lightly on the platform to give support while the swimmer is holding himself balanced in the starting position awaiting the pistol shot (Fig. 7-1, *B*).

The grip of the toes is made with the second joint of the great toe flexed over the edge of the platform, the second toe curled slightly over the third, fourth, and fifth toes assist slightly in the drive but give mainly lateral support. The grip of the toes also inhibits forward loss of balance.

The swimmer should never permit his body to sway on the mark. If the body is swaying backward at the pistol shot, the swimmer cannot project his body forward until the body has reached the end of the backward sway and has again recovered to the point of balance. This accounts for some swimmers being caught flat-footed. If a swimmer is caught back on his heels when the pistol is fired, he may partially overcome it by suddenly lifting his toes and the balls of his feet. This action removes the forward point of support and allows the body to drop rapidly forward.

It has been the custom for swimmers to start from a flat-footed position on the edge of the pool. The success that sprint runners met with the use of inclined starting blocks on top of the track suggested that an inclined starting block might be of advantage to the swimmer. An investigation of the use of starting blocks in the swimming start showed quite conclusively that inclined starting blocks are a disadvantage to swimmers in leaving the mark, as far as starting time is concerned.* However, the inclined starting platform is still being used in international Olympic competition.

Position of the knees. The proper amount of flexion of the knees in the starting position is one in which a straight line passing from the tip of the shoulder to the ankle bone will pass just in front of the knee cap (Fig. 7-1, *B*). A greater knee flexion would cause the heels to be lifted and the center of weight to be shifted forward to a position over the toes. In this forward position the swimmer is less stable and is effecting too great a tension on his extensor muscles. The knees should be so bent that the heels can rest lightly on the platform and further flexion and extension can take place freely. In this position the swimmer is well poised and is ready to execute a powerful drive from his mark.

Position of the hips. The degree of flexion of the hips depends on the choice of starting position. If the full-crouch position is used,

the flexion is nearly complete, causing the trunk to be held in a horizontal plane, the hips held at about the same level as the shoulders (Fig. 7-1, *B*). If the semicrouch position is used, the shoulders are held above the level of the hips. In both positions the hips are held far enough behind the center of support so that that portion of the body in front of the base is counterbalanced.

Position of the head and eyes. In the starting position when the swimmer has placed the feet on the mark, he then looks down the course of the pool to a point near the water level at the end of his lane on the opposite side of the pool. The head should be raised high enough so that the swimmer can easily see this point (Fig. 7-1, *B*). In this position the eyes aid in holding a steady balance for an appreciable length of time and also aim the flight of the body when leaving the mark.

Position of the arms (Fig. 7-1, *B*). The arms hang downward loosely from the shoulders, with the elbows slightly flexed.

Now that the swimmer has assumed his starting position and is holding a steady balance, two further factors must be considered. They are, namely, breathing and attention.

Breathing. While the swimmer is awaiting the command, "Take your marks," he should take three or four deep breaths. During this period of increased ventilation, forceful expiration should be made in order to reduce the carbon dioxide content of the air in the lungs. When this is accomplished, the swimmer can hold his breath for a longer period of time, and thus breathing does not interfere with his arm mechanics in the early part of the race.

Deep breathing before a race can be overdone easily. Some swimmers are so sensitive to the changes in the blood caused by hyperventilation that they become dizzy after taking six deep breaths. Such dizziness may reduce balance and coordination and spoil the start. Hyperventilation at the start should

*Tuttle, W. W., Morehouse, Laurence E., and Armbruster, David A.: Two studies in swimming starts. 1. The use of starting blocks in swimming sprints, Research Quarterly **10**:89-92 (March), 1939.

be used during practice before attempting it during competition. Only a few trials are needed to establish the number of deep breaths that can be taken without discomfort.

Some experimenters have demonstrated that a few deep breaths of oxygen before a race will increase the performance over short distances This experiment met with the same success when regular air was substituted for the oxygen and the swimmers were kept ignorant of the change. Deep breathing (washing out the excess carbon dioxide) plus a psychologic factor (faith in the beneficial effects of oxygen) were evidently the causes of increased performance.

Preliminary hyperventilation is especially important in races of short duration. It requires approximately 20 to 30 seconds to swim the 40-, 50-, or 60-yard dash. With adequate ventilation previous to the start, only a few breaths are required during the race. Some top-flight swimmers swim the entire 50 yards without taking a breath.

If conditions were such that forced respiration could be continued until the moment before the swimmer entered the water, the beneficial effects of hyperventilation would be augmented. However, in order to maintain his equilibrium in a delicately balanced starting position while awaiting the pistol shot, the swimmer must halt the heaving movings of his thorax, which accompany forced respiration.

In addition to aiding the swimmer to maintain a steady balance in the "set" position, cessation of respiration also aids the swimmer to give maximum attention while waiting for the pistol shot.

If a swimmer frequently loses his balance while in the starting position or is a slow starter, the coach may check the swimmer's breathing habits to find if he is properly holding his breath in the starting position while awaiting the pistol shot.

A short and deep inhalation at the take-off acts to increase the swimmer's buoyancy and prevents him from sinking too deep during the plunge and glide. It also provides air, which further aids him to hold his breath without distress during the glide and the first few strokes.

A study of the respiratory habits of trained swimmers during the start of a race supports the following conclusions*:

1. Prior to the starter's command, "Take your marks," trained swimmers either use forced respiration or breathe normally. After the command, "Take your marks," as the swimmers assume the starting position and maintain a steady balance while awaiting the pistol shot, the breath is held at the end of a normal inspiration. After the pistol shot, as the swimmers prepare to leave their marks, a deep inspiration is made and is held.

2. The respiratory habits of trained swimmers are similar to those of trained track runners. The adaptation of respiratory habits to race situations is, in most cases, so natural that the athlete acquires proper habits through practice and without advice from the coach.

Attention. When the contestant is behind his starting station awaiting the starter's instructions, he sets about the task in the following brief moments to prepare himself for the race at hand: The swimmer's attention becomes closely fixed on the words of the starter as the instructions are given. He then makes the bodily adjustments by placing his feet on the starting marks in preparation for the signal "Take your marks." At this signal he carefully assumes his starting position, which he then holds for a period of momentary steadiness. It is during this period that attention must reach its peak. The swimmer is "set" for the gun; his breathing ceases, attention is diverted from the noises, movements of the spectators and other contestants are shut out, and his en-

*Morehouse, Laurence E.: The respiratory habits of trained swimmers during the start of a race, Research Quarterly **12**:186 (May), 1941.

tire attention is centered upon the pistol shot.

Attention occurs in waves, reaching a peak and subsiding continuously. Thus, the length of time the starter holds the swimmers at a steady balance in the starting position will affect the start.

It is a well-known fact that the interval of time that a starter holds swimmers on their marks is subject to individual variation. Some starters allow only a short interval and start the swimmers before they are ready, and others prolong the holding time so that the swimmers have passed their peaks of attention and the initiation of performance is prolonged when the pistol is finally fired. The optimum interval of time that a swimmer should hold a steady balance in a starting position on his mark has been found to be 1.5 seconds.*

Practice in responding to the starting gun should be repeated frequently enough so that the swimmer's response is automatic. The swimmer should be so conditioned to the starting gun that any sharp noise will cause him to initiate the movements of the start. The official who is starting a race should be aware of this conditioned response and should not penalize swimmers who are disturbed by such an outside noise before the gun is fired.

Leaving the mark. The act of leaving the mark may be divided into two parts, the drop and the drive.

Drop. The drop may be defined as that portion of leaving the mark that is concerned with shifting the center of the body weight to a position in front of the base of support so that force applied behind the center of weight in this position will drive the body forward. A well-executed drop requires skillful and rapid movements of the arms and legs to overcome the inertia of the swimmer in the steady balanced po-

*Tuttle, W. W., Morehouse, Laurence E., and Armbruster, David A.: A further study of the optimum time for holding a swimmer on his mark, Research Quarterly 11:53-56 (March), 1940.

sition. At the pistol shot, the arms are flung in an outward circular movement to the rear (Fig. 7-1, *C*). This action aids the body in moving forward. At the same time the body is continued forward by a slight extension of the knees and hips. At this moment a deep breath is taken and held.

The arms next reverse the swing from backward to forward. This is followed by a rapid body drop caused by a flexion at the hips, knees, and ankles. The heels now rest firmly on the platform until the body has almost reached the drive position and the ankles have been flexed.

Drive. The end of the drop occurs when the hips, knees, and ankles are flexed and the arms have been swung forward as far as the knees (Fig. 7-1, *D*). At this point the body is crouched and ready for a straightforward drive. If the arms are too far forward or too far backward at this point, much power will be lost.

The drive now commences with a powerful action of both the legs and arms. The legs propel the body forward by an extension of the knees and hips. The arms are swung forward from the knees until they reach a position slightly below eye level. At this point the swing is suddenly halted, transferring the forward momentum from the arms to the body.

The ankle is not extended until the arms are stopped. The ankles, being weaker joints than the knees or hips, are used to push the body forward only after it is well under way. At this advantageous moment they are snapped into extension, adding considerable force to the forward speed at the end of the drive.

One of the simplest starts has just been described. There are variations in this form of starting that have proved to be equally as successful and deserve consideration here. The swimmer would benefit by practicing all the good forms of starts and selecting the one that advances him to a 10-yard distance in the shortest interval of time. An experiment devised to seek the best start revealed that among expert swimmers the start that was regularly used by each proved to be the best for him and that variations in arm or leg action of the style he had learned tended only to inhibit him. A similar experiment with inexperienced swimmers showed that the start that contained the simplest movements was the most successful.*

Variations in the start. There are numerous variations in starting technique that are worthy of consideration.

The hand grab start. At the command "Take your marks," the swimmer bends forward and holds the front of the starting block with both hands for balance and support (Fig. 7-2, *B*).

When the pistol is fired, the swimmer pulls forward with his hands and arms and extends the knees forcefully, resulting in a very fast method of getting off the starting block (Fig. 7-2, *C*).

This start is rapidly gaining in popularity and has been used most effectively by many sprint champions.

Knee extension technique. The swimmer using this technique fixes his hips and uses only his knees in the manuever of the legs in the drop to the drive position. This start is suited for relay races, since the head is held downward and the swimmer can see his teammate approach the finish mark under him.

The starting position of the swimmer employing the knee-action technique is similar to the full-crouch start. Following the pistol shot, the circular arm action is applied. The head is held low to keep the trunk from rising. At the instant the arms swing forward following the pistol shot, the knees straighten, and the body is extended forward. The knees are then rapidly flexed, and the forward speed of the body is increased because of the shortened radius. By the time the knees have dropped to a

*Morehouse, Laurence E.: A comparison of the starting times of various forms of competitive swimming starts, Official aquatic guide, New York, 1941-42, A. S. Barnes & Co., p. 66.

position of full flexion, the arms have completed their circular movement and have arrived opposite the knees. The body is now ready for the drive, which is executed as described in the circular start (Fig. 7-1, *D*).

The knee extension technique can also be accomplished using the standard arm swing.

Knee dip technique. Although this type of start considerably reduces stability in the starting position, it yields a very fast start when it is once mastered. Some swimmers with a slow response time but with good equilibrium find that their starting times are markedly improved using the knee dip technique.

In the starting position the knees are held straight, not hyperextended, and the body is bent forward at the hips. The arms are held backward at a level slightly above that of the hips. The head is held well up.

In this stance the weight is carried further forward to a point at the front of the balls of the feet and just behind the toes. The body is held at a steady balance in this precarious position.

At the pistol shot the knees are promptly flexed, causing the body to drop forward toward the drive position. The arms are held backward as the body drops under them. When the body has nearly reached the drive position, the arms are swept downward. When the arms pass the knees, the drive is started and is carried out in the standard manner.

An additional speed-imparting skill can be added to this and other starts by those gifted with a high degree of equilibrium. While holding the steady balance awaiting the pistol shot, the swimmer can slowly lower the trunk so that, when the pistol is discharged, the body is already in motion. The force will be applied, then, in changing the direction of the motion instead of starting the motion from a position at rest. A steady balance must be held during this slow lowering of the body, since the competitor will be charged with a false start if he has gained unfair advantage by being off bal-

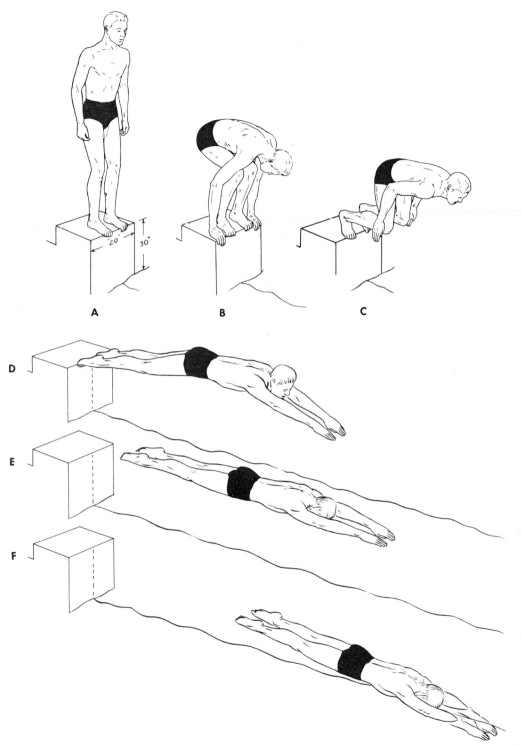

Fig. 7-2. A series of ideal form for performing the grab crawl stroke start. **A,** The preliminary erect, relaxed, yet alert stance. **B,** On the mark in a position of momentary steadiness, with the hands grabbing the starting block in readiness for gun signal. **C,** The arms and hands pull and push the body forward as the knees extend. **D,** Position of the body as it leaves the mark. Note the arms are driven forward and abruptly halted, just below the chin level. The head remains well upraised. **E,** The flight. The arms now line up with the body, and the head is lowered between the arms. **F,** The entry. For the underwater glide and initial strokes in surfacing, see Fig. 7-1, *H-J.*

ance in the direction of the start when the pistol is discharged.

Toe lift technique. The essential merit of this technique is its simplicity. The leg action is so fast, however, that the arm must react very fast in order to gather satisfactory momentum in so short a time as to be able to be coordinated with it.

This technique can be employed from the full-crouch position. The body is inclined forward, head up, arms back just below hip level, knees slightly flexed, and the toes in the regular gripping position. The center of weight is over the balls of the feet. At the pistol shot, the toe muscles are relaxed, and the support is removed from the front of the feet and transferred to the heels. This shift of support to a point behind the center of weight causes the body to drop forward at a rapid rate.

As the body commences to drop, the knees are flexed, and the arms are then quickly swung forward so that their action coincides with that of the knees at the initial stage of the drive (Fig. 7-1, *D*).

Some power is lost during the drive, since the arms have not gained sufficient speed. This deficit may be somewhat compensated for by the additional power gained from the swiftly falling body when the momentum is changed to a forward direction during the drive.

Motion picture studies show that nearly all sprint swimmers slightly relax the great toe and allow the weight to fall somewhat backward to the heels during the drop. This shift occurs naturally during all types of starts. The toe lift technique is merely an exaggeration of this natural tendency.

When the body reaches the beginning of the drive position, the toes again forcefully grip the edge of the pool. This prevents slipping and also provides a firm support for the drive from the edge of the starting station.

Flight. The swimmer leaves the takeoff with his body in a nearly horizontal position. His body follows a parabolic curve as it is projected forward through the air.

The extension of the ankle during the final part of the drive tends to throw the legs upward. If this is allowed to occur, the body will be projected toward the water at too sharp an angle, and the swimmer will enter too soon and in a disadvantageous position. In order to avoid throwing the legs upward, the toes should remain in contact with the takeoff until the ankles are fully extended (Fig. 7-1, *E*).

The angle of the takeoff should be nearly horizontal. A takeoff at an angle below the horizontal will result in an entry that is too near the starting mark, too deep, and lacking in momentum. On the other hand, if the takeoff is nearly horizontal, the entry will be at a greater distance from the mark, the body will remain near the surface of the water, and the glide will be longer and faster because of the advantageous application of force (Fig. 7-1, *E*).

As the swimmer leaves the mark, his head is held up, and his eyes look forward. Care must be exercised that the head is not held so high that the body becomes arched. In an arched position in flight, the swimmer frequently enters the water with his legs dragging, which results in retarding his forward motion.

If the swimmer keeps his head up until near the end of the flight and then drops it between his arms, he has a tendency to raise his arms and lower his legs. This type of entry is thought by some to facilitate the first strokes because the shoulders are not submerged and thus the arms are free to start stroking. Repeated observations have shown, however, that the extended shallow glide is faster than the leg drag and early arm action.

The head should be lowered to a position between the arms in the early period of the flight, preferably as the feet leave the marks (Fig. 7-1, *E*). In this position the body is held steady on a horizontal level, which facilitates a proper entry (Fig. 7-1, *F* and *G*).

Entry. If the takeoff has been performed

at a level approaching the horizontal and the body parts of the swimmer have been held in good alignment, the entry will be made at a maximum distance from the mark. The fingertips are first to enter, and the rest of the body follows at an angle of from 8 to 10 degrees beneath the surface (Fig. 7-1, *G*).

If the swimmer enters the water in a horizontal position, he will remain near the surface. If the entry is too angular, the swimmer will submerge too deeply, and his course will be curvilinear and time consuming.

As the body enters the water, it is held rigid. The fingers and palms are held in line with the arms, the feet and toes in line with the legs. The head is held low between the arms, and the back of the head in line with the upper surface of the arms. The arms are to be pressed against the sides of the head, and the thumbs and index fingers of the hands are held together. The whole body is in a streamlined position (Fig. 7-1, *G*).

Upon striking the water, the swimmer must press the arms downward in order to keep their alignment in the presence of the upward force of the water.

Observations have been made of the effectiveness of entering the water with the feet held in a narrow stride position so that the flutter kick can be commenced in the air or as soon as the legs are submerged. This early leg action was found to retard the forward motion instead of accelerating it.

Glide. As the body submerges, it is held stretched in the same streamlined position as during the flight (Fig. 7-1, *H*). The distance and speed of the glide depend on the impetus given by the drive from the mark, the extent of the trajectory to the water, and the resistance of the water to the body in its forward motion.

The water resistance is greatest at the surface and is heightened by the whirling or eddying motion of choppy water. The glide, then, should be just far enough below the surface to allow all parts of the body to escape these swirls.

The fingers do not usually have to be planed upward in order to guide the body toward the surface. As momentum is lost, the body rises toward the surface because of the buoyancy of most individuals whose lungs are inflated.

Initial strokes. When the speed at the glide is reduced to a point where it is no greater than the maximum swimming speed, the initial strokes should be made. The swimmer can cultivate in practice the feel of the speed by noting the sensation caused by the friction of the water against the surface of the body at various rates.

At this point, the legs start their drive, and the arm opposite from the breathing side executes the first arm pull (Fig. 7-1, *I*). This prevents the temptation to turn the head for air during the first arm pull. Turning the head is detrimental to arm action and body balance at this point, since the body is still low in the water and the head would have to be raised too high to get a breath. The swimmer should learn to hold his breath until he is well underway and his pace has been set. If adequate ventilation has occurred just before the start, this breathholding will not be uncomfortable.

The first arm pull is started while the body is still about 8 to 12 inches below the water's surface. The arm movement is started by depressing the hand and starting the pull backward. The elbow is then flexed, and the arm is drawn backward. The arm action does not start with a strong down stroke, since this would cause the body to be driven upward instead of forward, resulting in a loss of speed. The body is pushed forward and breaks to the surface with great speed (Fig. 7-1, *J*).

The head is held down during the first arm pull. It is then gradually raised to the swimming position with each succeeding arm stroke until the third arm stroke is reached. While the initial arm is pulling, slight supporting pressure is exerted on the other arm. This places it in readiness at the proper depth to start the arm pull as soon as the other arm has finished its stroke.

A forceful kick during the initial strokes lends stability to the arm action and aids in driving the body forward to the surface. The rhythm of the legs should coincide with the arm action from the beginning. A narrow, fast kick tends to cause a swimmer to speed up his arm action to a faster rate than that which he has been accustomed to using. If rapid leg action is started early, the arm action should not be started until the leg action has been reduced to the rate that is synchronous with the arm speed. The optimum speed of the initial leg and arm strokes is that which approaches the rate of the regular swimming rhythm.

Chapter 8

Coaching the sprint crawl stroke

The modern crawl stroke is the fastest and the most efficient stroke used by competitive swimmers today. In all freestyle events from the short 50- or 60-yard dash to the long distance races, the crawl stroke is universally used.

There are two forms of swimming the modern crawl. The first, the sprint crawl stroke, is used for short dashes in which the conservation of energy is not a factor, and the second, the distance crawl stroke, is used in races in which energy must be conserved and distributed over the course of the race. In the freestyle, races of 100 yards and less are generally considered as sprints. According to this definition, competitors who must conserve their energy by swimming at a speed slower than their maximum in order to complete a 100-yard swim must consider this race as a distance swim. Until they have improved their condition to such an extent that they can swim the 100 yards at maximum speed, the race, to them, is not a sprint.

The essential differences between the methods of swimming the sprint and the distance crawl strokes lie in the duration of the arm and leg cycles and the manner in which each arm performs the first act of the pull after it has entered the water. In order to lengthen the duration of the arm and leg cycles for distance swimming, a gliding movement is added to the arm stroke. The glide occurs just after the arm enters the water and before the pull is started.

The duration of the glide depends on the pace desired. In the sprint crawl stroke the glide is reduced to a minimum, and the arm is pressed downward into the driving position as soon as it enters the water.

In order to obtain maximum speed, the modern crawl stroke is swum in the sprint style. This style is described in full in this chapter. Modifications of the sprint crawl that adapt it to middle-distance and distance swimming are discussed later.

CHARACTERISTICS OF SPRINT SWIMMERS

A wide range of difference will be found among top-flight sprint swimmers. Competitors with only one leg have been among the place winners in county and state championships. In general, though, one will find that top-ranking swimmers possess robust, symmetrical bodies. A large number of these have developed from weaklings and poorly skilled individuals to powerful and smooth performers.

There are certain characteristics that will aid in sprint swimming performance. These can be divided into three classes, anatomic, physiologic, and psychologic.

The anatomic qualifications are probably the most important. These represent the equipment of the swimmer. The efficiency with which he uses this equipment depends on his physiologic and psychologic functions. The frequently repeated rule that a good big man has the advantage over a good little man applies in top-flight sprinting.

A long hand will provide a good paddle, but it must be accompanied by powerful wrist and arm muscles if it is to be effective. Because of the wide range of movement of the shoulder girdle during sprint swimming, the muscles attached to this girdle must be flexible.

The muscles of the back and abdomen must be powerful, since they are the muscles of fixation of the thorax and pelvis. The vigorous arm and shoulder movements and the driving leg action must originate and operate from and upon stable bases if these movements are to be effective. The body that sags in the middle and wobbles during the swimming action will not be streamlined, and greater resistance will be met in the water.

The hips should be thin, yet powerful. The sides of the buttocks should slope from the back to the thighs. A buttock that is undercut presents an abrupt surface that causes a drag in the water. Ideally, there should be no fold under the buttocks; they should be small and flat. In other words, the buttocks should be shaped more like a torpedo than like a rowboat.

The legs should be long and slender with flexible and strong muscles. An item of great importance is the ankle. This joint must be of the type that allows a large range of extension. Such an ankle is usually slender, and the joints in the ankle and foot are loose. A simple test of ankle flexibility is made by sitting on the floor with the legs extended forward and turning the feet inward and downward in a pigeon-toed fashion in an attempt to touch the floor with all the toes. Full efficiency in swimming the crawl cannot be realized until this degree of extension can be reached. This movement can be developed in most individuals through constant application of the few simple stretching exercises.

The feet should be long, slender, and flexible in order to achieve a free fishtail action. A foot that presents a long lever will be an efficient paddle, since the leg muscles are capable of providing powerful action to it as the leg completes the upward and downward drive.

Individuals with short necks have diffi-culty in turning the head in breathing in the crawl stroke. In full-speed swimming the individual with a long neck can lift the head better in acquiring the desired planed position.

The foremost physiologic qualification is speed. A sprint swimmer must be a quick mover. He must have a fast response at the start and at the turn, and he must be capable of moving his legs at a high rate of speed in order to coordinate them with his driving arm action.

The muscles must be powerful in order to develop the tremendous horsepower needed to overcome the water resistance. As the speed is increased, the resistance of the water becomes greater, and consequently more power is required to keep the swimmer moving at a high rate of speed.

Endurance must be great, since the entire body is at work during swimming. The heart muscle must be well conditioned so that it can pump blood continuously to all of the working muscles. The circulation of blood through the muscles must be adequate to supply large quantities of oxygen and foodstuffs and carry away the waste materials. This condition is gained only through frequently repeated vigorous exercise for several weeks. This means miles of daily swimming, including "wind sprints," for at least 6 weeks before a competitive season. The result is an increase in the quantity of blood capillaries within the work muscles. The improved circulatory condition in the muscles is felt by an increased ability to extend the distance of a swim at a fast pace.

The sprint swimmer who must move his arms and legs at a continuously rapid rate over a distance often becomes tied up. This occurs most frequently in those who are poorly coordinated. These individuals require more energy to overcome the waste movements. The sprint swimmer must train rigidly in order to derive a perfect stroke coordination. Some swimmers are faster learners than others and achieve this measure of skill in a relatively short time. Others must devote hours of conscientious practice in order to reach this stage of training.

TECHNIQUE OF THE SPRINT CRAWL STROKE

The components of the sprint crawl are discussed in the following order: (1) body position, (2) leg action, (3) arm action, (4) coordination of the arms, (5) coordination of the legs and arms, (6) breathing, (7) coordination of breathing with the sprint crawl stroke, (8) sprint crawl turn, and (9) finish.

Body position. Nature has given streamlined bodies to fish, but the human body must be held in a position to follow the natural lines of streamlined flow in order to eliminate the turbulence that retards the motion of the swimmer.

Position of the head and neck. The head is carried up, with the face only in the water (Fig. 8-1, *A*). The water level varies from a position just above the eyes to one at the level of the hairline. This variation is in accordance with the height of the bow wave in front of the head and the buoyancy of the swimmer.

The wave in front of the head will be higher as the swimmer increases his speed and will lower as the speed diminishes. A

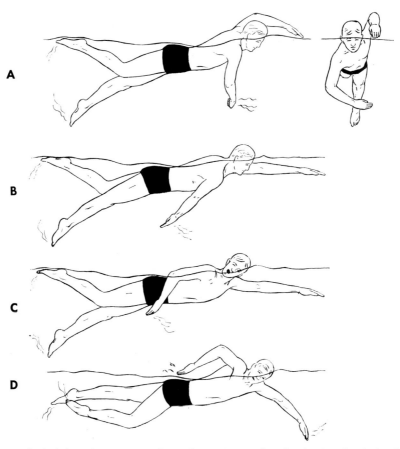

Fig. 8-1. A series of ideal form for executing the modern sprint crawl stroke showing the six leg beats and one revolution of the arm stroke cycle. These figures also show the counterbalance of the arm and leg action, the turning of the head in taking air in the stroke, and the body position in relation to the surface of the water. **B** and **F** show the looseness of feet and ankles during the beat action.

difference in buoyancy will also affect the optimum height at which the head is carried. A great many sprinters are exceedingly muscular and have a heavy skeleton. This type of swimmer does not float as high in the water as do individuals with lighter skeletons, less musculature, and more fatty tissue. The less buoyant individuals will thus swim lower in the water with the water level near the hairline, even at maximum speed.

The eyes are directed forward in a natural position and are not peering upward from under the eyebrows or sideward from the corners of the eyes. The eyes are the main aids in the control of the body position. If they are directed in an upward or sideward position, the body will be easily thrown out of equilibrium, and the propelling motion of the arms and legs will be inhibited. The eyes are centered or "spotted" on the forward plane of progression. When the head is turned for an inhalation, the eyes are moved with it but are quickly returned to the centered position and remain fixed in this position until the next inhalation. Any sideward rolling motion of the body should not alter the stability of the vision.

The nose and chin are also held in a cen-

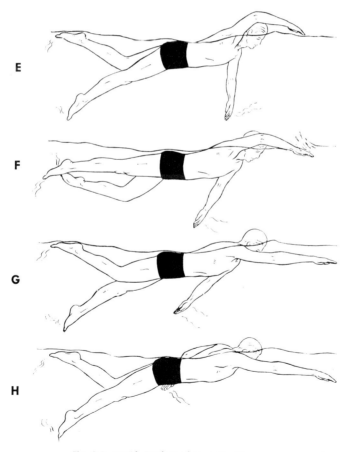

E

F

G

H

Fig. 8-1, cont'd. For legend see opposite page.

tered position, and, except for the turn of the head for breathing, they do not oscillate with any rolling movement of the body. After the inhalation they also recover to the center. The head cannot be held steady if the neck is too rigid. In this condition, any movement of the trunk is transmitted to the head.

It is commonly observed that if the head is returned too far past the center position during the exhalation phase of the crawl stroke, an unbalanced leg action will result. This reduces the driving power of the legs and thus should be avoided.

The chin is carried forward, away from the throat, except when turning for air. When the head is turned for air, the chin is tucked into a position in front of the shoulders and in line with the armpit so that a relatively smooth surface is presented by the under side of the face, neck, and chest wall (Fig. 8-1, *C*) so that the water can flow under them with little resistance and the mouth will be in the trough formed by the bow wave flowing around the head.

The chin should not be held so far forward when centered that wrinkles appear in the back of the neck. This rigid posture is most likely to be found in individuals with short necks. A strained position of the neck will result in early fatigue, since constant turning of the head in this position requires a greater effort. A rigid neck position usually is accompanied by a rigid body position also. In this condition muscles must work against each other as well as against the resistance of the water, and additional work must be done to overcome this additional load.

Although the head moves independently of the shoulder girdle and upper spine, the proper position of the head is aided by an accommodating posture of the shoulder girdle and upper spine. Likewise, a good body position is dependent on the posture of the head and neck.

The speed developed by the powerful movements of the sprint crawl stroke will naturally elevate the head and shoulders. The swimmer, therefore, does not need to lift his head and shoulders. In fact, they are pressed somewhat forward and downward, giving the impression of swimming downhill.

A common fault of sprint swimmers attempting to get a good head position is to raise the head and neck too high. In this position too much energy must be dissipated by exerting the downward force of the arms, which is necessary to hold the head high. Such a position also causes the lower trunk to compensate by sinking into the water. The stream of water flowing past the body in motion then offers additional resistance as it is broken into turbulence as large volumes of water close in over the back and are sent whirling off in eddies.

Position of the shoulder girdle and upper spine. The position of the shoulder girdle during the sprint crawl is designed to permit the maximum power and efficiency of the arm strokes. The shoulder blades should be held flat.

The shoulders are raised forward in the direction of the movement of the body. In this position the arms are able to execute a stronger pull, and the shoulder blades can move freely during the recovery.

The upper spine is also flexed slightly forward. In this position the sprint crawl swimmer presents the appearance of being somewhat hunchbacked (Fig. 8-1, *B*). This position affords a more powerful arm action because of the more mechanically advantageous position of the arm depressor muscles, mainly the pectoral muscles located in front of the chest and upper arm. It also places the trunk in a more streamlined position. The whole surface of the thorax and abdomen is flattened. As the swimmer propels himself through the water, his body level under the surface is parallel with the surface of the water, and the water can thus pass under this plane with the least amount of resistance as the result of turbulence.

Resistance is further eliminated by this plane position as the back and hips ride high in the water and a smooth, thin stream flows along the sides and past the hips in an unbroken sheath. The swimmer in this position experiences the sensation of swimming downhill. A common error in the position of the shoulder girdle and upper spine is to exaggerate their forward position. In this overly arched position, mechanical advantage of the arms is decreased, and power is therefore diminished. A high position of the upper spine also tends to result in a marked depression of the lower back and hips (Fig. 8-1, *B*), and large quantities of water are allowed to swirl over them and further energy is lost.

Position of the hips. During the sprint crawl stroke the hips remain level. They serve as a base for the articulations of the legs. The hips are carried slightly lower than the shoulders and move through the water just below the surface (Fig. 8-1, *B*).

The position of the hips varies among individuals, since the contour of the hips differs widely.

The water flows over narrow hips and small buttocks in an unbroken stream, which causes very little resistance. Those with smaller, streamlined hips can carry them higher and out of the water, with the legs well down in the water, so that the body is held level and the legs are in the most favorable position for the propelling action of the flutter kick. Swimmers with large hips should submerge them more than those with small hips in order to permit the water to flow smoothly over them. The extra power from the larger muscles helps to compensate for the increased resistance.

Position of the legs. The legs are held in a loosely extended position. The ankles and knees pass close by each other in a supple movement. An efficient leg action appears as though the legs were made of rubber.

During the sprint crawl stroke the legs move well under the surface (Fig. 8-1) in order to gain maximum traction in the water. No propulsive force is gained by any part of the foot when it is out of the water;

therefore, the feet should be beneath the surface at all times. If the hips are allowed to sink too low in the water, the feet are likely to be raised too high, and they break through to the surface and lose power.

Another common fault in the leg position is to allow the heels to drift apart in order to accommodate the toeing inward. In this spread position the legs lose some of their driving power, and the outward surfaces of the legs present a resistance to the forward motion of the swimmer.

In most individuals the proper alignment of the body position can be checked by drawing a straight line from the midpoint of the shoulder joint through the midpoint of the hip joint, the line being extended backward past the feet. If the body is in proper alignment, this line will pass exactly through a point that is midway between the ankle joints when the legs are fully spread in the stride position at the end of each beat (Fig. 8-1). In this position the legs are operating directly behind the body, providing the force in the most effective manner.

Leg action. The action of the legs in the sprint crawl stroke has been termed the "flutter kick." Because of its general usage and also because no really descriptive term has yet been assigned to it, the leg action will continue in this treatise to be called the flutter kick.

The legs neither "flutter" nor "kick" but oscillate forcibly and regularly, serving to push the water backward with each upward and downward beat. In order to derive maximum force from the leg action, the swimmer must have trained and strengthened his leg muscles to endure the continuous vigorous motion of the flutter kick. This may be accomplished by daily drills with the aid of the kicking board. While using the kicking board, the swimmer should ascertain that the body position simulates that of the regular sprint crawl position. Many bad swimming habits can result from careless use of the kicking board. The swimmer should strive not only to get his legs in top condition, but also to train his legs to perform in a manner that will allow him to derive the greatest amount of drive from each beat of the legs.

The most efficient sprint crawl leg action is one that resembles the action of a fish's tail. Although the swimmer's legs move in a vertical plane and the fish's tail in a horizontal plane, their propulsive action is derived from the same principle. The swimmer's leg propels him forward with both the upward and the downward swing just as the fish's tail propels him forward with each sideward swing.

The swimmer's leg, however, possesses a structural limitation that is not present in the tail of the fish. His knee joint restricts movement to a backward one only. If the knee joint allowed movement forward as well as backward, the swimmer could use his legs in the same range as that used by a fish during swimming. In order to compensate for this structural limitation, a slight variation from the fishtail action is made as the downward beat is completed. If the reader would sit on the edge of his chair and, leaning back slightly, go through the motions of pedaling a bicycle, he will get a good concept of what the compensated fishtail action ought to be. Note the action of each joint as well as the movements of the limbs. The pedal is pressed with the ball of the foot on the forward and downward stroke. The knee is straightened on the downward stroke, and then the foot is pressed more firmly against the pedal as it is pushed backward and then slightly upward. As the foot presses upward, the knee bends again, and the pushing power is diminished. This bicycle action can be observed in Fig. 8-1, *D* and *F*.

In the water the swimmer's leg action and range of motion are nearly identical to that of the bicycle rider. In riding a bicycle the pressure is always exerted on the balls of the feet, whereas in swimming the crawl stroke the pressure is exerted alternately on the soles of the feet in the upward tread and on the instep in the downward tread. Another example is to lie on a stool face down and pedal an imaginary bicycle.

The movement in the flutter kick leg action originates at the hip joint and is transmitted through the thigh to the knee joint. In whiplike motion the wave passes from the knee to the lower leg and next to the ankle and finally to the foot, which is lashed about like the free end of a rope that is being snapped. The initial movement is in the hips in both the upward and downward beat.

At the beginning of the upward leg movement, the thigh is slightly flexed upon the hip, and the knee and ankle are extended (Fig. 8-1, *D* and *F*). With the extension of the hip, the water is pressed backward by the back of the thigh, and the body is moved forward. This backward flow continues along the back of the leg and is finally whipped backward and upward by the sole of the foot. The flow of water is thus forced backward with ever-increasing speed, and, as it leaves the foot, the snap of the ankle sends the water backward with a tremendous driving force, thus propelling the body forward.

When the leg finishes its upward beat, the hips and knees are slightly flexed, and the ankles are extended (Fig. 8-1, *D* and *F*). The downward beat of the leg starts with the leg in this position. As in the upward leg beat, the action starts from the hips. A small flexion at the hips sends the water washing backward along the front of the thigh. The knee is then extended (Fig. 8-1). The water is thus driven backward along the anterior surface of the leg and down over the ankles as the body is driven forward.

The toes are turned inward in a pigeon-toed fashion during the down stroke (Fig. 8-1) in order to contact more water with the tops of the feet. Toeing in during the down stroke pushes the water backward at a more effective angle, since the foot can be extended farther in this position.

In order to execute an efficient leg drive

in this fashion, the leg muscles must be flexible, powerful, and able to relax to such an extent that they exert only a minimum of tension upon the joints that are being moved by their reciprocal muscles. Swimmers' muscles, when relaxed, give the appearance of being loose and elastic.

The advantage of possessing large feet and flexible ankles is apparent when the mechanics of the flutter kick are considered. The effectiveness of the kick will be limited by the degree of extension of the ankles. The lashing action of the foot provides the major propulsive action of the legs. If the ankle is stiff and movement limited, this lashing action is lost, and the legs do not provide their share of the propelling force.

The feet act as paddles, and swimmers with the largest feet naturally have the most effective paddles. The ideal foot for swimming is long, thin, broad at the instep, and flexible.

The upward leg action is as effective in propelling the crawl swimmer forward as the downward action. The slight knee flexion and powerful ankle extension as the leg completes its upward sweep contribute to the fishtail action, which is capable of sending large amounts of water backward from the sole of the foot. This fishtail action is inhibited on the downward movement because of the anatomic limitation of the knee joint to flex both ways. The small amount of propelling surface presented by the instep as compared with that of the sole of the foot is also a restricting factor in the downward beat.

The width of the flutter kick stride should be from 18 to 26 inches, depending on the length of the swimmer's legs and the speed with which he moves. Because of the refraction of the water, the stride appears much narrower and appears to be from 12 to 18 inches wide.

Turbulent surface water that is swirling and eddying is an inhibiting factor to the driving force of the legs. The legs act best

well below the surface of the water because surface water agitated by other swimmers or by waves striking against the side of the pool presents less traction than deeper water that is undisturbed.

Common faults in the sprint crawl leg action are as follows: (1) kicking with the legs too near the surface, (2) spreading the legs laterally so that the heels are beyond hip width, (3) kicking away from the vertical plane, especially during inhalation, (4) holding the ankles in a rigid extended position, (5) holding the feet toed inward during the upward stroke, and (6) holding the knees in a rigidly extended position.

Recent analysis of films in studies made at the University of Indiana* indicate that a large number of most highly skilled crawl stroke swimmers have an arm pattern that resembles an inverted question mark. Bernoulli's principle or law states that fluid pressure is reduced wherever the speed of flow is increased. Counsilman suggests that the swimmer pitch the angle of his hand in relation to its path through the water to serve as an air foil or propellor to provide forward propulsion to the swimmer. The theory involves moving a large amount of water over a short distance and constantly striving to move still water rather than moving a small amount of water over a greater distance. To achieve this result the swimmer must endeavor to move his hand in an elliptical pattern in order to continue encountering still water. This most interesting theory should motivate more scientific studies in the very near future.

The following description of the sprint crawl stroke involves the ideal mechanics utilizing the drag force theory of propulsion.

Arm action. The arms provide about 85% of the total power of the sprint crawl stroke. Slight adjustments in body position and leg action made to accommodate the

---

*Counsilman, James E.: The application of Bernoulli's principle to human propulsion in water, Indiana University, 1971, University of Indiana Press.

arm action are fully justified. In the sprint crawl stroke, the arms alternately drive forward into the water with reasonable force to pull the body forward over the surface. The arm, which completes the stroke, is then quickly recovered out of the water and placed in position in the water for the next arm stroke. For the purpose of analysis the sprint crawl arm stroke may be classified into the seven following components: (1) entry, (2) support, (3) catch, (4) pull, (5) push, (6) release, and (7) recovery.

Entry. The arm must enter the water in such a manner that it is immediately placed in the most favorable position for a forceful stroke by taking hold of as much water as possible. In the sprint crawl stroke the hand begins its propulsive action as soon as it penetrates through the water's surface and the pressure is felt in the hand and fingers.

For the purpose of this discussion the arm entry is defined as that period in the crawl arm cycle that starts when the hand passes in front of the shoulder following the recovery and ends when the arm is finally in the supporting position.

As the hand reaches forward and the arm is driven for the entry, the shoulder is held high and not allowed to reach forward to its fullest extent. Although the forward displacement of the swimmer's shoulder would increase the extent of the reach several inches, this displacement places the shoulder at a distinct mechanical disadvantage for the propulsive arm action. A shoulder displacement also tends to result in a sideward movement of the body, which impedes forward progression.

With the shoulder in a fixed position, more of the body weight is held over the arm and represents potential energy for the arm drive. The shoulder and arm muscles are also in a better position to draw the arm downward and backward through the water as it passes under the central plane of the body.

The arm is dropped into the water directly in front of the shoulder. The shoulder remains high (Fig. 8-1, *E* and *F*), and, as the arm contacts the water, the hand and forearm are pressed downward. The tip of the elbow is pointing sideward and is held in this position to prevent hyperextension of the elbow and also to prevent the shoulder from dropping as the arm is pressed downward.

As the arm is pressed below the surface of the water, the swimmer's shoulder moves forward, not downward, so that as pressure is applied to the hand and forearm, the body weight moves over the arm as it goes into the catch. This action gives the sprinter the sensation of swimming downhill. Actually, however, the shoulder and the rest of the body are moving straight forward on a level with the surface of the water.

When the sprint crawl swimmer is at full speed, the bow wave in front of his head and shoulders causes the surface water in front of him to swell up into an inclined plane (Fig. 8-1, *E*). It is along the surface of this plane that the arm enters the water. The angle at which the arm drops into the water depends, therefore, on the height of this wave, which, in turn, depends on the velocity, size, and body position of the swimmer.

Common faults in the sprint crawl arm entry are (1) smashing the arm into the water with too much force, which splits the water and allows a great deal of slip, (2) pressing the hand into the water with the little finger leading, (3) turning the elbow downward as the arm is pressed into the water, thus allowing the shoulder to drop, (4) reaching too far forward by displacing the entire shoulder girdle, which results in a loss of power and a disadvantageous position for the use of the body weight, and (5) reaching forward with the hand too high above the surface of the water, or (6) dropping the hand into the water too soon before the arm is properly extended.

Support. In the sprint crawl stroke, the arm and hand serve to propel the swimmer forward as soon as they enter the water and continue this propulsive action until they are removed for the recovery. The main propulsive action does not begin until the arm is in a favorable driving position below the surface of the water. The interval elapsing between the entry and the position at which the arm starts its major propulsive action is the supporting phase of the sprint crawl arm action.

As the arm enters the water, it drives forward and downward on a line parallel to the center line of progression. The fingers are forward and slightly downward. The tip of the elbow is pointing outward, and the elbow joint is slightly flexed so that there is approximately a hand's length of extension remaining as the arm presses forward and downward into the water. The shoulder is held high and somewhat drawn inward to the side of the face (Fig. 8-1, *E* and *F*).

The angle at which the arm slides through the water during the supporting phase of the arm stroke depends on the swimmer's speed. If the speed is slow, the angle is less, and the arm glides at a depth just below the water's surface. If the speed is fast, the elbow is bent further, and the arm is thrust into the water at a slightly deeper angle. The reason for this variance is obvious. At slower speeds a greater support is needed to maintain the body elevation, therefore, a more shallow slide should be used to prevent bobbing up and down with each stroke. At faster speeds the water pressure on the face and chest is greater, and the body elevation does not need to be supplemented by as much additional support by the arms.

In the sprint crawl stroke this supporting phase is reduced to the minimum required to stabilize the body position. The arm is thrust into the water in a manner in which very little emphasis is given to support, but much is given to propulsion.

During the brief glide the fingers and palm are pressed downward, and the water beneath them is forced backward under the forearm, thus generating propelling power.

By pressing downward with the hand and slightly elevating the elbow tip and shoulder, the widest portion of the forearm is presented to the water. In this position the arm is sliding downward, with the weight of the body moving forward over it. The water is forced up the under sides of the arm and is passed under the chest. This action produces the effect of rolling a barrel under the arm. At top speed, great pressure downward and inward is applied to the hand and forearm as the arm is extended into the water to the catch position. This technique causes the shoulder and body to slide forward over the propelling arm (Fig. 8-1).

The arm does not glide into the same place through the surface that the hand has entered but is pressed forward and downward into the water.

Common errors in the supporting phase of the sprint arm action are as follows: (1) extending the elbow fully, (2) completely elevating the shoulder girdle, (3) dropping the elbow and shoulder to a position below the hand level, (4) rotating the elbow downward, (5) overcupping the hand, and (6) abducting the hand to the right or left so that the fingers are not in forward alignment at all times.

Catch. During the supporting phase, the arm is pressing downward and backward. The major force is directed downward. As the arm is further depressed, the major force is directed backward, and the propulsive action of the arm is increased. At the point at which the major force of the arm action thus shifts from downward to backward, the catch is made. In most sprint swimmers, the catch takes place when the hand is from 5 to 10 inches below the surface of the water and pressure in the hand is felt.

The catch is a quick inward movement of the hand and arm devised to place the arm in the most advantageous position for the large depressor muscles to act during the following pull and push phases of the sprint arm stroke. While the arm is being placed in the position that results in maximum muscle teamwork, the pressure on the water, which has been obtained during the supporting phase, must not be lost. This is accomplished by a quick inward movement of the hand followed immediately by a similar movement of the forearm and then likewise with the upper arm. This motion results in turbulence behind the hand, which increases the water resistance and thus adds to the frictional force that prevents the arm from slipping through the water. If the hand and arm are pulled too slowly, they will travel too far before traction is gained, and the effectiveness of the arm pull will be diminished. It is for this reason that faster turnovers of all the competitive strokes are strived for by modern competitors and coaches. In order to master this fast turnover of the crawl stroke, intensive training must be undertaken to prevent the swimmer from "spinning his wheels," that is, losing synchronized timing between the arms and legs.

The catch brings the hand to a position in front of the axis of the body (Fig. 8-1, *A* and *B*) so that the center of body weight is balanced over the driving arm. If the body weight is carried to one side of the driving arm, it will result in an inefficient lateral motion similar to the sway of the body while walking with the feet widely spread.

The elbow continues to be directed sideward so that the widest part of the forearm remains in contact with the water that is being forced backward. The upper arm is brought to an approximately vertical position in front of the shoulder so that the large muscles can best act to draw the arm downward and backward.

Pull. At the end of the catch the arm has gained traction in the water and has been brought into position for the most propulsive phases of the arm stroke. From the point of the catch until the arm is below the top of the head, the arm pulls the body forward. If the swimmer allows his arm to be pulled directly under the shoulder before the push and drive are started, the shoulder passes over the hand, and the arm is in a disadvantageous position to deliver a powerful drive. During the pull as well as during the push that follows, the water is forced directly backward. The arm is acting nearly vertically to the forward direction of the swimmer and, in this manner, is in the most advantageous position to deliver the forward drive. When the arm is in this position, the muscular energy used in swimming is most efficiently applied. As the arm is depressed, the hand is pulled along a line below the axis of the body, and the elbow is gradually flexed in order to maintain the movement of the hand in this plane. The arm in this position closely resembles a boomerang (Fig. 8-1, *A*). The hand and forearm are swept downward and serve as a base of anchorage for the shoulder to be pulled forward over them. While the shoulder is riding forward over the anchored hand and forearm, the traction must not be lost by allowing the depression of the hand and forearm to lose speed through the water. In order not to yield its hold on the water, the hand describes a feathering action, or sculling motion, by an increased flexion of the elbow, which moves the arm and hand inward and slightly upward toward the chest. The broad part of the forearm continues to remain in contact with the water, which is being forced backward.

There are three reasons why the elbow should be flexed during the pull. First, it places the hand and forearm beneath the body where they can exert their force more nearly in a line with the body, thus reducing lateral motion. Second, the lever arm is shortened so that more speed can be attained. With the shortened lever, the weight to be moved is nearer to the fulcrum and thus less energy has to be expended in order to move the weight. Third, the transition from the pull to the push is more easily made.

Swimmers of the stocky type, with short arms and a heavy and powerful shoulder girdle, may reduce the amount of elbow flexion in order to obtain a longer and more propulsive stroke. A slight elbow flexion and feathering action during the pull are necessary to maintain balance to prepare for the transitional movement.

Push. The transitional movement from the pull to the push is accomplished by drawing the upper arm toward the body so that the arm can be drawn powerfully backward. This adjustment is made just before the arm passes under the shoulder so that it is in the proper position for the drive, or push.

The arm has maintained traction in the water so that, when the powerful push is made, the arm will meet with sufficient resistence to drive the body forward. As the arm is brought under the shoulder, the upper arm remains vertical to the surface, and the forearm is gradually extended (Fig. 8-1, *C*). As the arm approaches the front of the hip in completion of the push, the hand is whipped backward to give a last additional hand and wrist drive to the arm stroke. The propulsive action of the arm thus ends with the hand just below the hip. It is very important to note that throughout the push phase of the arm driving into the release, a progressive lift of the shoulder is executed to accommodate this entire arm and shoulder movement. When this action is thoroughly mastered, it will supply a powerful driving force to the entire arm and hand in completing the propulsive phase of the arm. The shoulder then continues to lift and move progressively forward with the arm through the recovery to the entry.

Release. At the completion of the arm-push-drive, the continued shoulder lift-action also accommodates the arm lift from the water and aids the arm to swing naturally into the recovery phase. In the sprint crawl stroke the water is released at the point at which the propulsive force of the arm stroke is progressively diminishing. If the arm is pushed backward too far, the body will be forced downward, and its level will be lowered.

The propulsive force of the arm stroke starts to diminish when the hand is opposite the hip. The hand is well below the surface and must be deftly driven from the water by the wrist and forearm without impeding forward progression. At the termination of the hand whip, the shoulder and elbow are near the surface, and the hand is beneath and behind the elbow with the palm facing backward and upward. As the forearm and hand release their pressure on the water, the elbow and shoulder are raised from the water and are elevated until the hand leaves the water, executing one fourth turn inward, palm facing the body just behind the hip joint.

If the arm stroke is ended after only a short drive and the release is made in front of the hip, much propulsive power is lost, and the recovery is opposed by a great deal of water resistance. Likewise, if the hand is carried upward past the hip joint too far before the release is made, the body will be pulled under the water, and the arm will be inhibited in its recovery.

Comment: Actually, the shoulder action and the shoulder arm muscles are the real motivating force of the crawl arm stroke. Too much stress cannot be placed on the shoulder movement to compliment the arm action throughout the entire arm stroke cycle.

Recovery. The action of the arm from the release to the entry is termed the recovery. During the recovery the arm is carried forward out of the water from a position with the hand near the hip to a position with the hand ahead of its shoulder in preparation for the entry. The arm recovery is best accomplished when the shoulder has reached a position in its lift so that the water level is just below the armpit.

The action of the arms from release to recovery is continuous throughout. At no point are the arms arrested in their movement. A common fault is to pause the arms at the end of the release and at the beginning of the press. This practice causes momentum to be lost with a resulting loss of propulsion.

During the sprint crawl stroke, the recovery must be well controlled and executed in such a manner that the head and body position are not altered and that no lateral motion is affected. The driving action of the legs and opposite arm, likewise, must not be inhibited by the recovery.

At the completion of the propulsive action of the arm stroke, the water is released. The entire arm and shoulder are immediately lifted from the water by raising the elbow until the hand clears the surface. The forearm and hand are then elevated in an outward and forward circular motion with the shoulder acting as the axis. The forearm executes a quarter turn, and the hand is carried forward with the palm facing inward and downward and the thumb forward (Fig. 8-1, *A*). As the elbow is carried forward, its elevation is maintained above the level of the hand for the remainder of the recovery and the entry. The forearm is nearly horizontal as the arm is carried forward past the shoulder. The hand remains in a line with the forearm. As the hand passes the head, the arm reaches forward. The upper arm is brought forward near, but not touching, the side of the head. As the arm thus reaches for the entry, the shoulder girdle is maintained in an elevated position, the tip of the elbow is above the shoulder level and pointing laterally, while the forearm points downward from the elbow as if to spear into the water at the point of the hand entry. The fingers are pointing forward into the water with the palm parallel with the water's surface and the wrist is slightly flexed downward (Fig. 8-1). The arm is now in a position preparatory to the entry.

There are many other styles of arm recovery during the sprint crawl stroke. Other styles include those in which the elbow is carried either high or low and the arm is recovered with the elbow either high above the shoulder or close to the surface of the water. These low, high, and medium recoveries with both the flexed and extended elbow have been used by different record-breaking sprint swimmers.

Timing of the arms. In the sprint crawl stroke, the opposition rhythm is recommended. That is, in the cycle of the entire stroke, the recovery of one arm is approximately opposite the propelling arm. This method almost entirely eliminates the slide between the arm entry and the catch (Fig. 8-1). This technique gives the sprinter the desired faster turnover of the entire arm-stroke cycle without actually going into a "dig-in-type" of stroke. The student should study the illustrated figures in Fig. 8-1 very carefully and note the position of one arm in relation to the other. This style of swimming the crawl, in order to obtain greater speed for both sprinting and distance competition, is being employed by most of the modern, top-flight swimmers.

Timing of the arms and legs. In the sprint crawl stroke the cadence of the legs is faster than that of the arms. This results in a motion that at first appears to be an unnatural one, since it is unlike that used by man while walking and running. In walking and running the arms serve to counterbalance the driving action of the legs by swinging in an opposite direction to the legs. The legs and arms thus move in a 1-to-1 ratio during walking and running. In the crawl, however, the leg-to-arm ratio is 3 to 1. The legs perform three beats to each arm movement, or six beats to each complete cycle of both arms.

An analysis of the mechanics of the six-beat crawl stroke reveals that it is as truly balanced as is the counterbalancing action of the arms and legs in walking. That is, both arms and legs should be evenly balanced, one with the other. Not all top-flight swimmers have an evenly balanced leg action in relation to the arms. If they are unbalanced, compensation is made with the arms in order to obtain rhythm, counterbalanced, and a comfortable feel of coordination during competitive action. In order to facilitate a description of the timing of the arms with the legs in the sprint crawl, the stroke is divided into six parts, and each part is discussed as a separate unit. The part of the stroke that is performed with the most regular rhythm is the leg action.

The legs move upward and downward in uniform periods, and each upward and downward beat of the legs marks a certain regular phase of the stroke. For the purpose of uniformity, the timing of the arms in relation to the legs is described in Fig. 8-1 in six parts. Each part commences with the instant the legs are completely spread in the stride position at the end of each beat.

It is impossible for the coach to detect errors in timing of the arms and legs of a swimmer sprinting at full speed by simply trotting by his side and watching his coordination. By the use of portable television units and slow-motion and still movies, however, an analysis is made possible. Many of the newer pools are equipped with underwater observation windows through which such pictures may be taken.* Many coaches have made use of underwater cameras for this purpose. If such equipment is not available, photographic records must be made above the water's surface. Above-water pictures are valuable even though the splashing and turbulence disrupt the actual movements and analysis is made difficult.

Once the record is obtained, a comparison may be made with the illustrations presented in Fig. 8-1, and the action of the swimmer compared with that described in the text. The coach and swimmer can study the timing and other mechanics of the stroke and determine objectively where the fault lies.

If the underwater movie method is not used, the coach must resort to an analysis of the arm action alone and then the leg action alone while the swimmer swims and attempts to detect an unbalance caused by faulty mechanics. For example, the coach

may watch the arm action during a certain phase of the crawl stroke when the right arm enters and the left arm should be completing its drive and vice versa, as the left arm enters, the right arm should be completing its drive (Fig. 8-1, *A, B, E,* and *F*).

Technique of breathing. Expiration through the nose and mouth under the surface and inspiration through the mouth above the surface is the traditional form of breathing in swimming the sprint crawl stroke. Although the nose is a natural inlet as well as outlet in the breathing mechanism, there are several objections to expiring under water through the nose alone. The nasal openings are very small to exhale all the air against water pressure. To exhale against the water, a forceful expiratory pressure would be required. This forceful expiration through the nose against the water resistance causes mucous discharge to pass toward the nasal and frontal sinuses and the middle ear and increases the liability to auto-infection.* When air is forced out through the mouth, the pressure against the ears and sinus regions is practically eliminated.

Experiments indicated that sprinters usually released air slowly through the lips or nose until just an instant before the head is turned out for the next inhalation and a forceful expulsion is made through the mouth. This is often called the "explosive" method.†

During inhalation, air should be taken rapidly through the mouth. As a general rule, inexperienced swimmers swimming the crawl stroke will fix the abdominal and back muscles, thus interfering with the function of the diaphragm. This rigidity occurs most frequently among swimmers who depress the hips too far, causing the fixation in the abdominal region and in the lumbar region. The tension in these groups of muscles is

*Armbruster, David A.: Underwater observation windows, Intercollegiate and Interscholastic Swimming Guide, Spalding's Athletic Library, No. 491, pp. 71-73, 1940.

*Taylor, H. Marshall: Otitis and sinusitis in the swimmer, Journal of the American Medical Association 113:891 (Sept.), 1939.
†Aycock, T., Graaff, L., and Tuttle, W. W.: An analysis of the respiratory habits of trained swimmers, Research Quarterly 3:199 (May), 1932.

relieved by lifting the hips, which in turn permits deeper breathing.

Breathing may disturb the leg kick and arm rhythm. One can lie face down in the water, releasing the air with the head under the surface, and swim with the legs alone for some distance even after the air is expelled with no interference with the force of the leg kick. The same is found to be true when both arms and legs are used in the same manner. Thus the interference occurs not from diminishing the fixing action of the abdominal muscles, but from either faulty head turning mechanics or from depressing the hips.

One seldom has difficulty in inspiring if the mouth can be turned easily above the surface. In fact, usually too much air is breathed in too early in a race and not enough is expired. If the swimmer breathes regularly early in a race, he should not breath so deeply but should increase the depth in proportion to the air requirement. The expiration should be adequate, or carbon dioxide will soon build up within the tissues and fatigue will set in early. Expert swimmers who have skillfully mastered breathing and relaxation of the abdominal muscles seldom have difficulty in breathing when under the exertion of swimming at great speed.

The question as to the number of breaths to take in a sprint race has always been a point of debate. It is a foregone conclusion that, if the head is turned less often, the fast rhythm of the arms and legs is least disturbed and, therefore, greater speed is developed.

The number of breaths to take during the sprint races depends on individual differences such as breath-holding ability, relaxation, and the ability to accumulate an oxygen debt. One cannot lay down a "hard and fast" rule as to the number of breaths to take. However, in a 40- or 50-yard sprint, almost any good swimmer can cover the first length with one or two breaths and take only two or three breaths coming back. Some swimmers need to breathe with every other stroke after the first length. Others can breathe with every third arm stroke, which is a very good method if the swimmer can breathe properly on both sides. This method also tends to impart greater relaxation to the shoulder stabilizer muscles and maintain greater balance. A well-trained sprinter can swim the entire 50 yards without taking a second breath. The breath-holding interval should not be long enough to cause the swimmer to fight for air. This fault is recognized by a "wild eyed," taut, drawn expression upon the swimmer's face as his mouth is lifted high out of the water to get air.

Lifting the head out of the water for air at the turn slows the sprinter. At the start, and in coming out of the water after the glide, the head should not be turned for air on the first arm pull since the head is then too far below the surface. The swimmer should first get under way with at least four to six arm pulls. The head must rotate on its central axis and should not be raised backward or lifted sideward during breath-taking. The most important duty of the head other than the part that it plays in breathing is to keep the body on an even keel and maintain symmetrically balanced arm and leg strokes. The head must be turned for air and recovered as quickly as possible. For this reason the face is held below the surface most of the time to maintain equilibrium. At the proper moment in the stroke, the head is turned so that the least amount of interruption to the stroke balance will occur and the least amount of time will be consumed.

Between inhalations the face should be directly forward (Fig. 8-1, *B*). This plane should not be disturbed during the stroke other than during inhalation regardless of what the arms or shoulders are doing. The neck must be relaxed in order to isolate the movement of the head from that of the shoulder girdle. Many swimmers have the sensation of having the head aligned with the spine, when in reality it is turned toward the breathing side. This often causes swimmers to bear toward that direction across the racing lanes. Then, too, some swimmers will permit the chin to oscillate back and forth with the movements of the shoulder girdle while the arms are stroking and recovering. Relaxing the neck and holding the chin and nose on dead center will remedy this fault. Another fault commonly committed by the swimmer is to fail to recover the chin and nose fully to or slightly beyond center. Such a fault will inhibit the action of the opposite arm, especially in the push phase. The eyes should be on a horizontal plane so that the eyes can look ahead in almost normal forward vision. The tips of the shoulders should also be raised, and the upper spine should bend to conform to the planing position in sprinting.

As the body gains in speed and considerable friction occurs under the face, neck, and body, the swimmer should experience and actually feel that he is pressing down upon the water as he pulls and pushes his body forward over the water. The friction under the body created by the speed attained should not actually be permitted to force the body too high, but high enough to keep the water off the back as far down as the hips. When this position is assumed, breathing is then a simple matter. With the body in this position, a bow wave is created that curves around the head and sweeps in a downward curve on either side of the head at an outward angle. This in turn creates a deep trough inside the bow wave next to the body. The aim in turning the head to get air is to get the mouth into this trough and not into the bow wave. To accomplish this purpose, the head must turn on its longitudinal axis. The chin is turned to the side and pressed in close to the throat as the mouth is opened. The eyes play an important part in turning the head correctly to this point. They must sweep from the forward line of vision and focus on the surface of the water just in front of the chin and mouth. Many swimmers make the mistake of looking for-

ward while turning the head. This causes the chin to move out into the bow wave, and for this reason it must be lifted farther to the side in order to get air. As the body rolls to the opposite and the supporting arm slides from its balanced alignment, the pull and push phases of the arm stroke are shortened. While the head is being turned to the side for air, the water streams down under the chest. While turning the head, the face should be pressed against the resistance of the water to keep the water away from the front of the face (Fig. 8-1, *C*). If the head is permitted to lift away from the water, the planing effect of the face is lost, and the bow wave is broken, which causes difficulty in clearing the mouth to take air quickly.

The mouth should not open until the lips are clear of the water. Air is then taken in in the form of a gasp.

The mouth is closed immediately after air has been taken, and the head is quickly recovered in order to put the body again on an even balanced keel. During the entire movement of the head, the water level should always be maintained constant. There should neither be a sideward nor an upward or downward movement. To prevent a tendency toward lateral movement while turning the mouth out for air, press the head slightly toward the supporting arm, since the head is likely to be moved toward the side to which it is turning to get air. When the head recovers to the center, air is expelled immediately if a breath is to be taken at the next stroke. If more strokes are to be taken before air is again inhaled, the breath should be held and air bubbles should be permitted to escape until just an instant before the head is again turned out for air. Then the air that remains should be forced out in one larger bubble. This release of air should be skillfully timed so that the exhalation is finished as the lips and nose are breaking out to the surface. With the air being released in one large air bubble instead of emitting a series of small bubbles, the water is cleared away from the mouth by the air bubble as the lips break through to get a fresh supply of air.

All crawl stroke swimmers should learn to breath on both sides. The reasons for this are obvious. A sprinter is not always able to come out even at every turn so that he can turn but one way. Thus, after he completes his turn he can take a breath as soon as the body is aligned at the surface. Finally, turning the head at certain intervals, especially during the fatiguing part of the race, releases shoulder girdle and neck tensions. After turning the head several times to the right and left, even though air is not always inspired, the competitor feels immediate relief if fatigue and muscular tension have already set in.

Relation between turning the head for breathing and the arm and leg cycle. The beginner usually breathes by turning the mouth to the side for air in the same rhythm with the breathing-side arm. This seems to be a natural method. The head thus turns for air just as slow or as fast as the cadence of the stroke. This method is inefficient, however, since it causes the head to remain at the side too long for the purpose of getting air. Whenever this unskilled method is used, one can almost always find that the body lies off keel, principally on the side opposite the breathing side. The body should be flat on the chest with the face forward on front dead center for a period at least twice as long as the time required to take a breath and return to the swimming position. It is the function of the head to maintain the body on an even keel, and this function is impaired if the head spends a large part of its time in getting air. This not only throws the body off balance, but the whole stroke equilibrium is disturbed and speed is reduced.

While turning the head to the side of inhalation, the body must remain stable so that neither the arms nor the legs are caused to deviate from their normal range of movement. In order to accomplish this maneuver, certain adjustments must be made. The neck must be relaxed in order that its movement can be isolated from that of the shoulder girdle so that the shoulder girdle will not be tilted to the opposite side to permit mouth inspiration. The opposite arm must have just entered the water for countersupport before the head is turned to the side for air. The head should start to recover as the breathing-side arm is lifted out of the water and should be fully recovered when the breathing-side arm is directly at the side of the head in the recovery. These accommodations permit the head to remain forward and on center four full beats of the legs. This permits the body to ride steadily and gives the arms and legs freedom to function without interference from the head. When improper breathing causes the body to roll, the arms and legs are less propulsive. Poorly timed head mechanics is a detrimental factor to speed. The well-trained swimmer should make every effort to turn his head for air and return it independently of the cadence of his arms. The head must move to and from air at a greater speed than the cadence in which the arms are moving. One can easily test the detriment of breathing by swimming the length of the pool at top speed without turning the head for air over the entire length and then swimming it at top speed, breathing with every stroke cycle. The former method will be very much faster. Note, too, how symmetrically balanced and smooth the arms and legs function when the head is maintained on dead center.

The breathing method referred to in the preceding may be designated as the two-count system. Note how skillfully the head is timed into the whole movement of the arms and legs. If the swimmer breathes on the right side, the head is turned at beat three (Fig. 8-1, *C*). The right arm is completing its push. The left leg is driving down for counterbalance in turning the mouth to the surface as well as for lifting the arm out of the water. The left arm is gliding forward and downward for the catch. At beat four, the right leg beats down while the head quickly recovers all the way to dead center (Fig. 8-1, *D* and *E*). At the beginning of beat four the recovery arm is just ready to enter the water. The inhalation has been accomplished in two counts or two beats of the legs. Therefore, the body remains balanced four out of six leg beats. The body on its keel and both legs and arms performing undisturbed for four beats in each stroke revolution is a tremendous factor toward greater speed and less energy expenditure.

If the swimmer breathes on the left side, the head is turned to get air during count six (Fig. 8-1, *F*). Another way to time this method other than by the count is to turn the head to the side the instant the opposite arm is beneath the surface. Care must be taken not to turn the head prematurely, that is, before the hand enters the water. The head is timed with the opposite breathing-side arm as it is entering the water. In either method the head should be fully recovered when the breathing arm has arrived in its recovery to a point directly at the side of the head. The sliding arm begins its pull as the head is completing its recovery.

A common error in this method is to drop the shoulder downward after the head has been recovered and after the breathing-side arm has entered the water. A shoulder drop in the crawl stroke violates sound mechanics in speed swimming. The shoulders must remain over the arms during the entry and propulsive phases. A shoulder drop is often caused by failure to maintain the head on dead center during exhalation. In turning the mouth for air, the head should not lift away from the pressure of the water, but both chest and the underside of the face should lie against the pillow of water while air is inhaled.

Common errors in breathing technique. Other common errors resulting from faulty head-turning mechanics are the following:
1. Lifting the chin forward and sideward to get air results in dropping the opposite elbow and shoulder, which causes the opposite arm to slide laterally. It also disturbs the leg balance, and propulsive force is dissipated.
2. Not fully recovering the head results in loss of body balance. The opposite shoulder drops, and the opposite arm pulls too wide, thus failing to complete the push drive phase. The pull is premature. The recovery-side arm has a tendency to freeze or lock at the entry.
3. Opening the mouth with the lips stretched back too far results in strangulation caused by water entering the mouth. Facial muscles become tense. The lips should aid in guiding the water away from the mouth.
4. Moving the head out of its longitudinal axis results in a loss of symmetric arm and leg action and disturbs body balance, and thus propulsive force is lost.
5. Breathing on one side only may result in the neck and shoulder muscles becoming cramped and the inability of the swimmer to see the field on both sides during a race.

Turn. Modern swimming facilities provide a target in each lane 60 inches from the end of the pool. Since the crawl stroke turn does not require the competitor to touch the wall with his hand, this warning target can be a great asset in judging the exact instant to start the execution of the no touch turn. Swimmers who cover considerable distance on their last arm pull will initiate their turn prior to reaching the warning mark. Those who complete the turn with less distance will wait until they have reached or passed the warning mark. However, the swimmer must learn to judge the distance from the wall without depending on the warning marker, which may not be visible or may not exist in all facilities. The basic turn is initiated from a position in which both arms are extended forward and assist the somersault action by pulling downward and to the rear or one in which the arms trail at the sides of the body and assist the somersault action by pressing downward and forward. (See Fig. 8-2.) The head can be

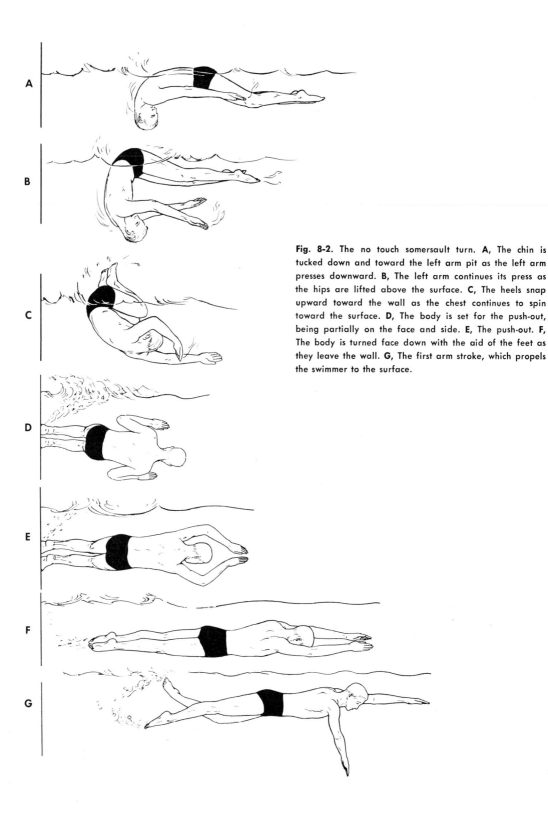

Fig. 8-2. The no touch somersault turn. **A,** The chin is tucked down and toward the left arm pit as the left arm presses downward. **B,** The left arm continues its press as the hips are lifted above the surface. **C,** The heels snap upward toward the wall as the chest continues to spin toward the surface. **D,** The body is set for the push-out, being partially on the face and side. **E,** The push-out. **F,** The body is turned face down with the aid of the feet as they leave the wall. **G,** The first arm stroke, which propels the swimmer to the surface.

a key factor in executing the quarter turn of the body. As the chin is lowered it is directed toward the left armpit and continues to press in this direction until the feet hit the wall. The resulting position should be such that the right side of the swimmers body is facing the bottom of the pool. Continuous practice should determine the exact amount of pressure to apply to the head action. Some swimmers may prefer to turn the chin under the right armpit, resulting in a left side down position. Many variations of the turn exist depending on the skill of the swimmer and what works most efficiently for him.

The following points should be noted.

1. When the head has passed the vertical, the hips should be above the water surface, the heels snap toward the buttocks.
2. The knees remain bent until the feet hit the wall, unless the swimmer has misjudged the distance and is short.
3. The back must remain rounded and the chin must continue to press toward the armpit until the feet are positioned for the push off.
4. The arms should assist in the somersault and immediately be positioned in a streamlined manner for the push off.
5. The amount of pressure applied to the head and shoulders will determine the depth of the position of the feet when they contact the wall.

Finish. The finish consists of the approach to the finish wall and finish hand touch.

Approach to the finish wall. In the sprint events, especially in the 100-yard crawl stroke, in which the swimmer must rely upon endurance to finish with a burst of speed, too often the finish is made in poor form and the race is lost. A great many swimmers just lower the head and "barrel" in for the finish. This is a grave mistake. Even though the swimmer experiences a sensation of driving harder, in reality his speed is diminished. The reason his stroke feels more powerful is that his arms are going faster. The lowering of the head lets the water support the body,

whereas, when swimming with the head and shoulder girdle elevated, the body is to some extent supported by the arms and legs. With the body held in sprinting position, the arms and legs are given additional purchase on the water at a more advantageous angle, and the arm speed provides the greatest traction.

In the approach to the finish some swimmers are coached to watch the field to see if they are gaining or losing. If the field is ahead, an occasional glance should suffice, but the swimmer should not look at the field every stroke, especially if he is tired or nearly "spent," because by looking forward he lifts the chin out and turns the head poorly and destroys stroke balance. Good sprinting form must be maintained at any cost in the approach to the finish.

Finish hand touch. In the touch at the finish, a swimmer should never reach out and slide in to the touch, but he should come in swimming hard and drive the hand in to the wall above the finish and stop short of it only an inch or two, with no more slide left. When one reaches, he stops swimming, and usually his head lifts up out of the water and the feet sink before the hand has touched. This situation is tragic for the swimmer in a close finish. He should swim until one hand hits and then stop swimming. If the hand touches under water, it is because he was sliding in too far. However, if one does slide in and touches underneath the surface, he then should not drive the other arm in just to make sure the judges will get his finish. If the hand touches in such a situation, the official is bound to judge him by the arm that comes in last, even though he did touch under water with the first. The judge is likely to be influenced by the action of the swimmer himself, by the fact that the swimmer knows whether or not he touched with the first hand. If the other hand is thrust forward, the judge will assume that he did not touch with the first. Even though a judge stands right over a lane and looks down, it is sometimes difficult to see if the touch has actually been made. If the judge is standing at the side, the angle of refraction of the arm under the water makes it difficult for him to judge as to where the touch is actually made. It is practically a guess. Should there be a question as to whether the underwater touch beat the opponent's touch above the surface in a close race, the touch above the surface is usually awarded the race.

Electronic timing devices. When electronic timing devices are used to judge and time the race, additional factors are involved. The sprinter must touch his lane finish plate with sufficient force to activate the mechanism. If he is swimming close to the lane markers he must be sure his finish touch is made on the plate in his lane, not the adjoining lane. Various electronic timing devices will differ in the construction of the finish plate. A few practice finishes with the attention of the coach prior to the meet should help prevent a poor finish in the race.

RACING FUNDAMENTALS

The sprint race is one in which the maximum speed is maintained throughout the entire race. For practically everyone who swims in competition, a distance of 25 yards can be considered a sprint event. The swimmer simply plunges into the water and swims at his top speed over the whole distance.

As the racing distance is extended to 40, 50, or 60 yards, younger and inexperienced boys and girls will have to reduce their speed in order to finish the race. They cannot, therefore, consider these distances as being sprints.

At 100 yards, only seasoned, top-ranking competitors can cover the distance at top speed without regard for conservation of energy. A survey of split times of champions for the 100-yard crawl stroke shows that the time for each consecutive lap becomes greater from the start to the finish. This means that the swimmers had not made any attempt to reduce their speed at any point during the race but rather attempted to swim at top speed throughout. The cumulative

factor of fatigue caused their speed to be reduced as the race progressed.

Swimming as fast as one can go does not mean making the arms and legs move as fast as possible. There s an optimum rate of movement that produces the greatest swimming speed for the individual. Fast, flailing movements of the arms only cut the water open and very little hold on the water is gained.

As soon as the sprint swimmer enters the water, he should attain the rate of movement that will produce the maximum speed and attempt to maintain this speed throughout the race. A common tendency among inexperienced swimmers is to break this optimum rhythm when they notice that they are being passed by a competitor or that they are behind the field. To break rhythm invariably results in an easily recognizable decrease in speed and, consequently, the loss of the race.

Thus, the answer to the swimmer's question, "How shall I swim this sprint race?" might well be, "Get off your mark as fast as you can, with a powerful dive. Come out of your glide swimming, not fighting the water, and build up into the rhythm of your greatest swimming speed. Hold your rhythm at this speed throughout the race to the best of your ability."

In order that a swimmer may compare his split times with those of champions, Table 8-1 is presented. By referring to this table, the swimmer can notice the part of the race that was swum too slowly. The next step to be considered is, then, the reason for this reduction in speed. The cause commonly is found to be improper breathing techniques, and these should be checked carefully. Improper breathing is usually associated with tying-up, and the swimmer often complains of being tired at this point.

The sprinter should not survey the field of competitors during a race. By lifting his eyes and head forward and sideward to look for his competitors, he drops his opposite shoulder and throws his body off balance,

Table 8-1.* Ideal split times for various racing times in the 100-yard crawl stroke (25-yard course)

ELAPSED DISTANCE (YD.)	ELAPSED TIME (SEC.)	SPLIT TIME (SEC.)
25	8.9	8.9
50	19.5	10.6
75	31.2	11.7
100	43.0	11.8
25	9.1	9.1
50	20.1	11.0
75	32.1	12.0
100	44.0	11.9
25	9.5	9.5
50	21.2	11.7
75	33.6	12.4
100	46.0	12.4
25	10.0	10.0
50	22.1	12.1
75	35.0	12.9
100	48.0	13.0
25	10.5	10.5
50	23.1	12.6
75	36.5	13.4
100	50.0	13.5
25	11.0	11.0
50	24.0	13.0
75	37.9	13.9
100	52.0	14.1
25	11.5	11.5
50	25.0	13.5
75	39.4	14.4
100	54.0	14.6
25	12.0	12.0
50	26.2	14.2
75	41.0	14.8
100	56.0	15.0

***How to use Table 8-1:** (1) Select your best total time that you now swim for the 100-yard freestyle race. (2) Record your own split times from this race and compare them with the split time divisions made by swimming champions. (3) To improve your best time for 100 yards, use the split times shown for the next faster total race time.

the rhythm of his arm and leg strokes is interrupted, and speed is lost.

Sprint swimmers have a tendency to race the arms at a faster rate of speed than is possible to attain with the legs. This causes a loss of rhythm between the arms and legs and can only result in a loss of speed. If a faster rhythm is desired to close a margin or provide a burst of speed at the finish, the speed of the leg action should be just as great as that of the arm action. The speed ratio between legs and arms is then balanced and will result in greater propulsive speed.

TEACHING AND LEARNING PROCEDURES OF THE CRAWL STROKE

Various methods have been used to teach the crawl stroke. Many instructors use the "whole" method in which the entire stroke is taught as a complete unit. They claim that this method saves time and the results are superior when working with learners of above-average ability. The whole-part method teaches the stroke as a unit, then breaks the stroke into its component parts, consisting of leg drills, arm drills, breathing drills, and finally putting the parts together as a complete stroke. The part-whole method consists of teaching the arm, leg, and breathing skills separately; then combining the skills with emphasis on coordination and timing.

SUGGESTED PROCEDURE OF TEACHING THE CRAWL STROKE USING THE "WHOLE" METHOD

The instructor explains the entire stroke to the class. When facilities and equipment are available, the use of slide projectors, moving pictures, charts, and other visual aids can be of help to the instructor in his presentation.

The instructor may demonstrate the whole stroke in the water or he may have a skilled swimmer demonstrate while he comments on points to be stressed. The whole stroke is attempted by the class using carefully selected floating devices as aids. The floating devices should permit freedom of movement of the arms and legs and enable the swimmer to regain a standing position easily. Each member of the class is assigned a partner and while half the class practices the stroke, the partners or other half of the class observes and constructively assists their respective partners.

When confidence and progress have been achieved, the floating devices are removed. The class continues to practice the whole stroke. During rest breaks advice is given by the instructor and partner.

The instructor then checks the stroke of each member of the class. Poor mechanics and faulty technique may be noted on a prepared skill sheet and are discussed with the pupil. Following an explanation as to what is to be done to improve the stroke the pupil is asked to repeat his performance attempting the suggested changes. The swimmer is then encouraged to continue practicing the whole stroke, concentrating on the aspects indicated by the instructor.

SUGGESTED PROCEDURE OF TEACHING THE CRAWL STROKE USING THE "PART-WHOLE" METHOD

The instructor explains the entire stroke to the class gathered before him. He then explains and demonstrates each part of the stroke.

Kick. The kick is explained on land and demonstrated by the instructor (see the discussion of leg action earlier in this chapter). Land drill for this kick is not recommended because of the limitation of the thigh action on the down movement.

Water drill. The water drill is practiced using the side of the pool for support or, if out-of-doors, arm depth shallow water with the hands supported on the bottom. The class faces the wall of the pool, with left hands grasping the hand rail with the elbow bent down against the wall directly beneath the hand, giving support to its shoulder which is maintained at a submerged level. The right hand reaches down against the wall, arm extended and directly under the right shoulder, but far enough down until both shoulders are level and horizontal with the surface of the water. The chin is submerged with the water level just below the lips. The body is extended out to the

rear by the aid of the hand supports, until the entire body is just under the surface. With the shoulders and chin at this level and the back relaxed, a deep arched sway back is eliminated. This position of the body affords the proper freedom of action for the legs to perform this kick.

Half of the class will perform and execute the kick, while the other half will observe his designated partner and offer constructive criticism. The partners then change, the student teacher becoming a pupil and the performing pupil now acting as a teacher. The instructor moves among the class correcting outstanding errors.

These kicking drills can be given for a duration of from 2 to 5 minutes at a time, or may be repeated with rest intervals. As the class begins to relax into the movements, a full respiration can now be added with each series of six beats of the kick. At first, breathing can be done with the face out of the water; then in and out of the water with each respiration within the six beats. At first, the instructor may count off, in a loud voice, the desired cadence and tempo, then let the class pick it up individually, and each student performs at random. (See discussion of breath control, Chapter 2.)

Kick board drill. The student is instructed to hold the kick board with both hands and the arms fully extended along its sides, just far enough ahead so that the near end of the board is just beyond the face. This position of the board will permit the head to move in and out of the water for breathing practice along with the kicking exercise across the pool. If the class is large, flights can be staggered moving all the way across the pool, with proper rest intervals.

During these exercises the instructor will stress hip lift to a constant maintained point near the surface. This is controlled by emphasizing the down beat of the kick so that the foot action is just under the surface. If the kick is properly performed, a boiling effect of the water rather than a splashing effect results. The instructor will also urge the class to mentally concentrate on using a six-beat rhythm or cadence, which action will later in the learning progression fit itself naturally to the arm stroke coordination.

These drills are continued until all members of the class can make progress across the pool. The instructor devotes most of his attention to the slower students. Any practical floating device may be substituted for the kick board.

Water drill without kick board. The student lies on the surface of the water, face down, the body and arms extended. In this position the class is again staggered in flights and instructed to kick as far as possible without a breath, then stop, catch air, and again push-off from the bottom and in this way continue across the pool. This drill

may be performed with half the class interchanging, with each partner as teacher and pupil. At this point the kick board can again be reverted to, and the class is now urged to cover a greater distance with continuous kicking and breathing—even as far as 100 or 200 yards.

Arm stroke and breath control. The class is again staggered in flights, this time walking across the pool, with the body bent forward to the water level and using a windmill action of the arms. This arm action is sometimes referred to as an alternating opposition rhythm. The primary purpose of this phase of learning is to recover the shoulder above the water. Maintaining a good shoulder lift throughout the entire arm recovery is of great importance in the success

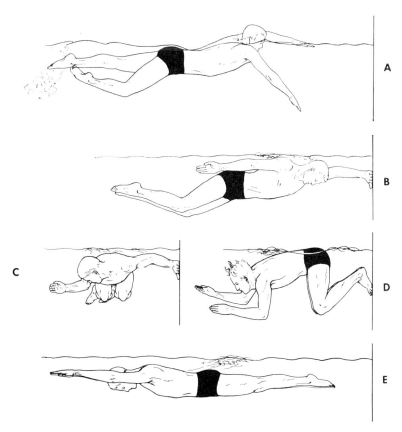

Fig. 8-3. A series of ideal form showing the elementary crawl stroke lateral turn. **A,** The approach to the wall. **B,** The start of the turn. **C,** The position of the body at the quarter turn. **D,** Body set for push-out. **E,** The body in the glide position after leaving the wall.

of learning the crawl stroke. Continue these drill repetitions with the added skill of breathing, the head turning techniques, and timing with the arms.

At this point the class is urged to walk slowly across the pool while concentrating on learning these timing techniques. Continue many repetitions of this drill while the instructor points out glaring errors. (See discussion of technique of breathing earlier in this chapter.) During this drill the student can practice turning the head to either side, or both sides, while these learning habits are being formed. The instructor constantly stresses shoulder lift during the arm recovery and also that the shoulder lift must be maintained until the hand and arm have entered the water. He should also stress pulling the arm down under the body during the propulsive phase. When these skills have been sufficiently learned, the instructor demonstrates in the water a lower and bent elbow recovery, as well as a bent arm pull under the body. (See discussion of arm action earlier in this chapter.)

Whole stroke. When the class has sufficiently learned the skills of the head action in breathing, the arm recovery, and pull, the whole stroke is now attempted by coordinating the six-beat kick with the arm and breathing action. Some instructors get best results during this learning phase by using supports as an aid.*

Again the instructor will urge the student to successfully complete as many individual stroke repetitions as possible, with breathing. When he is successful in completing more than four strokes with supports, the supports can be removed. The student is urged to strive for an ever-increasing number of strokes consecutively. It is then a question of increasing the distance during each class session until the student can swim easily and comfortably, breathing with relaxation.

*Brockway, David L.: The effectiveness of flotation aids in the teaching of beginning swimming, Masters thesis, 1961.

COMMON PROBLEMS IN LEARNING THE CRAWL STROKE

I. Failure to breath during each arm cycle
   A. Possible cause
      1. Student only partially exhales
      2. Arms moving too fast
      3. Head turning too late
      4. Eyes closing
      5. Whole body lifting
   B. Suggested cure
      1. Practice bobbing, complete exhalation
      2. Practice standing slow arm drill, with inhalation and exhalation on each cycle
      3. Turn head to breathe just as the breathing arm enters the water
      4. Turn head rather than lifting the whole body in breathing
II. Poor body position
   A. Possible cause
      1. Fear of inhaling water rather than air results in head and shoulders in high, hip and legs in low position
      2. Pause of hands above water surface prior to entry
      3. Dropping the elbow and using the arms to attempt to lift the body high in the surface
   B. Suggested cure
      1. Swim several strokes without breathing, eliminate pause above water surface
      2. Reach forward and downward as the hand enters the water as if trying to touch the bottom of the pool at the far side; attempt to achieve the sensation of swimming downhill
      3. Discourage arching the body and allowing hips to drop, instead assume more of a hunchbacked position with hips up
III. Ineffective leg action
   A. Possible cause
      1. Dorsiflexion of the foot
      2. Legs kicking too fast
      3. Legs too stiff and tense
      4. Too much knee bend with legs kicking high out of the water
   B. Suggested cure
      1. Practice kick with swim fins, the added surface will assist the foot to plantar flex
      2. Bracket drill with the instructor guiding the movements of the pupils legs with his hands
      3. Use slow motion action of the legs

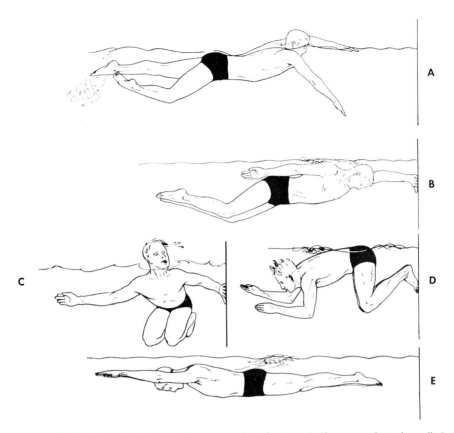

Fig. 8-4. A series of ideal form showing the distance crawl stroke turn. **A,** The approach to the wall. **B,** The start of the turn. **C,** The head is elevated above the water's surface, permitting the swimmer to take a breath. **D,** Body set for push-out. **E,** The body in the glide position after leaving the wall.

THE ELEMENTARY TURN

The beginner, in learning to turn, is usually taught by the instructor to use the hand touch.

Lateral turn. This turn is sometimes called the closed turn because the head is held under. As the hand touches the wall about 6 to 10 inches under the surface of the water, the elbow should be bent slightly so that momentum can be utilized (Fig. 8-3, *B*). Simultaneously with the hand touch, the legs are tucked tightly, with the knees together. Then the turn is made with the body remaining flat on the chest, the feet are tucked under to form a pivot upon which the body spins. The head and shoulders whip away from the arm that is against the wall and the hips move around toward the wall (Fig. 8-3, *C*). The free arm assists the turn by whipping the hand in a sculling motion, starting from the side of the hips and sweeping outward and across to the chest in a short, quick, vigorous movement. The touching hand is quickly removed from the wall and tucked close to the body as it is brought to a position alongside the other hand under the head (Fig. 8-3, *D*). The feet are driven against the wall, the arms are extended with a thrust and the head is lowered between the arms in the glide position.

In the glide the body must be held straight, not arched (Fig. 8-3, *E*). It should glide slightly upward. The body should be stretched from toes to fingertips, with the legs held close together.

This turn should be taught using both the right and the left arm touching the wall. It can also be used for turning in the side strokes.

Head-out turn. This turn is also called the open turn because the head is lifted out for air. This type of turn is used primarily for recreation distance swimming. It is used in competition when the swimmer wishes to check the number of laps he has completed or to acquire an additional breath when needed. This turn is executed in the same manner as the preceding turn except that as the hand touches the wall, the knees are tucked and brought up underneath the body, pivoting along its longitudinal axis, thus eliminating the lateral spin. The head is elevated and air is taken as the turn is executed (Fig. 8-4, *C*).

Chapter 9

Coaching the middle-distance and the distance crawl stroke

The distance crawl stroke is used in the races in which energy must be conserved and distributed over the course of the race.

In modern competitive swimming of today, the 200-yard freestyle is no longer considered a middle-distance event but a sprint race for world class swimmers. The distance crawl stroke is used by most swimmers in races of 500 yards and over.

The distance crawl stroke is built around the idea of getting a swimmer rapidly through the water with the least possible expenditure of energy. The distance crawl stroke resembles the sprint crawl stroke, except that the distance swimmer strokes with a minimum output of energy yet maintains effective speed. Relaxation is stressed and the whole action is smooth. The distance crawl stroke further differs from the sprint crawl stroke in that the trunk angle is slightly flatter and takes on a stretched appearance; the arm action is less strenuous, and the strokes are longer and more deliberate; the height of the recovery arm may be slightly lower than in the sprints; the six beat kick may or may not be broken, and the breathing is deeper.

Training for the distance events is performed quite differently than for the sprint events (see training, Chapter 16). We will not attempt to recommend an ideal style for swimming the distance events because of the number of variations being used in the kick. Many distance swimmers employ the use of an interrupted, or broken kick, tempo. There are, however, quite a number of good swimmers who adhere to the six beat kick throughout the entire distance. Swimmers who use the broken kick tempo, or drag style kick, are usually very buoyant. They depend on the arms to provide the propulsive force, using the minor beats of the kick for counterbalance and one or two major beats to compliment the propulsive force of the arm action.

Those swimmers who use an interrupted or broken tempo kick may revert to a regular six-beat sprint crawl kick in the closing moments of a distance race.

There are some individuals who possess the speed of a sprinter plus the stamina and endurance of a distance swimmer. These are ideal qualifications for the 200 and 500 yard freestyle events. Occasionally in dual meet competition a sprinter may swim in the 200 or 500 yard event to gain endurance. The distance swimmer may enter the same events to gain speed.

Whenever an event is long enough to warrant special emphasis to be placed on endurance, the problem of effort distribution immediately becomes a factor. The longer-distance swimmer must learn to pace his race so that he can efficiently distribute his energy over the entire distance in accordance with his own energy capacity. The longer distances are not injurious to the swimmer if he is physically prepared for prolonged exertion. This preparation is accomplished through a systematic training and conditioning program of work in which the cardiorespiratory system adjusts itself to the gradually added stress and strain brought about by increased distances at greater speeds.

TECHNIQUE OF THE DISTANCE CRAWL

Body position. The body rides slightly lower in the surface of the water than in the sprint crawl stroke because the speed is slightly less. The distance swimmer should bear in mind that as the speed is reduced the body position will naturally be altered and the body level will be slightly deeper in the water; as the shoulders are lowered in the water, the hips are somewhat elevated to prevent body sag. The shoulder girdle muscle fixation should be less than in the sprint crawl stroke. The muscles are less tense and allow the shoulder girdle to move freely in relation to the trunk.

Position of the head and neck. The eyes are directed forward. The water line is slightly below or above the hairline depending on the length and flexability of the neck. The head and neck must be relaxed. Any tenseness of the neck will result in a general overall tightening of the arms and upper body.

Position of the hips. The hips should be positioned well up in the surface of the water. Buoyant individuals will achieve this position naturally, whereas less buoyant swimmers must rely on the arms and legs to support the hips.

Leg action. The technique of the distance flutter kick is, in principle, exactly the same as that discussed in the sprint kick. There is, however, a general difference in the width of the stroke of the legs. This is because the slower the speed, the wider becomes the leg stroke. The reason for this is that the legs must obtain traction in the water, and when they kick less rapidly, less propulsive action is obtained. Therefore, wider action of the legs increases their pressure against the water and provides the traction.

Drag kick. There are some distance swimmers who have a very ineffective leg action but a fast and powerful arm action. These swimmers will then rely upon a reduced leg stride called the "drag," or broken tempo flutter kick. There is in this type of kick just enough hip and knee action to feather the legs with the legs held almost straight and merely giving counterbalance to the arms. There will be just enough effort expended in the kick to maintain the body near the surface and every effort should be made to offer as little surface friction along the legs as possible. The water must slip smoothly under, over, and past the legs.

ARM ACTION IN THE DISTANCE CRAWL STROKE

In order to slow the arm action and allow greater relaxation, the arm in the distance crawl stroke is allowed to glide forward during the catch. However, to obtain the longer catch, the arm reaches out to enter at a very shallow angle and then slides into the catch. Then the elbow is bent more in order to shorten the arm lever so as to obtain greater driving power by driving the arm almost straight backward with some downward pressure. During the distance crawl stroke, while the swimmer is using the gliding arm stroke, he relies upon a flattened arc to propel his body forward. This gives the body efficient forward action from the drive as the elbow and wrist extend in a follow-through delivery. After the completion of this arm delivery, the elbow is then bent again and lifted above the surface, and the forearm is flung around laterally to the reach and entry. Unless one has an efficient driving leg action kick to support a sliding arm stroke, the swimmer should reduce the slide and rely upon the arm action for nearly all of the power.

Reach. The reach may be made from either a high bent-elbow or from a low bent-elbow recovery. Both types are commonly followed.

In the high recovery, care should be taken not to let the forearm hang down vertically from the elbow because then the hand is too close to the armpit during recovery. When the elbow extends for the reach from this position, the hand usually overreaches in nearly every case, and the shoulder is dropped before the hand entry. The reach is made slightly slower than in the sprint type. However, if it is too slow the shoulder will roll down. Again in this type of stroke the shoulder must remain above the arm during the propulsive arc. The arm should not reach to its full extension above the surface. From the high bent-elbow recovery, the arm comes down from above for the entry. In the low bent-elbow recovery, the reach is very close to the surface and goes into the entry slightly sooner, usually with a press type of entry similar to the one described in the sprint stroke.

Entry. The arm should be pressed into the water, and it should continue under the surface to the catch and pull. It should be constantly pressed at the wrist and hand, not the elbow and shoulder, to allow the shoulder to move over the arm. The press allows contact to be held with the water while waiting for the completion of the leg cycle. The entry should not be prolonged because the loss of arm propulsion will be far in excess of the very slight advantage given to the legs by the delay.

Glide or support. During the glide the pressure should be felt in the fingers. This causes the arm to glide downward slightly below the level of the shoulder, which causes the body to rest on that arm, but the shoulders and head are not permitted to lower. The water level at the head should remain constant throughout the entire glide. Throughout the glide the elbow should never be stretched or overextended. There should be a natural full reach and elbow extension. The tip of the elbow should be pointing to the side, not downward, during the glide. If the tip of the elbow is pointing downward, the elbow has been extended too far and will cause the shoulder to drop below it. The action of the arm from entry to catch must be rapid and forceful yet be skillful in preparing itself for an effective catch. The phase from entry to completion of the release must be executed fast and skillfully in order to assure a fast turnover of the propulsive arm stroke, so that the opposition rhythm balance is maintained with the recovery arm. (See Fig. 8-1.)

It is during the glide phase of this stroke that the shoulder joint should be extended forward after the elbow joint has completed its extension. The shoulder is submerged in the water. This increases the length of the arm leverage as it commences the propulsive phase. The body glides on the arm from the drive of the other arm and from the constant flow of power delivered from the flutter kick.

If the arm is permitted to glide on or just barely under the surface, it is too shallow, and the entry has lost some of its propulsive effectiveness. The entry to the catch should be a propulsive phase of the stroke, even though minor in force to the major propulsive arc. The arm, while sliding, should move downward. From the study of underwater movies, the actual depth of proficient swimmers, riding below the surface, is approximately 6 to 10 inches at the completion of the glide. From above the surface it appears very much shallower and has the appearance of 2 to 4 inches in depth.

Catch. The catch is effected at the completion of the glide in the same manner as described in the sprint type of stroke. The pull or catch is initiated in the hand; then the forearm and upper arm follow in rapid succession. The elbow should never lead during the pull phase. The mechanics of the adjustment from pull, or draw, to push and drive takes place exactly the same way as it is performed in the sprint crawl stroke. Some swimmers use a decided elbow bend, almost a boomerang position, whereas others use a slight bend in adjustment. Whenever a decided bend is used in order to maintain good leverage in the movements, care should be taken not to let the hand move too far outside the line of the opposite shoulder, otherwise the mechanical advantage of the pull and drive is lost.

Pull, drive, and release. The pull, drive, and release are identical in mechanics to that of the sprint type of stroke. The essential difference in the release from that of the sprint type is that it occurs farther back.

As a general rule it takes place slightly beyond the hip joint. It is also essential in the release to notice if each hand has the same length of drive to the point of the release so that balance is maintained.

Recovery. The recovery of the arms may be accomplished as described in the sprint crawl arm recovery. Some swimmers employ a quick recovery, sometimes called a "flip" recovery, whereas others usually use a slightly slower recovery. Most distance swimmers recover the arm in a low, outward sweep of the entire arm, maintaining the hand well out from the elbow, with the arm rotator muscles adjusting the hand and elbow for the proper entry.

Timing of one arm with the other arm. A very simple and accurate timing method can be used. The recovery arm is used as a guiding basis. As the recovery arm is entering the water, the driving arm must be well beyond the shoulders in its concluding drive. In executing this significant and dominant phase of the timing technique, one should experience the same feeling as in ice skating. For example, in skating, as one drives with the hindmost leg, the foremost leg swings forward to contact the ice to receive the force of the driving leg. This same principle is true in the crawl stroke, that is, the driving arm under the body transfers force and momentum onto the entering arm. (See Fig. 8-2, *A* to *D*.) Note how this timing has established the opposition rhythm of the arms as well as the legs. The legs will naturally "dovetail" into the arm and shoulder movement for counterbalancing action of the entire stroke. Once this timing pattern has been established, it is very easy to maintain it throughout the distance to be covered. The weight of the body must not be shifted onto the recovering arm as the catch and pull begins but must be shifted when the recovery arm is in the water and is in a position to furnish support. It is this timing point that many swimmers miss. The speed derived from this type of stroke is in a large part the result of this timing. One derives a feeling of continu-ously sliding downhill if the entire stroke is performed well.

Timing ratio of the arms and legs in relation to each other. The same timing is used as described in the sprint crawl stroke, except that when an arm slide is used, a slightly longer kicking stride is necessary to coordinate with the arms.

RELATION OF THE HEAD TURNING FOR BREATHING TO ARM AND LEG ACTION

There is little difference in the timing of the head other than has been discussed in the sprint crawl stroke. Even though more time is allowed for the taking of air because deeper breathing is essential in distance swimming, actually no less time is or should be consumed in going to the air and in coming away from it. However, many inexperienced swimmers will, because they are stroking slower, move the head more slowly to and away from the air. This will disturb the whole stroke rhythm as well as body balance.

The distance swimmer must learn to turn the face equally well to either side for air. Occasionally, by alternating the breathing side, the shoulder muscles gain rest and relaxation.

Common errors in head action technique. A common error is either not turning the head fast enough to the point of inhaling or recovering it back to dead center after air is obtained. This is usually caused by a rigid neck. If fatigue sets in too early in a race, breathing should be checked to see if it is adequate and properly executed.

One should not retard the recovery arm as it approaches the point of entry. This fault permits the shoulder to lower and submerge before the hand enters. The hand must drop immediately into the water as it nears the point of entry.

RACING FUNDAMENTALS

Usually the middle-distance swimmer must also swim a distance event in a dual meet. A swimmer who is well trained and is in good condition can swim both races and does not need to harbor the feeling that he must conserve his energy in the first event in order to turn in a good performance in the second. In fact, the seasoned competitor will improve the performance of his second event by the warming-up influences of his first race.

Adjustment to the pool. Swimming pools are usually laid out in lanes. (See rules for outdoor and indoor competition.)* In dual competition the swimmer may have the opportunity to select his own lane. In narrow pools he should choose inside lanes. Outside lanes are not conducive to fast swimming because of constant agitation of water below the surface caused by waves reverberating from the walls. The swimmer should observe before the start of the race the lane in which a rival is stationed.

In a strange tank the swimmer should observe both ends of the tank to see that his turning wall is free of any obstruction. If the tank has lane markers on the bottom of the pool, he should observe if it has a warning mark 4 feet from the turning wall. If surface lane markers are used and should a swimmer hook an arm over one of them, he should not stop but continue until he is in the clear. If the swimmer has a balanced arm stroke, he will seldom swim out of his lane. Too often a swimmer will forget himself and watch his rival. A swimmer should not glance at the field at every stroke. Such an error causes the stroke to become unbalanced and results in a loss of speed.

Speed in the early part of the race. The rate of speed in the early part of a distance race usually depends on how thoroughly the swimmer is schooled in pace. However, it also depends on the ability of the swimmer.

The rate of speed at the beginning of a race is faster than at any other part, but it

*Amateur Athletic Union of United States, Official swimming rules, published annually by Amateur Athletic Union, 233 Broadway, New York, N. Y.; also, National Collegiate Athletic Association, Intercollegiate and Interscholastic swimming guide, Official rules for swimming and diving, published annually by National Intercollegiate Athletic Bureau, New York, N. Y.

must not be prolonged beyond the swimmer's ability to carry out his race plan. A burst of speed at the start by an opponent need not be met, since he is bound to revert to a slower rate of speed somewhere just ahead unless he is an exceptional swimmer.

Although the first 100 yards of a middle-distance race are important, one cannot win a race in the first 100 yards. The inexperienced swimmer is likely to forget this. He should school himself in pace so thoroughly that he can swim 100 yards at any given speed within his capacity and not misjudge it more than 0.5 second. In midseason the distance swimmer should be checked many times on the 100 yards at varying speeds so that he gets a sensation of the speed he is traveling. This will assure him of never being drawn out too far at a greater speed than his endurance will permit. If too little is spent in the first part of the race, he can distribute the remainder of his speed over the remaining yards. The inexperienced swimmer is more likely to win with such a plan until confidence and sufficient experience are gained. The loss of a race in the last 100 yards is often caused by a misjudgment of the first 100 yards.

The top-flight middle-distance swimmers can adopt a race plan of going out with the gun and staying out ahead. The top-flight swimmer is one who has had considerable racing experience and can swim a "rugged" 100 yards and go well beyond that distance. This depends on ability and competitive experience. The beginner should adopt a predetermined plan and then perfect it as he gains in experience, ability, and confidence.

Maneuvering for position. If a beginner has hopes of winning a race against a more experienced rival, he must not give him more than two body lengths lead in the early stage of a middle-distance race, if he is to overtake him in the final sprint. If one desires to take the lead and stay out, he must be willing to pay the price. Some swimmers simply lack confidence in taking a lead but are willing to swim along with the field and then challenge in the final sprint.

When two rivals are of equal ability, it may or may not be desirable to be out in front throughout the entire race. If one does relinquish the lead to an opponent of equal ability, it should not be greater than one and one half body lengths. This is commonly called the danger line in racing tactics. Very frequently in such a close race, one relies upon the other to be carried along at an optimum stroke cadence and keeps the leading rival near enough to sense quickly any change in tactics. Frequently a leading rival will go out at a terrific rate of speed with the idea in mind of causing his rival to press his stroke, throw him off his stroke rhythm, and in this way outmaneuver him to the finish.

An experienced swimmer knows his own best pace and will not allow a competitor either to entice him into early exhaustion by a great effort early in the race or cause him to swim so slowly at first that even an all-out accelerative effort will not enable him to finish well. Swimmers are in lanes by themselves and can be attentive to their own pace.

Passing an opponent. A distance swimmer who relinquishes an early lead to his rival may wish to challenge in the later stages of the race. He may attempt faster turns after the first half of the race and gradually build up the margin relinquished. Some swimmers like to sneak up and pass a less alert rival on a blind lap. These tactics may cause a less experienced swimmer no end of worry. Passing a swimmer is costly, and the passer must be prepared to pay the price to stay ahead and meet a counterchallenge.

In the final stages of a race, if a margin must be closed, it should be closed gradually. The swimmer should close the margin early enough in the final stages of the race so that it is within the limits of accomplishment. If the opponent is tiring rapidly near the finish, then a final effort is made to overtake him. The swimmer must always be on the alert in going for the finish and use good judgment by swimming in good form and not making a "dog fight" out of the finish. It is well for him to keep in mind that his rival may be tiring more rapidly than he is. In other words, while in the water be alert and smart at all stages of the race.

Meeting a challenge. The start may be considered as the first challenge in a middle-distance race. When the field gets underway, the swimmer must decide if the speed of his opponents is approximating that of his own plan or whether it is too fast or too slow. He has the option of either electing or rejecting the challenge. He may desire to conserve his energy early in the race and then in the closing seconds of the race elect to challenge for the lead.

A challenge may occur at any stage of the race. One may be swimming at his own best pace and may ignore passing tactics of an opponent. On the other hand, one may accept the challenge with the idea of breaking down excessive amounts of energy being spent by the challenger and later reducing his stroke cadence. Quite frequently in a race a swimmer must decide quickly which is the wiser plan to follow, even though it does not fit into his predetermine race plan. In the last 50 yards of the race he should be ready to meet any challenge if he has hopes of winning the race. Middle-distance swimmers may well follow the rule of swimming the first part of the race with the head and the last part with the heart.

Disastrous effects may be the direct result of accepting a challenge at a most inopportune time of a race if the challenge interferes seriously with the effort distribution of the accepting swimmer.

Pace. A swimmer should be thoroughly disciplined and schooled in the technique of pacing. Perhaps the ideal way to swim a middle-distance race is to be able to distribute the rate of speed and effort evenly in proportion to the distance covered. The swimmers who are breaking the records are swimming the first part of the race at only fractions of a second slightly faster rate than the latter part of the race.

Table 9-1. Ideal split times for various racing times in the 200-yard crawl stroke (25-yard pool)

ELAPSED DISTANCE (YD.)	ELAPSED TIME (SEC.)	SPLIT TIME (SEC.)	ELAPSED DISTANCE (YD.)	ELAPSED TIME (SEC.)	SPLIT TIME (SEC.)
25	9.8	9.8	25	12.0	12.0
50	21.8	12.0	50	26.1	14.1
75	34.0	12.2	75	40.6	14.5
100	46.25	12.25	100	55.2	14.6
125	58.50	12.25	125	1:10.2	15.0
150	1:10.80	12.30	150	1:25.3	15.1
175	1:23.15	12.35	175	1:40.5	15.2
200	1:35.00	11.85	200	1:55.0	14.5
25	10.4	10.4	25	12.6	12.6
50	23.0	12.6	50	27.3	14.7
75	35.8	12.8	75	42.4	15.1
100	48.7	12.9	100	57.6	15.2
125	1:01.6	12.9	125	1:13.2	15.6
150	1:14.6	13.0	150	1:29.0	15.8
175	1:27.6	13.0	175	1:44.8	15.8
200	1:40.0	12.4	200	2:00.0	15.2
25	11.0	11.0	25	13.2	13.2
50	24.1	13.1	50	28.5	15.3
75	37.5	13.4	75	44.2	15.7
100	51.0	13.5	100	1:00.0	15.8
125	1:04.6	13.6	125	1:16.2	16.2
150	1:18.2	13.6	150	1:32.6	16.4
175	1:31.9	13.7	175	1:49.1	16.5
200	1:45.0	13.1	200	2:05.0	15.9
25	11.6	11.6	25	13.8	13.8
50	25.3	13.7	50	29.7	15.9
75	39.3	14.0	75	46.0	16.3
100	54.4	14.1	100	1:02.5	16.5
125	1:07.6	14.2	125	1:19.3	16.8
150	1:21.9	14.3	150	1:36.3	17.0
175	1:36.3	14.4	175	1:53.4	17.1
200	1:50.0	13.7	200	2:10.0	16.6

A general plan is presented and recommended showing the beginner how energy may be distributed effectively for the middle-distance swimming races (Table 9-1).

Maintaining the stroke rhythm. To maintain and preserve a smooth, relaxed, and economical stroking cadence from the starting stages through the challenges and to the final stages of a race is a most commendable achievement in competition. If one is too easily excited under racing conditions so that the mind is diverted from the stroke rhythm, one can hardly expect to maintain any stroke balance. Sometimes swimming near the path of another swimmer's feet causes one to lose hold of the disturbed water.

In the middle distances one should turn the head occasionally to both sides for three reasons: first, to relax the neck and shoulder girdle muscles; second, to facilitate respiration; and third, to observe the position of his opponents.

TEACHING AND LEARNING PROCEDURES

For teaching and learning procedures for the crawl stroke, see Chapter 8.

Chapter 10

Coaching the back crawl stroke

The back crawl stroke is of more recent origin than that of its sire, the crawl. Since its origin in approximately 1912, its speed has been improved more than either the crawl or the breast stroke. A comparison of the fastest times recorded for the four strokes from 1912 with those of the present time is given in Table 10-1.

When the back crawl stroke first became known as the fastest means of swimming on the back, the preferred technique of stroke mechanics varied widely among coaches and swimmers.

Some of the questions considered were: Should the arms be recovered straight or bent? Should they be placed in the water behind the head, straight back from the shoulder, or outside a line with the shoulder? Should the arms be pulled deep or shallow? Should they be pulled straight or in a bent position? Should the head be carried in line with the body or held up facing the legs? Should the body roll more than in the crawl stroke? Through a long process of trial and error, a general agreement had been reached as to the best style so that we had but one style universally accepted. This style will be called the Kiefer style, since it was introduced by him. Practically every world's back stroke record has been established by Adolph Kiefer. However, the modern trend of the top-flight swimmers is now away from this style and favors a more vertical recovery of the arms. It is believed that a faster turnover of the stroke is obtained through the latter.

One must bear in mind that in swimming the back crawl style the man is on his back, and structural limitations at the shoulder joint prevent him from pulling the arms through the propulsive phases under the body as in the crawl stroke. However, to partially offset this limitation, he is able to maintain his breathing apparatus above the surface, which is a great advantage. The fact that the swimmer does not need to turn or lift his head out to the side or to the front for breathing air, as is the case with the crawl, breast, and dolphin butterfly strokes, makes this stroke one of the most mechanically balanced of all the competitive strokes. Because no head-turning mechanics are required for breathing, resistance to water is minimized, and, as a result, this is the smoothest of any of the swimming strokes.

PHYSICAL QUALIFICATIONS FOR THE BACK CRAWL SWIMMER

Almost anyone endowed with ability in water and better than average strength can

Table 10-1. A comparison of speed for the four competitive strokes (1912 to 1972)

STROKE	1912 100 YD. (SEC.)	1972 100 YD. (SEC.)
Crawl	0:58.0	0:45.00
Butterfly*		0:47.98
Back crawl	1:12.0	0:51.29
Breast	1:10.0	0:56.83

*Note: The dolphin butterfly stroke was not originated until April, 1935, by Armbruster and Sieg. Sieg's best time for 100 yards at that time was 1:00.2.

swim the back crawl stroke reasonably well. However, those who have ambitions of reaching the top should possess reasonably good height of at least 5 feet 11 inches, with large hands and feet and a snakelike type of build. Along with this, they must be endowed with strength and endurance. The 200-yard back crawl is probably one of the most difficult races on the college swimming program. A fast flutter kick is essential for speed. There are many boys who have long rubbery legs but who do not possess either the power or speed to drive them fast enough for either 100 yards or 200 yards to be top-flight swimmers. Many shorter-built swimmers are endowed with extremely fast driving legs and powerful arms and make up for their lack of long legs and arms by their speed and endurance.

The back crawl swimmer moves his arms and legs at about the same cadence as the sprint swimmer, and yet he must cover a distance that is beyond that of the 100-yard sprint. His physiologic characteristics are, therefore, a combination of the sprint crawl and the middle-distance swimmer.

He must be able to move his legs rapidly, he must have powerful arms and flexible shoulders, and he must also have a considerable amount of endurance. His sense of rhythm must be well developed.

TECHNIQUE OF THE BACK CRAWL START

The back crawl stroke start requires an entirely different technique than the crawl, breast, and butterfly strokes. In most instances the back crawler is put to a disadvantage in competition because of the lack of a secure foot support. This is a disadvantage that should be corrected. Some type of starting blocks* should be made with a hand bar for the competitor to grasp (Fig. 10-1, *A*). With the use of adjustable starting blocks, it has been proved that the starting time for back strokers is significantly

*Valett, Herbert B.: An experimental study of the back stroke start in swimming with the use of starting stirrups, University of Iowa Thesis, 1948.

faster. The bar can be constructed so that it is in line with the starting wall. A more advantageous start could be made with hand rests approximately 18 inches above the surface. Adjustable footrests upon which to place the feet should be constructed to prevent slipping and to give substantial support to the foot to any depth beneath the surface. With this equipment a more powerful start is made, which would enhance the flight through the air and give an advantage to the start similar to that of the other events.

Starting position. If no starting rail is available, the hands grasp the scum rail about shoulder width or spread slightly wider than shoulders. The feet take a position beneath the hands parallel to each other and spread hip width. The toes are from 0 to 4 inches under the surface and are never spread farther than the width of the hips. The feet are placed firmly against the wall (Fig. 10-1, *A*).

Another position of the feet is a walking stride stance, with the toe of one foot placed about level with the heel of the other foot. Either of these two methods of foot placing and spacing is used.

The body must assume a closely bunched tuck with the hips placed close to the heels. The body is out of the water. The arms may be held either straight or slightly bent at the elbows.

If a handrail is used, it should be grasped with the first two joints of the fingers, and the heel of the hand should take a position below the hand grasp on the hand starting rail. At the signal to start, the hand throw can be executed faster with the quick extension of the wrist against the hand rail.

The above stance is assumed (Fig. 10-1, *B*) when the starter gives the command, "Take your marks." At the report of the gun, the body is catapulted backward as if it were crouched upon a powerful compressed spring that was suddenly released (Fig. 10-1, *C*).

Leaving the mark. The aim of the throwaway action in the back stroke start is to

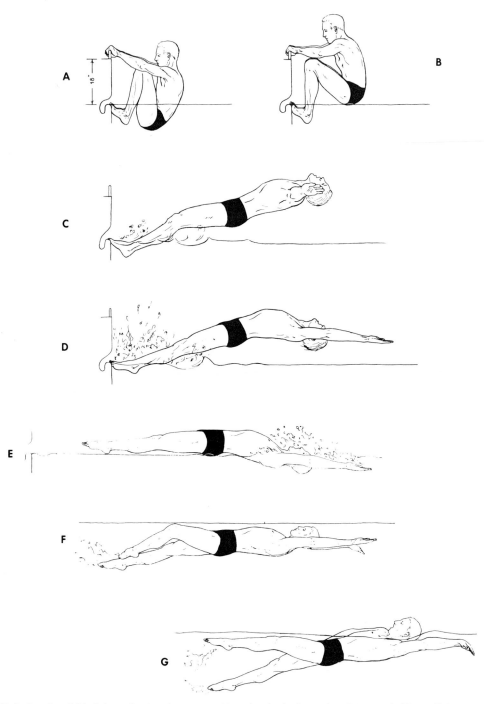

Fig. 10-1. A series of ideal form showing the start positions for the back crawl stroke start. **A,** The preliminary stance. **B,** The "set" position. **C,** The hands have pushed from the block, the arms reach laterally toward the entry. **D,** Leaving the mark. **E,** Body entering the water. **F,** The start of the stroke at the end of the glide under the surface. **G,** The position of the body as it comes to the surface.

make a backward racing dive by projecting the body out over the surface, entering the water, and utilizing the momentum derived from the start in the glide under water.

At the gun, the starting movement consists in releasing the hands with a wrist snap, and driving the arms vigorously backward laterally, not upwards, to a full arm extension beyond the head and in line with the spine. (See Fig. 10-1, *B* and *C*.) This arm movement is executed with tremendous speed. The head is driven backward simultaneously with the arms. The legs then begin extending at the knees and hips with explosive speed. When these joints are fully extended, then the ankles are extended. The final snap of the ankles gives added speed to the body. This should throw the body into a stretched position with the back slightly arched and the hips well above the surface of the water (Fig. 10-1, *C*). If no handrail is provided and the body is sitting in the water at the start, the hips must be lifted at the throw-away; otherwise they will drag through the water, causing resistance.

The swimmer should grasp the handrail in the starting stance, with the toes at the surface line. In this position the body can be driven far out above the surface with a very much faster start and a greater penetrating power into the water.

Entry. The position of the body is somewhat arched so as to gain a clean-cut entry at the proper angle. As the hands enter the water, the head is held well back between the extended arms (Fig. 10-1, *D*). The arms are fully stretched beyond the head, in line with the spine. The wrists should be held straight in line with the forearm. A common error is to hyperextend the wrists, which causes the body to glide too deep into the water. The hands and arms should be separated the width of the head and the neck and face. The moment the head and shoulders have entered the water, the head should be raised in order to prevent the body from going too deep.

Glide. The glide under water should be continued to a point at which the speed derived from momentum slows to a rate equaling that of the swimming speed. Overanxious sprinters have a tendency to start stroke action prematurely and thus do not take full advantage of the momentum gained from the start.

As the momentum is retarded to the swimming speed in the glide, the flutter kick begins just before the arm stroke action begins.

During the glide, air may either be expelled gradually or held until just prior to breaking through to the surface.

Breath control in the back stroke start. When the arms are thrown back laterally beyond the head, away from the starting wall, the chest region is lifted and expanded, causing air to rush into the lungs easily through a wide-open mouth (Fig. 10-1, *C*). The breath is held during entry and during most of the glide.

When one is lying on the back under water, the opening from the nose into the throat is directly down. In this position water can enter very easily, causing considerable respiratory distress to the inexperienced back stroke swimmers, especially during the glide phase of the start and also at the push-out at the turn.

There are several ways to prevent this distress of water entering the throat by way of the nasal passage. One method is to curl the upper lip and press it up against the external nasal openings. This closes them entirely and prevents water from entering the outer nasal and sinus regions. At the instant before swimming into the surface of the water and at the moment the nose has cleared the surface and the outer nostrils are free of water, the exhalation is started and the upper lip is removed. The mouth is then opened for an inspiration. A more conventional method is to expire air slowly through the nose continuously throughout the glide from the start and also throughout the push-out from the turn. This method is most difficult to control by a beginner because, while lying on the back, the swimmer finds the pressure of water difficult to overcome by a sustained expiration. This pressure causes the air held in the lungs to be forced out through the nose unchecked early in the glide. When the air has escaped in this manner, the inexperienced swimmer then finds himself just as helpless to prevent water entering the lungs through the nose before he comes to the surface.

Start of the stroke action. The arm stroke action begins while the body is still under the surface (Fig. 10-1, *E*). The swimmer

then comes up forward to the surface swimming.

While the first arm begins its pull under water, the other arm should remain firmly anchored under the surface and straight ahead in line with the body. Downward pressure on this arm is necessary to keep it under the water and prevent it from shooting out of the water. Maintaining the arm under the water streamlines the body and eliminates considerable resistance. The arm that is pulling should pull fast and hard. This first pulling arm should bend at the elbow

Fig. 10-2. A series of ideal form for executing the back crawl stroke showing the six leg beats and one revolution of the arm stroke. These figures also show the counterbalance of the arm and leg action and the position of the body in relation to the surface. All of these figures show the stroke, body from both sides, and head-on positions. **A,** The right arm has completed the drive as the left arm enters and catches the water. **B,** As the right arm recovers, the left arm starts the drive. **C,** Note the opposition rhythm of the right and left arms, also the bent arm drive. **D,** Opposition rhythm of the arm stroke.

to effect quick forward propulsion to the body, which is already moving fast from the start.

If the initial pulling arm is pulled in a straight-arm position, it will lead to two errors: first, it will push the body out of the water instead of driving it straight ahead; second, the straight arm cannot pull through the water fast enough to maintain the speed. The body must come out of the glide swimming fast. The head should be raised as the first arm is pulled (Fig. 10-1, *F*).

In the alternating type of initial arm action, the body slides through the surface under continuous application of power. The body rides on a supporting arm, which is preparing itself to catch the water the moment the other arm releases the water. As the body is swimming out into the surface, the stroke continues with regular rhythm. The head has been raised to the proper position in the next two or three arm strokes.

TECHNIQUE OF THE BACK CRAWL STROKE

The arms perform in reverse order to the crawl stroke. The back stroke is more easily mastered than the crawl, breast, or butterfly strokes, because it does not have the complex breathing skills to be mastered. The

Fig. 10-2, cont'd. E, The left arm is slightly bent for relaxation as it lifts out of the water for the recovery. The shoulder lift is also shown. **F,** The arm is again straight in the recovery. The height of the arm above the surface is also shown. **G,** Note the position of the legs, hips, and shoulder. **H,** Note the head and right arm as the left arm prepares to enter the water.

arms move in a regular cycle in opposition to each other. The kick is similar in action to the six-beat crawl kick.

Once the stroke is mechanically mastered, it seldom gets out of line. Sometimes a strong swimmer who is not highly endowed with motor skills makes a very fine back crawler.

Position of the body in swimming the back crawl stroke. The body is held nearly in a horizontal position and is maintained as near the surface as possible, with the hips just low enough to keep the legs under the surface (Fig. 10-2, *A*). The hips should not sag downward. The body should constantly be maintained in a stretched position. The chest and abdomen are flattened so that the water slipping around from the side of the head and neck can wash smoothly over the shoulders and chest with as little resistance as possible. The back of the spine presents a slightly convex position to the water. The back is curved just enough to cause the small of the back to conform to a continuous curved line from the hips to the shoulders. Stretching the body and relaxing the spine will place the body in this position.

Position of the head. The head is carried in line with the body (Fig. 10-2, *B*). The position of the head aids materially in forming the proper spinal curve. It also aids in balancing the body. The chin should be lowered reasonably close to the throat so that the eyes can easily see toward the feet. The back portion of the head below the ears should ride under the surface. The head in this position serves as a rudder. The position of the head in the water will vary somewhat with characteristics of the individual and the amount of speed generated. Usually the lower tips of the ears are at the water level.

The eyes, nose, and chin should be centered on the line of progression. Under no circumstances, except when glancing for the turn, should the chin move out of this alignment regardless of the movements of the shoulder girdle while stroking. In spite of a slight rolling of the body caused by the shoulder action of the arm stroke, the chin must remain centered and pressed down toward the throat. The body requires this stability of the head in order to maintain body alignment and balance during the stroke action.

Position of the neck. A long, flexible neck is a definite aid to a back-stroke swimmer because it offers a lesser amount of resistance to water than a short neck. In both the short- and the long-necked individuals, relaxation is essential. Unless the neck is relaxed, the chin will not be able to remain fixed while the shoulder girdle is oscillating. However, if an individual has a long neck, then instead of having to hold the body in an angular position in order to elevate the head, he can hold the body in an almost horizontal line, with the shoulders completely submerged (Fig. 10-2, *C*). The neck is projected upward, with the chin tucked toward the throat, and the back of the head presses into the water. In this position the water washes down smoothly over the entire length of the body.

Position of the shoulder girdle and upper spine. Ordinarily a swimmer who has a normal spine while walking will have the proper contour of his shoulder girdle and upper spine if he tucks his chin in, stretches the body, and relaxes the spine and neck (Fig. 10-2, *A*). In this position the cervical spines, from the shoulder to the base of the skull, will form a convex curve in line with the thoracic spines. A hunchbacked position would diminish power because the back muscles would be stretched and the pectorals would be shortened. The shoulder girdle muscles should be stretched daily to keep them supple and strong throughout the season. It must be remembered that the arms in the back crawl stroke work in reverse gear. Therefore, if the pectorals are allowed to become shortened when the arms reach back for the entry, they will prohibit the arm from stretching backward comfortably, and the body will have to roll over too much to accomplish a proper entry. The pectoral muscles should be stretched thoroughly so that there will be no resistance to the freedom of the arm action, especially in the recovery and the entry where efficient muscular performance is absolutely essential to great swimming speed performance in back stroke swimming.

The major characteristic of swimming the Kiefer style of back crawl is in the method of recovery. The arms sweep back from release to entry in a low, lateral swing. We recommend that in learning the back crawl stroke the beginner should first be taught the Kiefer style, or lateral arm recovery. This style has several advantages for the beginner over the style that employs a high vertical arm recovery for the following reasons: First, one is not apt to sink one's face or splash water over one's breathing equipment, the nose and mouth, causing unpleasant choking and strangling. Second, because of the structural limitation of the shoulder socket, if the arm is recovered vertically, the shoulder socket tends to lock itself just as the arm is extended overhead and about to enter the water. In this position the forearm and hand cannot be placed into the water unless the body is rolled over or the arm rotated, palm facing outward and downward. However, if the arm is swung back low over the surface and placed into the water just outside the shoulder joint, with the palm down, the joint does not bind and lock itself; neither does the body need to roll over to accommodate the movement.

The third advantage to this style is that the arm will not go into the water as deep as it usually does following a vertical recovery. By going deep, both the latissimus dorsi and the pectoralis major muscles are placed at a mechanical disadvantage. In the shallow pull both of these muscles pull with a very good mechanical advantage.

The modern trend in back stroke competition is definitely going to the high or vertical arm recovery. The advantages of the high arm recovery are as follows: First, it affords a faster turnover. Second, the recovery at the completion of the arm drive, a more natural continuous movement, is obtained, rather than a change of direction by swinging the arm laterally away from the body to initiate the recovery phase as is the case in the Kiefer style. Third, if the arm completes the drive and starts into the recovery, the thumb breaks through the surface first, then the hand and entire arm need only execute a quarter-turn inward in order to unlock the shoulder socket for an easy entry (Fig. 10-2, *D* and *E*.)

Position of the hips and lower (lumbar) spine. A common tendency for back strokers is to permit the hips to sag downward. This is brought about by carrying the head too high and rounding the neck and shoulders too much. This is true in the crawl stroke as well as the back crawl stroke. This sag is eliminated by stretching the body while swimming. Not only should the body be stretched in order to lift the hips, but downward pressure must be exerted on the two points of support—the arms as they enter and press and the down beat of the kick. The upper brim of the pelvis is tilted backward to straighten a deep curvature of the lower back (Fig. 10-2, *C*).

The hips do not have as much oscillation as in the crawl stroke. There is, however, just enough undulating movement in the hips for counterbalance between the beats of the legs and the pelvis.

Lateral sway of the hips should be eliminated. This is usually caused by overreaching in the arm entry.

Action of the legs. As in the crawl stroke, the six-beat kick is the most efficient and practical because of its natural counterbalance rhythm in stroke cadence with the arms.

There is little difference between the back crawl flutter kick and the crawl kick, as far as mechanics are concerned. The hip, knee, and ankle joints undulate the same way in either kick. There are, however, two essential differences (Fig. 10-2).

First, the feet do not kick into or break

through the surface. However, the legs lie just under the surface, and at the completion of the up kick the leg has straightened at the knee, but the knee and foot have not kicked through the surface. Underwater study of champions, including Kiefer, reveals the absence of air bubbles in the back crawl. This does not support the theory that air bubbles give added friction for the feet to get traction in the water. By the use of the underwater camera method, it is seen that the air bubbles pass backward at an angle and do not again come in contact with the other leg in either the down or up beat in either the back or the crawl flutter kick.

The second significant difference between the two flutter kicks is that, on completion of the up beat, in the back crawl kick the upper surface of the leg is on a straight line with the upper surface of the hips, abdomen, and chest.

In general, in the back flutter kick, the foot and toes bend inward in the up kick more so than in the down beat of the crawl kick. They do not remain in pigeon-toed position on the down beat. On the down beat the foot may or may not be fully extended.

In the up beat the knee bends and then quickly straightens to create a whiplike action in the ankle. During the bend of the knee, the inexperienced swimmer will very often bend or lift the knees too far and break the surface. This should be avoided. The water should be permitted to slip or wash down over the legs from the hips downward and not be retarded or resisted by poking the knee through the surface. To streamline the legs and avoid this knee lift, the legs should be stretched from the hips toward the feet. If the knee is lifting, the foot is not pressing against the water and is naturally ineffective. On the up stroke, the knee bends and does rise to the upper level of the body but does not break water. When the knee straightens, the foot whips up so that at the completion of the knee extension the leg is in a straight line with the upper surface of the body.

The axis of action for this kick is in the hip joint as in the crawl stroke. At the completion of this up kick, considerable water is thrown above the surface. The initiating movement is in the thigh, driven by the power of the pelvis and thigh flexors and hip extensor muscles. Initiating the movement in the thigh creates an action in the foreleg and foot, giving them an appearance when in motion of waving fishtails. Power is transmitted downward through the legs by means of pressure at effective angles against the resistance of the water, giving this back flutter kick its propulsive force in water.

The most frequent errors are those of holding the head either too high or too far back. Holding the head high will round the back too much. Holding it too far back will flatten it. Lifting the hips and thighs above the surface of the water will cause too much surface friction and therefore slow the speed. Each individual should experiment with head level to find the best level for creating least resistance to forward speed. Anatomic characteristics make some differences among different individuals. Sometimes the legs are held too stiffly and not relaxed to give free play to the joints. This is especially true in the action of the ankle.

Arm technique and mechanics of the back crawl stroke. The movements of the arms in the back crawl stroke differ from those of the crawl stroke in mechanics. However, arm-and-leg cycle ratio is 1 to 6, the same as in the crawl stroke.

Recovery of the arms. When the hand has completed its drive at the side of the thigh and below the hip (Fig. 10-2, *E* and *F*), the initiating movement in the recovery is started with the hips rolling slightly to the opposite side to give counterbalance to the opposite arm recovery. The shoulder lifts slightly as the body weight is shifted over onto the opposite arm as it enters. The elbow of the recovering arm bends slightly as the arm is lifted out of the water (Fig. 10-2, *F*). The wrist is turned so that the palm faces toward the surface. It droops slightly to permit it to relax and drain the water from the arm as the arm lifts out of the water. Bending the elbow slightly as the arm is lifted out of the water serves the three following essential purposes: First, it releases the tension of the arm flexor muscles and permits them to rest. Second, it permits the water to wash down the arm and drain off the fingertips as the arm is lifted out of the water, thus reducing the added weight of a curtain of water, which is a retarding factor to speed. Third, the palm is turned toward the body, so that the thumb side of the hand will break through the surface.

The moment the fingertips have cleared the surface, the arm moves overhead vertically in line with the outside of the body to the entry. The wrist can be slightly drooped during the recovery.

A slight error is to maintain a bent elbow throughout the entire recovery, thereby causing the shoulder and elbow to enter the water before the hand and wrist enter.

Entry. The entry should follow the recovery without any retardation. The movement of the arm is slightly accelerated just prior to the entry. As the fingertips enter the water, the arm should be pressed into the water and should disappear immediately below the surface. This is the most important timing point in the arm action of the back crawl stroke. There are far too many back crawlers who believe that their entire wrist, hand, and forearm are in the water at the entry when actually only the shoulder is submerged and half the forearm is projecting above the surface.

The correct hand entry is with the palm facing the surface (Fig. 10-2, *E*). The wrist is slightly flexed at an angle of nearly 60 degrees. The fingers are parallel with the line of the arm. The wrist should be straight, not abducted. The palm is now in a position to slide forward and into the water ahead of the shoulder, the same as in the crawl stroke. The outer extremity of the arm, that is, the outer edge of the wrist, hand, and fingers, presses into the water and gives

support to the whole body and prevents the shoulder from dropping below the hand. The hand should be pressed in quickly. When the hand approaches the entry position, it must enter before the shoulder. It should not be smashed but forced and pressed, so that the arm will slide down to the catch and pull effectively.

The hand should enter the water not more than 6 inches outside the shoulder line. The left hand should enter about 1 o'clock and the right hand at 11 o'clock, if one is swimming toward the face of the clock. The entry should be a quickened movement in order to keep the shoulder above the hand. If the movement is slow, the shoulder will ease down below the hand.

Press-slide. In the back crawl stroke, as in the crawl stroke, there is a definite momentary press-slide phase (Fig. 10-2, *A*). Even though brief, it is present in top sprinters, and it is there for a very definite purpose.

The hand and forearm press downward and slide forward to a very shallow depth in preparation for the catch. This is not deep, as in the crawl stroke, but just inches under the surface level. In this position the muscles that depress the arm have a good mechanical advantage. The shoulder is behind as well as above the arm in its drive. The palm is faced downward at an angle so that during the pressing phase, pressure is felt on the fingers.

During the entry, the body should not roll into the arm. After the arm has entered, the head and body are moved toward the extended arm. The trailing hand pushes as the recovering arm is extended. This slight inclination toward the sliding arm also helps to lift the opposite arm out of the water. A sensation of driving forward is achieved.

There is but little roll of the body in this type of back crawl stroke. The fundamental movement occurs in a loose, flexible shoulder socket, which gives the arm the freedom of action it requires. Tight-shouldered individuals cannot swim this stroke until they loosen their shoulder girdle by using daily stretching exercises for the shoulder girdle muscles.

There are some authorities who believe that the arm should enter and "dig" or go immediately into the drive. There are some very good back crawlers who use such a type of stroke. This is a more or less "windmill" type of stroke sought by those who use purely an opposition type of stroke, thereby gaining a faster "turnover" stroke that results in greater speed. However, it reverts back to the smash entry, and with a smash entry it is doubtful if a full cycle of six full-measured kicks can be executed on one stroke revolution. Again, there are some coaches who advocate anchoring the arm into the water and watching the body go by. This is the sensation one has when the stroke is properly executed, but actually the arms are not anchored. They definitely drive through the water, even though it seems that the body goes by stationary arms.

Catch, pull, and push drive. The catch, pull, and push or drive phase of the back crawl stroke will be considered as a whole, rather than broken down into its separate parts. In this stroke it is possible to pull the arm through to the release in either of two ways, straight or bent.

STRAIGHT ARM PULL. There are really few back crawlers who keep the arm straight after they have been swimming for several years. In learning, a swimmer will find that it is best to start with a straight arm pull. Later, the skill of bending the elbow for the push drive phase can be learned. There are, however, many top swimmers using the straight arm pull. Any strong, rugged boy can successfully use the straight arm pull all the way from the catch to the completion of the drive. If the arm is long, it requires powerful muscles to drive the arm through very fast. The straight arm back strokers usually develop a slow, lazy-looking pull. In sprinting, the swimmer must move the arms more rapidly through the water, and the hand must fasten onto the water

and not be permitted to slip. The longer-armed boys who are less rugged would find a more productive speed stroke with the arm bent at the elbow. In this way the lever arm is shortened, which gives greater advantage to the muscles.

The catch in the straight arm pull is no different than for the bent arm pull. The fingers, hand, and wrist must not be fixed. They resist when pressure is applied against them. The first movement of the catch is in the fingers and the hand, which curve and press downward and backward with a quickened movement. The palm is faced outward and toward the feet as the pressure is increased in the pull. The arm pulls very shallow in this movement, approximately 2 to 6 inches under the surface, until the hand and arm reach a point directly out from the shoulder, where the depth is increased to 8 to 16 inches. From this point to the release the whole arm presses downward to the finish on a plane in line with the body and against the leg. The palm is faced rearward and completes its drive tight alongside the thigh, executing a quick push at the finish.

BENT ARM PULL. The bent arm pull and drive is now almost universally used by all competitors. The catch is started with the hand and fingers the same as in the straight arm action. The pull is at a greater depth and is slightly faster. Instead of being stretched out to its full length as in the straight arm pull, the arm reach is gradually shortened as the pull progresses. A firm grip upon the water is maintained with the hand by bending the elbow down. When the arm and hand have reached a point just slightly ahead of the line with the shoulder, a mechanical adjustment takes place. The shoulder girdle is prepared for the transition from a pulling or drawing action to a pushing or driving action. During this transition the propulsive force is not weakened, and no dead spot appears in the pull. On the contrary, during this phase the forearm muscles spring into action and begin a powerful forearm drive, followed by a continued contraction of the depressor muscles of the arm. As the forearm executes this drive, the elbow is bent downward and slightly forward and moves in advance of the wrist and hand. The action is similar to that of a baseball pitcher who is in the act of throwing with the arm poised over and behind the head. The elbow is brought forward slightly ahead of the ball, but, as the powerful forearm flexors come into play, the forearm and the hand give a final flip to the ball as it leaves the hand in the followthrough stages. The back stroke swimmer uses the same arm action as the baseball pitcher in order to throw the water to the rear, enabling him to get great speed for the drive. The swimmer's hand describes a letter "S." If swirls appear on the surface during any part of the arm drive, the hand and arm are pulling too shallow. Although the hand does come very close to the surface in this stroke during the forearm whip, the hand in this movement should not break into the surface or pass through the surface water, for it will lose its hold against the water.

At the completion of this drive, the arm and hand finish at the side of the thigh as in the straight arm action. This type of propulsive arm drive should prove to be ideal for the long- and weak-armed individuals. It is a movement that can advance the arm with speed and force through the water in the propulsive phase. Sometimes swimmers are unable to pull a straight arm through the water fast enough during the latter portion of the race when they are fatigued. The bent arm type of drive is then used to advantage.

Release. The hand and fingers complete a whip or push from the wrist in the final stages of the drive of the arm in both the straight and the bent arm styles. The hands press the water directly backward and downward toward the rear. At the same time that the upper arm and elbow are actually squeezing the water out from between the arm and body, the hand and wrist snap in

an attempt to give a final push just before the arm has released its hold on the water. This final whip finish of the hand, arm, and shoulder gives a lifting impetus out of the water quickly and smoothly with the thumb uppermost as the hand breaks through the surface, and moves rapidly into the recovery phase (Fig. 10-2, *B* and *F*).

There are a great many coaches who advocate a feathering motion in the final stages of the drive. This is simply sculling with the hand. The idea is to give the arm a greater propulsive finish to its drive. Some back crawlers employ this sculling motion very skillfully. Whatever is gained in propulsive power is likely to be lost in the additional time it takes to complete the movement. The opposite arm must make up somewhere else the time lost in the stroke revolution. This delay usually takes place in the recovery or the glide.

There is another claim that this sculling of the hand is a supporting movement to the hips and that it holds them at the proper level. A hip sag can be eliminated by maintaining a constant stretch to the body with pressure placed on the arms during the entry and pull phase of the arms and slight emphasis placed on each down beat of the legs. This method gives sufficient support to maintain the hip elevation.

Timing of one arm in relation to the other. In the back crawl stroke there is no independent movement of one arm from the other. It is just like an elementary windmill action. One arm is always directly opposite the other throughout the entire revolution of the arm stroke cycle (Fig. 10-2). Both arms should be even with the shoulder since one is recovering and the other is pulling as they pass each other at the shoulder line. As the driving arm arrives at the side of the thigh, the recovery arm enters the water.

If the recovery arm is too slow, the drive of one arm is completed while the recovery hand of the other arm is still in the air. This is a very common error in timing the back crawl stroke, and, when it is violated, the swimmer permits his shoulder to drop and the body to roll toward it.

Another serious error is to permit the arm to pause too long at the side of the body at the completion of the drive. This causes the body to lose momentum as the catch is made, and the body moves along in a jerky manner. As one arm is completing the drive, the recovering arm must be entering the water (Fig. 10-2, *A* and *E*) so that the body drives forward onto the arm entering. One must experience two sensations in swimming the back crawl stroke. As the arm enters the water, one must have the sensation of moving forward on it. Again, when it pulls, one has the sensation of going past the hands.

Pulling the arms too deeply below the surface lessens muscular advantage as well as secures an ineffective purchase on the water with the arm and hand.

Timing the arms and legs. Some back stroke swimmers rely upon the feel of smooth rhythm to judge their timing. Sometimes this method does not give accurate mechanical timing, since there may be some part of the stroke deliberately delayed for which some other part must either mark time momentarily or gain time to offset the unbalanced movement.

When this stroke is perfectly timed, the back crawl stroke is performed even smoother than the crawl stroke because there is really nothing to disturb its working parts from a symmetrical balance. This stroke also falls into the category of a fast, executed, turnover type of stroke, the same as do all of the other competitive styles of strokes.

Breathing while swimming the back crawl stroke. While swimming the back crawl stroke, the swimmer will find that breathing is just about as elementary and simple as when walking. However, the traditional method of expiring through the nose and inhaling through the mouth is strictly adhered to. If one should inspire through the nose, he is almost certain of sniffing droplets

of water into the throat and causing strangulation. The chance of breathing in through the nose in the back crawl stroke is a chance a swimmer cannot afford to take. One splash of water into the nose may cause the loss of a race as well as some most distressing moments.

In former styles of back stroke recovery techniques, a curtain of water from the arm as it passed over the face caused considerable difficulty. With the present lateral and vertical arm recovery, this water hazard has been eliminated, and breathing can now take place under almost normal conditions except when the swimmer is under water at the turn or start. The tension of the abdominal muscles in the back crawl stroke during the up kick inhibits freedom of action of the diaphragm in breathing for the untrained swimmer. A swimmer who trains daily and increases the daily load of work in proportion to conditioning these abdominal muscles eventually becomes very efficient and permits almost normal breathing, even during strenuous racing.

The number of breaths per length depends on the individual. For distances of 100 yards or more, breathing every stroke throughout the race is almost essential.

Technique and mechanics of head action in the back crawl stroke. The most stabilizing factor of the entire back crawl stroke is the head position. The head is fixed, with the chin and nose remaining constantly on a central plane, while the body rotates about it on its longitudinal axis, even though the body oscillates slightly from side to side with each arm pull. In order for the head to be maintained in a steady position while the body oscillates during the stroke action, the head action must be isolated from that of the trunk. This is affected by maintaining a relaxed neck. By maintaining the head in a centered position, the body rides on an even keel and is prevented from rolling (Fig. 10-2). It also prevents lateral sway, which would move the body out of alignment. The head should lean in the same direction as the line of progression. The swimmer should not look around more than necessary because each change of head position is likely to alter the body position and the timing of the stroke. The inspiration and expiration phases are carried on in a normal way. Inspiration takes place through a wide-open mouth, with the lips curled out away from the teeth. Expiration should be through the nose to prevent strangulation and to maintain the nasal canals clear of water droplets.

Back stroke tumble turn. The reach to the wall is made with a drive under water just as the reaching inverted hand is about 12 to 16 inches from the wall. The head is lowered back with the arm. The hand dives to a depth of about 6 to 10 inches under the surface. The elbow bends so that the head comes close to the wall (Fig. 10-3, *A*). Air is taken just before the head is submerged. The free-arm shoulder is slightly dropped. The body is brought into a very

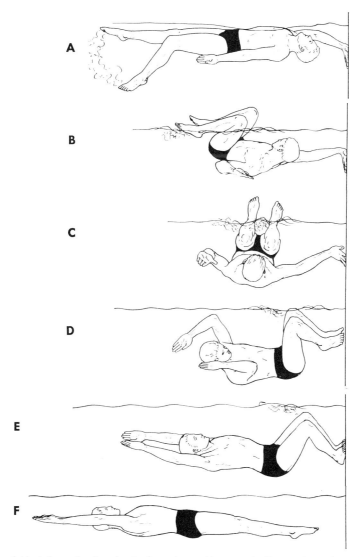

Fig. 10-3. A series of ideal form showing the back stroke tumble turn. **A,** The touch at the wall. **B,** The tuck. **C,** The turn. **D,** The completed turn. **E,** The driving position. **F,** The glide after push-out.

close tuck position, throwing the knees at an angle over the shoulder of the contact arm (Fig. 10-3, *B*). As the knees come over, the body has already half turned around and is nearly flat on its back (Fig. 10-3, *C*). By use of the contact arm on the wall and a sculling motion of the free hand, palm inverted, the remaining half turn of the body is made while at the same time the feet plant themselves against the wall (Fig. 10-3, *D*). The head should incline toward the angle of the knees, which is a partially oblique plane. This turn is not a somersault. The head in this turn is a guide and controls the entire turn, especially the placing of the feet on the wall. The body spins directly on its back while tucked. In the tuck the knees should not spread apart. The body is now in push-off position. The arms are poised ready for the thrust, and the elbows are flexed, palms up, one on either side of the head close to the ears, just over the shoulders. The chin is tucked down toward the throat (Fig. 10-3, *E*). A vigorous drive of the legs is made, while at the same time the arms are thrust out to full extension beyond the head for the coast to the surface (Fig. 10-3, *F*).

This turn is often confused with the somersault turn. The body does not somersault but merely permits the trunk and head to submerge, with the trunk remaining in a horizontal plane throughout the entire turn. This turn is called the tumble turn. It is similar in general principles to the touch, tuck, spin, and push with head out as explained in the sprint crawl turn. This turn is the fastest of all the back stroke turns. In approaching the wall for the turn, speed is of utmost importance to flip the turn fast. Coasting to the wall slowly will result in a poorly executed turn.

Finish. A great many sprinting back crawlers make a serious mistake of turning the head to the side when pressed for a close finish. Instead of turning, they should press the head back into the water deeper in the last two or three firm strokes so that the approaching end can be seen over the forehead. This also gives a longer stretch to the body as well as permits the touching arm to drive low over the shoulder to the finish wall or finish curtain. In this manner the swimmer can accurately judge the distance to the finish wall, and the fully extended arm reach can be thrust at the wall with tremendous speed. In this way the swimmer can gain at least a foot advantage in reach over an opponent who remains in swimming position. However, the head should not be lowered earlier than the last two or three arm strokes.

The touch on the finish wall should be made with the fingers reaching downward and the palm of the hand flattened against the wall. This prevents injury to the fingertips.

The back stroker, while in the natural swimming position, is tempted to watch the other competitors in a race. This is wrong because it keeps his mind from concentrating on the number of strokes to the approaching finish. Not only that, but he is not centering the head on its longitudinal axis and will cause his body to flounder from side to side, which loses speed for him when speed is most needed.

Another error often made in approaching the finish is to look for the finish wall over one shoulder. In doing so, the opposite arm will never take the full reach, the stroke is shortened, and rhythm is lost right at the finish where driving speed is absolutely essential. Furthermore, fixing the eyes on the finish wall over one shoulder as he approaches causes him to veer to the opposite side, and the touching hand will reach the wall at an angle to the side of the wall. The head should be centered and lowered, and the hand should reach directly back in line with the spine.

Many swimmers rely upon markings on the ceiling when swimming in indoor pools. Roped markers should be stretched above the center of each lane for the back stroke races, for both indoor and outdoor races, to aid in guiding back stroke competitors. Surface lane markers should also be of a contrasting color about 10 feet from the end wall as a warning to the back stroker. End walls above the surface should also be of a contrasting color from the surface so that they can be easily distinguished through the water-blurred eyes of a back stroker. A wall that is not easily distinguishable to water-blurred eyes often causes an optical illusion of the wall appearing either farther away or nearer than is actually the case. This causes the swimmer to reach for the finish or turn either too soon or too late, which may mean the loss of a close and hard-fought race.

Back strokers should be constantly trained to keep driving their legs as they are reaching for the finish. They often cease all stroke movements when reaching for the finish. This should never be tolerated in practice. While reaching for the wall and just inches short, the swimmer should hold the finishing arm straight and on the surface as the legs drive him in.

As a general rule, if the reaching arm for the finish is less than 14 inches short of the finish, the arm should lie on the surface, and the swimmer should rely upon the legs to drive him home to the finish. If the fully extended arm is farther than approximately 14 inches away from the finish line, the arm should be pulled through and the other arm driven into the finish wall.

RACING FUNDAMENTALS

Pace. The 100-yard back stroke can be grouped in the sprint event, and, for all purposes of training, the sprint type of training should be followed as discussed in the sprint crawl stroke.

In the 200-yard event, a large amount of endurance combined with speed is essential in competition. The stroke cadence is just slightly slower than that used for the 100 yards. Usually the 100 yards elapsed time on the way to 200 yards varies just from about one to two seconds. It is practically

full sprinting effort. A great deal of sprinting, as well as distance endurance swimming, is necessary in training for this race. The standard table (see Table 10-2) for the 200-yard back stroke should be carefully studied in planning for competition. Both the sprint and middle-distance techniques of racing fundamentals should also be studied.

A common error of racing in this style is to look over to the side or over the shoulder to watch an opponent. This should be avoided, and, if done at all, the head should again be centered after each glance. When one does glance to the side, the body rides off keel, and the opposite arm does not take its full reach. A back stroker should cultivate a sense of knowing where a rival is with only occasional glances in his direction.

TEACHING AND LEARNING PROCEDURE

The back crawl stroke is demonstrated before the class. The instructor explains the advantages of the stroke and the major characteristics. The instructor then breaks down the stroke into its component parts and teaches them to the class.

Back crawl kick. Land explanation and demonstration are again given by the instructor.

Land drill. The class is seated on the side of the pool, with the legs extended over the water. The hands are placed just behind the hips for support. The legs move up and down from the hips in an alternating action. Emphasis is placed upon keeping the feet and toes pointed in an extended position. The knees bend to facilitate the desired whip action in the legs. The instructor corrects the individual's faulty technique and stresses the positive desired action to the group.

Water drill. The water drill is practiced, using the side of the pool for support. The pupil stands facing away from the side of the pool and leans backward in order to rest the neck on the scum gutter. The hands reach up and grasp the gutter above the

Table 10-2. Ideal split times for various racing times in the 200-yard back crawl stroke (25-yard pool)

ELAPSED DISTANCE (YD.)	ELAPSED TIME (SEC.)	SPLIT TIME (SEC.)	ELAPSED DISTANCE (YD.)	ELAPSED TIME (SEC.)	SPLIT TIME (SEC.)
25	11.5	11.5	25	13.0	13.0
50	25.1	13.6	50	28.2	15.2
75	38.9	13.8	75	43.6	15.4
100	53.0	14.1	100	59.4	15.8
125	1:07.2	14.2	125	1:15.4	16.0
150	1:21.5	14.3	150	1:31.6	16.2
175	1:35.9	14.4	175	1:47.9	16.3
200	1:50.0	14.1	200	2:04.0	16.1
25	11.5	11.5	25	13.4	13.4
50	25.0	13.5	50	28.9	15.5
75	38.6	13.6	75	44.8	15.9
100	52.4	13.8	100	1:00.8	16.0
125	1:06.3	13.9	125	1:17.2	16.4
150	1:20.2	13.9	150	1:33.8	16.6
175	1:34.2	14.0	175	1:50.5	16.7
200	1:48.0	13.8	200	2:07.0	16.5
25	11.4	11.4	25	13.8	13.8
50	24.8	13.4	50	29.6	15.8
75	38.3	13.5	75	45.8	16.2
100	51.8	13.5	100	1:02.3	16.5
125	1:05.4	13.6	125	1:19.2	16.9
150	1:19.0	13.6	150	1:36.2	17.0
175	1:32.6	13.6	175	1:53.2	17.0
200	1:46.0	13.4	200	2:10.0	16.8

shoulders. Elevate the hips to a supine position. Where the side of the pool cannot be utilized, a partner may be used to give the needed support. Half the class executes the kick action while the other half observes a designated partner and offers constructive criticism. The partners change, the teacher becoming the pupil and the pupil acting as a teacher. The instructor moves among the class correcting outstanding faults.

Kick board drill in the water. The pupil is instructed to lie on his back, in the water, holding the kick board on his chest by wrapping both arms over and across the board. The pupil is instructed to bend his knees to assume the above position, lean backward slowly, and place the back of the head and ears into the water. The feet and knees then extend, resulting in a supine floating position with the body supported by the kick board. The drill is continued until all members can make progress across the pool. The instructor devotes most of his attention to the slower students. Any practical floating device may be substituted for the kick board.

Water drill using kick without floating device. The instructor reviews the hand sculling action. The class reviews the use of sculling with a back float, hand sculling just outside the hips and well below the surface. Half of the class attempts to kick approximately 40 yards; using the sculling action of the hands to help maintain a high hip position, just beneath the water surface, is encouraged at this point. Partners observe and offer constructive criticism. The remainder of the class attempts the skill.

Kick 200 yards. At this point the pupil is encouraged to depend only on the kick for support and forward progress. The hands are held at the sides of the body, arms relaxed. The goal of each student is to complete 200 yards without stopping. If he is forced to stop, he rests momentarily and again continues.

Kick test. The arms are extended and stretched beyond the head, beneath the surface. The hands are held together. The head is lowered so that the chin is on the chest. The pupil attempts to kick 20 or 25 yards in this position.

Back crawl arm action. When the pupil is skilled with the kick to the point at which he can make suitable progress through the water without depending on the arms for support, he is ready for instruction in the arm action. The straight arm low recovery action is taught to the beginner, because water is less apt to be thrown over his face, and progress is rapid. (See discussion of low arm recovery earlier in this chapter.)

Hand action explanation and demonstration is given by the instructor. Major points such as arm position, recovery, entry, and propulsive force are discussed.

The class, now standing erect, imitates the instructor, slowing going through the arm action. Faulty technique is noted and corrected.

Water instruction by the instructor. The class is assembled about the corner of the pool deck where all can see and hear the instructor. The instructor is supported by a member of the class while demonstrating the arm action.

Water drill. Pupils stand in shoulder-depth water, holding the arms out straight to the sides of the shoulders and moving the arms forward and backward in opposition to each other. The pupil is instructed to imagine that a broomstick is held behind the neck and to extend the arms to the sides on the imaginary stick. This gives the student the feeling of moving the arms in opposition to each other, which action is significant in learning the action of the back crawl arm stroke.

Walking backward across the pool. Pupils bend their knees to maintain a neck depth level of the surface. Emphasis is placed upon lifting the shoulders first in the recovery. The elbows are kept straight throughout the entire action. During the entire recovery the palm is held facing the surface, and the head is held still with the chin on dead center.

The student is instructed to breathe regularly, inhaling through the mouth and exhaling through the nose. This skill is repeated until the pupil achieves desired relaxation, coordination, and rhythm.

Whole back crawl stroke. The instructor demonstrates the whole stroke. The body position and timing between arms and legs are stressed.

The student now practices the whole stroke and is encouraged to make as many stroke repetitions in succession as possible before stopping. The student is cautioned not to race the arms ahead of the six-beat kick but to work easy and relaxed.

At this point the instructor gives a great deal of his attention to encourage regular and natural breathing. During most of the learning progression previously discussed, the student has employed very irregular breathing habits. Swimming easy and relaxed will aid the student to breathe normally. He should be taught to inhale through the mouth and exhale through the nose. Nose clips are not recommended.

Chapter 11

Teaching and coaching
the breast stroke

The breast stroke was the first of the competitive swimming strokes. Its original form has been altered more than the other strokes. The dolphin butterfly stroke was developed as a form of the breast stroke (see Chapter 1). Since 1956, the dolphin butterfly stroke has been recognized as a separate competitive event and is discussed in Chapter 12.

TECHNIQUES OF THE BREAST STROKE START

The various stances and techniques of the takeoff described for the crawl stroke start also apply to the breast stroke start. *Deep breathing* while the swimmer stands ready to take his mark is especially important in the breast stroke, since the first stroke of the race is swum under water. Three or four deep breaths will enable the swimmer to hold his breath much longer without discomfort.

Line of flight. There are some authorities who recommend a slightly higher line of flight than that used in the crawl stroke start. They recommend that the head be lower and the arms dipped for a deeper entry than that used for crawl stroke starts. Caution should be used in deviating too far from the traditional line of flight used for the crawl stroke start; otherwise, penetrating power is lost.

Another method of attaining a deeper glide is to adopt a slightly sharper downward angle of flight than is used in the crawl stroke start. The slightly sharper downward angle of flight is the most generally adopted method for the breast stroke start.

Entry. The entry, in all respects except that of the angle, is exactly as described for the crawl stroke as far as position concerning the arms, head, body, and legs. The angle of entry is slightly deeper than in the crawl stroke start because of the fact that a full stroke is permitted under water.

Glide under water. The body, whether the glide is shallow or deep, should be maintained in a straight position from the fingertips to the toes. Preserving this body alignment at the point of entry and throughout the glide depends largely on the action and position of the head. The head should be held between the arms and low, with the chin tucked in. This position will do a great deal to streamline the swimmer's body and will offer the least resistance while keeping the body at proper depth.

Since the breast stroke is the slowest of all the competitive strokes, it is essential to get all the speed advantage possible from the start. The body will glide with less resistance beneath the surface than on the surface. Therefore, the swimmer can make greater speed by remaining under water on his first stroke. The breast stroke swimmer is now limited to one complete stroke under water at either the start or after the push-off of the turns. The purpose of this rule is to keep the swimmer on the surface.

Swimmers differ as to physical contour and have different resistances to water. Some swimmers have low water resistance and slip through the water without any apparent slowing down during the glide after the start, after the push-out from the turn, and during the glide following a stroke. Others with higher resistance may drive just as powerfully but seem to drag down to a stop as if brakes were applied. A swimmer who has slow speed in the glide under water should be carefully checked with the watch to study accurately just where the starting momentum has subsided to a swimming speed and where he should begin to swim. As the swimmer progresses under water, he should gradually bear upward so the angle is not too abrupt as he strokes to the surface. He should never lie much deeper than 2 feet before the break to the surface is made.

Technique, mechanics, and timing of the underwater stroke. The underwater breast stroke is discussed here for purposes of class instruction. (See NCAA and AAU rules.) The underwater breast stroke differs in technique and mechanics from that generally used on the surface. The essential difference between the underwater and the surface stroke is in the length of the arm pull. On the surface, the hands and arms are not pulled very far beyond the line of the shoulders in the traditional breast stroke. If they are pulled fully beyond the shoulders, the hands no longer can hold the body and head well up out of the water. This will cause the head to drop below the swimming level of the surface, and the swimmer will bob excessively. While the swimmer is under water, this is not true. The arms can be pulled all the way back to the hips and still not alter body balance.

The full arm pull may be executed in two ways:

1. The arms may be pulled by sweeping them laterally and holding the arms almost entirely straight. The arms should not be pulled downward because the downward press would push the body up toward the surface. During the lateral sweep of the arms, they should actually pull slightly below the line of the body so that at the finish of the pull the hands are actually pressing upward, which aids in pressing the shoulders and head down-

ward and helps to maintain the body in its straight course. The body, while submerged, usually tends to float upward because of buoyancy. The swimmer must acquire skill with the hands in order to maintain the proper plane of the palms throughout the arm drive and to cause the body to remain under the water in a straight line of progress.

2. The second method, which is more generally used, is to pull the arms with the elbows bent in a boomerang position. The upper arm is carried almost in a horizontal line with the shoulder, and the forearm is directed vertically downward and inward. In this movement, the hands start the action with a quick digging hold of the water, and from there the arm drive is continued. The forearms press outward slightly, and, when they arrive almost in line with the shoulders, a transition takes place from a pull action to a swift push or driving inward action to the hips. The arms finish alongside the hips, fully extended, with palms upward. Here the arms drift momentarily during a brief glide on the momentum gained from the powerful arm stroke. The arms should be permitted to drift in this position, but not too tightly to the body, so that the water can wash and flow down the arms and sides of the body freely. If the arms are held too close to the body, the water is pocketed between the arm and body and thus increases resistance. The arms should drag in line with the back. During this arm pull, the legs are held straight but relaxed and slightly spread so that the water freely washes down the legs without interference from turbulence between the legs.

The legs remain straight while the arms start the recovery movement. In the recovery of the arms, the elbows are bent, and the arms slide closely along the under side of the body to a point under the chest or chin where both hands join palms down. This movement continues uninterrupted, and the arms thrust forward to the fully extended gliding position.

The recovery of the legs begins just as the hands are about to join under the chest. The legs should recover in a fairly rapid movement with not too much of a drag, or the timing point with that of the arm thrust is likely to be missed. The leg drive should be executed when the arms are not quite, but almost, fully extended in the forward thrust. The arm pull starts as the legs begin their drive so that both arms and legs act together. The legs thrust and whip in their propulsive drive. At the completion of the leg drive the body again glides momentarily from the momentum gained from the leg drive. The leg drive, as well as the arm drive, is an individual unit of power in the underwater stroke. Some swimmers prefer the arm pull to begin almost immediately upon the completion of the leg drive, or as soon as the legs have closed from the kick.

Surfacing. There are two essentials to bear in mind in breaking to the surface:

1. The body should be at the proper depth below the surface of the water just before the breakthrough. If the body is too deep, the angle that the body must make to reach the surface in one stroke is too sharp, and the forward speed will be decreased. Additional loss of speed from rising at too abrupt an angle comes from expending forward motion when the body shoots above the swimming level. This deviation from good form will also force the legs too deep for good propulsion on the first kick.

2. The break to the surface should be initiated by the kick, not the arm pull. This is accomplished in the following way: When the arms are thrust forward from under the chin, they should be directed at a slight angle toward the surface. At the same time the head is raised, and the legs drive the body upward. However, when the body arrives at the surface, it should be sliding forward, not upward. When the legs drive the body

to the surface, the arms are already placed in pulling position. This method prevents any break in forward motion that would cause the legs to lose traction. According to all present competitive rules, the start of the second arm pull must not occur until the head has surfaced.

TECHNIQUES OF THE ORTHODOX BREAST STROKE

General position of the body. The position of the body in the orthodox breast stroke in the water does not differ essentially from that described in the crawl stroke. The body must be maintained in a streamlined stretch, but at the same time in a comfortably relaxed position. This is controlled principally by the position of the head. During the glide phase of the stroke the head should be held comfortably well up and maintained there (Fig. 11-1, *A*). This is especially difficult for individuals who have short necks. The head in this position is in front of the center of weight of the body and in this position will tend to balance the legs over the center of weight.

Classification of leg kicks. Many attempts to improve the orthodox breast stroke kick have been made in order to keep it abreast with the arms. Rather than relying upon the traditional kick, which consists of a wide knee spread and wide whiplash of the legs, new methods have been devised. The knee spread has been narrowed, the heels have been lifted, and the downward thrust has been executed in a circular motion. Many variations are used.

The variations of the kicks were naturally developed because of anatomic limitations of breast stroke swimmers. Some swimmers are naturally crotch bound, which prevents a wide knee or leg spread. Others are very flexible and supple and possess a wide lateral range of leg movement. It was formerly believed that the wider the spread of the legs, the greater was the propulsive force that could be obtained because more water could be squeezed out from between the legs while

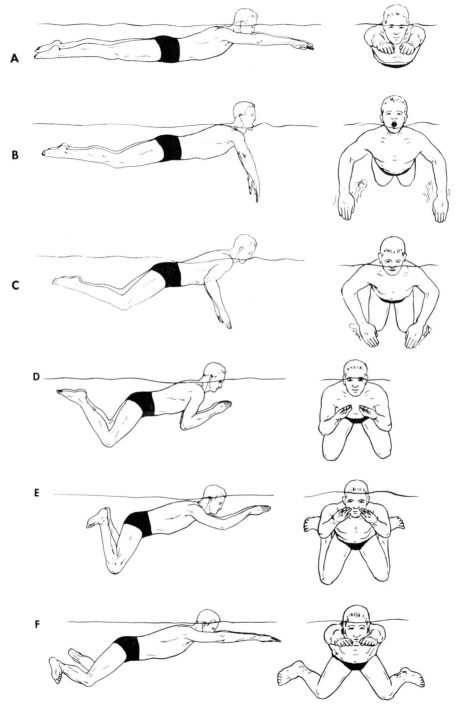

Fig. 11-1. A series of ideal form for executing the orthodox breast stroke. **A,** The legs are closing, and the arm pull is started. **B,** The head is lifting to clear mouth for air. **C,** Both arms and legs begin the recovery at the completion of taking air. **D,** The hands are preparing for the forward thrust, and the legs are preparing for the leg drive. The feet should be well spread. **E,** The ideal timing position to start the leg drive in relation to the arm thrust forward. **F,** The arms are in the downhill coasting position, and the legs are completing the drive.

completing the leg drive. However, this theory was discredited when crotch-bound swimmers with a narrow knee and leg spread seemed to get as much, and in some cases more, propulsive drive from this narrow thrusting drive than did others using the wide whipping drive.

Coaches now generally select the type of kicks to be used according to the physical attributes of the individual; that is, the height, strength, and build determine the general type of kick to be used.

Orthodox kick. This kick is almost obsolete in competitive swimming but is taught in swimming classes and is still popular for recreation swimming. The kick may be used most efficiently by swimmers with short, powerful legs. The kick is started from a moderate spread of the knees. Both legs are rotated outward so that the feet turn out and remain extended so that the soles of the feet almost face each other (Fig. 11-1, *C*). The knees are spread wide, and, as the heels are drawn outward to a spread, they are drawn as closely as possible toward the hips (Fig. 11-1, *E*). There should be a continuous rapid-action recovery and leg drive. From this position, the feet may either be drawn out as far as possible or partially turned out and the toes flexed toward the knees so that, as the thrust is being made, the soles of the feet immediately engage the water (Fig. 11-1, *F*). Just prior to the knees becoming fully extended, the thighs are driven and squeezed together. The feet extend fully during this whip phase. This movement, if accurately timed, gives a tremendous propulsive whiplash to the legs. The squeeze or snap of the legs should continue from the whiplash, so that the feet do not lose hold of the water. Too often in this kick, swimmers do not follow through in this squeeze movement but instead permit the legs to drift together, and therefore the kick loses some of its effectiveness. As speed is reduced, force is lost. The kick is performed with a thrust, whip, and squeeze. As the legs close, they should relax and drift slightly apart. There is a counteraction from the end of the down

kick, which gives the swimmer a feeling of lift of the legs to the surface.

Whip kick. This kick corrects for weak mechanical advantage in swimmers with long legs. Its action is to recover the knees using a narrow spread. The thighs are pressed down while the legs and heels are drawn, just under the surface, toward the hips. The heels are drawn up to the outside of the hips. Here the toes and feet are turned outward and immediately go into a quick outward and inward circular thrust, with the thighs snapping together just prior to the knees being fully extended. This entire kick is executed from a narrow knee spread. This type of kick not only corrects for the wide knee spread with a poor mechanical advantage but also permits the legs to force the water back along the longitudinal axis of propulsion.

A variation in this kick in the propulsive phase or drive phase may be made. Instead of driving the legs and feet outward and inward in a circular motion, they are driven and directed downward, and the thighs are driven backward and together just prior to the full extension of the knees. This gives the knees a rotation inward and an upward movement, giving the foot a screw-drive effect. The down drive, theoretically, gives greater resisting force against the foot, whereas in the backward inward snap of the thighs and knees the powerful hamstring extensors spring into action to assist the thigh adductor group of muscles. Caution must be exercised in manipulating the feet on the downward thrust so that the toes are turned down and drawn toward the knees when the legs are "cocked," so that the soles of the feet engage the water on the downward action of the feet. This type of kick gives the leg action a vertical range of movement as well as a lateral range. This kick is very effective in propulsion, especially if the swimmer is endowed with a long, broad pair of feet and powerful legs.

Modified whip kick. Swimmers with medium long legs will do best to maintain a moderately narrow kick. The recovery of the legs is similar to the recovery in the short-legged individual, except that the feet and the knees are not turned out nearly as wide. The heels are drawn up very close toward the hips and well spread. From this point the feet are turned out, and the outward circular thrust is made. The motion is a circumduction with the hip joint as the axis. The water is engaged at the start of the thrust with the inside of the foot as the knee begins to extend. Before the knees are fully extended, they execute an inward and backward snap, giving a simultaneous whip to each leg, which gives tremendous propulsive power.

In all types of kicks a common error is to draw the knees too far forward. The most effective results from the breast stroke kick are obtained by not flexing the thighs upon the pelvis farther than approximately a 45-degree angle with the spine. This limitation streamlines the thighs and causes the water to slide under the legs as they are drawn up.

The heels and feet should be drawn up as closely to the line of the hips as is anatomically possible. The feet there are able to engage the water nearer to the line of the hips. In this way, the feet are able to hold and push the water over a longer range, giving the legs a greater area for propulsive pressure against the water during the leg drive. Too many swimmers are likely to kick the feet diagonally back, rather than pressing the feet directly out from the hips, before the backward thrust is delivered. The legs are drawn up quite rapidly and immediately start the thrust.

Orthodox arm stroke action. The arms pull simultaneously in a lateral, downward, and backward movement. From an extended position in front of the face the arms are pulled to a point under the upper chest. Here the hands join each other and are thrust forward to the starting position. The entire movement is continuous and uninterrupted. In the traditional arm stroke, the hands should never pull more than a few inches beyond the shoulder line. Most top-flight breast stroke swimmers, for the shorter sprint events, use a very short arm pull, to a point just ahead of the chin, and a very narrow, fast, leg kick, in order to obtain a faster stroke turnover for greater speed. If the hands are pulled too far beyond the shoulder line, the support is taken from under the shoulders and head, and the body sinks, causing body balance to be destroyed. When the hands release pressure upon the water, they should relax.

Press-catch with arms and hands. The catch begins from the glide position (Fig. 11-1, *A*). The arms are extended in front of the face at a depth of 4 to 6 inches below the surface. The catch is initiated with the arms stretched forward and the fingertips and hands turned downward. The wrists flex slightly in a quickened movement. At the same time, the shoulders lift in an attempt to get the shoulders over the forearms and behind the press and pull so that the water level at the face is not changed.

Pull and push. The pull is very similar to the crawl stroke pull except the movement in the breast stroke is made laterally as well as downward in a semicircular movement. The path of both hands may best be described as drawing the upper half of an elongated letter O. The fingers should direct the path of the arms. The catch begins by a quick press and pull outward and downward of both hands and forearms. At the same time the shoulder blades rotate forward, giving the arm tremendous mechanical advantage in the shoulder arm-push position while the arms are still well in front, but at 8 to 15 inches in depth. Both arms give lateral balance and support to each shoulder, and the center of body weight is not altered. While both arms are pressing and pulling, the shoulders tend to be lifted out of the water (Fig. 11-1, *B*). The lift should be minimized and converted into forward motion along the surface.

The pull phase of the breast stroke is of short duration and really is a continuation of the press-and-catch movement. It is during the press-and-catch movement that the shoulders adjust themselves for the push phase. The press-and-catch draws and lifts the body. The movement must be a quick and forceful action of the hands and fore-arms. In order to perform this with skill, an active, flexible, strong wrist joint is absolutely essential.

The hand must have freedom of movement while in the water. During the press-and-pull phase the hand should be slightly flexed at the wrist in order to hold the water against the arms. Some water is allowed to wash down the arm to give greater planing resistance against the arms. If the arms pull with the wrist set at a slight angle, a greater resistance is obtained by deflecting the water from the heel of the hand toward the finger-tips. With the wrist cocked at an angle of 20 degrees, the wrist flexor muscles have a good mechanical advantage during the catch-and-pull phase. The wrist straightens as the shoulders move forward to get in front of the hands and arms. Although the swimmer does not actually anchor the arms in the water and then draw the body over them, he appears to do so. The swimmer should not be misled by this appearance and strive merely to set the arms in the water. He must actually pull and drive them through the water so that water will slip off the arm and form suction swirls behind the hands and arms, which give traction with the water. With a quick movement of the hands at the catch, swirls form that give greater propulsive efficiency earlier in the stroke. The water pressure should be felt in the palm. The fingers should not be flattened to full extension but to a very slight saucer shape. This gives greater strength to the fingers and is less fatiguing. During the catch-and-pull phase of the stroke, the arms should be spread downward, until the hands have reached a depth of 14 to 16 inches. At this depth the arms are still ahead of the shoulder line, and maximum propulsive force has been attained.

There is a great deal of difference of opinion as to how the arms should complete the push phase and the recovery. There are two generally recognized methods. In one, the elbows spread wide, and the hands pull in under the elbow and toward the chest wall, followed by an elbow squeeze toward the body. The other method is to pull the elbows back and toward the body with the hands and forearms following the elbows. Those favoring the first method rely chiefly upon the rotator muscles of the upper arm and the forearm flexors to assist the rotators in driving the forearm downward and inward. When the arms are on a line with shoulders, the upper arm and elbow are then squeezed in to the under side of the chest wall. The hands follow, planing at an angle and pressing against the water.

Those favoring the latter method advocate a flexed elbow leading the arm in a movement backward and inward to the underside of the upper chest wall. Here the pulling force is not from the weaker upper arm rotators but from the powerful arm depressors. In both movements, the elbows begin to flex early in the catch-pull phase of the stroke and increase in flexion as the drive continues through its maximum depth and to the completion of the arm stroke under the chest. The theory is advanced that in the wide-spread elbow technique there is more arm surface area presented against the water. To offset the weakness of the muscles brought into action in the movement, the swimmer should train to strengthen these muscles.

Swimming speed can be increased by shifting from a wide lateral arm movement to a more downward movement to get the arms under the body. Speed is also the chief objective in breast stroke competitive swimming. To obtain greater speed in this, the slowest of all the competitive strokes, the range of hand and arm movement is shortened, and the hands take on an appearance of sculling in a horizontal plane to obtain faster turnover speed of the entire stroke cycle.

Release and recovery. The pull phase in the breast stroke is actually completed when the hands have released backward pressure, which occurs when the hands arrive at the upper chest wall. This release is accomplished with a wrist whip, and the hand rotates upon the wrist joint, forcing the water to the rear. The hands are then relaxed and recovered to a point under the chest. This is a common method of release and recovery. A more skilled method is to continue the press of the hands at the end of the push toward a point near the chest, still pressing the water down and back and then releasing the pressure and cocking the wrists so that the fingers point forward from under the chin, palms down. Although the movement is one of recovery, the hands actually do not release the pressure of the water while they complete the elongated letter O.

Arm thrust. The thrust is a continuation of the release and the recovery. There must be no separate motion of release, recovery, and thrust. It must be continuous. At the beginning of the thrust, the hands are aligned together under the chin, palms down and the elbows close to the sides of the chest (Fig. 11-1, *D*). The thrust should be as streamlined as possible, with the least amount of resistance offered by the elbows and the shoulders. In some swimmers less resistance is obtained if the hands are separated from 3 to 6 inches during the thrust and glide. This depends on the physical characteristics of the individual swimmer.

When the arms are being thrust forward, they should be moved rather quickly at an upward angle, but not thrust out of the surface or even close to it (Fig. 11-1, *E*). When the arms are nearly fully extended, downward pressure should be made upon the hands and forearms. They glide deeper and cause the body to slide downhill. The whole technique is as if an obstruction such as a partially submerged log is lying across the path of the swimmer, and he glides his hands up and over the submerged log and coasts down on the other side.

Arms in glide position. The glide position of the arms may be made with the hands aligned together or with the hands apart (Fig. 11-1, *A*). Under no condition should the arms become so relaxed that the elbows assume a slight bend and the hands and forearms fail to press slightly to afford a planing surface to the upper part of the body. If the arms are permitted to spread, water will be carried along between the arms and against the head and cause considerable resistance to the forward gliding motion. The arms should remain comfortably straight, so that water washes down the arms in a straight path and passes on underneath the chest wall to the rear. At the end of the glide and just prior to the catch for the next stroke, the hands should be submerged 3 to 6 inches in depth.

Timing the arm action to synchronize with the leg kick action in the orthodox breast stroke. There are two types of timing to be used, depending on whether a wide or narrow knee spread is being used.

Timing of the orthodox, or wedge, kick. The arms pull lateral to the shoulders; then the legs recover (Fig. 11-1, *B*). The arms then recover to a point under the chin and go immediately into the thrust (Fig. 11-1, *D*). While the arms are recovering, the legs are spreading and turning the feet out, poised for the leg drive. When the arms are almost fully extended in the thrust, the leg drive is made (Fig. 11-1, *E*). The start of the leg recovery in the stroke must be fast. There must be no hesitation or slowing down between the leg spread and the leg drive.

Timing in the whip kick. The difference in timing in the narrow knee spread and the wide knee spread is that it does not take so long to recover the legs in the narrow spread as it does in the wide knee spread. Therefore, in order to coordinate with the arm stroke, the knees should not be recovered until the hands are recovered to the front and lateral side of the head or the chest wall. The drive of the legs is made at the same time in the arm thrust as in the wide knee spread. The legs lift up into the recovery very quickly, and this movement can be executed while the arms move from the chest wall to the proper point in the arm thrust.

When a swimmer with a wide kick attempts to learn a kick with a narrow knee spread, he must readjust the timing of the recovery of the legs in relation to the arm recovery. Otherwise, difficulty will be experienced in the timing of the stroke.

In both types of kicks, the arms should remain in the glide position until the legs have closed from the kick. Then the catch in the next stroke may be started immediately after the legs close for a sprinting type of stroke. For longer distances, more time may be consumed in the glide position after the legs have closed, depending on the individual's strength and condition.

In short races the swimmer uses a quick, narrow kick with a quick pull following the kick, almost entirely eliminating the traditional glide following the stroke. Top-flight breast strokers no longer depend on a resting glide but train and condition themselves to eliminate as much of the glide as possible in order to acquire great speed. He, therefore, naturally speeds up his stroke, not only by shortening the glide, but also by speeding up the execution of both arm and leg action. The quick spread of the knees is narrow so that the legs may execute the kick movement as fast as the arms execute the arm movement of the stroke. This quickened kick movement has geared up the orthodox stroke to a higher speed level. This geared-up ratio tends to give the orthodox breast stroke an almost continuous propulsive action, rather than single units of power delivered at intervals in series. The entire stroke must have a rapid turnover. Usually one who uses a long glide will start the arm pull slowly as a means of gathering himself to deliver a powerful leg stroke. This slower gathering-up phase has been discarded, and instead more strokes per length of pool are used.

Timing of the head action in breathing for the orthodox breast stroke. Generally there are two types of timing of the head action used to synchronize and balance the arm and leg action.

1. The better method is to elevate the chin for air as the arms go into a stretch-and-press action, and, by the time the mouth has cleared the surface, the arms go into the catch-and-pull. The head must be maintained high after air has been taken and must remain on the surface throughout the race except at the start and turns. This tends to ride the body high on the surface and prevents it from bobbing up and down, thus reducing resistance.

2. The second method is delaying the head lift in the arm pull. The chin is lifted for air after the arms have passed well back beyond the catch to about the point where the pull ends and the push begins. Unless one is skillful, this delayed head action causes the body to lift out of the water too high and to unbalance the arm and leg action. Considerable motion will be wasted. In the action of lifting the chin for breathing, the level of the body should be kept as nearly constant as possible. The body should remain in alignment with the level of the water and the forward plane of progress.

The head is not lifted backward, but the mouth is drawn forward to the air above the surface (Fig. 11-1, *B*). When the eyes appear above the surface, they should focus on the surface in front of the mouth and be on guard for any choppy movement. The mouth is opened, and, simultaneously with the opening, air should be gasped quickly. The mouth may be opened with the lower lip extended forward beyond the upper lip, curled out to ward off wavelets around the mouth on the surface. Another method of opening the mouth is to catch the tip of the tongue behind the lower front teeth and then "belly" the tongue forward into the mouth opening, leaving a narrow opening above the bulge of the tongue and the upper lip.

A most frequent and common error in lifting the head for air is to lift it backward out of the water, as if trying to press the ball of the head back between the shoulder blades. This faulty head movement is very detrimental to both forward progression and body balance. The head should be moved toward the line of progress, not against it.

Very often a swimmer will pull the arms too slowly during the press-catch-and-pull to accommodate the head lift in getting air. This slow arm action at the inception of the arm stroke retards accurate mechanical timing in stroke performance. In practice, a quick and independent head action should be stressed, especially in the longer distance workouts. The longer the distance of workout, the more a fault is liable to be practiced.

Another common error is usually developed in slow long-distance workouts. This is a "frozen" wrist joint. A wrist joint should be flexible and sensitive at all times to the pressure of the water.

Coaching methods and techniques used for daily practices. The following land and water drills, used in daily practices, aid in the development of arm and leg action.

For the development of the leg action. Four methods of leg development are suggested to be used. One is Danish gymnastics for stretching the ankle ligaments and stretching the crotch muscles. Abdominal muscles should be strengthened as well as the back extensors by using body-bending and leg-lifting exercises and wall weights. Second, the heavy kicking board should be used early in the season and continued throughout the season with the load increased or decreased as the leg strength and skill develop. Some swimmers can perform the kick without the kicking board by holding the arms extended beyond the head. For other swimmers this position arches the back too much and therefore should not be practiced without the board. Breast strokers should also use a type of fast kicking movement by whipping the legs continuously without a pause at any point. This improves the leg flexibility. The third method is to use an elastic check rope and belt. This can be made from several bicycle inner tubes, with one end fixed to a rope attached to a belt at the swimmer's waist and the other end fastened to a wall. The swimmer then kicks against this resistance. The fourth method

is to practice the dolphin breast stroke kick, which will aid in maintaining a limber, supple back and rubbery legs.

For the development of the arm action. Here again land drills may be used as a way of stretching shoulder joints and strengthening arm and shoulder muscles by use of weights and wall weights. The use of the elastic check rope and belt is perhaps the best method for conditioning the arms. The breast stroker should develop himself until he is sturdy and rugged. The hands should not flatten to a hyperextension of the fingers during the press and propulsive phase, nor should the fingers be over-cupped. The fingers and the wrist joints should be slightly bent in flexion to give the finger, hand, and wrist flexor muscles a greater mechanical advantage, especially during the press-catch-and-pull phase of the stroke. This position of the hand and arms also gives proper tonus to the arm muscles and thus delays fatigue as late as possible in the race. Special attention should be given to keeping the neck relaxed. Tension on the neck muscles will cause early fatigue that will spread quickly to the other muscles of the shoulder girdle group.

Breast stroke turn. The breast stroke turn consists of the approach to the wall, tuck, turn, push-off, glide, and stroke.

Approach to the wall. A swimmer must drive into a turn, not coast in slowly. Momentum gathered must be utilized to carry the body well up to the wall and for the tuck and turn. The swimmer should come into the wall with his hands about 4 to 8 inches apart. The head is lowered just before the hands contact the wall. The hands are placed flat on the wall. The elbows bend until the head almost touches the wall.

Tuck. The tuck of the legs is made simultaneously with the bending of the elbows. With a slight sideward pressure of the hands the hips are pivoted along the longitudinal axis of the body.

Turn. The head should lift out, and the mouth should be turned to the side to get air. The upper back should rise during the first half of the turn. If the turn is to the left, the left arm is jerked away from the wall and assists in the spin by a scooping motion across the chest. It then meets the other hand, which has been on the wall and is now on its way forward. The body turns at a point slightly less than an arm's length away from the wall. When all these movements are timed perfectly, the body first rises slightly then sinks in rhythm for the push-off.

Push-off. The feet are set against the wall just as in the crawl push-off. The feet and knees are set at a hip-width position against the wall. The knees are then extended, and the body is stiffened. Simultaneously with the drive of the legs against the wall, the hands, which have joined under the chin after assisting in the turn, are now thrust forward simultaneously with the push-off. The body is directed forward and slightly upward, so that the head will break the surface before starting the second arm pull.

Glide and stroke. In the glide the body should remain absolutely straight from fingertips to extended toes. The back should not

Table 11-1. Ideal split times for various racing time in the 200-yard breast stroke (25-yard pool)

ELAPSED DISTANCE (YD.)	ELAPSED TIME (SEC.)	SPLIT TIME (SEC.)	ELAPSED DISTANCE (YD.)	ELAPSED TIME (SEC.)	SPLIT TIME (SEC.)
25	12.0	12.0	25	14.2	14.2
50	27.0	15.0	50	31.6	17.4
75	42.5	15.5	75	49.4	17.8
100	58.0	15.5	100	1:07.4	18.0
125	1:13.5	15.5	125	1:25.4	18.0
150	1:29.1	15.6	150	1:43.8	18.4
175	1:44.7	15.6	175	2:02.0	19.0
200	2:00.0	15.3	200	2:20.0	18.0
25	12.4	12.4	25	14.8	14.8
50	28.0	15.6	50	33.0	18.2
75	43.8	15.8	75	51.4	18.4
100	1:00.0	16.2	100	1:10.0	18.6
125	1:16.2	16.2	125	1:28.6	18.6
150	1:32.6	16.4	150	1:47.5	18.9
175	1:49.0	16.4	175	2:06.6	19.1
200	2:05.0	16.0	200	2:25.0	18.4
25	13.0	13.0	25	15.6	15.6
50	29.0	16.0	50	34.2	18.6
75	45.6	16.6	75	53.2	19.0
100	1:02.4	16.8	100	1:12.4	19.2
125	1:19.2	16.8	125	1:31.8	19.4
150	1:36.3	17.1	150	1:51.2	19.4
175	1:53.4	17.1	175	2:10.8	19.6
200	2:10.0	16.6	200	2:30.0	19.2
25	13.6	13.6	25	16.4	16.4
50	30.4	16.8	50	35.4	19.0
75	47.6	17.2	75	55.1	19.7
100	1:05.0	17.4	100	1:15.0	19.9
125	1:22.4	17.4	125	1:35.0	20.0
150	1:40.0	17.6	150	1:55.0	20.0
175	1:57.8	17.8	175	2:15.2	20.2
200	2:15.0	17.2	200	2:35.0	19.8

be arched. The head should be held low between the arms. The arms may be held together at the thumbs or separated, depending on the individual. Legs also may be slightly separated or held together. Anything that causes resistance to forward progression should be minimized.

Finish. In general, the finish is no different from the approach to the wall in the turn. However, in a close finish when the swimmers' heads are even and it looks like a tie or dead heat, one swimmer may be going into the pull of another stroke while the other swimmer is thrusting the arms forward in the recovery. The latter will appear to finish first. The one who is approximately an arm's length away from the finish at the end of the glide has the disadvantage because he cannot afford to coast in, even with the head low, since most of this momentum is already spent. He must, therefore, outwit his competitor and effect a quick catch of the hands and thrust for the finish without the kick. A full stroke would use up too much time and pull his head too close to the finish mark, and he would arrive at the finish with the hand touch too late to win the race. In this situation, the swimmer should accurately measure the remaining distance to the finish in terms of strokes with the head held high and the eyes having clear vision to the wall, so that, when his body has arrived close enough to the wall, with the last arm thrust he hits the finish at full arm extension. The head should be held up even though air is not taken during the last two or three strokes. The swimmer should not turn the head to the side and watch his competitor as the finish is approaching. He should look straight ahead at the finish.

TEACHING AND LEARNING PROCEDURES

The stroke is explained and demonstrated before the class. The instructor then breaks down the stroke into its component parts. He explains, demonstrates, and teaches each part to the class.

Breast stroke kick. Land explanation and demonstration are given by the instructor.

(See discussion of kick earlier in this chapter.)

Land drill. It is difficult to give land drill for this kick unless canvas backless stools are available.

Demonstration in the water. The instructor demonstrates the kick after he has demonstrated the whole stroke before the class. In his explanation and demonstration he emphasizes the following:

1. The amount of knee spread in the recovery of the kick; that is, if narrow or wide spread is to be used
2. How far to flex the thigh upon the hip joint in relation to the body during the recovery phase
3. When and where to cock the ankles; that is, flexing the feet toward the knee joint just prior to the leg drive
4. During the kick phase, how to drive the thighs together before knee joints are fully extended (This technique, if executed properly, with fairly relaxed legs, results in the desired whiplash of the leg drive.)
5. That the kick is the major propulsive function of the entire stroke, not the arms

Water drill. The water drill is first practiced using the side of the pool for support. This phase of the drill gives best results if the partner system is used. The partner stands just in back of the performer's legs in order to best give aid with hands to correct faulty movements.

Another good teaching method is for the instructor to place himself on a deck stool, in view of the entire class, supported at the sides of the pool, following and imitating the kick movements of the instructor. He may use the count system if desired. For example, on count 1, he drags the legs slowly during the recovery phase so that the class is able to follow. On count 2, the heels are separated, and the ankles cocked. On count 3, the drive is executed. On count 4, the legs are held together straight for a definite pause.

Kick board drill. When the kick is sufficiently learned at the side of the pool, the kick board is employed for best results because the swimmer is able to breathe above the surface and continue practice of the kicks over a longer period of time. One after another, flight waves can be sent across the pool in rapid sequence. This drill is performed with the face out of water.

As the class progresses, the breathing skill can now be added as the flights move across the pool. The instructor demonstrates when and how breathing is executed in the stroke. (See discussion of breathing earlier in this chapter.) The face is lowered and raised in and out of the water, between extended arms supported on the kick board and just behind the board. Air is inhaled during leg recovery and expired during leg drive and glide during the pause of the kick after completion.

Another skill can be added to the kick and breathing, that of using the arms with the aid of the kick board. This is performed by drawing the kick board down under the chin while the legs are executing the recovery phase. During this movement the face is lifted out of water, and air is inhaled. As the drive of the legs is now executed, the arms thrust the board forward to the starting position, while the face is again lowered and air is expired during the glide phase. At the completion of this entire exercise, the pause and glide received from the impetus of the kick are stressed by the instructor. This exercise is given to prepare the student for the whole stroke coordination. This exercise is very helpful to the student, since the whole stroke coordination of the breast stroke is very difficult for most students to grasp. It is therefore very essential that the student is well schooled in the kick and performing the preceding preliminary coordinating exercise. Too much emphasis cannot be placed on overlearning the kick.

Arm stroke water drill. The arm stroke is again explained and demonstrated by the instructor as the class is gathered about him in a large circle in waist-deep water. In this formation the class will bend down to the water level and imitate the instructor going slowly through the movements of the hands and arms. After sufficient practice by the class, flights are formed to walk slowly across the pool, taking one step forward as the arms are executing the forward movement from under the chin. After a pause the arms then pull sideward and downward to shoulder level in the propulsive phase. As the recovery and arm thrust are again executed, the second step forward is taken. This exercise of both arm and leg movements gives the student the sensation of a glide, which is so greatly desired in the learning of the whole stroke.

The breathing skill can be added to this drill as the class progresses. (See discussion of breathing technique.)

Whole stroke drill. If no supports are being used, the class can lie on the surface, face down in the water, and attempt to execute three or four strokes without a breath.

Some instructors favor a partner system, with the partner in front, catching the hands of the performing partner at the end of each stroke. He holds the hands momentarily to emphasize the glide at the end of the stroke.

Other instructors favor supports placed under the body as an aid, without partners. This method is advantageous, because then the student can move all the way across the pool without a stop. Regardless of which system is used, the student is constantly urged to take as many unhurried stroke repetitions as possible without a stop. To obtain best results in this phase of learning the coordination of the stroke, supports as an aid are highly recommended.

Once the stroke has been quite well mastered by the class, the instructor then stresses the finer timing movements and skill techniques of the stroke.

DISTANCE ORIENTATION

The student is now urged to swim farther each class session without stopping to rest. The instructor should at this point commend distance achievement accomplished by the students.

Chapter 12

Teaching and coaching the dolphin butterfly stroke

The dolphin butterfly stroke was developed at the University of Iowa in 1935.* This stroke is a further development of, and a step forward in, speed in the different types of breast stroke swimming. If changes could be made in the arm stroke of the orthodox breast stroke and still stay within the scope of the competitive breast stroke rules, then it would seem logical that the leg stroke could also be altered so long as the legs performed in unison, as to the arms. The flying arms were powerful and created greater speed, but the two movements, flying arms and orthodox breast stroke kick, were not a good basic mechanical combination of movements. The kick was a retarding type of action compared to the faster, more powerful action of the flying arms. Retarding factors in the kick action had to be eliminated. A kick had to be developed that eliminated a recovery phase as well as the tail suction it created behind the legs. This was the dominating factor that led me to create this stroke.

The discovery of this stroke was merely an assembling into a perfectly timed combination of skills of arm and leg actions, which had already been known for years. The kick was a simultaneous undulating action similar to a double flutter kick.

*Armbruster, D. A., and Sieg, Jack: The dolphin breast stroke, Journal of Health and Physical Education 6:23 (April), 1935; Armbruster, D. A.: The new dolphin breast stroke on trial, Swimming Guide, New York, 1937, American Sports Publishing Co., p. 52.

TECHNIQUE OF THE DOLPHIN BUTTERFLY STROKE

The dolphin butterfly stroke is definitely dominated by the kick, which resembles the tail movement of a flat-tailed dolphin.

Kick. The leg action is exactly like that of the flutter kick in the crawl stroke. The feet have the same slant on the up beat as the crawl kick. The knees bend as the legs pass the central axis of body progression. At the end of the up stroke, the feet relax (Fig. 12-1, *A* to *D*). At the beginning of the down stroke the toes are turned inward, the foot is hyperextended. On the downward stroke of both legs, the knees are somewhat bent until almost the end of the down beat. The knees straighten quickly, giving a tremendous downward whip to the feet. While this whip is completing its downward stroke, the thighs are already in the upward motion, causing the loose knee to straighten as the whole leg continues upward. The up stroke is started with the legs straight until the legs reach the central axis of progression where the knees again bend in order to effect the propulsive action of a fishtail. As the legs wave up and down, they press backward against the water at an angle as the water washes down the legs. This action supplies the propulsive power of the kick.

The kick has several better and more efficient principles for delivering speed than does either the alternating crawl flutter kick or the orthodox breast stroke kick. First, there is less resistance at the thighs than in the crawl flutter or the traditional breast stroke kick. Second, there is less retarding resistance to forward motion than an alternating motion of the legs. Third, there is no waste return motion such as in the orthodox breast kick recovery. Fourth, there is no counterpropulsive reaction caused by motion opposite to the direction of progress. For example, the orthodox breast stroke kick has a reciprocating jerk so that, when the legs kick backward, the kick ends with a jerk caused by the backward momentum of the feet.

In the dolphin kick both the legs and trunk weave up and down in the water, placing the axis of motion somewhere in the spine, well up in the shoulder region. In the crawl flutter kick the axis of motion is in the hip joints. In the dolphin kick the whole body weaves as if made of rubber.

Arm action. The arm action includes the entry, support, catch, pull, push, release, and recovery.

Entry. The entry of the arms should be at a point in front and in line with the

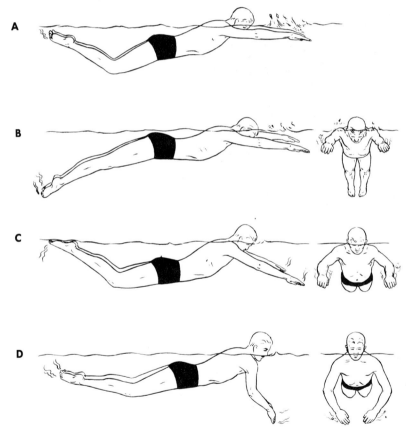

Fig. 12-1. A series of ideal form for executing the dolphin butterfly stroke. These figures also show the ideal position in relation from both side and head-on of the body in relation to the surface. **A,** The legs have completed the up drive and are beginning to drive downward. The arms are in the glide-and-catch position. **B,** The legs complete the first down beat, and the hips get an action-reaction upward. The arms press and spread into the downward catch. Note position of the entire body. **C,** The legs are beating upward to complete the first beat of the kick. The arms have completed the catch-and-pull and are beginning the push phase of the stroke. The head is kept in line with the body. **D,** The legs begin the second down beat while the arms are well in the push phase of the stroke.

shoulders. The arms are naturally extended and relaxed, with the hand slightly bent down at the wrist (Fig. 12-1, *A*). The hands and arms should be dropped into the water rather than carelessly smashed into the water. The hands enter the water about 10 to 12 inches apart. The resistance of the water should be felt on the palms during the entry.

Support. The arms and hands serve to propel the swimmer forward as soon as they enter the water and continue this propulsive action until they are removed for the recovery. The main propulsive action does not begin until the arms are in a favorable driving position below the surface of the water. The interval between the entry and the position at which the arms start their major propulsive action is the support phase of the dolphin butterfly arm stroke. The support phase aids in maintaining a desirable body position in the water. It is not a glide but rather a downward and slightly outward press of the hand and forearm that is timed with the

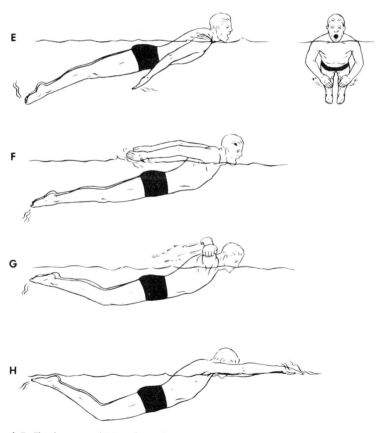

Fig. 12-1, cont'd. D and **E,** The legs are driving down through the axis of progression while the arms have released the water and begin the recovery. Note at this point air is being taken. **E,** During the push drive, air is taken as the legs complete the down beat. **E** and **F,** The arms are midway in the recovery, and the legs begin the final upward beat in the stroke revolution. Again note action-reaction of arms and legs. **F,** Shows the arms clearing the surface and the legs beginning the up beat. **F** and **G,** The arms are about to complete the arm stroke revolution. The legs continue the up beat to complete the arm stroke revolution. The legs continue the up beat to complete the two-beat leg kick revolution. (See **G** and **H.**) **G** and **H,** Show the low straight arm recovery and entry. The legs have completed the up beat and are in position for the next stroke cycle.

downbeat of the legs. As the hands move downward the shoulders follow in a dropping movement that helps to facilitate an elevation of the hips, resulting from an action–reaction of the legs in their downward drive. During the dropping movement of the shoulders, care should be taken not to allow the shoulders to become lower than the level of the hands. If the shoulders drop below the hands, the result is a decided mechanical disadvantage in the arm pull. In the shorter sprint events, the drop of the head and shoulders are decidedly reduced and retained at a higher level.

Catch. The path of the arm action with its changing directional line of drive can best be described by the hand forming an elongated and reversed letter S if one were to look down upon the stroke. The hands first press outward, then inward, and, as the arms finish the stroke, they again press outward. The initial outward movement takes place during the support phase. The catch starts at the completion of the down kick of the legs. The catch takes place as the arms finish their outward movement and begin their inward action. This transition consists of a quickened skillful movement involving the supination of the hand and forearm. The pressure of the water must be maintained in the hand and forearm during the catch action.

Pull. The pull immediately follows the catch and continues until the hands are in a position immediately below the shoulder level. During the catch and pull the elbows move slightly outward, and, just before the shoulders are over the hands, the arm and shoulder action shifts from a quick press to a push action. There is an element of lift during the support, catch, and pull, but this lift should be kept to a minimum. Forward, not upward, motion of the body should be the objective. This is based upon mechanically sound principles, giving advantageous leverage as well as efficient muscular action. The principle is exactly the same as that applied in the crawl arm action.

Push. The push phase of the arm action begins at a point at which the hands reach a position slightly ahead of the shoulders at the end of the pull. As the transition from pull to push takes place, the elbows turn toward the chest wall, and the hands almost meet under the body as the arms drive back, toward, and on a line with either hip in a direct push (Fig. 12-1, *C* to *E*). The push of the arms coupled with the second downward drive of the legs results in a powerful forward thrust of the body. As the arms approach the front of the hips in completion of the push, the hands whip backward to give a last additional drive to the arm stroke.

Release and recovery. After the hands push and drive backward from shoulder to hip, each hand releases the water just beyond the hip joint (Fig. 12-1, *E* and *F*), knifes outward to the surface, and moves rapidly into the recovery.

The arms should recover in a low, lateral, sweeping movement above the surface, with rotation of the arms to accommodate the movement (Fig. 12-1, *G*). A rapid initial forward movement carries the arms forward to a position opposite the shoulders, with the elbows and the little fingers of each hand slightly facing upward. The arms are held as relaxed as possible in this position. As the arms pass the shoulders, there is a rotation at the shoulder joint that accommodates the forward movement. The rotation continues until the palms are facing downward. In this position the arms are in readiness for the entry. While the hands are in the air during the recovery, the body has a tendency to sink. This sinking of the body can be reduced by a rapid recovery. Those swimmers who are less buoyant especially should stress the point of recovering the arms as quickly as possible without smashing them into the water.

The body should progress over the surface at as nearly a constant level as possible; undue climbing and dropping results in increased resistance and slower speed.

Timing of the arms and legs. The best

rhythm found for this stroke was two beats of the legs to one cycle of the arms. Since the kick dominates the stroke, the timing elements should be analyzed from its action. There are some top-flight swimmers now using only one beat of the legs to one cycle of the arms. This action needs further experimenting. The first timing movement is begun (Fig. 12-1, *A*) with the arms in the support phase, just after entering the water. The legs at this point are driving downward in their first beat.

The arms catch and press into the pull while the hips elevate at the end of the downbeat of the legs (Fig. 12-1, *B*). In Fig. 12-1, *C*, the arms are pulling while the legs are driving upward. Note the counteraction of both arms and legs in relation to the hip in Fig. 12-1, *B* and *C*. In Fig. 12-1, *D*, the legs begin the second downbeat, and the arms are making the transition from the pull to the push phase. Note the pigeon-toed feet and the narrow spread knees on the downbeat. In Fig. 12-1, *E*, the legs have completed the second downward beat, and the arms have released the water and are beginning to recover. Note how both the arms and legs are in line, since the arms have completed the push. The body at this point is in its highest position and is in readiness for the inhalation of air in the breathing cycle.

Fig. 12-1, *F*, shows the arms already rotated in the recovery, while the legs are moving upward in the second kick. Fig. 12-1, *G*, illustrates the legs completing the upward drive as the arms are about to enter the water.

The most troublesome difficulty many swimmers fall into, after having learned the stroke, is in obtaining the best timing movements of the arms and legs. The basis of the fault lies in the fact that the swimmer does not pull the arms through the water fast enough nor recover the arms fast enough. He should also check the kick and shorten the range to adjust to the faster arm action.

Timing of breathing with the arms. At the end of the push phase of the arm action, the legs have finished the downbeat of the second beat of the kick. The body at this point is at its highest position, and it is the ideal time to inhale the air in the breathing and stroke cycle. Buoyant swimmers may start the exhalation of air immediately following the inhalation. Those less buoyant should retain the air until just prior to the end of the push phase of the arms and then exhale in a strong blast, through the mouth. It is very common to breathe once every two strokes. However, the swimmer must consider the possibility of building an oxygen debt in a race over 100 yards. The question remains, does the ease and mechanical advantage gained by breathing every other stroke give the individual performer an advantage in this method over the possibility of paying for an oxygen debt later in the closing moments of a race?

Start. The techniques and mechanics of the moving parts of the dolphin butterfly start are no different from those presented for the crawl stroke start. (See Chapter 7, Figs. 7-1 and 7-2.)

The entry and glide technique also are the same as that described for the crawl start.

The swimmer comes out of the water, from the glide, flying on the very first arm pull, since more swimmers can fly faster on top of the water than swim under it.

The distance to be traveled under the water in the glide to the beginning of the first stroke depends also on the penetrating power derived from the start and the velocity maintained, which, in turn, depends on individual characteristics. Some men are more streamlined in physical contour and present less frictional resistance to the water. However, most any swimmer should be out at least 18 to 20 feet before beginning the first stroke. Starting too early in the glide will slow down the speed of the stroke.

When the hands and arms spring into action, the arms should press and pull downward, slightly wider than the shoulder width, and pull toward each hip. The pull should be executed in such a way that, as the body pops through the surface, it is in a forward movement, not upward.

Dolphin butterfly turn. There are very few differences between the techniques in the dolphin butterfly stroke turn and those used in the conventional type. In the approach one should time the strokes so that as the arms recover they lunge into the wall above the surface. The head remains lowered. In case the throw of the arms is short, the momentum will drive the body forward into the wall. The turning mechanics are the same as in the conventional breast stroke turn. After the turn is made with both hands, one hand is removed to execute an outward finning action that aids in turning the hips around during the tumble movement. When the turn is completed and if the swimmer is sprinting, the push-off should be shallow so that the body can immediately be driven to the surface on the initial arm stroke.

Table 12-1. Ideal split times for various racing times in the 200-yard dolphin butterfly stroke (25-yard pool)

ELAPSED DISTANCE (YD.)	ELAPSED TIME (SEC.)	SPLIT TIME (SEC.)	ELAPSED DISTANCE (YD.)	ELAPSED TIME (SEC.)	SPLIT TIME (SEC.)
25	10.2	10.2	25	12.6	12.6
50	23.0	12.8	50	28.1	15.5
75	36.1	13.1	75	43.8	15.7
100	49.5	13.4	100	59.6	15.8
125	1:02.9	13.4	125	1:15.6	16.0
150	1:16.6	13.7	150	1:31.9	16.3
175	1:30.7	14.1	175	1:48.4	16.5
200	1:45.0	14.3	200	2:05.0	16.6
25	10.8	10.8	25	13.4	13.4
50	24.3	13.5	50	29.4	16.0
75	38.0	13.7	75	45.6	16.2
100	51.9	13.9	100	1:02.0	16.4
125	1:06.0	14.1	125	1:18.6	16.6
150	1:20.5	14.5	150	1:35.6	17.0
175	1:35.2	14.7	175	1:52.8	17.2
200	1:50.0	14.8	200	2:10.0	17.2
25	11.4	11.4	25	14.2	14.2
50	25.5	14.1	50	30.8	16.6
75	39.9	14.4	75	47.6	16.8
100	54.5	14.6	100	1:04.6	17.0
125	1:09.3	14.8	125	1:21.9	17.3
150	1:24.3	15.0	150	1:39.5	17.6
175	1:39.6	15.3	175	1:57.2	17.7
200	1:55.0	15.4	200	2:15.0	17.8
25	12.0	12.0	25	14.6	14.6
50	26.8	14.8	50	32.0	17.4
75	41.8	15.0	75	49.5	17.5
100	56.9	15.1	100	1:07.1	17.6
125	1:12.4	15.5	125	1:24.9	17.8
150	1:28.2	15.8	150	1:43.1	18.2
175	1:44.2	15.9	175	2:01.5	18.4
200	2:00.0	15.9	200	2:20.0	18.5

Finish of the dophin butterfly stroke. For the finish, the same principles apply as recommended in the finish of the traditional breast stroke.

Coaches should train swimmers to practice the finish approach just as much as they practice starts and turns. There seems to be no advantage to practicing starts and turns consistently if the swimmer is destined to lose in the last 10 yards of the finish what he gains by a good fast penetrating start and fast turns earlier in the race.

By referring to Table 12-1, the dolphin butterfly stroke swimmer can plan his race in accordance with the ideal split times throughout his race.

TEACHING AND LEARNING PROCEDURES

Land drill. The class is seated on deck on the side of the pool. Legs are extended out above the pool water. Arms are extended backward with the hands placed on the deck supporting the body. The instructor reviews and demonstrates a single one leg action of the back crawl kick. The class practices the movement with one leg. The instructor then demonstrates the action of the dolphin kick —both legs moving up and down as a single unit—following the same pattern as previously executed with one leg. The class continues to practice the action.

Water bracket drill using the side of the pool for support. The instructor reviews the key points of the crawl stroke kick. The class then executes the crawl stroke kick, concentrating on the mechanics of its action. The instructor now demonstrates the dolphin kick, waving both legs up and down similar to the crawl but as a single unit. Action–reaction will necessitate movement of the hips and upper body, which is encouraged at this point. The drill is continued until all members can keep the legs together in the execution of the kick.

Underwater drill. The student is instructed to push from the side of the pool so that the body is in a submerged prone position. The hands and arms are held loosely at the sides of the body. In this position the kick is practiced, keeping the eyes open to avoid submerging too deep. Repeat several times until all pupils get the feel of the propulsive movement of the fish-taillike action.

Side drill. The students push off on their right side and execute the kick several times. The breath is held, and the eyes are focused backward toward the legs to observe their action and technique. Repeat on the left side. Alternate right and left.

Back drill. The kick is practiced in a supine position.

Kick board drill. Using the board as a floating support, the student attempts to kick 200 yards while on the face. If he is forced to stop, he rests momentarily and continues until he has covered the full distance. During this exercise the student should attempt to hold the up and down action of the hips to a minimum. When the class becomes proficient to the extent that all can cover the distance, they are ready for instruction in the arm action technique.

Arm action of the dolphin butterfly stroke. The instructor should review the coaching techniques of this stroke in this chapter and then discuss and demonstrate the arm stroke action, stressing important points.

Land drill. The land drill is preceded with flexibility exercises of the shoulders. Pupils face the instructor and imitate his arm action. The instructor emphasizes the keyhole action beneath the surface followed by a speedy and relaxed arm recovery. He also cautions the class not to drop the shoulders at the arm entry.

Shallow water drill. Pupils take position and stand in waist-deep water. The legs are spread with the knees bent. The body is inclined forward at the hips so that the shoulders are in the water. The class simulates the arm action as taught in the land drill.

Leg support drill. A kick board or other floating device is used to support the legs in a floating position. The swimmer uses his arms to propel him through the water, with the face in the water. As he improves this skill, he is encouraged to elevate his head toward the end of the arm push and inhale. (See Fig. 12-1.)

Combined arm and leg action. It has been observed by us that, if the swimmer will utilize the arm action and merely trail the legs, the legs will move up and down slightly, twice during a complete arm cycle, because of body action–reaction. The swimmer then attempts to lengthen the size and range of this natural movement of the legs, until he feels the balance and power from the kick. If he has difficulty in recovering the arms above the surface, a common problem in learning and coordinating the whole stroke, the beginner should pull and recover the arms at a greater speed. This faster arm action not only aids coordination but also helps to prevent the shoulders and head from sinking during the arm recovery and entry.

The beginner has a tendency to lengthen the range of movement in the kick. As he becomes skilled, he should strive to shorten and minimize the size and range of the kick.

The up and down action of the hips caused by action–reaction from the kick should also be held to a minimum.

The instructor should stress the point at this time of too much up and down movement of the head and shoulders during the breathing action. This is commonly known as "climbing" to get air, instead of moving the head and shoulders forward to inhale (see the discussion of breathing in this chapter).

TWO-PART METHOD OF TEACHING THE DOLPHIN BUTTERFLY STROKE

Another approach in teaching the timing of the whole stroke is the two-part method. Part one starts from a prone glide position with the arms extended forward. The pupil is instructed to lift the legs during the catch and pull action of the arms. As the arms start the pushing phase of the legs kick down, the chin is elevated forward, and air is inhaled. The pupil is then instructed to lower the head and pause. The arms are held at the sides of the body at this point. After a pause of from 3 to 5 seconds part two is initiated. The legs move upward as the arms recover above the water. The student is instructed to kick down and glide as the hands and arms enter the water.

The swimmer is encouraged to move slowly and to concentrate on the coordination of the arms and legs. The pause and glide are shortened gradually and finally eliminated.

Chapter 13

Teaching the dolphin crawl stroke

Ever since the introduction of the dolphin butterfly stroke at the University of Iowa in 1935, we have periodically experimented with a stroke that could possibly prove to be as fast as, if not faster than, the crawl stroke—namely the dolphin crawl stroke.

Early experimentation with the alternating overarm crawl action and the dolphin kick proved discouraging. The flat body position with the hips moving up and in a vertical plane seemed to inhibit relaxed head action in breathing and to somewhat curtail a rapid turnover of the arms.

Observation of a group of swimmers going through a drill using the dolphin kick only, while keeping their arms at their sides, revealed that several swimmers would rotate the hip girdle when turning the head to breathe. Swimmers turning their head to the left to breath would drop the right hip and elevate the left hip. The resulting kick was a sideward downward movement, rather than straight up and down movement in the vertical plane. Not only the hips but the whole body would roll to accommodate breathing.

First trials utilizing the body roll in the whole stroke resulted in better breathing patterns for the majority of the group. Some swimmers experienced difficulty in timing when they would over roll, or roll to both sides, or use too large a kick.

To achieve balance and timing of the arms with the legs, the downward beat of the legs should occur during the push phase of the propelling arm. The opposite arm is entering the water and is pressing forward and downward in the support phase. "Two up and down beats take place during one complete arm cycle in the sprint stroke." (See Fig. 13-1.)

Most sprinters in early trials will tend to time their arms with the leg kick, resulting in a rather slow turnover. If greater speed is desired the kick can be shortened so as to be in balance with a faster turnover of the arms.

Distance swimmers have experimented with a single up and down beat to each arm cycle and have found it less fatiguing than the double kick. Allen, working with a small group of varsity swimmers after the regular swimming season, found that after a week of practice with the dolphin crawl stroke one swimmer was able to equal his best freestyle time for 50 yards. It seems logical to conclude that the dolphin kick is indeed faster than the flutter kick; that if those individuals endowed with a natural dolphin kick would devote the practice time and effort to excel in the dolphin crawl stroke it could prove to be as fast as, and possibly faster than, the crawl stroke.

TEACHING THE DOLPHIN CRAWL STROKE

A suggested procedure for teaching the dolphin crawl with the body roll is as follows:

1. A water demonstration of the whole stroke
2. A support drill for the dolphin kick using the side of a swimming pool, the shallow water area of a lake, or a partner for support. Swimmers are encour-

aged to lower their heads under the water and observe the up and down movement of their legs. Begin with a large slow kick, gradually shorten the size and range of the kick and increase the cadence. (See Chapter 12.)

3. A 10 yard underwater dolphin kick drill:
   a. Repeat on right side
   b. Repeat on left side
   c. Repeat on the back

d. Repeat moving from prone to the right side, to the back, to the left side
e. Repeat rotating in the opposite direction

4. A surface dolphin kick drill

Arms are held at the sides of the body, the chin is extended forward. Turn the head to the left to breathe. Rotate the hips by elevating the left hip to accomo-

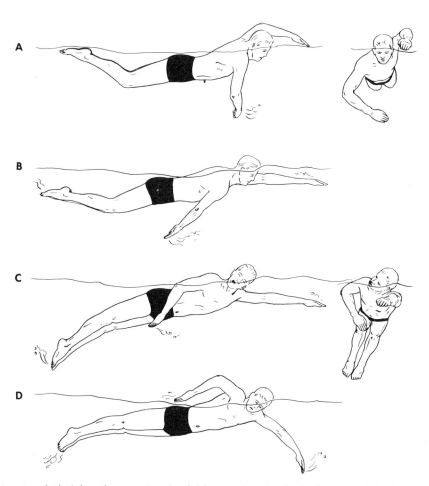

Fig. 13-1. A series of ideal form for executing the dolphin crawl stroke. **A,** The legs start their downward thrust as the right arm starts its push. **B,** The legs are halfway through the downward kick as the left arm enters the water. **C,** The proper breathing timing. **D,** The legs have started upward as the right arm recovers. **E,** The legs start their second downward thrust as the left arm starts its push. **F, G,** and **H,** The timing for completing the arm cycle.

date breathing. Repeat the drill turning the head to the right to breaths; rotate the hips by lifting the right hip.

5. A crawl stroke arm drill with the legs supported by a pull buoy or other floating device. Rotate the hips as the breath is taken.

6. Swim the whole dolphin crawl stroke slowly without breathing. Concentrate on the timing of the kick in relation to the arms. Kick down during the push motion of each arm.

7. Continue to swim the whole stroke; add body roll and breathing. Gradually shorten the range of the kick and increase the speed of the arms.

The degree of body roll and the size of the kick will vary with the individual swimmer. He should strive for a natural, relaxed, well-coordinated stroke.

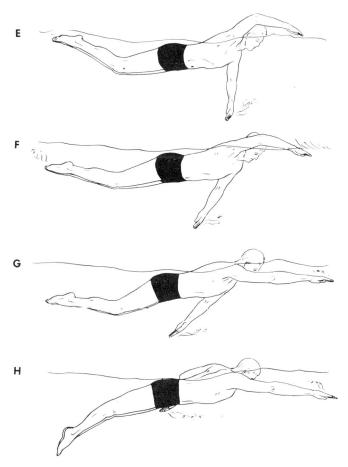

Fig. 13-1, cont'd. For legend see opposite page.

Chapter 14

Relay racing

Relay racing is that form of competition in which two or more men swim the same specified distance, one relieving the other at the end of the distance.

Relay racing is fun for most swimmers as well as spectators because of its spirited competition. Each portion of the relay race is designated as a "leg." Points in relay racing run very much higher than in an individual race. For this reason relays become the highlights of the meet.

TYPES OF RELAY RACES

There are usually two types of relays in swimming: medley (including the four competitive styles of swimming) and the freestyle relays, which may be classified as sprint and middle-distance races, that is, for each individual portion of the race. The length of each leg is quite definitely standardized for high school, college, and Olympic competition. Other types or varying distances come under the heading of noteworthy relay performances. The standard types are as follows:

High school:
1. 200-yard medley (75-foot pools) (4 x 50)
   160-yard medley (60-foot pools) (4 x 40)
   (Four swimmers on each team, each to swim one fourth the distance; first, back stroke; second, breast stroke; third, butterfly; fourth, freestyle)
2. 400-yard sprint freestyle relay (75-foot pools) (4 x 100)
   400-yard sprint freestyle relay (60-foot pools) (4 x 100)
   (Four swimmers, each to swim one fourth the distance)

College and AAU:
1. 400-yard medely relay (4 x 100)
   (Four swimmers on each team, each to swim one fourth the distance; first, back stroke; second, breast stroke; third, butterfly stroke; fourth, freestyle)
2. 400-yard sprint freestyle relay (4 x 100)
   (Four men on each team, each to swim one fourth the distance)
3. 800-yard freestyle relay (4 x 200) (college championship meets)

Olympic and AAU:
1. 800-meter freestyle relay (4 x 200)
   (Four men on each team, each to swim one fourth the distance)
2. 400-meter medley relay (4 x 100)
   (Four swimmers on each team, each to swim one fourth the distance; first, back stroke; second, breast stroke; third, butterfly; fourth, freestyle)

ARRANGEMENT OF A RELAY TEAM

When selecting members of a relay team and the order in which they swim, a coach must first consider a number of factors as to the qualifications of the candidates before making a decision. A number of these factors are as follows:
1. Who is a fast starter and calm under fire of competition?
2. Which one will swim best when behind?
3. Who swims best when in the lead?
4. Who is the weaker competitor?
5. Which lead-off man will give the most stability to the team?
6. Which anchor man will give the most confidence to the team?

Another question that must be answered is whether all men should be selected on a tryout basis; that is, for the particular meet for which a tryout is held, should those who win be on your team because they were fastest on the day of the tryout?

Some coaches will rely entirely upon tryouts. Others will wait until well along in the meet to see how certain individuals performed in earlier races and then nominate the men for the relay team. If a meet is close and depends on the last relay event, some coaches will often select, at the last minute, a slightly slower man but one who has been tried and true. This is selecting on a percentage basis and is considered an advisable procedure. One cannot take chances and experiment when the meet is close. A faster man may be an "in and outer," or an inexperienced man may fold up when the going gets tough. After the men have been selected, the next question to be decided is: In what order should they be placed in competition? We must now go back to the preceding questions as to personal characteristics and qualifications.

For the sake of simplicity, let us list the men in the order of their speed as 1, 2, 3, and 4, respectively. The most commonly used order is 2, 3, 4, and 1. This arrangement places the weaker man in the number 3 position, with two good men in front of him and the fastest man behind him. This shoud give the weaker man confidence.

Another commonly used plan is 2, 4, 3, and 1. This places the fastest man at anchor and the second fastest in the lead-off position, with the weaker man in the number 2 position. This arrangement is made with the hope that the second fastest man will hold is own or hand over a lead to the weaker man. Should those two men lose the lead, there are still two good men left to make up lost yardage.

Another order of swimming the sprint relay, and one that is often used to confuse opponents, is to arrange the competition in the order 1, 2, 3, and 4. The idea is to put the faster man out in front to get the lead and the number 2 man to further gain or at least hold the advantage, so that by the time the weaker "anchor" man comes up, he has been given a substantial advantage. In case things do not go well for him, he still has quite a margin. In each race, the team standing in the meet and the opponents' possible lineup should be the determining factors in arranging the team. If a lineup has been decided upon before meet time, a last minute change is likely to disturb the composure and confidence of the team.

TECHNIQUE OF THE TAKEOFF

The swimming takeoff in relay racing differs from that in track relay racing. In track the competitor receives a baton from his predecessor within a limited zone. He then must carry this on and pass it to his succeeding teammate. Such passing cannot be accomplished in swimming relay racing.

In the swimming relay the preceding swimmer finishes his "leg" by touching the finish wall. Poised above this finish lane and wall is the succeeding teammate who takes off as soon as his teammate touches the wall. There is some latitude given the swimmer at the touch-off comparable to the zone advantage given a runner. The starting swimmer may be in motion, such as arm swing or body lean, but his feet must not leave the takeoff wall until his teammate has touched it. In competition this is checked in two ways: (1) A takeoff judge stations himself in such a position that he can place his finger on the foot of each swimmer (after the first one) and at the same time see the end of the pool, and he judges whether the swimmer leaves his position before the preceding swimmer touches the end. (2) The more common method is the honor system. The judge stations himself at the side of the finishing end of the pool and merely observes that the rule is not violated.

There are several methods by which a swimmer may judge when to start his windup for the takeoff. The swimmer must use his own judgment about when to begin preparation for his takeoff. A safe method is for the swimmer to begin preparation for his takeoff when the head of his teammate is approximately 3½ feet from the finish wall. When the teammate's head reaches this point, the starting swimmer can drive with tremendous force and still have his feet on his mark when the "leg" is finished. The finishing swimmer must practice driving in with the finishing hand in order to time it perfectly. The starting swimmer must observe and practice judging a distance of 3½ feet. He looks down at the swimmer below him but must hold his head well up. If the head is held low, he is likely to lose balance, or, when he does dive, he is likely to dive short.

In a shorter sprint where speed is greater, a 4-foot margin can be allowed.

In breast stroke swimming in the medley relay, the following swimmer may allow not more than 2½ feet from the head to the finish wall since the speed of the incoming swimmer is slower.

Chapter 15

Training and conditioning

Training is a general term. It encompasses the adjustments the athlete must make to the competitive situation. These include the development of skill and the development of specific physical fitness for special events. The process of physical fitness development is termed conditioning. A conditioning program consists of regimens of diet, exercise, and other practices that strengthen the organism and increase its mobility and endurance.

Practice of the special event is the best single form of training and conditioning for competition. But this is not enough. Repetitions of the event in swimming or diving does not provide the degree of conditioning needed for maximum performance. In fact, once a peak of condition is reached, a program consisting solely of daily practice of the swimming or diving event will be accompanied by a deterioration of physical condition. The athlete gradually becomes weaker, loses endurance, and his performance declines.

To achieve and maintain top condition and continue to break through the barriers of performance the conditioning program from preseason through the championship period must extend in many directions. The swimmer must exercise against progressively heavier resistances to develop strength, and he must work at progressively higher workloads to develop endurance.

Before commencing these and other regimens of conditioning, the athlete should be given a thorough medical examination. The physician will determine that a strenuous program is not contraindicated by some organic defect or other health problem. Although wholesome good health does not assure maximum performance (sick athletes often break records), strenuous exercise may be dangerous under many conditions such as rheumatic heart disease. The athlete's physician will examine the athlete's heart and lungs at rest and during a test exercise, will study his bones and other tissues using roentgenograms, and will analyze his blood and urine for signs of metabolic or other disorders. During the competitive season the athlete will be referred by the coach for medical review if unusual responses occur or if the athlete does not react normally to conditioning regimens.

In addition to the medical evaluation, the initial physical examination ideally includes an assessment of physical fitness. Estimates of excess body fat, muscular strength, joint mobility, and cardiopulmonary response to exercise form the basis of individual conditioning routines.

Conditioning for athletic competition requires a drastic modification of lifestyle. Exercise must be balanced by rest and dietary adjustments so that a gradual process of adaptation can keep abreast with the progressive application of physical stress. The key to a successful adjustment of lifestyle is regularity. Sleep is more refreshing if regular hours are kept. Food is digested better at regular mealtimes. Work and study are more productive when scheduled at regular hours.

The use of tobacco and alcohol is not compatible with best performance in swimming and diving. Drugs other than those medically prescribed have no place in the sports program. These restrictions may seem severe, but once the new lifestyle is established, the athlete experiences a new level of well-being. When the satisfactions and rewards of improved performance are added to the feelings of well-being, the burdens of the restrictions and the rigors of a conditioning regimen are cheerfully borne.

NUTRITION

The diets of swimmers and divers need no special modification. A wide variety of wholesome foods consumed in amounts necessary to maintain normal body weight will sustain energy requirements.

The optimum body composition for swimmers and divers has not yet been computed. An optimal body fat component is probably close to 10% in males and 18% in females. Although fat increases buoyance, it also contributes to drag in swimming, since it represents an added resistance that must be overcome by arm and leg propulsion. Excess fat in divers spoils their aesthetic appearance.

Long-distance swimmers, in events lasting 30 minutes or more, may save energy by added buoyancy of more body fat. Fat also serves to insulate against loss of body heat in cold-water swims. The thickness of folds of the skin on the waist, back, thigh, and the back of the arm are valid indicators of body fat. None of these skinfolds should exceed 1 inch in thickness ("an inch of pinch") in swimmers or divers. This skinfold indicator is more accurate than body weight in estimating excess fat. During training, body weight may increase while fat is decreasing because of an increase in muscle mass. A combination of exercise and dietary restriction guarantees fat reduction. There is no universal diet for weight reduction.

"Crash" diets should be avoided by athletes. A rate of weight loss in excess of 2% of body weight per week (3 pounds per week in a 150-pound person) may endanger the health and performance of the athlete.

The practice of dehydration to reduce weight is unsound. Withholding fluids or using heat baths to "dry out" the body disturb metabolic processes and deteriorate health and performance. The wearing of impermeable clothing while exercising to induce water loss is dangerous, since it imposes abnormal stress on cardiovascular and temperature-regulating mechanisms.

If the athlete is reducing weight by partial starvation, eating fewer calories than he is using each day, closer attention needs to be given to the type of foods eaten. A reducing diet consists of high bulk-low calorie foods, such as raw vegetables and fruits and lean meats and fish. If the diet restriction is severe, one in which the calorie intake is less than half of the amount utilized, supplements of vitamins and minerals may be added to prevent deficiencies.

B-complex vitamins and vitamin C are important to athletic performance, but supplementing a nutritionally adequate diet with vitamins has no beneficial effect. In climates where there is little sunlight, vitamin D in fish and eggs offers an effective replacement. Ultraviolet radiation treatments are helpful in providing vitamin D. The exact function of vitamin E has yet to be determined. If vitamins are used, the time-release type are recommended.

Mineral supplements, such as iron, are also ineffective if the diet is nutritionally adequate.

A nutritionally adequate diet for swimmers and divers consists of 5,000 to 6,000 calories, provided by foods from dairy products, meat, fish and eggs, vegetables, fruits, and cereals. Breads and cereals made of whole grain or enriched with vitamins and minerals are preferred to the refined variety.

Water intake should be copious. Thirst is a poor guide to the fluid needs of the body for circulation, metabolism, and temperature regulation.

There is no basis for omitting fats or any other class of foods from the athlete's diet. Fats are useful foods and the athlete should not avoid an egg or a glass of milk in the ordinary diet because of the fat content.

Proteins are essential for normal growth. The athlete must have at least 50 grams of protein a day just to repair and rebuild the tissue damaged during heavy muscular work.

Carbohydrate is the chief fuel for continuous work. It yields more calories per unit of oxygen than fat or protein.

Frequent, light meals are better than two or three heavy meals each day. Omission of breakfast decreases athletic performance.

The meal before an athletic contest or an exhaustive practice session should be eaten about 3 hours prior to the event. This relieves the drain on the circulatory system by both the absorption of food and the demands of activity and allows digestive processes to be nearly completed. A small liquid sugar supplement just before activity prevents hypoglycemia (low blood sugar), which affects strength, endurance, and coordination.

Heavy, prolonged exercise lasting more than 1 hour, such as marathon swimming, is benefitted by glycogen supercompensation or superglycogenization. Increased glycogen stores in the muscles leads to better performance. This benefit of carbohydrate loading does not apply to events of short duration such as 100-yard sprints.

Carbohydrate loading for marathon events is accomplished by a diet-work regimen outlined in the following countdown (C = contest):

C minus 3 to 6 days—Exercise muscles to exhaustion to empty glycogen content and enhance resynthesis of glycogen. Keep the glycogen content of exercised muscles low by diet consisting almost exclusively of fat and protein.

C minus 48 hours—Shift to carbohydrate-rich diet. Taper off exercise to permit rebuilding and repair of muscle tissue. Continue carbohydrate-rich diet. Avoid fats. Eliminate bulky foods, such as lettuce and tomatoes, and eliminate highly spiced foods.

C minus 24 hours—Active rest. Very easy work-out. Continue carbohydrate-rich diet. Avoid fats.

C minus 3 hours—High carbohydrate precontest meal, such as oatmeal, toast and jam, sweetened tea with lemon. Avoid glucose pills, sugar cubes, honey, and other concentrated sugars that draw fluid into the digestive tract and dehydrate the body. Avoid salt tablets for the same reason. Reduce protein to the minimum. Avoid fats.

C minus 90 minutes—Liquid meal such as Sustagen or Nutrament.

C minus 30 minutes—Sweetened tea with lemon, either hot or iced. Avoid excess amount of sugar.

C plus 1 hour—Starting at the first hour and repeating every 30 minutes during the performance drink cold sweetened tea with lemon. If the pool water is warm, add small amounts of salt to the beverage to prevent cramps.

REST

The amount of sleep required by the athlete is an individual matter. Eight hours of sleep in each 24 hours is an average amount. If an athlete sleeps more than 9 hours he may be deconditioning.

Healthy sleep habits are founded on the following principles:

1. Muscular activity leading to general muscular relaxation and normal fatigue promotes sleep.
2. Calculate the hour of retirement by subtracting the number of hours of sleep required from the time required to awaken to start each day without hurrying. Establish the habit of retiring regularly at this hour.
3. As you undress for bed, shed your worries with your clothes. Freedom from anxiety promotes better sleep.
4. If nervous excitation is marked or physical fatigue unusual, soak in a hot bath before retiring.
5. Have the sleeping room dark, well

ventilated, and as quiet as possible.

6. Avoid excessive bed covers. These inhibit movement and are fatiguing because of the extra weight that must be supported during the night.

7. If an electric blanket is used, do not employ it as a heating pad. Sweating and other forms of heat dissipation during the night require effort and are fatiguing.

8. Go to bed to relax, rest, and sleep. Relax by letting the bed support your body weight.

9. Arise at a regular hour, regardless of feelings of early morning fatigue.

10. Stay awake all day. Do not take a nap.

RELAXATION

The secret of effortless swimming or graceful diving lies in a conservation of energy—the lack of oppositional movement or excess tension and an effective utilization of momentary rest periods. Such "relaxed effort" starts with the vagotonia of training, exhibited by lowered resting heart rate, and a release of the muscular tension that accumulates because of emotional problems and the strains of present-day living.

The athlete can learn to relax at will and should learn it early in the season. The following relaxation drills are helpful:

1. While sitting comfortably, deliberately tense parts of the body, such as the thighs, and then let the tension go. Repeat several times, each time letting go further and further so the tension is less and less. Do the same with other parts of the body, then with the whole body.

2. Practice the same tensing and letting go procedures while swimming. Swim one lap while tensing the muscles and then swim the return lap letting the tension go out of the muscles. Repeat several round trips and finally swim two laps slowly and easily and as loose and relaxed as possible.

3. While floating in the water, practice tensing and letting go until all muscles are

relaxed and let the waves toss you around.

WARMING UP

Preliminary exercises before strenuous activity may not prevent injury, but they may increase speed and efficiency of movement. Passive warm-up, such as massaging the muscles to be used, has a pleasant and relaxing effect on some athletes. The benefit, if any, is probably psychologic, acting to motivate or to reduce anxiety, depending on the individual and his trainer. An active warm-up may consist of a light swim using the strokes to be employed in the event or "on deck" exercises such as running in place or hopping for 2 minutes, emphasizing ankle action. Then static stretching exercises are performed to complete the warm-up. Dynamic, or ballistic, stretching exercises are apt to cause muscle soreness and may decrease range of motion.

Warm-up exercises should not be strenuous and should not cause body heat storage—both are fatiguing and diminish performance. Keep in mind that in most contestants the first 100 yards is the best performance for the day.

MOBILIZATION

The following static stretching exercises are used to increase the flexibility of swimmers and divers.

1. *Trunk stretches.* From a prone position, let the pelvic area remain on the floor while elevating the upper body by extending the arms to a full push-up position.

2. *Back stretcher.* From a sitting position with legs extended and toes pointed, grasp the ankles or outer borders of the feet and let the head and shoulders fall to rest on the knees or close to them.

3. *Toe pointer.* Sit on the feet with the toes and ankles stretched backward. Balancing the weight with both hands on the floor behind the hips, rock backward slightly allowing the knees to be raised from the floor.

4. *Shoulder stretcher.* While standing, reach behind the upper back with the right hand and bring the left hand to the upper back from below and grasp the fingers. Relax the shoulders to bring the hands together. Repeat, reversing the hands.

5. *Lateral stretches.* While standing with arms overhead, grasp each elbow with the opposite hand. Bend sideways from the waist and allow the muscles of the shoulders and thorax to stretch. Repeat on opposite side.

STRENGTHENING MUSCLES

Practice of the swimming or diving event by itself is not sufficient to develop peak muscular strength. In strength development by swimming there comes a point at which gains cease. This is because the resistance of the water no longer overloads the muscles. On-deck exercises or special exercises in the water permitting gradual increases in loading must be used to supplement the daily swimming or diving workout.

Loads must be applied in the manner that simulates the movements and the forces applied in the actual performance or the action will not be strengthened. This is an example of the SAID principle of *S*pecific *A*daptation to *I*mposed *D*emand. Devices used in the water such as ropes with adjustable friction attachments to provide drag, elastic rope arrangements, or vanes worn by the swimmer as a brake in the water facilitate specific loading. On-deck strengthening exercises can be made specific by various bench arrangements for barbell and dumbell exercises, wall pulley exercises, drag or elastic ropes, and isokinetic exercises.

Such devices should allow the swimmer to "swim through" his exercise in a horizontal posture. Peak resistances in exercise should be applied at the exact position that peak resistances are applied by the arms, shoulders, and legs during swimming or by the legs and ankles during diving. Many ingenious devices to apply the SAID principle are now available.

Swimming is essentially an arm and shoulder activity, and diving involves the legs and ankles. Strengthening exercise routines are directed toward these areas of the body. Sprint swimming with the feet attached to a large float will develop arm and shoulder strength.

Explosive strength. The swimming start and the diving takeoff require one or two brief near-maximum contraction efforts. This type of strength is achieved by exercising against maximum loads at a rapid speed of movement in only 1 to 5 repetitions. This set of repeated work can be performed periodically after 2-minute rest periods or while different muscle groups are being exercised. The number of sets are progressively increased as strength improves. Load is kept at a maximum.

Systems of fixed weight can provide the benches and loading arrangements for explosive strength exercises specific to swimming. Divers can perform a jump-and-reach maneuver while wearing a belt filled with lead shot tightly fixed to the waist. Progression in explosive strength is achieved in this exercise by gradually filling the belt with increasing amounts of lead shot, adding about one-fourth pound each session.

Strength endurance. The type of muscular strength that supports a long continued series of contractions against moderately heavy resistance is needed most by swimmers. This is strength endurance and it is achieved by exercise that is graded by adding heavier loads while maintaining the number of repetitions. For swimmers the number of repetitions can be set by counting the number of strokes required for the event (that is, 60 strokes with each arm for the 100-yard sprint). The rate of exercising can also be set to simulate the rate of arm or leg movement. If the swimmer's strength is known his strength endurance exercise regimen can commence with a load representing 50% of his maximum strength.

Resistance swimming is an effective means of developing strength endurance. The actual swimming style is performed with resistance added by hand paddles, drag vanes worn on the waist, pulling a sea anchor, or swimming in clothing to add drag. To develop strength endurance, periods of maximal effort should last for 5 to 10 seconds, alternating with brief rest periods.

Exercises for explosive strength development can be practiced during alternate periods with exercises for strength endurance development. Twice daily bouts on each type of exercise are not much more productive of strength development than exercising once a day.

AEROBIC ENDURANCE

The ability to continue work of high intensity for a long period is a function of the oxygen intake, or aerobic capacity. The rate of oxygen intake is limited by many factors, such as the flow of oxygen from the lungs to the bloodstream, the power of the heart to pump blood from the lungs to the muscular tissues in large quantities, and the flow of oxygen from the blood to the muscle tissues. These factors are affected by the adjustments the circulation can make to return the blood from the tissues to the heart, and the quality of blood and muscle tissues to take up, store, use, and release oxygen. All of these functions are improved by a certain type of exercise.

To improve aerobic endurance the exercise must be of sufficient intensity to tax the metabolic, circulatory, and respiratory systems, and it must be applied for sufficient duration to demand that all adjustments to exercise be completed. The problem in developing an aerobic endurance regimen is that the swimmer usually exhausts one system (such as cardiovascular) before other systems (such as cellular-metabolic) are taxed. A solution is interval training.

Interval training consists of interspersing high-intensity exercise with low-intensity exercise. The low-intensity periods allow a certain degree of recovery so that more high-intensity work can be accomplished during the practice session.

The goal in aerobic endurance exercise is to raise the swimmer's capacity to swim at a high speed for a longer time. This is achieved through interval training by a step-by-step process:

1. Determine the swimmer's probable best rate of swimming in his event. This rate is slightly (5%) faster than he can go for the entire distance of the event at the present time.
2. Establish the length of the interval of high-intensity swimming. The interval can be based on either time or distance (for example, one length of the pool). The high-intensity interval should be about one fourth of the total time or distance of the event.
3. Compute the split time for the length of the high-intensity interval.
4. Establish the rate of swimming during the low-intensity interval. The rate should be easy, but not so slow as to be tiring; swim with a relaxed, almost effortless stroke.
5. Compute the split-time for the length of the low-intensity interval.
6. Set a practice distance that is about twice as long as the swimmer's event.
7. Tabulate a schedule of interval training in which the length of high-intensity intervals remains the same and the length of the low-intensity interval is very gradually diminished. More high-intensity intervals will be added to complete the total distance as the length of the low-intensity intervals is shortened.
8. Practice interval training daily or on alternate days. This regimen will become exhaustive when the length of the low-intensity periods is reduced about 50%.
9. Construct a new table based on a recycling of the above procedures, starting with a reestablishment of the swimmer's probable best rate of swimming in his event. Recent time trials are used

for this value. Reset the new high-intensity rate. Establish split times.

10. When the above table of work has been completed, again adjust the intervals, and so on.

Staleness. Endurance conditioning can become boring to the point of staleness in which the swimmer reduces his work load. Performance will be affected if preventive or remedial measures are not taken.

Introduction of a variety of substitutes for interval training add interest without reducing workload. Some of these are:

1. *Dauerlauf.* A relay of three swimmers in which one is swimming while the other two rest.
2. *Fartlek.* Cruising interspersed with peak efforts then a return to cruising "as the spirit moves one." Swimming in pairs sparks the spirit of playful mini-competition.
3. *Tempolauf.* Very short all-out bursts of speed interspersed with short periods of recovery swimming. After a period of complete rest or a period of some lighter form of activity the tempolauf is repeated.

Progressive loading. During the entire season the work must be very gradually increased in order to prevent deconditioning. This progressive loading can be applied by alternately increasing each of seven variables: (1) the load of resistance, (2) the number of repetitions in each set, (3) the number of sets, (4) the rate or speed of movement, (5) the frequency of practices per week, (6) the intensity of the activities performed during rest periods, and (7) the duration of the work periods in relation to the rest periods.

SEASONAL PLANNING

The period *between seasons* is the best time to make drastic changes in the athlete's skill. Motion picture analysis and evaluations of body mechanics are studied with the athlete, and improved forms of movement are tested. Those that appear to be effective are incorporated into the athlete's style by special drills. Throughout the period between seasons, the athlete remains physically active to sustain a moderately high level of physical fitness for his event.

During the *preseason* period no new drastic changes in the style are attempted. Training consists of perfecting the athlete's form of movement. A transition from conscious attention to movement details to reflex action is accomplished. Emphasis turns from skill to strategy. At least an hour of practice each day is devoted to physical conditioning. At least 6 weeks is allowed for conditioning so the process can be very gradual to avoid injury and overfatigue. Exercises to develop strength, endurance, and flexibility are individually prescribed and each athlete proceeds at his own pace. If group drills are used, allowance is made for individual differences in condition and rate of conditioning. Pairing of athletes according to condition levels permits "buddy" workouts and provides some companionship to relieve monotony. Competition during weight training or interval training is discouraged, since it destroys progressive overload schedules and invites injury. Time-trials and mini-competitions in intersquad swimming meets are delayed until after the third week of preseason conditioning. Injured or unfit athletes are excluded from these trials.

The season of *competition* does not mark the end of the processes of training and conditioning. Adjustments in skill are limited to single, minor alterations in movement patterns, such as head position. Mental set is all important here. A harmonious power-tension balance is achieved by allowing movements to be more forceful just by a slight relaxation of the tension in elongating muscles. The quickness of execution of starts and turns is accelerated by repetitions until the skills are overlearned to the level of unconscious action. The sense of pace is refined by stopwatch checks until split-times are invariable. The separate arts of mental practice and reflex execution are mastered. Self-adjustment of anxiety levels by focusing on the completion of the event, breath control, or other awareness techniques is achieved. Physical conditioning exercises are continued with lessened frequency but with gradually increasing load. Staleness is prevented by scheduling meets with opponents of near-equal ability, and by permitting diversions and variety in practice sessions.

The *postseason* period is the time for analysis and evaluation of individual performances and methods of training and conditioning. Decisions are made regarding style changes and further adjustments the athlete should make before the next season of competition. Physical activity levels probably should be tapered-off, rather than suddenly shifting from a high to a low energy level. A period of rest for a week after the final meet is usually a welcome relief.

ENVIRONMENT

Travel involving sitting for a long time has a deconditioning effect and may cause constipation and motion sickness in some athletes. Time zone changes affect circadian rhythm and may impair appetite, digestion, wakefulness, and sleep. Changes in temperature, humidity, and altitude affect body functions and endurance.

The solution to these problems is to travel early to recover from travel fatigue and allow acclimatization to the new environment. Acclimatization is nearly complete in about 3 weeks at the new site.

If early travel is not feasible, the adaptation may be partially promoted at home by a gradual shift in hours of working, eating and sleeping. Adjustments in pool temperature toward that of the host will help acclimatize the athlete.

During travel the athlete should not remain seated for more than 50 minutes during each hour. He should increase his fluid intake and eat extra fruit or other high bulk foods to prevent constipation. If motion sickness is severe the team physician may prescribe a remedy that is not too sedating.

SELECTED READINGS

Annarino, Anthony A.: Developmental conditioning for physical education and athletics, St. Louis, 1972, The C. V. Mosby Co.

A.C.S.M.: The Encyclopedia of Sport Sciences and Medicine, Lemon, 1971, The Macmillan Co.

AAHPER: Nutrition for athletes, a handbook for coaches, Washington, D. C., AAHPER, 1971.

Astrand, P. O., and Rodahl, K.: Textbook of work physiology, New York, 1970, McGraw-Hill Book Co.

Beisler, Arnold: The madness in sports: psychosocial observations on sports, New York, 1967, Appleton-Century-Crofts.

Bourne, P. G.: The psychology and physiology of stress, New York, 1969, Academic Press.

Dintiman, G. B.: Sprinting speed, Springfield, Ill., 1971, Charles C Thomas, Publisher.

Dubos, R. J.: Man adapting, New Haven, 1965, Yale University Press.

Edholm, O. G., and Bacharach, A. L.: The physiology of human survival, New York, 1965, Academic Press.

Hardy, J. D., Gagge, A. P., and Stolwijk, J. A. J.: Physiological and behavioral temperature regulation, Springfield, Ill., 1970, Charles C Thomas, Publisher.

Jokl, E.: The physiology of exercise, Springfield, Ill., 1964, Charles C Thomas, Publisher.

Jokl, E., and Jokl, P.: The physiological basis of athletic records, Springfield, Ill., 1968, Charles C Thomas, Publisher.

Klafs, Carl E., and Arnhiem, D. D.: Modern principles of athletic training, ed. 2, St. Louis, 1969, The C. V. Mosby Co.

Lee, D. H. K.: Physiology, environment, and man, New York, 1970, Academic Press.

Moore, J. W.: Psychology of athletic coaching, Minneapolis, 1970, Burgess Publishing Co.

Morehouse, L. E., and Miller, A. T.: Physiology of exercise, ed. 6, St. Louis, 1971, The C. V. Mosby Co.

Morehouse, L. E., and Rasch, P. J.: Sports medicine for trainers, ed. 2, Philadelphia, 1963, W. B. Saunders Co.

Morgan, W. P.: Contemporary readings in sport psychology, Springfield, Ill., 1970, Charles C Thomas, Publisher.

Novich, M., and Taylor, B.: Training and conditioning of athletes, Philadelphia, 1970, Lea and Febiger.

Rasch, P. J., and Burke, R. K.: Kinesiology and applied anatomy, Philadelphia, 1971, Lea and Febiger.

Roby, F. B., and Davis, R. P.: Jogging for fitness and weight control, Philadelphia, 1971, W. B. Saunders Co.

Scholz, A. E., and Johson, R. E.: Body conditioning for college men, Philadelphia, 1971, W. B. Saunders Co.

Selye, H.: Stress of life, New York, 1956, McGraw-Hill Book Co.

Shepard, R. J.: Endurance fitness, Toronto, 1969, University of Toronto Press.

Shepard, R. J.: Alive man, Springfield, Ill., 1971, Charles C Thomas, Publisher.

Shepard, R. J., editor: Frontiers of fitness, Springfield, Ill., 1971, Charles C Thomas, Publisher.

Simonson, E., editor: Physiology of work capacity and fatigue, Springfield, Ill., 1971, Charles C Thomas, Publisher.

Spackman, R. R.: Conditioning for gymnastics, Springfield, Ill., 1970, Charles C Thomas, Publisher.

Spackman, R. R.: Conditioning for wrestling, Springfield, Ill., 1970, Charles C Thomas, Publisher.

Taylor, A. W.: Training—scientific basis and application, Springfield, Ill., 1971, Charles C Thomas, Publisher.

Thomas, V.: Science and sport, Boston, 1971, Little, Brown and Co.

Vanek, M., and Cratty, D. J.: Psychology and the superior athlete, London, 1970, The Macmillan Co.

Chapter 16

Specificity of training

The remarkable assault on the record books that has taken place in competitive swimming over the past 20 years has led to speculation about the reasons for the improvement in record times that has been seen in virtually every event. Some attribute much of this progress to the great influx of athletes into the sport. Others point out that improved stroke mechanics and nutrition must account for some measure of the improvement in record times. Virtually everyone, however, agrees that swimmers of today are faster than those of 20 years ago, primarily because of the training in which they engage.

Coaches have been greatly interested in training methods because of their desire to have knowledge of the most effective ways to produce desired physiologic changes through various kinds of training programs. They traditionally have constructed training programs on a hit or miss basis—by simply using things that work and casting aside those that do not. Even this method, over a period of many years, has led to training programs that are productive and more or less scientifically correct, because those methods that work are, for the most part, those that *are* scientifically correct.

Scientists, too have been interested in this area and have been active in producing information of great interest and use to the coach. Perhaps the most interesting single concept that science has contributed to thought in the area of training methods in recent years has been that of *specificity of training*. This concept, which applies to both strength and endurance training, has been reflected in current training programs conducted by top-flight coaches, even

though most programs have been based on empirical rather than scientifically accurate data. Virtually all of the current successful programs in swimming use the concept of specificity of training. Thus, swimmers who are successful are training primarily in the strokes in which they expect to compete. It is also important to note that, as the period of competition approaches, the swimmer must do progressively more and more of his training at or near the pace at which he expects to swim his event.

SCIENTIFIC BASIS FOR SPECIFICITY OF TRAINING

The concept of specificity of training in endurance training exists because of the physical and physiologic requirements of the various events (Fig. 16-1).

As can be seen in Fig. 16-1, the metabolic systems that pay the cost of exercise are indeed specific. In an event such as the 1650-yard freestyle, some 85% of the energy cost of the event is paid for by the aerobic metabolic system. To be successful in this event, a swimmer must have a well-developed cardiorespiratory system and a large aerobic capacity (that is, the ability to absorb a large amount of oxygen per unit of time). Although strength is somewhat important in such an event, it is not as important as in a sprint event and is relatively unimportant when compared with the necessity of having a well-developed aerobic metabolic system. The aerobic system can be developed through training.

When compared with the 1650-yard freestyle, the 50- and 100-yard freestyles have strength and metabolic requirements that are entirely different in nature. In the sprints

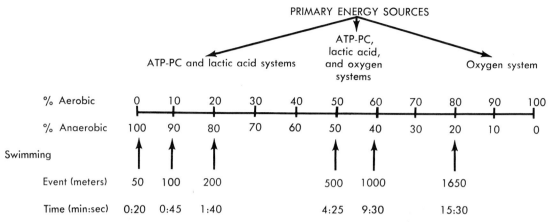

Fig. 16-1. The approximate percentage of contribution of aerobic and anaerobic energy sources in selected track events. (Adapted from Mathews, D. K., and Fox, E. L.: The physiological basis of physical education and athletics. Philadelphia, 1971, W. B. Saunders Co.)

muscular strength appears to be a requisite for success, and the anaerobic rather than the aerobic energy sources would appear to be important. In the 100-yard freestyle, for instance, 85% to 90% of the energy cost of the event is paid via the anaerobic energy systems as compared with 10% to 15% that is paid for by the aerobic system. The capacity of the anaerobic system, which furnishes most of the energy cost of the sprint events, can be developed through training. It must be stressed, however, that a change in the capacity of any metabolic system, which takes place through training, is most effectively achieved through a training program that stresses, specifically, that system.

Aerobic training

In order to stress the aerobic system, most training authorities of today tend toward great volumes of work done at comparatively low heart rates (that is, below 150 in most people). This training can be done either continuously, as in marathon training, or in interval training. In either method, however, it must be noted that the total distance of the work done is an important factor. Marathon runners, whose energy requirements are almost entirely aerobic,

train from 100 to 250 miles per week, running continuously at training distances of from 15 to 30 or 40 miles, mostly at a slow pace. Interval training, which is designed to stress the aerobic system, is discussed later in this chapter, but it might be said that the principle is a large number of repetitions of 50- to 200-yard swims with rest periods shorter than 30 seconds.

It is the purpose of aerobic training to stress the aerobic metabolic system. Physiologic results of this kind of training are as follows:

1. Training effects on the heart
   a. An increase in the thickness of the walls of the ventricles; an increase in the strength of the working heart muscle.
   b. An increase in the number of capillaries in the heart muscle per unit of volume, enabling the heart to better nourish itself and to remove the by-products of contraction.
   c. A decrease in the heart rate at rest and at any submaximal level of work. This allows for more diastolic filling time, and thus the stroke volume of the heart increases.
2. Training effects on the working muscles
   a. Although this type of training will

not lead to great strength in the working muscles, adequate strength to do this submaximal type of work is developed.

b. Over a long period of time, that is, several training years, it is possible that aerobic training will lead to a shift from white to red fibers in the muscle. Although the muscle loses, through this shift, some of its explosive power, it is better equipped to do submaximal work of long duration because of the increased amount of myoglobin within the muscle and because the mitochrondria, the power plants of muscle where the aerobic processes take place, increase in both size and number.

c. Aerobic training is also likely to lead to an increased capillarization within the muscle.

3. Training effects on the metabolic systems
Although both anaerobic and aerobic training lead to an increase in the athlete's maximum oxygen consumption, aerobic training leads to a high degree of efficiency of the aerobic system. The athlete is able to work at a higher percentage of his maximum oxygen consumption before the muscles begin to produce lactic acid.

Anaerobic training

People who train for the anaerobic events would find that training of the type mentioned previously would leave them poorly prepared for the sprint events. It should be remembered that during the 1920's, when virtually all swimmers trained by what might be called general distance training, the record for the 100-yard freestyle was 51 seconds, whereas in the 1972 NCAA Championships, it took a time better than 46.0 to qualify for the championship finals.

Much of the training for the sprint events is done by the interval training method. In this type of training the work performed is

very hard, frequently driving heart rates to 180 beats per minute or over. The rest period between innings of work is never less than 30 seconds, and may be as long as three to four times that of the work interval. Another type of training that is used to prepare sprinters is referred to as sprint training. This specialized form of interval training employs short sprints, usually not in excess of 100 yards. These are done all-out, with a rest period of several minutes between, to allow the athlete to come to nearly complete recovery. The physiologic effects of anaerobic training are as follows:

1. Training effects on the heart
a. Although there is a decrease in heart rate at any submaximal level of work, the overall effects on the efficiency of the cardiorespiratory system are apparently not as pronounced as is the case with aerobic training. Basal heart rates are seldom as low in sprinters as in aerobically trained athletes.

b. Some increase in the weight of the heart takes place, apparently as a result of hypertrophy.

2. Training effects on the working muscles
a. As a result of overload during this heavy muscular work, some hypertrophy of the muscles involved in swimming, and a concomitant increase in the strength of these muscles, is to be found. However, even though this is a long-term effect of this kind of training, muscular strength is so necessary to success in the anaerobic events that many athletes go to an outside system of resistance exercise, such as weight training, to increase strength gains.

b. The heavy work of training in the anaerobic events, over a long number of years, might be expected to lead to a shift in fiber type within the working muscle. This shift leads to an increase in the number of white fibers to be found in the muscle and increases the ability of the muscle to contract rapidly and with great force.

3. Training effects on the metabolic systems
    a. Anaerobic training, just as aerobic training, leads to an increase in maximum oxygen consumption.
    b. Anaerobic training leads to an increase in the amount of lactic acid that an athlete can produce, leading to an increase in the amount of energy available from the lactacid metabolic system.
    c. Anaerobic training may lead to an increase in the energy available from the alactacid energy system.

TRAINING SYSTEMS

Throughout the last 50 years of competitive swimming, a number of schemes have been developed for the conditioning of athletes. Although for the most part some of these methods, such as general distance training, have been discarded, there are several systems, which are productive, in common use today. The common ones, and their strengths and weaknesses, are described below. Successful training programs, regardless of type, have some common denominators. A few of these are listed below.

1. They are progressive. They begin at the start of the training season with moderately taxing workouts and get progressively harder. It is necessary to overload any physiologic system to make it improve.
2. They stay, for the most part, within the capacity of the individual. Following the workout, the athlete should be tired, but the feeling of fatigue should diminish and disappear in a few hours and should not linger from day to day. Exhaustion is the enemy; it retards progress.
3. They are specific in nature, leading a person to train at speeds that are progressively closer to the speed at which he will wish to swim when he competes.

4. They stress the appropriate metabolic systems.

Distance training

This type of training is used extensively in the track world for the preparation of marathon and distance runners. It involves comparatively easy continuous swimming for long distances. The ultimate goal of this system is aerobic endurance. Using heart rate as an indicator of stress, it would be usual to find heart rates that are quite low. In this kind of training, runners may train at heart rates of around 150 beats per minute. However, because immersion in the water produces bradycardia (a lowering of the heart rate), the swimmer's heart rate will be somewhat lower. A heart rate of 130 beats per minute, on the average, would be a good figure. Some athletes might be able to swim distances of 2 to 5 miles at heart rates of 140 beats per minute. However, if a given level of work produces fatigue, which tends to make the individual stop, the purpose of this type of training is being defeated. The intent of this kind of program is to stay within the capacity of the aerobic system. This system has application to modern training for swimming, although it is never used exclusively. It is used by many coaches during the early part of preseason training to lay the broad aerobic base that is thought to be essential even in the training of sprinters. Its contribution, however, is not only in the improvement of the capacity of the aerobic system but also in the adaptation of the body to physical stress and fatigue. It is a building block for the more strenuous forms of training to follow.

Fartlek training

Fartlek training, or speed play, is a method of training that has been used by many runners, dating back to the Finnish champion, Paavo Nurmi. It is a type of training in which a runner runs through country of varying scenery, now walking, now jogging, and occasionally sprinting. In track, it can be a very pleasant way to train because of the low-pressure setting. It should be noted that this method is based on periods of high stress interspersed with periods of comparatively low stress. It is this aspect of the program that has led some authorities to consider it a predecessor of interval training.

The individual athlete must learn to work with this type of training to derive maximum benefit from it. In this system as in any other, improvement is not without cost. It should be treated as a progressive system in which the average workout for each training week should be more stressful than the average workout of the week before.

The fartlek system does have some application to training in swimming. However, it is not as widely used in swimming as in track, because the environment is different. The runner can run along beaches or in the woods, deriving pleasure from the change of scenery, but it is difficult to create a parallel situation in a 25-yard swimming pool.

Again using heart rate as an indicator of stress, the accomplished swimmer might swim for a time at a comparatively relaxed heart rate of 130 beats per minute. Occasionally, he might speed up for a couple of hundred yards, so that the heart rate speeds up to 140 to 150 beats per minute, and once in a while add a 50 to 100-yard sprint, strenuous enough to raise the heart rate to 165 to 180 beats per minute, again followed by several minutes of relaxed swimming at quite low heart rate.

The problems with this kind of training are several. First of all, we should realize that unsupervised swimming of this kind tends to be without the kind of stress that will produce change. Although a knowledgeable swimmer who is highly motivated might profit greatly from this kind of training, the less than dedicated athlete tends to omit the stressful portions of the program that produce the training effect. In addition, the charm of possible changes in scenery that make this program attractive to runners are not available to swimmers, and this tends to be a boring way to train.

The benefits to be derived from this program, assuming motivation on the part of the athlete and also assuming that the program includes adequate progressively applied stress, are great. Because a properly applied program might be expected to stress both the anaerobic systems as well as the aerobic systems, this training method is useful for a wide range of events from the sprints to the middle distances.

Interval training

Interval training is a training method that employs alternating periods of work and rest. Although other training systems, such as fartlek training, have employed alternating periods of work and, at least, comparative rest, interval training is unique in that there is precise control over each of the variables with which it is possible to change training stress. Interval training is comparatively new to swimming, dating back to the late 1940s, when William Peterson, the swimming coach from Northwestern University, divided the 1500 meter swim into 16 × 100 yard swims and a 40 yard sprint in order to train William Heusner, NCAA champion and member of the 1948 Olympic team. The original work on interval training, however, was done by German track coach Waldemar Gerschler and a physiologist, H. Reindell, in training the outstanding German runner, Rudolph Harbig, in 1939.

Interval training consists of several variables, each of which can be maneuvered to alter the stress of the work being done. These are listed by most authorities as follows:

1. The distance to be swum
2. The pace at which the distance is to be swum
3. The number of repetitions of the training distance
4. The rest interval between swims
5. Activity during the rest period

6. The frequency of training

As can readily be seen, altering any of these variables can change the intensity of the workout. Much has been written about the role of each of these variables in the building of a sensible system of exercise. Some of these thoughts, which will be of help in constructing a training program using interval training methods, are presented below.

Distance. Although several different distances might be utilized in making up an individual workout, the workout should have a central theme. Some authorities suggest that one fourth of the competitive distance would be a good average training distance. Others have stated that, from a psysiologic standpoint, the length of the work period should not exceed 30 seconds and that periods of work in excess of 90 seconds are not productive. However, to be practical, in swimming, work periods of less than 30 seconds would limit training to 50 yard-50 meter sprints. Since the chief problem with interval training is boredom, it can be readily seen that a training program consisting of mile after mile of swimming only 50-yard sprints would be successful only with a highly unusual athlete.

The successful training program for the sprint events, 200 yards and less, is likely to include, across a training year, distances from 25 to 800 yards. It is clear that it is possible to swim 25 yards at a rate that is faster than could be maintained over the 800 yard distance. Therefore, since one of the objectives of the training season is to get the individual to swim progressively at paces that are closer and closer to the pace at which he will compete, most of the longer swims appear early in the training season, and the average length of the distances swum becomes progressively shorter throughout the season. Within 4 weeks of the championship meets, virtually all training for events of 200 yards and shorter is done at the competitive distance or less. It should be remembered that it is not the training dis-

tance itself that is important, but the amount of stress that can be applied through swimming repetitions of that distance.

Repetitions. The number of repetitions to be done per workout day leads one to a consideration of the total amount of work to be done per day. Some trace authorities advocate total daily training volumes of from 2 to 3 times the competitive distance. However, Emil Zatopek, the Czechoslovakian Olympic champion is said to have done as many as 60×400 meter runs in a single workout. One reads of workouts in swimming in excess of 15,000 meters per day, but few programs seem to include more than 8000 to 10,000 yards per day on a regular basis. This total distance tends to be progressively less throughout the season for sprinters, as the intensity of their workouts increases, but because of the kind of adaptation required in the distance events, the volume remains comparatively stable as the season progresses. It can be said that good swimming programs usually include, even for sprinters, at least 3000 to 4000 yards of swimming per day, right up to the time of the taper for the season's major competitive events. The point should be made here that the stress involved in swimming a distance is more important than the distance itself as an overall factor in producing a training effect.

Pace. The pace at which an individual swims the repetitions that comprise a workout is the most effective way to control stress. Theoretically, a person could condition himself by swimming the same workout all season long, altering only the speed with which he swims. If the speed increase was done in a progressive fashion and provided enough stress, there would be a definite training effect. However, only a highly unusual person could fail to be bored with such a program.

The overall purpose of altering pace in a workout is to change the amount of stress provided by the workout. This amount of stress is indicated by exercise heart rate, which can be determined by taking a 6-second carotid pulse immediately after exercise. In fast interval training, the pace should be fast enough to bring the heart rate all the way up to 180 beats per minute and perhaps even slightly beyond. It will be noted that during a training season the speed with which the workout must be swum involves, to accomplish heart rates of 180 beats per minute, increases throughout the season as the swimmer adjusts to the work load.

Rest. The length of the rest interval in interval training has been much discussed, some authorities stating that it should never be less than 30 seconds. However, in actual practice, coaches have found that it is practical to vary the rest period from 5 seconds to several minutes, depending on the goals of a particular workout. A usual practice in fast interval training is to allow the heart rate to fall to at least 140 beats per minute between repetitions within a given set of swims, and to allow recovery to at least 120 beats per minute between sets.

That the recovery interval is important is beyond question. Much of the adaptation of the heart itself takes place during the recovery interval immediately following exercise. It is at this time that the stroke volume of the heart is highest. It is also during this period that the alactacid portion of the oxygen debt is paid off; about half of it, or 1 to 1½ liters, during the first 30 seconds of recovery. The replenishment of this portion of the oxygen debt gives the athlete the opportunity to swim the next repetition slightly above what can be done entirely aerobically without increasing the amount of lactic acid in the blood. This may work to the athlete's advantage, since in really exhausting work, such as is seen in competitive events, the amount of lactic acid in the blood is the limiting factor. It is also this factor that may curtail workouts if the work level is too high, or if the rest period is not long enough to allow replenishment of the alactacid energy source.

Many times conditioning programs are constructed using the rest interval as the means with which to apply stress. This is usually done with athletes who compete in the aerobic events. It is possible here because the net effect of shortening the rest interval is to force the individual to work aerobically if he is to complete his workout task. As the rest interval is shortened, the athlete simply has less opportunity to replenish the anaerobic energy sources. The swimmer is very sensitive to reduction of the rest interval. Many authorities say that this is the most difficult of the variables to maneuver. An athlete will notice moderate changes in pace or total distance far less.

Activity during the recovery interval. Virtually every coach who has done extensive work with interval training has discovered that the recovery interval cannot be a period only of rest. Some movement is necessary so that the kneading action of the muscles squeezing on the veins will promote the return of venous blood to the heart and lungs. Without this muscular action, blood tends to remain in the extremities, and the exercise metabolites are removed from the working muscles much more slowly. Some moderate activity, then, should be maintained during the recovery interval. This might be as little as treading water using the arms and legs. Track men frequently walk or even jog the recovery interval for these same reasons. It is my feeling that the worst thing to do during the recovery interval is to lie quietly on the pool deck. This kind of inactivity does not promote venous return, and the resulting time required to achieve recovery to a given level is lengthened.

Some coaches have attempted to add other methods of conditioning to the recovery interval, having their swimmers do such things as push-ups, sit-sups, or shock cord work between swims. Although this can be very productive if done between sets or at other times during the day as a part of the work out structure, I feel that such activities during the recovery interval within a set drastically alter the total stress that can be tolerated during swimming and makes more difficult the construction of a progressive conditioning program.

Frequency of training. It is the tendency with most of us, when considering total work load, to assume that the more work one does the greater are his chances of success. As one reads the training literature, one can't help but be impressed by the workouts that have been done by such greats as Mike Burton, the 1968 Olympic champion at 400 and 1500 meters. Indeed, some runners have assumed that in order to do better than a great athlete, such as Emil Zatopek, it would be necessary to do more work than he did. The overall idea seems to be "the more work, the better."

In another area of the sports world, this has not been found to be true. Competitive weight lifters do not, even at the world class level, do heavy lifting every day. Rather, their workouts consist of three to four workouts per week, usually with a day of recovery between workdays. The apparent reason for this is to allow the body to recuperate, to adjust, to rebuild.

Current literature indicates that this concept may be applicable to some events in swimming. Recent studies conducted at The Ohio State University indicate that in anaerobic training, there is no difference in training two, as compared with four, times per week, provided the week by week intensities of the workouts for the two groups are matched.

A method of training that, in part, uses this principle is the so-called Oregon system of training, in which training days of hard work are interspersed with days of comparatively light work. The proponents of this system in the swimming world claim that this is an effective way to ensure week by week progression, because the danger of greatly overworking an individual is lessened, despite the fact that the days of heavy work can indeed be hard.

It would not seem wise, on a basis of current information, to keep a swimmer entirely out of the water for several days per week for the purpose of recovery. However, people who train for the sprint events may soon be doing heavy water work only 3 to 4 days per week, using the off days, which would include only comparatively light water work, for weight training, work on starts, strokes, turns, and so on.

The exception to the above would appear to be those events that stress primarily the aerobic metabolic system. Apparently from what is known at this time, great volumes of training are necessary over a period of years to produce maximal changes in the cardio-respiratory system. Exercise bradycardia is produced in virtually all athletes who train for events that require endurance, but the phenomenally low resting heart rates (low thirties) seen in some athletes who participate in the distance events are not a usual characteristic of sprinters. Stroke volume also is apparently increased by aerobic training, and distance athletes develop, as a result of their training, the ability to perform at extremely high percentages of their maximal ability to absorb oxygen without having to rely on an input of energy from the anaerobic systems.

Since this kind of aerobic endurance, developed over a period of years, is apparently stimulated by great volumes of training in regular training sessions, it would seem prudent to suggest to the young swimmer that he train at least 5 to 6 days per week.

The question of the advisability of training more than once per day arises whenever coaches get together. It is well known that most of the national and international level competitors train more than once each day, and that most good college programs include training at least twice each day. The reason for this is apparently that the athlete can stand more stress if it is administered in more frequent but smaller doses. This is a sensible approach even if the training one does is done essentially three or four times per week, although there is at present no experimental evidence to back it up.

Specialized interval training

Within the broad concept of interval training as a method that employs alternating periods of work and rest, several types of training systems, each with its special use have been developed. Some of these, which are appliclicable to training in swimming, are presented below. The following table, adapted from Fred Wilt's fine article, shows the contribution made by each of the training systems to the factors necessary for success in speed swimming.*

Fast interval training. As can be seen in the above table, fast interval training is intended to develop anaerobic endurance of the kind so necessary in the events of 200 yards and less and also speed. The amount of stress should be controlled by heart rate, the exercise heart rate going to at least 180 beats per minute after the first couple of repetitions. The principle behind this kind of training is to increase the individual's ability to produce and to tolerate increasing amounts of lactic acid in the blood. The pace at which an individual swims will approach the speed at which he competes late in his training season. Recovery heart rates should come to 140 or below between swims within a set and to 120 or below between sets.

Slow interval training. Slow interval training is done at a slower pace, and as can be seen by looking at Table 16-1, the contribution of this training system leans toward the development of aerobic endurance, although some development of anaerobic endurance may result. Speed is not developed effectively through this system, which looks much like fast interval training when it is being conducted. Heart rates should only approach and should never exceed 180 beats per minute in this type of training, because beyond

*Wilt, Fred: Training for competitive running. In Falls, Harold B., editor: Exercise physiology, New York, 1968, Academic Press, pp. 395-414.

Table 16-1. Development of training factors according to types of training

Type of training	Percent contribution of type of training to		
	Speed	Aerobic endurance	Anaerobic endurance
Sprint training	90	4	6
Distance training	2	93	5
Slow interval training	10	60	30
Fast interval training	30	20	50
Repeat training	10	40	50
Fartlek training	20	40	40
Negative-split interval training	40	20	40

a heart rate of 180, stroke volume decreases, and there is a great increase in the production of lactic acid. Although recovery heart rates are allowed to drop as low as 120 in slow interval training, this happens quickly when compared with the recovery times in fast interval training, because the stress produced by the work being done is less.

Negative-split interval training. This form of interval training is similar to fast interval training and includes distances up to and including the competitive distance. Heart rates are allowed to drop to 120 beats per minute between swims because of the strenuousness and speed of the next swim. In this kind of training, the last half of each swim is required to be faster than the first half. This frequently requires an all-out sprint for the last fourth of the swim and produces heart rates in excess of 180. The primary contribution of this kind of training is to speed.

Repeat training. Repeat training in swimming is a specialized form of interval training in which the distances range from about three fourths of the competitive distance up to the competitive distance itself. Since the usual objective of this type of training is anaerobic endurance (although there is also a nearly equal contribution to aerobic endurance), the repetitions are done nearly all-out, raising the heart rate to over 180 beats per minute. Recovery periods may last several minutes, and the heart rate should have returned to a level below 120 beats per minute before the next repetition is begun. Two to six repetitions might be done, but these should be continued only as long as the pace can be maintained. Although an index for recovery has already been mentioned, it should be noted that recovery time must be adequate for the individual to swim at the required pace in order for this type of training to be effective.

Sprint training. Sprint training is similar in form to repeat training. In swimming, normally only distances up to 100 yards are included. Each of the two to five swims that is included in a set should be done all-out, raising the heart rate to over 180 beats per minute; and recovery times should be long enough to allow the heart rate to drop well below 120 beats per minute, possibly to 110 or below. The principal contribution of this kind of training is to speed. It is widely used in the tapering process, when the championship season is approaching.

Managing the workout in interval training

It is extremely important for the coach to help the swimmer understand the workout and to know what the objectives and target times are for each part of the workout, for it is only in this way that the swimmer can get the most of what the workout has to offer. In general, the principles for managing the workout, from the swimmer's standpoint, might be as follows:

1. Swim at an even pace. Each swim should be done so that the time for the last half of the swim is within 2 seconds of the first half. The emphasis, in order to do this, usually must be on the last half of the swim.
2. Manage each set of swims so that the times for each of the swims is within a second or so per each 100 yards of the average. Thus a set of 100-yard swims might vary from 1:00 to 0:58, a set of

200-yard swims from 2:12 to 2:08, and so on.
3. Manage each set of swims so that, within the above limits, the last swim of each set is the fastest one. Swimming the first repetition of the set all-out (except in sprint training), defeats the purpose of the workout. It will simply make it impossible to finish.

Constructing the workout. From the coaches point of view, constructing the workout requires an intimate knowledge of where the individual stands in terms of his ultimate goals. Although examples of the kinds of workouts that might be seen at various times during the season are included in this chapter, they are intended only as examples. No comprehensive day-by-day workout plan is presented simply because it would be meaningless. Workouts need to be planned individually, on a day-by-day basis, according to where the swimmer stands *at that time* in relation to his ultimate goal. The coach's responsibility goes beyond just conditioning the individual so that he will some day hit a desired time goal. The coach must also be aware that peak performances must be hit at the desired time in relation to the individual and team goals for the season. Some principles for achieving these objectives follow:

1. If the individual has speed and can take the race out fast enough to achieve his goals but dies in the last part of the race, endurance is the problem. His event should be analyzed to determine his metabolic needs during the race, as presented above, and the appropriate kinds of training should be included in his program to enable him to build the proper kind of endurance.
2. If the individual maintains a pace well but simply can't swim fast enough to to achieve his time goal, either technique or strength as it is related to swimming speed is his problem. Assuming technique to be adequate, those kinds of training that lead to speed, such as sprint

training or negative-split training, should be added to the program. In addition, it might be well, in the off season or the preseason, to include in the swimmer's program some resistance training, such as weight training.

3. If the individual appears to be handling his training program well but is approaching his peak too rapidly, do less speed work and lengthen the workout, including more endurance work in the program.

4. If the individual is approaching his peak to slowly, include more speed work in the program. Sprint training, negative-split training, and repeat training may be of help here. Remember that if these methods are to be properly done so that they can make their contribution, the workout may have to be shortened and more time for rest included.

THE TRAINING SEASON IN SWIMMING

A season plan for training in swimming is discussed here as it applies to the winter scholastic or intercollegiate seasons. It is realized that this is only half the picture, since today virtually all successful swimmers train and compete on a year-round basis. However, this picture is representative of a training cycle that could be repeated, after a brief layoff, in preparation for the summer season. The workouts presented here are really for purposes of illustration only. They are designed to show a progression in the intensity of the program as the season proceeds, but will not necessarily meet the needs of a particular individual as his status at any point is related to his goals for the season.

The workouts divide swimmers into two classes for training purposes; those in anaerobic events (sprinters, or those in events of 200 yards and less), and those in aerobic events (distance swimmers, or those in events of 400 yards and more). The workouts are presented as if the swimmer is working only once a day, but it is realized that

some will wish to work out two or even three times each day.

The training program is divided into four parts as follows:
1. Preseason training
2. Precompetition training
3. Competitive season training
4. Championship training

A discussion of the objectives of each portion of the training season, its objectives, and sample workouts are presented below.

Preseason training. Preseason training normally begins in October and proceeds through the month of November. The early part of this period is a time for adaptation of the muscular system to the extremely heavy work of the months ahead. The work of the first week or so should be only moderately taxing and should be well within the capacity of the individual. The work at this time is aerobic, for the most part, the training schedule being comprised mostly of fartlek training and slow interval training. Water polo is included in order to avoid the drudgery of miles of swimming months on end without a break. The early workouts presented apply to both sprinter and distance swimmers, and they work, for the most part, together. Although the work at this time is predominantly aerobic, the sprinter profits too, for he is laying the "broad aerobic base" so necessary for success in the sprint events. It is only late in the preseason period that the sprinters begin to specialize, doing more fast interval training. Work is done only 5 days per week and by late preseason a weekly pattern has been established as follows:

Monday—hard training
Tuesday—moderate training
Wednesday—hard training
Thursday—moderate training
Friday—hard training

The precompetition period. During the precompetition period, which lasts, ideally, from December 1 to mid January, the work for both groups begins to get difficult. The distance swimmer gets progressively less rest between work bouts in his slow interval training at race pace and does longer sets without a break. Some fast interval training begins to appear in his workouts.

The sprinter begins to do more and more fast interval work, much of it centering around his longest competitive event, the 200. His training up to this point has given him an aerobic base upon which to build, and at this point anaerobic work is being emphasized and speed work begins to appear. The weekly training pattern is the same as in the preseason period, except that the swimmer trains 6 days per week rather than 5. Monday, Wednesday, and Friday are moderate days, and Tuesday, Thursday, and Saturday are days of hard training. Many swimmers will choose to train twice daily during this period.

The competitive season. During the precompetition period and the early competitive season period much of the hard training that the swimmer does in preparation for the ultimate goals for the season is accomplished. Most swimmers will be trying to work twice daily, and more and more fast interval training appears in the training routines for both distance swimmers and sprinters. This, of course, reflects a shift in emphasis toward anaerobic endurance, although distance swimmers will continue to do large amounts of essentially aerobic work. At some time during the competitive season some negative-split training, repeat training, or interval sprinting will appear in the program, as they are needed, to increase speed. Large amounts of these should be used with caution, however, because they tend to increase the rate at which one advances toward a peak.

Because of the complication of the competitive meets, which are assumed to be on Saturday each week during the competitive season, the weekly training pattern must shift somewhat. A suggested pattern is as follows:

Monday—hard training
Tuesday—hard training
Wednesday—moderate training
Thursday—hard training (if Saturday meet is easy)
moderate training (if Saturday meet is hard)
Friday—moderate training (if Saturday meet is easy)
easy day, work on starts, turns, and so on (if Saturday meet is hard)
Saturday—meet

Championship training. This period begins about 2 weeks before the championship meet. It is during this period that one tapers off the training program in order to arrive at a physical peak for the championship meet. During this period the total distance becomes less, frequently less than half what it was during the competitive season. The swimmer should be well rested going into the championship meet. Care must be taken to see that he does not overwork at this time. More rest is given between swims, but the speed factor in the workout increases and more repeat training is done. Interval sprint training is used here, as at other times during the season, to accomplish its particular purpose, but it can be overdone, because if too much training is done this way it tends to tire the individual excessively. With sprinters, close to 4 days of nearly complete rest should be allowed before major championship competition. The swimmer should approach the meet rested and ready physically and psychologically.

TRAINING SCHEDULES

A series of training schedules is presented below, but I must again emphasize that they are only examples, intended to illustrate a progressive approach to training. Note that all are presented on a weekly basis except the schedules for the championship period. I believe that the workouts at this time should be so specific to the needs of the individual that an illustrative program for a week would be meaningless; therefore, only 2 days of examples are included. Please note also that the workout progression is based on intensity or overall difficulty of the workouts and is not solely related to the total distance swum.

The workouts are written using kicking, pulling, and swimming. Kicking is done using a kickboard, using the legs alone for propulsion; and pulling is done using the arms alone for propulsion, while supporting the legs with a small tube or floatation device. The sole purpose for kicking and pulling is to overload, specifically, the arms and legs.

EARLY PRESEASON TRAINING
Sprinters and distance swimmers

Monday

1 × 500	Kick	
1 × 500	Pull	
2 × 800	Swim (recover to heart rate of 120 beats per minute between swims)	

Water polo

Tuesday

1 × 400	Kick	
2 × 200	Kick—slow interval training	
1 × 400	Pull	
2 × 200	Pull—slow interval training	
1600 yd.	fartlek swim—sprint every eighth length	

Wednesday

2 × 300	Kick—slow interval training	
2 × 300	Pull—slow interval training	
2 × 800	Swim—(recover to heart rate of 120 beats per minute between swims)	

Water polo

Thursday

1 × 400	Kick	
1 × 400	Pull	
2000 yd.	fartlek swim—sprint every eighth length	
5 × 200	Swim—slow interval training	

Friday

2 × 400	Kick—slow interval training	
2 × 400	Pull—slow interval training	
1 × 1650	Swim	

Water polo

LATE PRESEASON TRAINING
Sprinter

Monday

4 × 200	Kick—slow interval training	
10 × 100	Swim—slow interval training	
4 × 200	Pull—fast interval training	
1 × 200	Swim—easy swim, work on stroke	
4 × 300	Swim—slow interval training	

Tuesday

1000 yd.	fartlek swim—set own pattern	
6 × 150	Swim—slow interval training	
1 × 800	Pull	
1 × 800	Kick	
5 × 100	Swim—fast interval training	

Wednesday

6 × 100	Pull—slow interval training	
6 × 200	Swim—slow interval training	
6 × 100	Kick—slow interval training	
1 × 200	Swim—easy swim, work on stroke	
4 × 300	Swim—fast interval training	

Thursday

3 × 400	Swim—slow interval training	
3 × 200	Pull—slow interval training	
6 × 150	Swim—slow interval training	
3 × 200	Kick—slow interval training	
10 × 50	Swim—fast interval training	

Friday

1 × 400	Swim—easy swim, work on stroke	
4 × 300	Swim—fast interval training	
1 × 100	Swim—any style, any speed, 3 minute time limit	
5 × 100	Kick—slow interval training	
1 × 100	Swim—any style, any speed, 3 minute time limit	
5 × 100	Pull—slow interval training	
1 × 100	Swim—any style, any speed, 3 minute time limit	
5 × 100	Swim—slow interval training	

PRECOMPETITION PERIOD
Sprinter

Monday

1 × 400	Swim—work on stroke, set own pace	
4 × 200	Swim—fast interval training	
6 × 100	Kick—slow interval training	
6 × 100	Swim—slow interval training	
6 × 100	Pull—slow interval training	
10 × 50	Swim—fast interval training	

Tuesday

4 × 200	Kick—slow interval training	
1 × 100	Swim—recovery swim, set own pace	
4 × 200	Pull—slow interval training	
6 × 150	Swim—fast interval training	
1 × 100	Swim—recovery swim, set own pace	
6 × 100	Swim—slow interval training	
6 × 100	Swim—fast interval training	

Wednesday

1 × 400	Swim—work on stroke, set own pace	
4 × 200	Kick—slow interval training	
4 × 200	Swim—fast interval training	
4 × 200	Pull—slow interval training	

1 × 100 Swim—recovery swim, set own pace
8 × 100 Swim—slow interval training

Thursday

4 × 200 Pull—fast interval training
1 × 100 Swim—recovery swim, set own pace
4 × 200 Kick—slow interval training
6 × 150 Swim—slow interval training
1 × 100 Swim—recovery swim, set own pace
6 × 100 Swim—slow interval training
8 × 100 Swim—fast interval training

Friday

1 × 400 Swim—work on stroke, set own pace
8 × 200 Swim—slow interval training
6 × 100 Kick—slow interval training
10 × 50 Swim—fast interval training

Saturday

6 × 150 Swim—fast interval training
6 × 100 Pull—slow interval training
8 × 100 Swim—slow interval training
6 × 100 Pull—slow interval training
2 × 200 Split 200's done as follows:
        swim 50, rest 30 seconds
        swim 50, rest 30 seconds
        swim 100, all out
        rest 3½ minutes or recover to heart
        rate of 100 beats per minute be-
        tween 200's, whichever occurs
        first

EARLY COMPETITION PERIOD
Sprinter

Monday

1 × 200 Swim—work on stroke, set own pace
6 × 150 Swim—fast interval training
6 × 100 Kick—slow interval training
6 × 100 Swim—fast interval training
6 × 100 Pull—slow interval training
10 × 50 Swim—fast interval training
1 × 200 Swim—recovery swim, set own pace
6 × 50 Swim—fast interval training, breath
        holding task (that is, breathe every
        other cycle)

Tuesday

1 × 200 Swim—work on stroke, set own pace
4 × 200 Swim—negative split interval train-
        ing
4 × 200 Kick—slow interval training
4 × 200 Pull—fast interval training
10 × 100 Swim—slow interval training
8 × 50 Swim—fast interval training, breath
        holding task

Wednesday

1 × 200 Swim—work on stroke, set own pace

4 × 200 Swim—split 200's (50, 50, 100, 20
        second rest between parts)
6 × 100 Pull—slow interval training
8 × 50 Swim—fast interval training
6 × 100 Kick—slow interval training

Thursday

1 × 200 Swim—set own pace, work on stroke
3 × 100 Swim—repeat training
4 × 200 Pull—slow interval training
4 × 200 Kick—fast interval training
1 × 200 Swim—recovery swim, set own pace
4 × 200 Swim—negative split interval training

Friday

1 × 800 Swim—easy swim, work on stroke
5 × 100 Swim—negative split interval training
1 × 400 Kick—easy kick
1 × 400 Pull—easy pull
8 × 50 Swim—fast interval training, breath
        holding task

Saturday

Swimming meet

LATE COMPETITION PERIOD
Sprinter

Monday

1 × 200 Swim—set own pace, work on stroke
5 × 150 Swim—negative split interval train-
        ing
6 × 100 Kick—slow interval training
8 × 100 Pull—fast interval training
1 × 100 Swim—recovery swim
10 × 75 Swim—fast interval training, alter-
        nate breathing first 50

Tuesday

6 × 100 Pull—slow interval training
8 × 100 Kick—fast interval training
1 × 100 Swim—recovery swim
4 × 100 Swim—repeat training
1 × 100 Swim—recovery swim
12 × 50 Swim—fast interval training

Wednesday

4 × 150 Kick—slow interval training
1 × 100 Swim—recovery swinm
4 × 150 Pull—slow interval training
8 × 100 Swim—fast interval training
1 × 100 Swim—recovery swim
4 × 75 Swim—sprint training

Thursday (important meet on Saturday)

4 × 200 Swim—split 200's done as follows:
        swim 50, rest 15 seconds
        swim 50, rest 15 seconds
        swim 100, all out

rest 3½ minutes or recover to
heart rate of 100 beats per minute, whichever occurs first

5 × 100   Kick—slow interval training
5 × 100   Pull—slow interval training
10 × 75   Swim—fast interval training
5 × 50   Swim—fast interval training, breath
holding task

Friday (important meet on Saturday)

1 × 200   Kick—easy kick
1 × 200   Pull—easy pull
4 × 100   Swim—split 100's done as follows:
swim 25, rest 10 seconds
swim 25, rest 10 seconds
swim 20, all out
rest 3½ minutes or recover to heart
rate of 100 beats per minute
1 × 100   Swim—recovery swim
6 × 50   Swim—fast interval training
Starts and turns, relay takeoffs

Saturday

Swimming meet

CHAMPIONSHIP PERIOD
Sprinter

Monday

1 × 200   Swim—easy
4 × 100   Kick
4 × 100   Pull
8 × 50   Fast interval training
Starts and turns

Wednesday

1 × 200   Swim
6 × 50   Swim—fast interval training
Starts and turns

LATE PRESEASON TRAINING
Distance swimmer

Monday

4 × 200   Kick—slow interval training
4 × 200   Pull—slow interval training
1,600 yd. fartlek swim—sprint every fourth
length
4 × 200   Swim—fast interval training

Tuesday

8 × 200   Swim—slow interval training
10 minute fartlek kick—sprint every fourth
length
10 minute fartlek pull—sprint every fourth
length
10 × 100 Swim—slow interval training, 30 second rest

Wednesday

1 × 500   Kick—time trial

1 × 400   Pull
4 × 100   Pull—slow interval training
1 × 1650   Swim
5 × 100   Swim—slow interval training
5 × 100   Swim—fast interval training

Thursday

1,000 yd. fartlek swim—vary speed on own
4 × 100   Kick—slow interval training
6 × 100   Pull—slow interval training
6 × 200   Swim—slow interval training
10 × 50   Swim—fast interval training

Friday

5 × 200   Swim—fast interval training
1,000 yd. fartlek swim, tumble turns, vary
speed on own
1 × 100   Kick
1 × 400   Pull
10 × 100   Swim—slow interval training, 30 seconds rest
400-yard time trial

PRECOMPETITION PERIOD
Distance swimmer

Monday

15 × 100   Swim—slow interval training, 1650
pace, 30 seconds rest
4 × 200   Kick—slow interval training
4 × 200   Pull—slow interval training
Split 800—done as follows:
swim 200, rest 45 seconds
swim 200, rest 45 seconds
swim 200, rest 45 seconds
swim 200, rest 45 seconds

Tuesday

5 × 400   Swim—slow interval training
1 × 500   Kick—time trial
8 × 200   Swim—fast interval training

Wednesday

20 × 100   Swim—slow interval training, 1650
pace, 30 second rest
2 split 400's done as follows:
swim 100, rest 30 seconds
swim 100, rest 30 seconds
swim 100, rest 30 seconds
swim 100, rest 30 seconds
3½ minute rest or recover to heart
rate of 100 beats per minute,
whichever occurs first, between
400's
6 × 100   Kick—slow interval training
6 × 100   Pull—slow interval training

Thursday

8 × 200   Swim—slow interval training
1 × 400   Swim—easy

1 × 500 Pull—time trial
1 × 400 Swim—easy
6 × 200 Swim—fast interval training

Friday

4 × 100 Kick—fast interval training
1 × 200 Swim—easy
4 × 100 Pull—fast interval training
1 × 200 Swim—easy
24 × 100 Swim—slow interval training, 1650 pace, 30 second rest

Saturday

20 minute fartlek swim, tumble turns, alternate breathing every fourth length
12 × 100 Swim—fast interval training
1 × 400 Swim—easy
1 × 400 Time trial

EARLY COMPETITION PERIOD
Distance swimmer

Monday

4 × 200 Kick—fast interval training
1 × 200 Swim—easy
4 × 200 Pull—fast interval training
1 × 200 Swim—easy
20 × 100 Swim—slow interval training, 1650 pace, 20 second rest

Tuesday

8 × 200 Slow interval training, 1650 pace, 30 second rest
4 × 100 Kick—fast interval training
4 × 100 Pull—fast interval training
1 × 200 Swim—easy
15 × 100 Fast interval training

Wednesday

24 × 100 Swim—slow interval training, 500 pace, 20 second rest
1 × 200 Swim—easy
4 × 100 Kick—fast interval training
4 × 100 Pull—fast interval training
1 split 400 swim done as follows:
      1 × 100, rest 20 seconds
      1 × 100, rest 20 seconds
      1 × 200, even pace, all out

Thursday

8 × 200 Swim—fast interval training
4 × 200 Kick—slow interval training
4 × 200 Kick—slow interval training
Starts and turns

Friday

15 minute fartlek swim, set own pattern
10 × 100 Fast interval training
1 × 400 Kick

1 × 400 Pull
Starts, turns, relay takeoffs

Saturday

Swimming Meet

LATE COMPETITION PERIOD
Distance swimmer

Monday

8 × 100 Kick—fast interval training
1 × 100 Swim—recovery swim—set own pace
8 × 100 Pull—fast interval training
1 × 100 Swim—recovery swim—set own pace
2 × 100 Swim—slow interval training, 1650 pace, 15 second rest

Tuesday

1 × 400 Kick—moderate pace
4 × 100 Kick—fast interval training
1 × 400 Pull—moderate pace
4 × 100 Pull—fast interval training
10 × 200 Swim—slow interval training, 1650 pace, 20 seconds rest
4 × 200 Swim—negative split interval training

Wednesday

20 × 100 Swim—slow interval training, 1650 pace, 15 seconds rest
1 × 100 Swim—recovery swim
1 × 400 Kick
1 × 400 Pull
3 split 400's done as follows:
      1 × 100, rest 15 seconds
      1 × 100, rest 15 seconds
      1 × 200, even pace, all out

Thursday

10 × 200 Swim—slow interval training, 25 second rest
1 × 500 Kick
1 × 500 Pull
4 × 150 Swim—repeat training, 6 minute rest

Friday

10 × 100 Swim—slow interval training, 1650 pace, 10 second rest
4 × 200 Swim—negative split interval training
Starts and turns

Saturday

Swimming meet

CHAMPIONSHIP PERIOD
Distance swimmer

Monday

16 × 100 Swim—slow interval training, 1650 pace, 10 second rest

2 × 200   Kick
2 × 200   Pull

Wednesday

8 × 100   Swim—slow interval training, 1650
          pace, 10 second rest
8 × 50   Swim—fast interval training
Thursday, Friday, Saturday—championship meet

SELECTED READINGS

Dintiman, George B.: Sprinting speed—its improvement for major sports competition, Springfield, Ill., 1971, Charles C Thomas, Publisher.

Doherty, J. Kenneth: Modern training for running, Englewood Cliffs, N. J., 1964, Prentice-Hall, Inc.

Down, Michael G.: Interval training—an appraisal of work-rest cycle applications to training for endurance running, Loughborough, Leicestershire, England, Physical education and industrial fitness unit, 1966, Loughborough University of Technology.

Heusner, W. W.: Specificity of interval training, East Lansing, Mich., Human energy research laboratory, 1963, Michigan State University.

Mathews, Donald K., and Fox, Edward L.: The physiological basis of physical education and athletics, Philadelphia, 1971, W. B. Saunders Co.

Shepard, Roy J.: Frontiers of fitness, Springfield, Ill., 1971, Charles C Thomas, Publisher.

Wilt, Fred: Training for competitive running. In Falls, Harold B., editor: Exercise physiology, New York, 1968, Academic Press, pp. 395-414.

Chapter 17

The fundamental techniques of teaching and learning basic diving

Once the swimmer has acquired sufficient skill to swim approximately 25 yards, he is ready to learn basic diving techniques. For the student who has never had the opportunity to learn diving, the new sensations that he will experience upon entering the water head first for the first time are foreign to him; and the teacher will find it nearly impossible to verbally describe these sensations and experiences to the student. It is more important that the student gain confidence in the teacher's ability to provide successful learning experiences for him. The teacher does this by preparing and following a proper progression of skills and ensuring that each skill is successfully learned before the subsequent skill is introduced.

The first dive that should be taught to the novice diver is the kneeling dive. The novice diver is asked to kneel on one knee at the side of the pool or pier. Depending on the type of ledge or edge of the pool, adjustments might have to be made in the diver's body position. Generally it is most desirable to start in a kneeling position on one knee. The diver curls the toes of one foot over the edge of the pool. This is to serve as traction and to aid in applying force when diving for the first time. The arms are placed overhead with the hands clasped together. Upon instructions from the teacher the diver elevates his hips so that his center of gravity is raised. At the same time he leans forward while pointing his hands toward the point of entry into the water, which is approximately 18 to 24 inches from the edge of the pool. During the process of raising the hips and leaning forward the diver simultaneously pushes off with the foot that is in contact with the edge of the pool. While pushing off, the head is kept down and the legs are stretched out. It may be necessary for the teacher to guide the diver to ensure that he does not land on his stomach. The key factors in learning this dive are the elevation of the hips so that the diver can rise off of the one knee while simultaneously leaning forward to permit gravity to pull him down as he falls toward the water. The head must be kept down with the chin tucked in closely to the chest and the hands reaching toward the point of entry. For youngsters the teacher or coach might find it convenient to help by lifting up the legs at the ankle or knee joint. This will ensure that the legs are above the head and prevent a belly-flop landing. This type of kneeling dive should be attempted from 3 to 6 times so that the novice diver will experience immediate success and develop confidence in his ability to execute this very fundamental dive as well as develop confidence in his instructor.

The next step in the progression is the continued practice of the kneeling dive with hips elevated a little further on successive tries. Eventually the diver will learn the standing dive. The successful standing dive can be done by flexing the knees slightly, reaching for the point of entry, which now will be about 3 to 4 feet from the edge of the pool, and pushing strongly off of the legs to ensure that the hands and head enter the water first. It is also important that the chin is close to the chest during these learning stages. If the diver is learning to dive for the first time at a beach or a lake that is equipped with a pier a foot or two above the water level, an alternate possibility to the kneeling dive, the sitting dive, could be learned. In the sitting dive the diver sits on the edge of the pier or the side of the pool and then by reaching out in front falls forward and rotates around the buttocks; thus, entering the water hands and head first. The disadvantage of the sitting dive is twofold. First, it is a little difficult on the fabric of the bathing suit. Second, if the ledge or pier is not high enough, approximately 20 inches or more, it is difficult to get enough rotation to guarantee that the novice diver will enter the water head first.

Once the fundamental kneeling or sitting dive is learned, the diver gradually should progress to a standing dive. The mechanics of the standing dive are very much similar to those of the kneeling dive. A great help for the early attempt of the standing dive is to have the diver lift one leg backwards while bending forward at the hips. This aids in forward rotation about the stationary foot and guarantees a head-first entry. During the learning of this skill the coach can assist the diver by elevating the lifted leg. This dive should be practiced at least six times before attempting the standing front dive from a 2-foot takeoff. This dive should be practiced at pool level at the side of the pool or from a very shallow pier to gradually higher and higher levels. Thus, the novice diver is taught the kneeling dive from the side of the pool and gradually progresses to the standing dive from a 2-foot takeoff and finally the standing dive from the 1- and 3-meter springboard. Once these skills are learned he is ready to progress to the proper techniques of the approach and the hurdle

step and then move on to the fundamental springboard dives.

LEARNING THE APPROACH

Since the action of the springboard will be quite strange to the beginner, the most desirable way to introduce the forward approach is by demonstrating the basic steps of the approach and the hurdle step on dry land or on the deck of the pool. The young diver should be taught to take three steps and the hurdle step. The hurdle is simply a continuation of the approach and consists of a one-foot takeoff followed by landing on both feet simultaneously. This can be demonstrated quite easily by the instructor and imitated by the beginning diver. If the diver practices the approach and hurdle for several minutes on the deck of the pool before advancing to the springboard, the learning process will be significantly accelerated. As the youngster learns to do a reasonably smooth approach on the deck, certain qualities that are characteristic of a good approach and a good hurdle can be emphasized by the instructor. These are as follows:

1. Walk erect. Keep the back straight with the eyes focused on the point that represents the end of the diving board.

2. Let the arms swing naturally. The arms may be swung together in opposition to the legs or they may be swung as in walking, the right arm backward as the left leg goes forward, and so on.

3. Get a good, strong jump off of the back leg during the hurdle.

4. Do not lean in the hurdle. Jump vertically off of the back leg. The length of the hurdle, depending on the size of the diver, should be at least 2 feet long.

5. Lift the hurdle knee very high during the hurdle. The thigh should be parallel to the deck of the pool, whereas the lifted leg should be perpendicular to the deck of the pool.

6. In the hurdle, coordinate the arm swing and the lifting of the knee. As the knee

is lifted, the arms are raised overhead. The arms and the knees work together in the hurdle. Upon landing, both feet should contact the end of the board simultaneously.

7. Upon contact with the board, the arms should have moved from a position over the head to slightly behind the hips.

All of the above cues should be used by the coach in teaching the novice diver the approach during the deck drill. Practicing the approach on the pool deck is also of value for the early stages of learning for the competitive diver who is trying to develop smoothness and consistency in the forward approach. Marking the correct length of the steps of each diver by placing strips of adhesive tape on the pool deck also aids in more rapid learning of a consistent approach.

Once the beginning diver has learned a consistent approach and feels comfortable and reasonably natural during the dry land or deck exercise, he is then ready to advance to the springboard. The first step on the springboard is to measure the length of the approach and the hurdle step. This is done by starting at the diving end of the board, turning around as if preparing to execute a backward dive, placing the heels flush up against the diving board edge and then taking the complete approach—three steps and the hurdle step in the direction toward the anchor end of the board. The spot at which the end of the approach and the hurdle are completed determines the starting point for the beginning diver. After measuring the length of the approach and the hurdle on the springboard, the diver is ready to practice them on the board. During the first several attempts of the approach and hurdle, the novice diver should not jump into the water but should stop at the board tip in order to ensure that the steps were measured properly. Once this is done the diver is now ready to add the front jump into the water. This skill should be practiced many times in order for the diver to develop a good sense of springing the diving board.

The trampoline serves as a valuable learning aid that helps the beginner develop the sense of the spring action of the diving board. If one is available, simple multiple bouncing can help the diver develop the springing action so necessary to good springboard diving.

It is quite essential during the learning phase of the approach and hurdle that the diver is not overcoached. If the instructor emphasizes the cues outlined above and analyzes the diver's weaknesses of the approach in primarily a gross fashion during these beginning stages, he will find that learning occurs more rapidly than if too many fine corrections are made. The instructor should keep in mind that the primary objective during this stage of teaching diving is to help the diver learn the basic fundamentals, and confusing the diver at this early stage of learning can result in a loss of self-confidence.

Riding the diving board

"Riding the board" is the term applied to the interaction of the diver and the springboard so that a smooth takeoff in which the diver uses the maximum energy of the board to attain height can be achieved. To appropriately ride the springboard, the diver must land very softly on the end of the board in order to avoid stomping it. The diver should land on the balls of the feet. Although slow-motion films of great divers indicate that most divers land nearly flat-footed, the process of a soft landing does require the diver to think of landing initially on the toes and subsequently on the balls of the feet. A good exercise for the beginning diver, which aids in learning the soft landing, is multiple bouncing on the end of the springboard. During the multiple bouncing the diver's back should be held erect. The feet should be slightly apart and the arms should circle. These movements will aid in maintaining balance and help the diver bounce in the natural rhythm of the board. The primary objective is continuous low bouncing in the natural rhythm of the springboard. Also if the diver is in rhythm with the board, the sound of the board will be very quiet during the bouncing process.

Jumping into the hurdle

Usually the beginning diver does not appreciate the importance of pushing off of the back leg during the jump into the hurdle step. There is a very good dry land exercise that helps emphasize the importance of this skill. If a pole is laid from a bench or an elevation of approximately 2 feet to the floor, the diver can practice hurdling over the pole at various heights. During this dry land exercise the young diver gets a chance to concentrate on pushing off of the hurdle leg without having to worry about the other important mechanics of the hurdle. This should be practiced several times and the diver should keep in mind that the toes of the hurdle foot should clear the pole while the driving leg is straight. In other words, when the diver pushes off the back leg during the hurdle step this leg is in full extension at the knee joint and hip joint as the toes pass over the pole. As a diver becomes capable of successfully hurdling the pole at a height of approximately 1 foot, he is ready to give more serious thought to the complex mechanics of the hurdle, which are described in Chapter 18.

LEARNING FUNDAMENTAL DIVES

Plain forward dive. The plain forward dive should be executed in much the same fashion as the standing front dive. It is mainly a plain dive that incorporates the approach and the hurdle step. As the diver springs from the board, he reaches for the water at a point 3 to 4 feet in front of the diving board edge in preparation for the entry.

Forward jackknife. Prior to attempting the jackknife for the first time, the diver should be introduced to the fundamental exercise of "jumping the hips up." The diver stands at the base of the springboard, places his hands flat on the diving board surface, and, while maintaining this hand position, jumps his hips up. This action closely resembles that of the jackknife. Once the diver has practiced this exercise several times, he is then ready to move on to the springboard and attempt his first jackknife. Care must be taken so that the "hip lifting" action occurs immediately upon takeoff. Care must also be taken so that the diver does not lean excessively. Excessive lean will make it impossible for the diver to complete the touch of the toes prior to straightening and entering the water. After touching the toes, the diver should look at the point of entry while reaching for it with the hands. This entry point should be approximately 3 feet in front of the diving board edge. The common mistakes that one will experience upon learning this dive are: (1) too much lean in the hurdle, and (2) lifting the legs up too far in front of the body. The first problem will make it impossible for the diver to complete the toe touch, and the second problem will prevent the diver from having adequate rotation and cause him to be short of the vertical upon entering the water.

Swan dive. The forward swan dive is probably one of the most difficult dives to execute consistently well in competition. However, the dive can be taught to the beginner without elaborating on the minute characteristics that make it such a difficult dive. Upon takeoff the diver should immediately place the arms in the swan or T position while simultaneously pressing the legs straight back so that they rise upon takeoff. There should be no flexing or bending at the hips. Flexing at the hips is the most common mistake made by beginners. The only way to correct this is to emphasize the simultaneous placement of the arms coupled with a strong hyperextension of the thigh at the hip joint upon takeoff.

Forward dive with half twist. Once a diver, regardless of skill level, learns a swan dive, he is then ready to move on to the forward dive with a half twist. The forward dive with a half twist is another very complex dive that has given many great divers difficulty throughout the years. However, for the recreational or beginning diver, the fundamental techniques that initiate the twist are quite simple. The easiest way to teach this dive is to start with a dry land or deck exercise. Have the diver point one arm at the floor and the other arm at the ceiling (or sky). Now upon takeoff from the springboard as the arms come through one arm should be pointed immediately at the floor (point of entry) and the other arm should be pointed directly overhead. This arm action, which is a simultaneous motion, should be done immediately upon takeoff from the springboard. The diver should not think of turning the body or turning the head or any type of twisting action. The eyes focus on the point of entry as the low arm points toward it. In other words, as the diver comes off the diving board, one arm points immediately to the sky or ceiling while the other arm points to the water. This action will cause the twist. The techniques of executing the half twist, which are employed by more advanced divers, are not the same as the learning techniques described here. The technique described above has proved to be very successful for the novice diver.

Backward takeoff dives. Before a diver can adequately perform a back dive or an inward dive, he must be taught how to use the springboard for a backward takeoff. Again, a dry land exercise should be incorporated here. Most children and adults have a basic understanding of the vertical jump. The action that is utilized in springboard diving in order to press the board in a backward standing dive is very much like a simple vertical jump. The diver bends at the knees and hips and then jumps off of both feet simultaneously. The arm action during the back press is somewhat unique. The arms first lift laterally to a position slightly above the diver's shoulders, then as the diver

bends at the hips and knees the arms circle and press down slightly behind the body at the hips with a slight bend at the elbow joint. Finally, the arms come through in front of the body as the diver springs off of his legs and makes his jump. This skill can be taught easily on dry land. The instructor should keep the coaching cues simple. The diver should be instructed to (1) rise up on his toes and lift his arms laterally to a point slightly above the shoulders, (2) bend at the hips and knees with the arms pressing down and slightly behind the hips, and (3) jump as high as he can, swinging his arms in front of the body overhead to a point of full reach. These three moves are done in a smooth systematic manner. Once the diver learns to do this reasonably well on the deck of the pool, he is then ready to attempt the back press on the springboard. He then should execute the backward press followed by a foot-first entry into the water. This back press and foot-first jump should be repeated several times so that the diver feels very comfortable with this new skill.

Back dive. The fundamental method for learning the back dive is the learning of the fall-off back dive. This dive does not incorporate springing the board with the backward press. The diver stands on the board in preparation for the back dive. The arms are held overhead with the hands clasped and the head is rotated back as far as possible. While keeping the rest of the body solid and firm the diver falls backwards, continuing to look for the water. If the diver follows these directions exactly, he will successfully execute the fall-off back dive. Gravity and friction do all of the work. The feet are in contact with the diving board and as the diver falls and looks for the water, the hands and head will enter the water first because gravity continues to act on these members while the feet remain in contact with the springboard surface. However, since the diver has never had the sensation of entering the water backwards before, he might have a tendency to change his head position or change his mind during this dive. Therefore, it is imperative that the instructor provide some manual guidance during the first attempt at this skill. The coach should hold the diver at the hips and at the same time verbally instruct him on the mechanics of the dive. As the diver begins to fall, the coach can assist by steering the diver into the water head first. An assist can also be made by lifting the legs of the diver to ensure that the head-first entry will result. The typical beginning diver needs assistance only on one or two attempts and then is ready to execute the fall-off back dive alone.

The diver must then overcome another fear barrier and put these two skills together and execute the backward spring dive. The mechanics are very much similar to the backward fall-off dive except that they include pressing the springboard. The key points to remember during the first attempt of the backward dive are as follows: (1) take a very strong bold press, (2) jump with as much a force as possible, and (3) put the head back early. If the diver follows this procedure he will more than likely be successful the first time he tries this dive. Common mistakes include putting the head back too late, and the exact opposite, swinging the arms and head immediately upon takeoff, thereby getting too much rotation. It will be up to the coach and the diver working together to resolve these common errors.

Inward dive (pike). The inward dive appears by the nature of its execution to be a dangerous dive. However, if properly taught and if the instructor understands the fundamental mechanics, it is nearly impossible for the diver to hit the board during the execution of this dive. The mechanics that prevent the diver from hitting the board are as follows: (1) the arms reach up over the head and thrust down toward the board as the diver jumps the hips up, (2) as the arms come down, they are applying a force toward the board, and (3) the reaction to this force is the force of the diving board acting through the diver's legs pushing the diver's hips up and away from the springboard so that the only way to incur an injury is by leaning into the board during the takeoff. If the instructor wants to be doubly sure of safety, it is possible to teach this dive by having the diver stand on one corner of the diving board rather than in the center and encourage a slight turning away from the board during the execution of the dive. Employing this teaching technique may introduce some bad habits later on. For the first or second effort this might be acceptable, however, it is not recommended to encourage the novice diver to use this technique more than twice.

Forward dive pike with a half twist. Another dive that the novice diver may learn is the forward dive with a half twist in the pike position. In this dive the diver executes a jackknife in the conventional manner. After the toe touch is completed, the diver points one arm directly at the point of entry while the other arm is brought across the pointing arm. This crossing arm action gives the necessary impetus to the half twist.

Forward somersault. The easiest way for someone to learn the forward somersault is by attempting it on the trampoline. The proper teaching progression on the trampoline, which can be accomplished in a matter of minutes, is as follows: first, the diver learns to multiple bounce the trampoline; second, the diver learns to stop the bounce, which is called the check. Next the basic drops on the trampoline should be learned. These include the knee drop, seat drop, front drop, and back drop. The knee drop, which is the easiest of the basic drops, should be learned first. After the diver successfully learns to go from the feet to the knees and back to the feet again and is able to repeat this cycle several times, he will be ready to learn the knee drop-front somersault. This is a very easy trick, and it takes more determination than skill to execute it successfully the first time. Immediately upon coming up off of the knees, the diver throws his head and his arms as hard as he can toward the mat. This initiates the somersault. The instructor should assist by "spotting" the diver during his first several attempts. This is done by guiding the head around during the somersault by keeping the hand on the neck of the diver. If the diver happens to be a youngster and changes his mind during a trial, the application of a small force behind the head of the diver will aid him in completing the somersault even if against his will. This spotting technique is valuable in the prevention of injuries.

Next, the diver is ready to take the forward somersault to the springboard. The forward somersault from the springboard is done precisely in the same manner as on the trampoline. Following the takeoff from the springboard, the diver immediately throws his head and arms down while lifting the hips up. The key point for the unskilled diver is to make sure that the head is thrown forcefully down. The somersaulting action will then, to a great degree, take care of itself.

After the somersault is learned it should be repeated several times the first day so that the diver develops the necessary confidence and will execute the dive more easily during his next practice session. As the dive is practiced the diver should then be taught to establish a good tight tuck position. It should be quite obvious to the instructor that during the learning phase of all dives most youngsters, and oldsters for that matter, who are new to diving are more concerned with survival than they are with form and finesse.

Backward somersault. The backward somersault can be learned in much the same fashion as the forward somersault. It can be learned either on the trampoline or on the springboard. In order to learn this trick on the trampoline, it is imperative that the instructor employ correct spotting techniques. The instructor should stand with one foot on the bed and the other foot on the solid trampoline frame. As the diver starts multiple bouncing, the coach should hold the diver at the waist of the diving suit.

This can be done either by clasping the material of the suit or by wrapping a towel around the waist of the diver. The somersaulting action in a backward somersault is initiated by throwing the arms and the head backward as the legs are jumped up to the chest. After three bounces the diver is instructed to attempt a backward somersault on the trampoline. When the diver throws for the somersault, the spotter pulls up on the towel in order to assist in the attainment of height, meanwhile the diver's legs are grabbed at the calfs and pulled over the top. Perhaps the obvious advantage of learning the somersault on the trampoline is that the young diver will have the security of the coach's immediate availability to aid him during the first few tries. However, this particular dive can be learned just as easily from the springboard providing that the diver is willing to *go through* with the dive as directed by the coach. The coaching cues are, as mentioned earlier, a strong jump after the backward press followed by thrusting the arms and head backward while the knees are simultaneously brought up to the chest. If the diver makes an honest effort to do this, he will successfully execute the backward somersault during the first attempt.

Any new dive should be practiced at least three times during the first experience. This is to ensure that the diver will develop confidence so that during the next practice session he will continue to do the dive with increased skill.

Reverse dive. Perhaps the most difficult dive for the novice to learn is the reverse dive. The feeling of jumping up and initiating a backward action toward the springboard will be extremely uncomfortable and most novice divers are very reluctant to try the reverse dive for the first time. However, a proper sequence can be employed, which makes this task much easier for the coach and diver. It is strongly recommended that the trampoline be incorporated in this learning progression. The diver should be taught the fundamental back drop on the trampoline by kicking one leg very high as in the act of kicking a football. While kicking the leg the diver leans backward falling off balance and lands on his back on the soft trampoline bed. After this is done several times, the diver is then ready to jump and bring both legs to the chest while keeping the chin down and rotate backwards to the mat. Here again the diver lands on his back. The diver can further do the backward drop in the pike position. Here the legs are brought up straight to a target made by the hands, which have reached up to a point slightly short of the vertical. The chin is kept in line. After the touch, the diver lands on his back on the mat. This skill should be executed quite a few times and the diver should have a very good back drop on the trampoline before progressing to the springboard.

The first reverse dive from the springboard should be executed in the simplest possible fashion—the tuck position. Once the novice has learned the back drop on the trampoline, it is just a matter of incorporating that technique into the forward approach and hurdle; instead of landing on the back in the water the diver continues to look for the water after the knees are brought up to the chest. This skill requires much more courage than talent during the first attempt. For some beginners who seem to exhibit a great deal of coordination, it is possible to teach the reverse dive initially in the pike position. Here the instructor should cue the diver to kick the legs *immediately* upon takeoff to the hands, which have set a target directly over the head of the diver. If the legs are kicked up soon enough, all that the diver has to do after the touch is to look for the water. Looking toward the water is a natural reaction for most divers while learning this dive.

Twisting somersaults. One of the major difficulties in coaching springboard diving is that of teaching the twisting somersaults. A twisting somersault incorporates the som-

ersaulting action of either a forward somersault, backward somersault, reverse somersault, or inward somersault as well as the inclusion of a pirrouette that defines the twist. More precisely, a twist is the act of rotation around the longitudial axis of the body. Before learning a twisting somersault, the diver should learn how to somersault independently as described earlier and should learn how to twist independently. Here again the trampoline serves as a wonderful learning device. The diver should attempt at first a half twist (half pirrouette) and then a full turn (a full 360° pirrouette). Eventually the novice will be able to work up to a one and one half or a double twist from the standing position in a relatively short period of time. These skills can be learned in a matter of minutes on the trampoline. Next the diver should execute the same skills from the springboard. These include the forward approach, hurdle and a half twisting front jump, full twisting front jump, half twisting backward jump, and a full twisting backward jump. Once the diver has mastered the basic standing jumps as well as good somersaulting technique both forward and backward, he is ready to put the two movements together and learn a forward somersault with one twist and a backward somersault with one and one half twists.

Forward somersault with one twist. The diver should have a very good forward somersault in the pike position before attempting this dive. The first skill is to execute the forward somersault pike with the arms held in a lateral or swan position during the entire somersaulting action. After this skill is learned, the next step is to incorporate a slight snap or straightening action of the body over the top of the somersault. That is, during the execution of this dive the diver starts the pike somersault and immediately snaps out very rapidly holding the arms in a lateral position. This snap should occur early in the dive and will provide enough impetus for the entire somersault to be completed. This dive is appropriately named the snap somersault pike. Note that during the execution of the somersault pike and the snap somersault pike, the arms are maintained in a lateral or swan position. The diver should be taught to play the entries of these front somersault pikes slightly short of the vertical. Once the twist is added, the twisting action will tend to carry the somersault a little further and therefore carry the diver beyond the vertical entry.

After the diver has learned a good snap somesault, he will be ready to add the twist. The easiest way to learn this is to add the twist just prior to entering the water. After the somersault, the diver should bring both arms in across the chest similar to an ice skater. More than likely the first try will not yield complete success. Usually a half twist results. The diver will eventually get to the full twist, and thus will have successfully completed the forward somersault with full twist. Occasionally the diver will have some difficulty getting beyond the half twist. Since the new twisting action is foreign to the diver, he will have a tendency to drop his chin and to try to sight the water during the twist. This is very undesirable during the learning of any twisting dive. The diver must make an effort as he completes the snap somersault to keep the head back and the body straight and to maintain the layout position during the twisting action. If the coach can emphasive these points, the diver will learn this dive more quickly. After the forward somersault with one twist has been successfully learned, the diver will be ready to move along to the backward somersault with one and one half twist. Here again the progression is very similar to the previous dive. The diver must be able to execute a backward somersault layout with relatively little difficulty. Once again, it is desirable to have the angle of entry short of the vertical. Keep in mind that the introduction of the twisting action has a tendency to carry the somersault. Once the diver executes a backward somersault layout to the

satisfaction of himself and his coach, he is then ready to introduce the twist. During the twist it is more desirable to start the twisting action just prior to entry into the water. In other words, to keep it simple, the diver thinks only of the back somersault layout. Just prior to entry the coach should call the diver on the twist, at which time the diver stretches out, thrusts the arms across the chest in the twisting direction, and pirouettes. If the head is held in line or slightly back and if the diver maintains a layout position and emphasizes the twist action from the shoulders and the hips, he will be successful in twisting smoothly. With successive tries, eventually the backward somersault with one and one half twists will be learned.

Note that in the learning phases there should be no discussion of how to stop the twist or in locating a spatial awareness for the diver. It is not important that the diver knows where he is in space. The twisting dives are essentially blind dives during the learning phase. After the diver becomes more experienced he will be able to sight the water or possibly the wall or some other landmark at the completion of a single or a multiple twisting dive. However, initially the sensations he experiences will be quite strange and he should be unconcerned with where he might be located in space.

The mechanics of the twist are fundamental to all twisting somersaulting dives, whether they incorporate a full twist, one and one half twists, a double twist, two and one half twists, or even triple twists. If a diver is pirrouetting in the proper fashion, he can stop the twist by the simultaneous action of thrusting out the arms away from the body and bending at the waist. The simultaneous use of both of these actions is necessary in order to appropriately stop the twist. During the learning stages of the full twisting somersault and the backward one and one half twisting somersault, the diver should be taught to stop the twist by placing the arms out in the swan position while simultaneously lifting up the legs into a slight pike position. This resembles the action of sitting in a chair when done correctly and enables the diver to sharply stop the twisting with a reasonable amount of finesse. This technique, however, is not taught until after the diver has learned to successfully complete the number of twists desired.

There are two general methods of utilizing the arms in initiating twists. These are the ice skater's twist as described here and the one arm behind the head–one arm across the chest technique. Both methods have been successfully used by skilled divers and the latter method is pictorially described in Chapter 18.

EXERCISES AND WEIGHT TRAINING APPLIED TO DIVING

Anything that will make a diver stronger will make him a better diver; therefore, any type of exercises or weight training that will improve overall body strength will benefit the diver. A word of caution must be noted and that is that the exercises must be selected so that flexibility is not lost while strength is gained. The following principles should be employed for all weight training —high repetitions at relatively low weights rather than heavy weights at few repetitions. The exercises should include the full range of motion of the body part exercised.

Exercises

Exercises for the abdominal region. A very critical part of the body that must be strengthened for most divers is the abdominal region. The following exercises are very valuable for developing this total area of the body.
1. *Bent knee situps.* These should be done daily about 20 to 50 times each, depending on the strength level of the individual.
2. *Leg lifts.* Here the diver hangs from a bar, generally the stand or platform serves as a very good device for this, and lifts the legs in a pike position so that the toes touch the bar. This should

be repeated approximately 10 times. The arms should be straight and the knees should be locked. This particular exercise firms up the upper abdominal area as well as strengths the psoas major muscle, which is the primary flexor of the hips. By repeating this exercise in the tuck position, where the legs are drawn up slowly and very close to the body all the way to the upper chest, the diver will strengthen the upper abdominal region. The legs should be lowered very slowly as well.
3. *Isometric situp.* In this particular exercise the diver lays in the supine position with the hands clasped behind the head and the knees bent. He then lifts his back off of the floor, keeping the back rounded, and continues the movement until the stomach muscles cramp up.

Exercises for arm and upper body development. The following exercises are very valuable for developing the arm and upper body:
1. *Chinups and pullups*
2. *Dips on the parallel bars*

Leg development. The following exercises are very valuable for developing the legs:
1. *Swinging leg circles.* Lying in the supine position, the diver raises both legs to about 3 to 4 inches above the ground and swings the legs violently to the left and then to the right as rapidly as possible until the leg muscles cramp up. This may require quite a few repetitions in order to achieve the desired muscle cramping.
2. *Isometric leg tightening.* Lying on his back, the diver tightens all leg muscles until cramping occurs. Repeat three times.
3. *Strengthening the hurdle leg.* As described earlier in this chapter, the diver should take approaches on the ground and hurdle up to a bench approximately 12 inches in height while emphasizing driving off of the back leg. Make sure that the back leg clears the 10- to 12-

inch height without any bending at the knee or hip joint.

Weight training

Intense weight training for the diver can build overall body strength, which will greatly aid the diver in attaining the height as well as in executing the explosive moves that are important to good diving. Weight training should be done on alternate days, and the emphasis on all of the exercises listed below is the use of the *full range of motion* of the body part exercised. This will guarantee that flexibility is not lost at the expense of gaining strength. During the execution of the weight training exercises, the diver should exhale on the force-producing phase of the exercise.

1. Arm and upper torso development
   a. *Lateral pullups.* A 5- or 10-pound dumbbell is placed in each hand. While lying in a supine position on a bench, the diver touches the dumbbells together, then with the elbows straight moves them to the swan position. Repeat up to thirty times.
   b. *Overhead pullups.* Lying supine on the bench, the diver brings the dumbbells from the arm entry position to the backward standing dive position. Repeat up to thirty times.
   c. *Arm circles.* Combine exercise one and two above. Do the circles in both the clockwise and counterclockwise direction. This exercise is excellent for loosening up the shoulders while simultaneously developing arm strength.
   d. *Bench press.* While lying supine on a bench the diver raises a barbell with weights to the full arm extension position above the chest. Start with approximately 50 pounds. Repeat exercise thirty times, progressively increasing weight.
   e. *Latissimus dorsi machine.* Here again emphasize light weights and high repetitions.
2. *Leg development*
   a. *Ankle raises.* Place a heavy dumbbell in one hand and while standing on an elevated ledge, execute one-legged ankle raises. Repeat thirty times. Use full range of motion of the ankle joint.
   b. *Squats.* A barbell with weights is placed behind the neck. From a standing position the diver executes half knee bends. The head should be held erect with the back straight. With the feet flat on the floor the quadricep muscles of the legs will be strengthened during this exercise. Again high repetitions are important.

Weight training should be done only as an addition to the diver's training program. It should not be used to replace a normal diving practice session. A great deal of time and effort is necessary to develop diving skill and the ambitious young diver would make a serious mistake by substituting weight training for a normal practice session.

Chapter 18

Coaching springboard diving

INTRODUCTION

Diving was developed in Europe as an outgrowth of outdoor aerial acrobatics and tumbling. It became a competitive sport in England in 1905. Fundamentally, diving consists in leaping from either a platform takeoff or a springboard takeoff and descending vertically into the water, either head or feet first.

Competitive springboard diving is really a form of aerial acrobatics. The water serves merely to ease the shock of alighting, just as a net catches the trapeze acrobat. Needless to say, springboard diving is as spectacular as it is intrinsically difficult and is related more closely to acrobatics than to swimming. It offers a thrill to the spectator as well as to the performer.

Diving consists in projecting the human body high into the air and there performing a series of breathless, swift, and gracefully controlled maneuvers, such as bending, twisting, and somersaulting. Then the body is suddenly righted and poised for a straight entry into the water. Springboard diving attracts and challenges the most stouthearted youth. It provides an opportunity to cultivate a supple and graceful body through skilled movements.

Some dives, when performed efficiently, cause the diver to move with the rhythm and tempo of "poetry in motion," especially such dives as the layout dives. Any dive performed in the layout, pike, or tuck position, whether slow or rapid in motion, must always have force, yet have the appearance of being performed with ease, comfort, and simplicity. When power and ease of performance are achieved, the dive is well balanced. When expertly timed and controlled, the springboard dive is a thrilling acrobatic feat. It leads to confidence and poise in body control.

An ambitious beginner who has hopes and aspirations of becoming a top-flight diver should first master the fundamental dives before attempting the more intricate dives. Then advancement will be easier, and the difficult dives will be more easily mastered. Many inexperienced divers, as soon as they are able merely to perform a dive, without any regard for good form, seem to be satisfied with their efforts. One should not stop here but should make every effort to "dress up" the dive by improving the style and mechanics, even to the smallest detail, in order to give the dive personality.

If the movements, such as the lift from the board, are not well timed, the dive will appear unbalanced, and will also seem to require great effort. Any dive, no matter how intricate, if well timed from the takeoff to the entry, will have the appearance of being performed effortlessly.

A diver must possess an awareness of muscular movement. In the performance of intricate dives, he must be able to make one group of muscles perform one movement while another group performs independent of the other group or groups. If a diver wishes to become a champion, he must possess perseverance, courage, and patience. He must be willing to spend several seasons developing fundamental skills in the elementary dives in order to go far in competition.

PHYSICAL QUALIFICATIONS

The build of a diver should be reasonably well proportioned. It is particularly advantageous to have a flexible shoulder girdle so that when the arms are extended overhead they can easily squeeze tight next to the head. When the legs are extended straight for the entry into the water, the aesthetic appearance presented by a graceful curve of the ankles and toes does much to improve the beauty of the dive. If the diver's ankle joint is not flexible, it will then be a definite detriment to his diving. Ankle exercises do improve the flexibility of the ankles. A diver could weigh 190 pounds and be over 6 feet tall and be just as great a diver as a man 5 feet tall, weighing 120 pounds, so long as each has a well-proportioned body and similar muscular coordination.

EQUIPMENT

Divers should be equipped with snugly fitting trunks of some type of elastic that conforms to the contour of the hips when the body is either bent or straight. The suit should be high-waisted, giving the diver a more pleasing appearance. The diver should have at least two suits, one for practice and another for competition.

TRAINING AND CONDITIONING EXERCISES

To attain a pleasing physique and maintain good poise and posture, a diver must practice some preseason and daily conditioning. A good diver must develop firmness in the muscles of his body, especially in the stomach and legs. There is considerable impact when the body strikes the water, and the diver must be strong and firm in order to hold his body in straight alignment for a perfect entry. All the muscles of the body must be held tense to keep the body from collapsing on the entry. Control of the stomach muscles is particularly important in many dives, especially in the back and reverse dives done in pike position. In these pike dives the muscles of the stomach contract to draw the legs close to the body, and then they extend to straighten the body and again are held taut at the entry.

To strengthen the stomach muscles, the diver should do sit-ups from the floor or from an inclined board. If the diver uses an inclined board, the feet should be attached to the high part of the board, and the head should lay on the lower end. After the diver is able to do this many times in succession, he should try holding an extra weight behind the head.

The legs and toes must extend firmly on the diving board on all takeoffs and must be held firmly throughout the execution and entry into the water. To strengthen the legs and toes, the diver lays on his back in a supine position and does repeated leg lifts. He should hang from a horizontal bar by the arms and do repeated leg lifts up to the bar. He should try to increase the number of times he does this exercise each day.

To exercise the flexibility of the ankles, kneel on a towel, with the toes pointing backward. Then, sit back on the ankles, and rock up and back, slightly supporting the body weight with the hands placed on the floor beside the legs. The knees will lift off the floor as the body rocks back on the ankles. This exercise is used to strengthen the ankles and increase the flexibility and should be practiced daily before and during the season. A towel should be kept beside the diving board, and before every dive the diver should turn his toes downward and exert a little pressure in extending the ankle. This will help to increase his thought and awareness of the toe point in the actual dive.

A number of stretching exercises are important at the beginning of a workout in order to loosen the muscles in the back, shoulders, trunk, and legs. Some of these exercises are as follows:

1. Run in place, lifting the knees high toward the chest.
2. Bend down, keeping the legs straight, and touch the ankles, then straighten up, and arch the back with the arms over the head.

3. Rock back and forth in the kneeling position while sitting on the ankles.
4. Jump up and down on the balls of the feet like skipping rope.
5. Stand erect, with the arms stretched laterally, and twist at the trunk from side to side. Bend over at the waist with the legs straight, and repeat the exercise.
6. Press into a handstand and balance without an arch in the back.
7. Stand with the back against a flat wall with the heels, calves, hips, shoulders, and head touching for a sense of posture alignment and correction. Tilt the pelvis back to straighten the spine, allowing just the thickness of the hand to be inserted between the spine and the wall.

DAILY WORKOUTS

A competitive diver with the aspiration of becoming a champion must enjoy a lot of hard work. A competitive diver should work out at least once a day and, if time permits, twice a day. When practicing once a day, the diver should first loosen up with some stretching exercises along with some practice approaches on the board. The diver should then execute about three each of the required dives and the optional dives. The diver may find it helpful to practice the first four compulsory dives in the pike and layout positions during the beginning of the season to aid in muscle tonus and orientation to body position in the air. Once the diver has completed his full list of dives, he should make repeated attempts at those that cause him the most trouble. The diver should experiment with new dives he wishes to learn at this time.

When practicing twice a day, the diver should not execute the compulsory and optional dives more than three times in each workout. The two practices should be separated by at least 2 hours of rest. In practicing from both the 1-meter and 3-meter boards, the diver should devote one practice session to the 1-meter and the other practice session to the 3-meter board. The practices from the different heights may be switched from day to day. The diver should occasionally start the second practice by executing the optional dives and then the required dives to add variety to the practice. He should then finish the practice with any particular dives that he wishes to give extra attention. At least twice each week, the second workout should be as though the diver were in actual competition; that is, he should do each dive on his lift of competitive dives without repeating any dive. Also, it is important to have someone judge his diving at this time.

The diver should be taught to create a visual picture in his mind before attempting a dive. When learning a particular technique, the diver should draw an imaginary picture in his mind and strive to achieve this very thing as he does the dive. Perhaps in a jackknife he will imagine that he is lifting his hips over an imaginary pole, wire, wall, or whatever he wishes in striving for the hip action involved. In a somersault, he may think that he has heavy weights on his feet and that he must throw them over his head.

The diver should visualize whatever image best describes the action to him and then perform it. The action and coordination of the dive should be thoroughly thought through by the diver before trying it. Once he has decided to try a dive and has launched his body into the air, he should go through with it as he has pictured it in his mind, and he will usually be successful. If the diver changes his mind in midair, he will generally make a bad landing and "take a beating." Therefore, it is suggested that once a dive is started, make every effort to finish it.

Water temperature is something the diver may have no control over, but, if he does, he should practice diving when or where the air temperature and water temperature are warm. Goose bumps and muscular coordination just do not go together.

Eating habits do not have to be restricted

or controlled for diving. However, the diver should not eat anything for at least 2 hours before a workout or competition.

A diver should never practice alone. First, it is not safe because the diver could possibly have an accident. Second, someone must observe and correct his technique if he is ever going to learn. A coach must observe the component parts of a dive. He does not simply note whether or not the body causes a splash forward or backward, but what action takes place from the time the diver takes off from the board until he enters the water. It is better to look at one single thing at a time. For example, if in a front jackknife the diver continually lands on his stomach and is short of the vertical entry, the coach should observe the action of the legs ONLY to see if they lift upward and backward to cause enough rotation. If the action seems right, then on the next few attempts he observes ONLY the action of the arms. Perhaps the diver touches his hands to his toes too far in front of him. Or possibly after the proper touch, he may be straightening his body and reaching too far forward with the arms instead of directly for the bottom of the pool. If there is no coach around, the diver can tell another diver or observer what to watch in his dive.

It takes attentive concentration to spot the errors in the takeoff as the diver leaves the board. The most common error is simply "rushing" into the execution of the dive as soon as the diver lands on the board after the hurdle. This, however, is not easy to correct and gives reason for mastering the required dives before spending much time on the optional dives. Thus, it is also valuable to spend a lot of time on board work, using the sand pit or, if none is available, just practicing the approach with jumps. When a diver learns to land on the end of the board in perfect balance, his dives will be more consistent, and he will be certain to gain more success.

Since skill in diving depends much on the building of one skill on another, the diver, whether a beginner, a novice, or a skilled performer, should pay strict attention to each detail underlying diving performance. The basic skills are not learned simply by the process of smoothing out a complete performance but are learned more easily by starting from scratch and practicing each step until it is learned thoroughly. Through this process, the first skills become a part of the diver's reflex behavior as the succeeding, more difficult skills are added to the performance.

If faulty skills are learned first, the unlearning and relearning of new reflexes are time-consuming, very difficult, and often discouraging to the learner.

TEACHING AIDS

Watching a champion diver at first hand is certainly a great inspiration and an asset in learning to dive. Not everyone has a chance, however, to see champion divers. Therefore, the next best thing is to study movies or slides. Motion pictures of diving champions in action provide excellent devices for helping the student learn the parts of each dive.

With the modern advances in motion picture projection, it is possible to stop the action precisely where you wish in order to study every detail of a dive at a precise moment. Slides, too, offer an excellent opportunity to study the mechanics of the dive at a given moment.

It is quite impossible for a person to know how he himself looks in a dive. It is very important to have motion pictures made of himself in order to observe his own technique. Watching one's self in an actual dive is a vivid way of observing mistakes. This is a much more impressive lesson for the diver than an explanation by a coach. Sometimes, viewing films is the only way a diver can actually "get the feeling" of the action involved in a dive.

Use of the trampoline. Basically, divers use the trampoline to aid in the quick development of muscular coordination, balance, and kinesthetic sense. The trampoline provides the diver with the opportunity to learn and attempt fundamental dives and advanced dives with the use of spotting and safety apparatus, which reduces to a bare minimum the chance of injury. Divers also find the trampoline useful in physical conditioning and in the development of endurance. They can learn certain diving techniques and body mechanics on the trampoline much faster than on the diving board. Many new dives have been perfected in recent years that were first tried on the trampoline.

Use of the dry land pit. In recent years the sand pit has been replaced by the port-o-pit, which is a large sack filled with foam rubber. This provides the diver with a much softer landing than sand and also allows him to land on his back, stomach, and so on, which is not possible when sand is used. Whatever type of dry land equipment is used, the diver can practice nearly twice as fast as in the pool, for he does not have to keep climbing out of the water. The pit permits the diver to practice diving techniques on dry land when a cold or minor injury may have prevented him from going into the water. The use of the dry land pit is usually emphasized just before and after the swimming season, but it may be very helpful during the season in correcting fundamentals. The approximate size of the pit is 8 × 14 feet.

It is imperative that the diver spend much time perfecting an approach with a good takeoff, since this is vitally necessary in the execution of a good dive. The diver will find the pit a great aid in obtaining this objective. In addition to the approach, takeoff, and practice jumps from the board in the pit, the diver can practice somersault dives, with feet-first landings, when using the sand pit, and various other landings when using the port-o-pit, from all five of the diving groups. Single somersault dives can be practiced with reasonable safety, but a safety belt should be considered when multiple somersaults or somersaults with twists are attempted. The important thing is to perfect the takeoff and the start of the somersaults, since the beginning actions are basically the same for the more complicated spins. When practicing with sand, it should be piled to within 2 feet of the board, for a long drop to the sand is very hard on the legs and ankles.

FUNDAMENTAL TECHNIQUES OF THE FRONT APPROACH, HURDLE, AND TAKEOFF

It is at this point that the various finer aspects of the finished performance should be instituted so that, as the diver repeats these polished movements, they become natural to him.

The approach to the hurdle consists of (1) mental and physical poise in the starting position, (2) the walk, (3) the hurdle, and (4) the takeoff from the board.

In the starting position, the diver should assume an erect, active position. The head is held erect, with chin in and chest well up, but not extremely exaggerated. The abdomen is drawn in. The center of body weight is over the balls of the feet, not over the heels. The back is erect, the arms are at the sides, and the palms rest at the sides of the thighs. The fingers and thumbs should be held straight and slightly squeezed together, with the palms flat from the moment the diver steps onto the board. The legs and heels are held together. The eyes are focused on the far end of the board, without lowering the head to do so.

While in the starting position, the diver is concentrating on the particular dive that he is going to perform. He should visualize his body going through the entire dive. Then he should concentrate on the approach and hurdle as he moves to take the first step. The eyes sight the end of the board throughout the approach until the feet are ready to alight on the board following the hurdle. The eyes then shift to an approximate point in the water where the entry will be made.

As the feet make contact with the board following the hurdle, the diver again concentrates on the dive to be executed. When performing dives requiring the diver to stand on the end of the board with his back to the water, he concentrates on the dive to be executed as soon as the arms are set in the backward stance. Before a large audience a diver in the starting position is a human magnet for hundreds of pairs of eyes that are attracted toward him. As he becomes quietly and deeply engrossed in concentration on his announced dive, so, too, will the audience come to attention. This moment gives him inspiration. All outside stimuli about him are blocked out, and everything is centered on the performance of the dive. Throughout the stance the diver should express confidence, strength, personality, and poise.

Walk. The walk must be smooth and forceful. A diver should not give the appearance of any awkwardness. If he is too tense, he will usually shorten his normal steps, and his hurdle will be too long.

The walk should consist of at least three steps before the hurdle. A natural walk is better for accuracy in dropping to the end of the board from the hurdle than one that is hurried or forced.

The first step is slightly shorter than the others, and each succeeding stride is slightly longer than the one previous. The takeoff foot in the hurdle should reach a point approximately 2 to 3½ feet from the end of the board. Some divers try to put too much power into the step just prior to the hurdle, causing the step to overreach and giving the body a crouched appearance or unbalanced position.

In the three-step approach, start the first step with the foot opposite the one used when kicking a football. Assuming the starting foot to be the right foot, it is then the left foot that is lifted in the hurdle.

In the four-step approach, start the first step with the foot used in kicking a football so that you will come out right at the hurdle step.

During the run the arms should coordinate in rhythm with the legs (Fig. 18-1, *C*). The arm swing should be natural and not exaggerated. The rhythmic run is best accomplished by swinging the arms slightly forward and backward from a hang at the sides of the hips. It is important that the arm swing be timed so that at the hurdle step both arms are ready to come forward from slightly behind the hips with the hurdle takeoff (Fig. 18-1, *C*). In the three-step run, the arm swing is very simple. The arms swing moderately from a shoulder hang, and the diver merely attempts to coordinate the movement with the run, as in walking. Then, at the hurdle step, the arms move simultaneously behind the hips and swing forward then upward and slightly lateral with the leap. The arms should be extended. In the four-step approach, the only variance from the three-step approach is that the diver starts the approach with the opposite foot. To obtain a smooth walk, it is important that the diver makes sure to alight on the heel of the foot in each step.

Hurdle and takeoff. In order to derive optimum lift from the springboard, the diver must drop onto the end of the board in such a manner that he is in the proper position to depress the board. The elongated jump or spring to the end of the board is known as the hurdle (Fig. 18-1, *C*).

The hurdle is basic for all front running dives. There are numerous basic techniques to be learned in an accurate hurdle to give a true and powerful lift from the board.

When placing the foot on the board on the last step (assume it to be the right) before the hurdle, the body continues to move forward until the center of body weight is over the ball of the right foot. The right leg is slightly bent at the knee. A powerful upward spring is given by extending the knee and powerfully extending the ankle (Fig. 18-1, *C*). Simultaneously with this movement the left leg, bent at the knee to form a 90 degree angle, is lifted, and the ankle and toes extend toward the board.

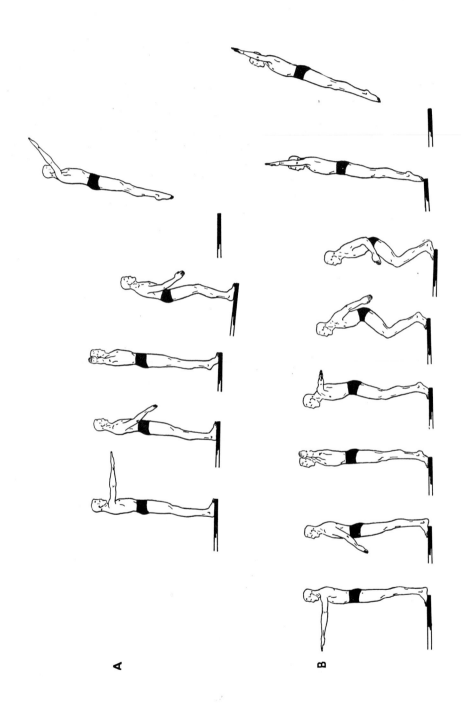

A

B

C

Fig. 18-1. A series of ideal form showing the various types of springboard diving takeoffs. **A,** Standing takeoff with body facing the water. **B,** Standing takeoff with body facing the springboard. **C,** Three-step run, hurdle, and takeoff.

The arms move forward and upward from slightly behind the hips. As the arms are lifted upward, the shoulder girdle is pulled up erectly from a slightly forward lean; the hips are pressed forward until the body is straight. The head is forward just enough that the eyes may maintain focus on the end of the board. The left leg is then quickly stretched downward as the right leg moves forward alongside. All of these movements should take place by the time the body reaches the highest point in the hurdle. Both legs and body are now stretched straight down toward the tip of the board (Fig. 18-1, *C*).

The hurdle leap must be accurately directed so that the body is at its highest point just behind the very end of the board. Here the body is prepared for the descent to the board. Too much power sometimes is attempted, causing the diver to crouch too deep during the approaching steps to the hurdle, which causes loss of springing power as well as rhythm and timing. The result is an unbalanced takeoff. The hurdle is an important skill and requires weeks and weeks of practice. In the descent, the toes, ankles, legs, and the entire body must be stretched and directed toward the end of the board. Check any overforward lean with the shoulders in the drop or descent. There should be approximately a degree or two of lean, just enough to place the center of weight of the body behind the tip end of the board.

In the descent from the hurdle, the arms are delayed in their descent until the weight of the body is about to drop onto the board (Fig. 18-1, *C*). Then the arms are driven downward slightly behind the hips, swept forward at the side of the hips, and then lifted upward. This delayed descent of the arms gives perfect timing with the board and with the takeoff. Most divers get the arms down too soon, which results in ineffective timing of the takeoff movement. The arm descent should be delayed because the board must be pressed down by the body

weight; then the arms are brought forward, transferring their downward momentum to the body at the end of their swing to assist in giving greater downward bend to the board. The descent should not be forced. One can only drop as fast as gravity permits. Some beginning divers will flatten the feet several inches above the board, with a slight bend of the knees, and then stomp the board for the takeoff. Most boards today are slow and flexible. They should not be stiff and quick. A stiff board causes the diver to stomp, which develops the dreaded shin splints. The diver should drop onto the end of the board with his feet settling as lightly as a feather.

An important movement takes place as the balls of the feet land on the board. About 1 inch from the board during the descent, the toes lift upward. The ankles remain extended so that the balls of the feet can contact the board first. As the feet come in contact with the board, the fall is broken, and the weight is distributed over the entire foot by letting the ankle flex gradually as the toes and balls of the feet, then the heels, alight on the board.

The knees and hips also act as shock absorbers and prepare for the lift. They flex slightly as the body drops onto the board. These mechanics prevent the diver from stomping the board and allow for a quiet descent.

With the weight of the body depressing the board, the knees and hips flex slightly as they take up the landing shock. While the board is being depressed further, the knees and hips cease to give, and the full weight of the body settles onto the board. As the board approaches its fullest depression, the knees and hips begin to extend and drive against the board, pressing the board farther toward the water.

As the board recoils, the knees and hips continue to extend and propel the body upward. When the board has completed the recoil, the knees and hips reach full extension, and it is then that the ankles execute the final lift that sends the body soaring into the air. The extension of the ankle and foot is vigorous, and even the toes contribute to the snap upward as the feet finally leave the board.

The action of the arms must be turned into this whole springing movement. The arms serve to control body balance and also to supply a further force in the depression of the board and upward lift of the body.

As the body is above the board ready to drop into it, the arms slowly move into a position in preparation for the downward swing as the body descends. The arms are outstretched, with the hands slightly more than shoulder width and just above head height. The palms are face downward and somewhat forward, and there is a comfortable flexion in the elbow joints.

The arms describe a slow outward motion, and, as the body nears the board, the slow outward motion is converted into a rapid downward and backward swing, with the hands reaching the hips just as the board is being depressed.

The arms move downward to a position just alongside and slightly behind the hips and then swing forward and upward with the palms of the hands facing the hips. This sudden change in direction from downward and backward to forward and upward transfers the downward momentum from the arms to the body. As the hands pass the hips, the downward extension of the legs against the board is made. The arms lift upward as the board is depressed to its fullest extent so that, as the board starts upward, the arms are nearly at shoulder level.

At this position the arms must be carefully controlled so that body balance will be maintained. The hands now aim upward to the required position necessary to guide the dive.

While practicing the hurdle, the diver should enter the water head first at the completion of the takeoff. This practice will drill the diver in the proper drop onto the board and in the proper angle of takeoff.

Bouncing up and down repeatedly on the end of the board is dangerous. An approach with a SINGLE bounce is reasonably safe and often very helpful in getting the feel of the board. Once the approach to a dive is started, the diver should go through with it and not balk.

Takeoff. As the lift from the board is executed, the arms extend forward and reach upward (Fig. 18-1, *C*). Just at what angle or how far the arms should reach depends on the dive to be performed. This will be discussed further with each dive. However, when the board is depressed to its maximum bend, the diver times the arms to reach beyond the head and in the intended line of flight of the body as it leaves the board. Too often the inexperienced diver swings the arms upward too abruptly or ahead of the recoil of the board and presents an awkward, unbalanced position. Note in each dive the position of the hands and arms as the feet leave the board. The eyes should be steadily fixed upon the tip of the board until the feet drop onto it. The eyes then sight down at the water until the arms begin their upward reach. What the eyes see after the arms are lifted depends on the dive to be executed.

The amount of lean in the body as it drops to the board in the hurdle also differs with each dive. In every forward dive there must be just enough lean to permit the center of the body weight to pass just beyond the base of support when the feet are on the end of the board. One must distinguish between proper lean and the common fault of falling forward. This moving-lean will give a faulty takeoff and reduce height and balance. A plain front header and the backward dive are half somersaults, and any somersault dive passes through a line of flight that is angular in motion. This angular motion can be obtained by merely having the body approximately one or two degrees off center. It might be said that there should be no forward movement at all once the desired degree of lean is obtained from the hurdle. Usually, angular forward motion continues once the diver has landed on the end of the board. The forward motion should be so slow and the lean so slight that it can hardly be perceived. To illustrate, place one end of a stick 5 feet long on the floor and perfectly balance it. Then move it just off its center of support. Notice that the early falling movement is so slow that it appears to be balanced. As gravity begins to take effect, the falling speed is accelerated.

With a diver, this falling fault usually starts in the descent of the hurdle if it has not been sufficiently counterchecked in the ascent of the hurdle. Through constant trials and practice, the diver acquires a sense of lean and just the exact amount of lean required during the ascent and descent of the hurdle necessary for the type of dive to be performed. He must, therefore, train to acquire different angles of lean at the takeoff for dives requiring a greater or lesser amount of lean to obtain a desired line of flight. These body leans may possibly vary only from 1 to 10 degrees. One may readily note that to achieve such slight angles consistently requires accuracy in performance. Unless this fundamental is thoroughly learned, a diver can never hope to perform consistently in competition. It is the amount of lean that determines the distance a diver goes out from the board. A diver must then not "groove" himself to learn one angle of takeoff for all dives, but he must be able to take off at several different angles of varying degrees, depending on the type of dive to be performed.

The flight will vary as the angle of takeoff varies. Some dives require a flatter line of flight than others. The center of motion of the body describes the line of flight. In layout dives the center is just slightly above the hip joint. In pike dives the center of motion is not in the body but just outside and in front of the hips. In the tuck position the center of motion lies just outside of the body, in front of the hips between the abdomen and the thighs. An attempt is made to group these dives as to the amount of distance of entry from the end of the board. They are as follows:

1. Those dives entering farthest from the end of the board with a more or less flattened line of flight; the plain headers, all of the forward somersault dives whether tuck, pike, or straight; the front dive with one-half twist and front dive with one twist in the layout position; and the forward somersault twisting dives

2. Those dives entering nearest the end of the board with a more vertical line of flight; the forward dive, pike; the inward group of dives; the jackknife dives with twists; all of the reverse dives including those with twists; and all of the backward dives

A common error most divers make is that, as the dives become more difficult to perform, the more hurried the hurdle and takeoff become. Then, too, there is a tendency to become more tense in the approach and hurdle, causing an inefficient takeoff. Divers must remember to be properly relaxed in the approach of a difficult dive and perform the preliminary arm movement of the standing takeoff slowly.

In the takeoff, the hands, arms, head, and shoulder girdle should conform to the intended angle and line of flight of the body at the exact moment the body stretches off the board. The eyes then assist the body in the air by constantly spotting or focusing upon some object to inform the diver as to his bearings and balance. The head of the diver should not move awkwardly out of body flight alignment for the purpose of focusing.

Height and line of flight. Height in diving is the vertical distance of the highest peak reached by the body's center of motion in the line of flight. The line of flight is the path described by the center of body weight from the takeoff to the entry. To obtain optimum height in a dive, all essential movements must be rhythmically timed and balanced from takeoff to the entry. If this is attained, the body lifts effortlessly into the air. Whenever one observes a diver making tremendous effort to obtain height in a dive, the body usually appears jerky in its motions and unsymmetrical or unbalanced. Muscular power must be skillfully controlled. Height, then, is a natural result when the run and hurdle are well controlled and timed.

Some divers have a natural gift of good springing muscles in the legs, so it is not practical for all divers to attain the same height. However, each diver should utilize all of the potential lift from the board. When this jumping force is properly transmitted through the central longitudinal axis of the body, the body will derive maximum height.

Entry. The point of entry of a dive should be at a point directly under the center of weight of the body, on a line with the descending flight of the body. From the surface, the line of flight should be projected directly down to the bottom of the pool. The diver's body should follow this projected line of flight to the bottom so that every part of his body will pass through the same opening in the surface of the water. In the feet-first entry dive, the pointed feet and legs must guide the body down this line so as to draw the shoulders and head into the hole without side, forward, or backward casts. Nearly every dive requires a different position of the body, legs, head, and arms to effect a good entry. A technique used by high platform divers to reduce the splash after a feet-first entry is to pull the toes up as soon as the feet are under water. This blunt entry cuts down the splash and leaves nothing but a mound of bubbling water.

In all feet-first dives, such as the inward somersault or the reverse somersault, the diver's body should be held straight with only a natural standing arch in the back. This will prevent splash or side casts. To prevent a large curvature in the back, the arms should be closed along the sides of the body with the palms of the hands curving along and slightly in front of the thighs just below the hips. This arm and hand position will prevent the elbows from protruding behind the line of the spine. The legs must be straight with the ankles extended, toes pointed, and the head held erect in all feet-first entries. If the mechanics of the dive are correct and well timed and the dive is not short, the arch is straightened to a minimum. If short, or over, then the amount of arch varies from a deepened arch to a straight line. Too much arch will never drive the diver to the bottom on a projected line with his line of flight but will cause him to veer just under the surface and cause his feet to splash on the surface if his legs remain straight.

In header dives the hands should be held extended. As a general rule in most types of dives, a smoother and less noisy entry is made when the hands are clasped one over the other with the thumbs locked and the arms held tightly against the head. It also presents a more streamlined effect to the head and shoulders when entering the water.

In the head-first dives, the head should be lowered slightly just as the hands clasp together for the entry. The back of the head should be well above the back line of the arms at the entry. The head in this position preserves the unbroken and continuous arch from the head down the curved line of the spine to the feet. In all head-first dives the arms, when extended above the head, should be pressing against the ears and in a straight line with the upper spine. If the arms are extended too far, the arch will be too great.

MECHANICS AND TECHNIQUE FOR THE TAKEOFF FOR BACKWARD DIVES (BODY FACING BOARD)

This takeoff is executed without a run. The back faces the water at the end of the board where the stance is assumed (Fig. 18-1, *B*).

Approach. The diver steps on the board

and assumes a momentary stance before executing the approach. In this position the diver must have confidence in his poise as well as be mentally alert for the dive he is about to perform.

The diver then walks briskly, yet poised, head and chest held high, and arms swinging naturally and alive as he takes natural, moderately spaced strides to the end of the board. Some inexperienced divers make the error of walking out too slowly and showing a nonchalant attitude. The eyes may spot the end of the board as he walks out to it, and the head should not be lowered. The head does an about face as the diver pivots with his feet and focuses his eyes on the rear of the board.

Pivot step. The pivot action of turning the back to the water may be performed in the following manner: The walk to the end of the board is identical to that used when making a forward approach except the hurdle is not executed. The diver starts toward the end of the board on the same foot as when performing the forward approach. When the foot of the last step in the approach is planted on the board, the body should be approximately 2 feet from the end of the board. The weight of the body is then placed on the ball of this foot, and the diver pivots a half turn. The pivot is controlled and stopped by stepping back with the other foot, after the pivot is made, and placing the ball of this foot near the end of the board. Part of the body weight is then transferred to the back foot to maintain balance. When balance is accomplished, the back foot is placed in position over the end of the board, and the forward pivot foot is moved back along the other foot ready for the stance.

Stance. With the back to the water, the arms are placed at shoulder height and shoulder width as the feet are placed in proper position. The body must be straight and not arched. The curvature at the small of the back must be straightened by tilting the pelvis back. The center of body weight rests on the balls of the feet and the toes. The heels are level with the board.

If a stance is assumed for any of the inward dives, the body should assume more of an incline toward the board, with the center of body weight over the big toes. This slight incline accommodates a more efficient hip lift at the takeoff. In a backward dive or backward somersault, the center of body weight should be well back in the heels, even though the heels do not rest on the board.

Takeoff mechanics of arms and legs in action. The arms are lowered slowly to the sides of the body so as not to off balance the diver. Throughout the entire preliminary arm action of the takeoff, the center of weight must be maintained over the base of support.

With the arms extended, they lift laterally and slightly forward from the sides of the body. The arms lift upward to either shoulder height or slightly above shoulder level. No matter to what height the arms lift, they must always move in front of the spine during the up phase of the arm swing. If the arms are moved behind the spine on the up swing, the shoulders pull back, the chest bulges forward, and the lower spine arches, which causes the body to lose its balance over its base of support.

As the arms lift, the body is raised well upon its toes (Fig. 18-1, *B*). The arms move up strongly enough to just ease the weight of the body off the end of the board. This sets the board in motion and in rhythm with the arms and legs for the remainder of the takeoff. A deep breath is taken through the mouth during this motion, and then the mouth is closed.

The initial arm lift is the most important phase of the mechanics of the backward takeoff, and the success of the dive depends on the accuracy of its performance. Usually a diver drives the arms up too hard and fast, which lifts the shoulder girdle high, causing the body to lift off the board (crowhop), which results in the body leaning backward prematurely at the takeoff.

The final downswing of the arms is now executed as the knees are bent in preparation for the final push on the board (Fig. 18-1, *B*). In this action, the arms drive down with force as far as the hips, where they suddenly change direction, further transmitting downward force, while the arms begin the final upswing. Together, with a sudden extension of the knees and ankles, the arms lift and reach up into the line of flight (Fig. 18-1, *B*). The diver should attempt to keep the arms straight throughout this entire action. While the arms swing down the heels remain above the board and the knees bend, the hips move back and down very slightly with the knee bent forward, extending beyond the toes as if to sit down on the heels. However, the body or trunk remains in a vertical line above the hips and does not bend forward. (See Fig. 18-1, *A*). This movement does not give the body a falling appearance. At the same time, it gives it true balance, and the diver is able to keep the body under control on the takeoff, as well as throughout the dive.

The movements for the standing takeoff, body facing the water, are very similar to those described for the takeoff with the back of the body facing the water (Fig. 18-1, *A*).

FUNDAMENTAL JUMP DIVES

The jump dives are devised mostly for the beginner so he may learn the proper approach and takeoff. The beginner should not attempt the advanced dives until he has learned these rudimentary skills of diving. The diver's proficiency should then improve rapidly because his technique is sound.

In all of the jump dives it is a question of balance in the air. This the beginner should control right from the takeoff. When in the air, he should rely upon the head and arms to accurately control the body. When consistency in balance is developed, the arms are relied upon less, and the head takes over in slight adjustments in midair.

The jump dives should first be attempted from a standing takeoff (Fig. 18-1, *A*). The technique used in executing the standing takeoff with the body facing the water is the same as that described for the takeoff with the back facing the water (Fig. 18-1, *B*). The only difference is that the diver can curl his toes over the board when facing toward the water.

When he has adjusted himself to the feel of the movement of the arms and legs with the board, he can proceed with the approaching run and hurdle as described in Fig. 18-1, *C*.

Front jump—straight. As the body leaves the board, the arms reach forward and upward at shoulder width to a position above the head. As the body reaches the peak of the jump, the arms stretch upward, fingers squeeze together, and the head and shoulders press backward to keep the body well aligned. After the peak of the dive has been reached, the arms move downward so that the hands are placed at the sides of the thighs at the entry. The head is held erect with the eyes sighting the water near the other end of the pool. At the entry, the toes stretched toward the water (Fig. 18-2, *A*).

Front jump—pike. The arms reach for the ceiling as in the front jump, straight. After the body has left the board, the legs should lift to a position nearly parallel with the water. The flexion is in the hips as the thighs are lifted. The legs are kept extended, the ankles stretched, and the trunk and head held erect throughout the dive. The arms are lowered toward the legs as the legs reach hip level in a horizontal plane. The ankles are brought up to touch the hands as the peak of the dive is reached. The body should straighten immediately after the peak of the dive has been reached. The hands simply slide along the front of the legs to the entry position in the front of the thighs. This dive requires a considerable amount of body control in order to effect a vertical entry (Fig. 18-2, *B*).

Front jump—tuck. This dive is harder to perform than the pike. The body is stretched

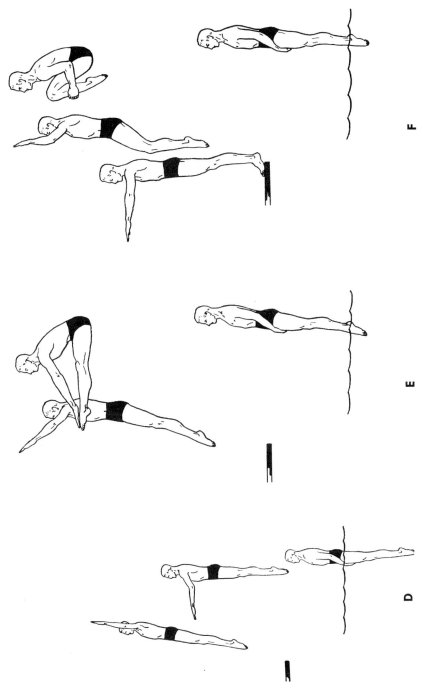

Fig. 18-2. A series of ideal form for executing the elementary jump dives. **A,** The standing or running front jump dive, layout. **B,** The standing or running front jump dive, pike. **C,** The standing or running front jump dive, tuck. **D,** The standing back jump dive, layout. **E,** The standing back jump dive, pike. **F,** The standing back jump dive, tuck.

momentarily as in the front jump, straight. After the body leaves the board, the knees are brought up to the chest, and the knees and ankles are held together. At the same time the hands are lowered and grasp the legs at the shins and pull them in so that the heels are brought toward the buttocks in a tight tuck. The hips and knee joints must be relaxed.

As the diver reaches the peak of the dive, he should hold his trunk firm and his head erect with the eyes directed forward. The tuck is held for a moment after he has passed the peak when the legs are released and shot downward. The hands slide down the legs and are held against the sides of the thighs at the entry (Fig. 18-2, *C*).

Backward jump—straight. As the body leaves the board, the arms lift forward to a position above the head. The arms are stretched upward. As the body jumps upward and backward from the board, the head and body must be held erect. A falling takeoff should be avoided. As the diver descends from the peak, the hands are lowered to the thighs, and a vertical entry is made.

If the feet tend to come out from under the diver, then the head should be tilted according to the direction in which the feet move. For example, if the feet move back on the jump, then the head should be dropped (Fig. 18-2, *D*).

Backward jump—pike. At the lift from the board in the takeoff, the body leans slightly backward. The center of weight is in the heels, which project beyond the board, as in Fig. 18-1, *B*. As in the front jump, pike, the hands lift forward and upward above and slightly in front of the head before the pike is made. The arms do not jerk to a stop, and they are not lifted to a full reach above the head, since either of these actions would cause a transfer of momentum from the arms to the body, and the body would be thrown out of alignment. The legs should be held extended, and the toes pointed. The hips should flex easily as the

legs are lifted to the pike. The legs are slightly short of horizontal when the pike is effected. The diver should unpike immediately after the peak is reached.

The entry should be made in the vertical position at a point from 4 to 5 feet from the tip of the board (Fig. 18-2, *E*).

Backward jump—tuck. The diver executes a straight back jump layout before the tuck is started (Fig. 18-2, *F*).

At the peak of the dive the head is erect, and the eyes are directed forward. The body is leaning slightly forward. As the knees are drawn up forward, the arms are lowered until the hands grasp the shins. The heels are held close to the buttocks, and the knees and ankles are closed tightly together. The toes are in full depression, and the ankles are extended.

The diver should untuck soon after the peak is reached and attempt to gain a vertical entry with the body in good alignment, not arched.

COMPETITIVE DIVING

All dives are combinations of the forward or backward dive with either a somersault or a twist in one of the straight, pike, or tuck positions. The first dive of each group is the fundamental movement, and succeeding dives contain added movements that increase the complexity of the dive.

In learning the dives the diver should accomplish the most elementary of the dives in each of the groups first. As these are mastered, the successively more difficult dives are attempted.

The following order may be used in learning all of the required and a few of the more elementary of the optional dives:

Order*	Group	Dive
1	I	Forward dive—layout
2	I	Forward dive—pike
3	II	Backward dive—layout
4	V	Forward dive half twist—layout
5	IV	Inward dive—pike

*See Rules for springboard diving, Intercollegiate Swimming Guide and AAU Swimming Handbook.

6	I	Forward somersault—tuck
7	II	Backward somersault—tuck
8	III	Reverse dive—pike
9	I	Forward one and one half somersault
10	III	Rerverse dive—layout
11	IV	Reverse somersault—tuck
12	IV	Inward dive—layout
13	IV	Inward somersault—tuck
14	I	Forward somersault—pike
15	IV	Inward one and one half somersault—tuck
16	II	Back one and one half somersault—tuck

SPRINGBOARD DIVING FROM THE 1- OR 3-METER HEIGHT

Forward dive—tuck. This dive is, in reality, a one half somersault. The one half somersault tuck dives require a great amount of body control in order to maintain the body in good balance and alignment throughout the flight in the air. It is helpful to perform these dives to improve the diver's control and alertness for a perfectly aligned entry into the water.

The dive begins the same as the plain front header. As the feet come in contact with the board at the end of the hurdle, the eyes are lifted from the board and look at the front wall. The arms reach overhead and slightly forward as the diver rises from the board. The face is held directly forward. As soon as the legs have made the final extension onto the board, the hips are lifted slightly, and the knees are brought forward under the chest. The hands lower to grasp the shins just as the knees are about to reach the chest. This contact in the tuck position is made at the peak of the dive. The head tilts downward slightly, keeping the eyes focused on the water. This causes enough rotation to put the diver's body almost in a complete head-foremost position. The legs are immediately snapped straight just short of the vertical alignment. The hands slide from the shins to the sides of the hips as the body straightens. Then the hands reach laterally outward and are stretched downward toward the water. The arms are pressed firmly against the head for the entry (Fig. 18-3).

A common fault in executing this dive is to bring the arms together too slowly and too near the surface of the water. The arms should be brought together quickly, since the body has fallen to within a few feet of the water.

Forward dive—jackknife, pike. The takeoff is made with the hands held shoulder

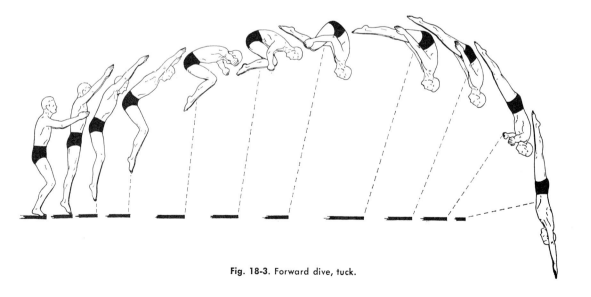

Fig. 18-3. Forward dive, tuck.

width apart in a modified reach above and in front of the head. The hips lift almost immediately on the takeoff from the board. The feet point straight down, the arms depress, and the hips lift above the head as the body rises to the peak of the dive. The eyes sight the water at the approximate point of entry. As the peak of the dive is reached, the hands are brought in contact with the feet. The legs at this point are in a vertical position, with toes pointing downward.

As the body drops from the peak of the dive, the arms reach toward the water. The legs then lift slowly as the body starts to open up, and the continued rotation of the body places it in a vertical position for the entry. As the legs lift upward, the arms reach downward to a position along the sides of the head, and the hands clasp together at the entry.

Common errors in executing this dive are as follows:

1. The head lifts on the takeoff, and the arms fail to reach overhead.
2. The hands touch the feet before or after the peak of the dive is reached.
3. In unpiking, the hands follow the legs back too far, giving the body too much rotation forward with the loss of entry control (Fig. 18-4).

Forward dive—layout. This dive is commonly known as the swan or plain front dive. It is, in reality, a one half somersault.

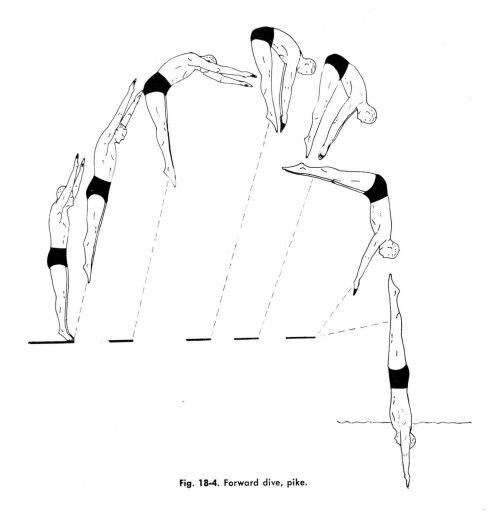

Fig. 18-4. Forward dive, pike.

The difficulty of this dive lies in the large amount of body control required to maintain the body in alignment throughout the flight through the air. As the feet come in contact with the board at the end of the hurdle, the eyes lift from the board and focus on a point at the other end of the pool that is usually lower than the height of the board. The face is held directly forward until after the peak of the dive has been reached. When the diver leaves the board, the body should stretch, with the feet pressing downward and backward. The arms raise overhead at a position wider than the shoulders and then spread out to a position straight from the shoulders with a slight angle forward. A line across the upper back should follow along the top of the arms when the body is in the layout position.

The whole body should be straight, and the legs held close together, with the toes pointed backward.

As the peak of the dive is reached, the body rotates forward around its center of weight, which is just above the hip joint. This rotation lifts the legs upward and levels the trunk so that the heels are just above the head level when the body is at its peak.

The rotation continues as the body falls from the peak, and the head remains in line with the body as the eyes shift to the point of entry. The hands clasp as the vertical entry is made.

The diver should reach for the bottom

Fig. 18-5. Forward dive, layout.

at a slight angle as he enters the water (Fig. 18-5).

Forward somersault—pike. After the reach upward is made in the takeoff, the hips are lifted up and over the body as the shoulders, arms, and head are lowered with chin in as the body rotates forward. Instead of touching the toes as in the front jump, pike, the hands grasp the back of the knees, and the elbows are held close to the hips. The hips are relaxed in order that the flexion can be deep. The legs are held extended and the toes are pointed.

As the body falls from the peak of the dive, the trunk is held firm, and the opening from the pike is started. The legs are pressed down and the head is pressed to an erect position with chin in. As the legs drop downward and the body straightens, the eyes focus at a point on the water well ahead of the point of entry as a vertical entry is made.

The pike should be initiated by lifting the hips up and over the head. With the upper part of the body curled under, the radius of rotation becomes shorter, which increases speed of angular rotation (Fig. 18-6).

Forward somersault—tuck. As the diver leaves the board the arms reach overhead and the eyes sight the water at the approximate point of entry. The legs then extend, and the hips push upward. At the same time the arms and head start a downward movement, and the body starts to rotate. When the hips start their upward movement behind the body, the knees draw toward the chest with the heels making an upward and backward movement toward the buttocks. The spinning motion is induced by the downward motion of the arms and head toward the knees. Caution should be taken not to bring the knees up to the hands.

The knees draw tightly to the chest by grasping the shins with the hands and holding the elbows close to the body. On passing the peak of the dive, the body approaches a "sitting" position at which time the tuck is released by letting the legs slide from the hands. When approximately three quarters of the somersault is completed, the legs ex-

Fig. 18-6. Forward somersault, pike.

tend with a slight bend in the hips. The legs then move down toward the water while the head and chest lift to bring the body to an upright position. The arms press against the sides, and the hands are placed on the thighs for the entry into the water (Fig. 18-7).

Flying forward one and one half somersault—tuck. This dive is more easily performed from the high board but is also a good dive from the low board if the diver obtains a sufficient amount of height from the spring.

The legs lift upward and backward as the feet leave the board and continuously press upward past the peak of the dive. The arms stretch sideward, and the body arches with the head up.

When the body has reached the peak of the dive and the legs are nearly vertical, a fast tuck is made and released when one and one quarter somersaults are completed. The radius of the body is shortened in the tuck, which greatly increases the speed of rotation. When the legs are released, the body begins to straighten with the arms

reaching for the water and the eyes sighting the water. The body completely straightens, with the arms stretched overhead and the hands clasped for a near vertical entry into the water (Fig. 18-8).

Forward one and one half somersault—pike. In this dive the diver should concentrate on his center of rotation, which is in front of his hips when the body is piked. This dive is very similar to the forward somersault, pike, but the rotation is exaggerated by the continual pressure of the hips backward and the head and shoulders forward. The hips must be relaxed so that the pike can be deep. The dive may be performed in the open or closed pike and, in this case, the open pike is demonstrated. The open pike requires the arms to be placed laterally at shoulder level during most of the dive.

While the body is descending from the peak, the diver completes one somersault and the water can be sighted.

The legs are driven backward and upward, and the trunk remains firm as the

Fig. 18-7. Forward somersault, tuck.

body straightens for the head-first vertical entry. The arms move laterally as they reach downward toward the water, and the head is brought between the arms as the entry is made (Fig. 18-9).

Forward one and one half somersault —tuck. The diver reaches overhead with his arms and sights the water directly in front of the board as his body lifts from the board.

The tuck is begun directly in the reach from the board, and the hips lift as the head and shoulders are depressed. The heels are brought sharply to the buttocks. The chin is tucked in as the head is brought to-

ward the knees and the back is rounded. The tuck starts to open when the body passes, in horizontal position, the one and one fourth turn. The legs extend and press backward as the body is straightened. This elongation of the longitudinal axis decreases the speed of rotation.

The arms reach for the point of entry, and the body slides down the parabolic line of trajectory and into the water.

A common error in executing this dive is that the arms do not reach high enough on the takeoff then move sidewards for the tuck, instead of straight down in front of the body (Fig. 18-10).

Fig. 18-8. Flying forward one and one half somersault, tuck.

Forward double somersault—tuck. With the increased complexity of the dive, the diver is likely to stomp the board with the idea that this will give him an additional lift from it. The diver should not stomp the board but should drop onto it with the toes pressing into the board and make use of the rocking action of the ankles and the full spring of the board in order to get ample height. To obtain greater height, a higher hurdle should be effected so that gravity acting upon the body from this height will increase the force exerted upon the board when the body lights onto it, thus bending it deeper. Naturally it follows that the deeper the board is being depressed, the greater will be the recoil, as well as the greater the lifting force imparted to the diver.

The forward double somersault, tuck, should only be done from the low board. It is probably the most difficult step in achieving the more intricate dives. The execution of the dive requires the diver to depend entirely upon feeling in opening from the tuck spin for the entry. There is only a split second of visual perception for adjusting the angle of entry. Success with this dive is dependent on determination and trial and error, since there will be many times when the diver will misjudge the snap open-

Fig. 18-9. Forward one and one half somersault, pike.

Fig. 18-10. Forward one and one half somersault, tuck.

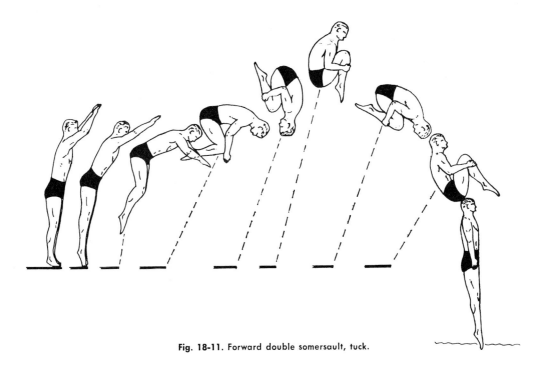

Fig. 18-11. Forward double somersault, tuck.

ing. It is much safer and easier first to learn this dive on the trampoline or the port-o-pit before attempting it from the board.

The emphasis is on the swiftness of the arm swing from the reach of the arms on the takeoff to the tuck position. As the body weight depresses the board, rock forward slightly and tilt the head down a little to sight the water as the arms reach upward in front of the head. Extend the legs and follow immediately with a snap up of the hips and feet in the direction of the forward spin. Almost simultaneously, the arms thrust downward toward the bendings legs as the hands grasp the shins and the head is pulled down hard. There is a feeling of "chasing the knees with the head and arms" and a continual tightening of the tuck. The diver holds the tuck tightly until he feels the body

turn into a sitting-down position. As he senses this feeling, he straightens his body, keeping the eyes open and the mind alert for a last split-second correction of body alignment. As the legs thrust downward, the toes point so that, as the feet strike the water, they pierce the surface with a minimum of splash and sound. The hands slide from the shins to the front of the thighs as the body straightens, and the shoulders press backward. The head is held erect with the eyes focusing far down the pool (Fig. 18-11).

Forward two and one half somersault—pike. The pike and the somersaults are made in the same manner as that of the forward one and one half somersault, pike, except that more power is applied in the spin and the dive is executed in the closed pike posi-

Fig. 18-12. Forward two and one half somersault, pike.

tion. The eyes lift toward the anticipated point of entry as the diver depresses the board, and, immediately as the board recoils, the diver rocks forward, lifting the hips and vigorously extending the ankles onto the board. The ankles and toes extend swiftly as to almost scrape the toenails on the board as the arms swing down in front of the body in chase of the legs. The legs move backward and upward over the body into the forward spin. The hands catch up to the legs and are clasped just behind and above the knees. It is important to clasp behind the legs, above the knees, rather than below the knees to ensure a faster spin.

As the diver increases the number of spins, he may have a tendency to close his

eyes. The eyes should be kept open at all times, and he should learn to orient himself to his surroundings throughout the dive. As the two and one half turns near completion, the head is tilted slightly down, and the eyes focus slightly forward where the water can be sighted. The hands reach slightly forward for the water as the legs press back, straightening the body for the entry, which should be made at an angle slightly short of vertical (Fig. 18-12).

Forward two and one half somersault—tuck. The diver should be able to do the forward double somersault, tuck, from the low board before he attempts the forward two and one half somersault, tuck, from the low or high board.

Fig. 18-13. Forward two and one half somersault, tuck.

The takeoff should not be hurried, and the tuck must not be started too soon.

The opening is made as the trunk is beyond the horizontal after two and one fourth turns have been made. The body snaps open as the arms release the legs, which quickly extend. The arms shoot downward and continually stretch toward the water as the legs straighten upward. This stretching movement gives support to the straightening of the legs as they spring open.

The diver should be alert for the instant the opening should take place (Fig. 18-13).

Forward three and one half somersault— tuck. In the initiation of a successful three and one half somersault, the emphasis is on getting into the tuck position as soon as pos- sible without rushing the takeoff and thus reducing the left of the dive. As the body weight depresses the board, rock forward slightly, and bring the head up erect with the eyes sighting the water where the entry is to be made. The arms simultaneously reach upward in front of the head. Extend the legs straight and follow immediately by an upward snap of the hips and feet in the direction of the forward spin. Almost simultaneously the arms are quickly forced downward toward the legs with the hands clasping the shins and the head pulling down hard. As the arms first reach downward for the shins, the arms should extend straight, making a reaction movement that aids the lifting of the hips to accelerate the rotation.

Fig. 18-14. Forward three and one half somersault, tuck.

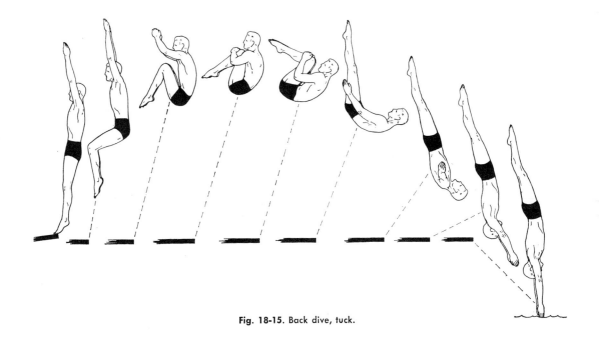

Fig. 18-15. Back dive, tuck.

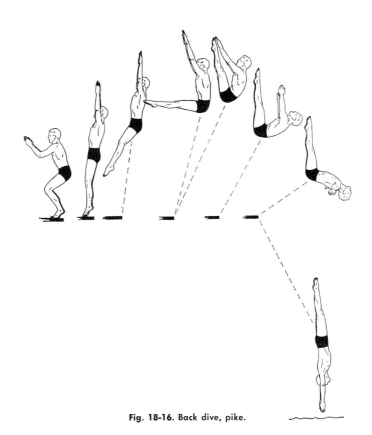

Fig. 18-16. Back dive, pike.

The emphasis is on "chasing your knees with your head and arms" and a continual tightening of the tuck. The diver holds the tuck tightly until he feels the head turning downward into the completion of the three and one half turns. The diver must sense instinctively when to straighten his legs and thrust his arms down toward the water. Straighten the body keeping the eyes open and the mind alert for a last split-second correction of body alignment (Fig. 18-14).

Back dive—tuck. The diver springs from the board as in a back jump. As the body rises upward and slightly backward from the board, the head and body must be held erect. In the lift the arms reach directly overhead and hold stationary while the knees lift up toward the chest. The hands are lowered to grasp the shins just at the instant the knees reach the chest. The hands clasp about the upper shins at the peak of the dive; then the legs snap upward, the body straightens downward, and the hands

slide from the knees to the sides of the body. The shin remains tucked toward the chest as the body is straightened for a momentary look at the legs. This instant peak orients the diver to the position of his legs, thus giving him better judgment for the entry into the water. Next, the diver swiftly extends his arms out laterally and downward toward the water for the entry, while the head tilts back to sight the water (Fig. 18-15).

Back dive—pike. After the arms press the board downward and the knees and hips flex, the diver sits slightly backward and jumps straight up. The arms aim directly overhead. The hips must not push forward. The emphasis is on stiffening the legs on the final thrust into the board and immediately lifting them up toward the hands. The stomach and thigh muscles contract very tightly. As the peak of the dive, the arms press slightly forward in the touch to "check" the legs overhead slightly short of

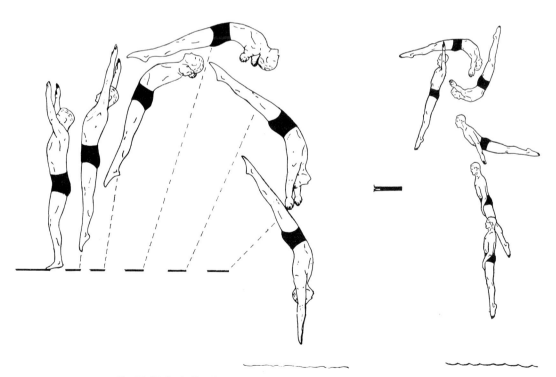

Fig. 18-17. Back dive, layout.

Fig. 18-18. Back somersault, layout.

vertical. The eyes peer where the hands will touch the instep. The head does not tilt back until a firm touch is made. To open out of the pike position, the diver must hold the leg muscles firmly as the stomach muscles relax for the body to arch back head-first. The head and arms press back simultaneously for the entry. The arms reach out laterally before closing together over the head for the entry (Fig. 18-16).

Back dive—layout. As the body lifts from the board, the eyes focus high on the rear wall. The arms reach upward slightly above shoulder level and spread laterally to a position at right angles to the body. At the peak of the dive the head tilts backward, and the eyes commence to look for the water.

During this head action, the back should be arched, and the knees and ankles must be stretched. The arms are brought together when the body has dropped to a point near the water, and the entry is made with the hands together and the head between the arms (Fig. 18-17).

Back somersault—layout. This dive is similar to the back dive except that the arms are lifted vigorously overhead, then extended laterally. The head and back continue arching backward until the body is well past the horizontal. The emphasis is on the initial arm thrust upward from the board.

The hands drop forward from the arm-spread position to the thighs as the horizontal is passed. The shoulders lift upright, and the eyes focus on the edge of the pool under the board as the entry is made (Fig. 18-18).

Back somersault—pike. The diver reaches overhead with the arms shoulder width

Fig. 18-19. Back somersault, pike.

apart, the eyes sight the hands as the legs are drawn up to the hands, which remain stationary. The hands grasp behind the legs slightly above the knees. The legs are released as the diver completes about three quarters of a somersault. The eyes sight the water as the body begins to straighten. The arms slide up the legs to the sides as the body straightens for the near vertical entry (Fig. 18-19).

Back somersault—tuck. The tuck is made soon after the upward reach so that the body is tucked at the peak of the dive. The tuck is made by lifting the knees to the chest and the hands grasping the legs just below the knees.

When the chest is horizontal to the surface and well above the board, the legs are thrust to full extension, and the toes are kept pointed. The head and shoulders are lifted erect so that the body is perfectly aligned at the entry.

As the body is opened, the eyes can focus on the board until the entry is made. The hands simply slide from the shins to the front of the thighs (Fig. 18-20).

Back one and one half somersault—layout. As the body leaves the board, the initial pull backward is made with the arms and head. The diver should not attempt to gain as much height in this dive as in the backward header but should use this energy to accelerate his backward rotation. This is obtained by vigorously swinging the arms and head back on the takeoff. Then as the legs life from the board, the arms are forcefully moved forward to the waist of the diver. This reverse action of the arms gives added lift and rotating motion to the legs. The back of the diver must be made supple in order

Fig. 18-20. Back somersault, tuck.

to decrease the radius of the body movement and obtain the desired speed to the rotation at the peak of the dive. The knees must be stiffened very forcefully as the legs are thrust upward. The board can be sighted between the first half to three quarters of the first somersault, which helps in adjusting the speed and position of the dive.

As the horizontal position is reached when one and one fourth turns have been made, the arms are thrust straight toward the water. The body should arch in the entry.

As the water is sighted, the head is adjusted so that a vertical entry is made with arms stretched, legs extended, and toes pointed (Fig. 18-21).

Back one and one half somersault—pike. After the vertical reach of the arms, at shoulder width, the legs lift upward between the hands and backward over the head in the pike position. When the body is piked, the head is stretched slightly backward. The hands grasp the backs of the knees and hold the legs in a pike.

Fig. 18-21. Back one and one half somersault, layout.

The pike position is held for a full somersault. When the body has made one and one quarter turns on the 3-meter board, the opening of the pike is made, and the body straightens for the entry. The diver must keep his eyes open, and he should see the board at the completion of the one and a quarter somersaults when the legs are in line with the board.

When the legs are aimed directly at the board, the opening is made. The legs are held as if anchored in position as the body drops away from the pike for the straightening before the entry.

The eyes do not spot the water until the body is nearly straight. The arms open laterally from the knees and reach for the water below the head (Fig. 18-22).

Back one and one half somersault—tuck. A full extension of the body is made as the diver leaves the board. The chest lifts as the arms swing up above the head in front of the face. The head also lifts up with the eyes directly sighting the hands. The knees then

Fig. 18-22. Back one and one half somersault, pike.

Fig. 18-23. Back one and one half somersault, tuck.

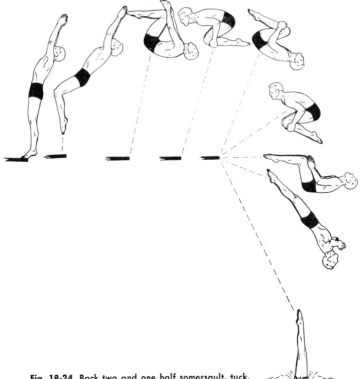

Fig. 18-24. Back two and one half somersault, tuck.

drive upward toward the hands. When the knees drive into the chest, the hands grasp the tucked legs just below the knees and pull them tight against the chest.

As the body completes one and one quarter somersaults, the hands release the legs just as the legs pass above the horizontal level. The legs extend with a snap as the arms quickly extend laterally over the head and the body straightens for the entry. In reaching for the entry, the back arches slightly, and the head tilts backward until the water is seen (Fig. 18-23).

A common error in executing this dive is reaching down for the legs on the takeoff, rather than lifting the legs to the arms that are overhead. The opening should be initiated by snapping the knees straight with great speed and holding them in place, and then the arms and head reach backward for the entry.

Back two and one half somersault—tuck.

The dive is started with the arms held straight at the elbows and at shoulder width as they reach directly upward and slightly backward. The toes, ankles, and knees extend forcefully to push the body upward. As soon as the legs have straightened in the

downward push on the board, the knees are lifted directly upward. The hips must not push forward. As the knees lift upward, the arms swing slightly forward to catch the shins. Immediately upon contact of the hands on the shins, the diver pulls firmly and tightens the tuck position into a close ball. As the diver senses the completion of the two and one fourth turns, he should feel the legs pulling up toward the board when the body is snapped straight. The legs straighten upward, aiming directly at the tip end of the diving board as the arms stretch directly at the water (Fig. 18-24).

Reverse dive (half gainer)—tuck.

The diver jumps forward and upward from the board, lifting his arms directly overhead and pointing his hands a bit forward as he rises from the board. Immediately as the diver jumps from the board, he begins to lift the knees up forward in front of the chest. The head is held erect, and the eyes are directed forward. The emphasis is on holding the trunk and arms steady as the knees lift up toward the chest. The arms lower just at the instant the knees reach the chest. The hands clasp about the shins momentarily at the peak of the dive; then suddenly the legs

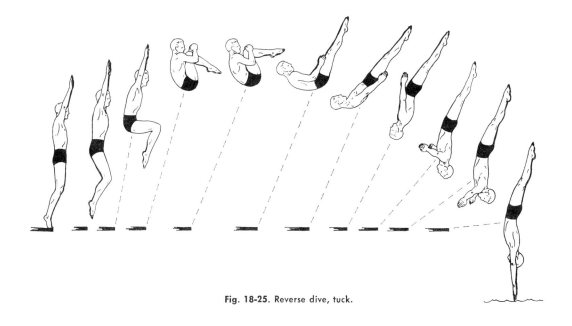

Fig. 18-25. Reverse dive, tuck.

snap upward, the body straightens downward, and the hands slide from the shins to the sides of the body. The chin remains tucked toward the chest as the diver straightens the body for a momentary look at the legs. This orients the diver to the position of his legs, thus giving him better judgment for the entry into the water. Next, the diver drops the head back and swiftly extends his arms laterally and downward toward the water until they are squeezed tightly against the head (Fig. 18-25).

Reverse dive—pike. This dive presents one of the most beautiful movements of the body when expertly mastered and controlled. The alternating movement of isolating the trunk from the legs during the lift and just the reverse during the drop is an esthetic achievement that requires a tremendous amount of practice to perform with finesse.

After the reach overhead with the hands held close together, the trunk is held firm, and the legs lift upward toward the hands. The feet touch the hands at the peek of the dive. The legs are very near vertical as the touch is made.

The unpike is made by dropping the body away from the legs as they are held just short of the vertical position.

The trunk should be relaxed as it falls away from the stretched legs and the arms are lowered laterally to a position below the head for a vertical entry (Fig. 18-26).

Reverse dive—layout. As the diver jumps from the board, his center of body weight (in the hips) should be directly over the base of support (balls of feet) so that the

Fig. 18-26. Reverse dive, pike.

body is easily projected forward and upward.

The hurdle and takeoff should be thoroughly mastered before any of the reverse group of dives are attempted. In learning the dives in this group the diver should jump out well away from the board until the mechanics and the body control are mastered. Then he may gradually move his dive nearer to the board. It is sometimes helpful for someone to hold a towel up high on the end of a pole, about 5 feet in front of the board so that the diver can aim the feet at it as an aid in moving the body out from the board.

The reverse dive, layout, is one of the most graceful of all the dives. It is, in its essentials, a backward dive from a forward takeoff. The diver actually gains distance in a forward direction; thus the name gainer was given to it. It is now called the reverse dive.

The arms lift to a spread position as the diver reaches upward on the takeoff. At the peak of the dive, the head and shoulders are levered backward, and the hips and legs are well stretched. The back arches over at the top of the dive as the head tilts back in search of the water. The arms remain in the lateral position until the water is seen and the diver approaches the water. The arms then close, the head is brought between the arms near the water, and the body straightens as it drops into a vertical entry (Fig. 18-27).

Reverse somersault—layout. At the takeoff as the arms swing swiftly overhead, the knees straighten abruptly, and the ankles and toes snap downward onto the board to thrust

Fig. 18-27. Reverse dive, layout.

the hips upward. The legs extend and the back arches as the diver leaves the board. The head pulls back in search of the water. As the body turns into the reverse somersault, the arms extend at right angles from the sides of the body.

As the body completes the three quarter turn, the arms lower to the front of the thighs, and the body is straightened for the vertical entry (Fig. 18-28).

Reverse somersault—pike. After the reach, the legs are brought upward where the hands grasp the backs of the knees. The hips are forced around the center of rotation by pulling the legs toward the chest. As the pike is made, the head remains in line with the body.

The diver stays in the pike position until over three fourths of a somersault is completed. The legs are then forced downward, and the head and shoulders are pressed backward as the toes reach for the feet-first vertical entry (Fig. 18-29).

Reverse somersault—tuck. After the body is stretched during the takeoff, the knees are lifted. The hands are poised above the head preparatory to grasping the shins just before the peak is reached and the knees are pulled sharply into the chest while the head remains in line with the body.

After the body has rotated backward so that the trunk is approaching the horizontal and the eyes are spotting the water, the legs move outward toward the tip of the board. The feet stretch toward the water, the head and shoulders are made erect, and the hands slide into position on the front of the thighs as a feet-first vertical entry is made (Fig. 18-30).

Flying reverse somersault—tuck. Perform the movements of the reverse dive, straight, until the body is falling away from the peak. The knees are then brought to the chest, and the hands pull the shins into a close tuck. This shortening of the radius of movement increases the speed of rotation considerably, and the body must untuck immediately so that the legs can be straightened downward

and a vertical feet-first entry can be made (Fig. 18-31).

Reverse one and one half somersault—tuck. In executing the reach on the takeoff, the arms reach shoulder width apart and above the face so that the knees can be lifted up to the hands for the tuck. The knees then lift to the chest, and the tuck is tightened by the pull of the hands just below the knees.

The tuck is held until a one and one quarter somersault is completed, and then the legs are released. The legs kick upward just above the horizontal line, and the arms reach laterally and stretch above the head for the entry. If the opening is made well above the level of the board, the diver will have sufficient time for a good stretch as the body is straightened before the entry (Fig. 18-32).

Fig. 18-28. Reverse somersault, layout.

Fig. 18-29. Reverse somersault, pike.

Fig. 18-30. Reverse somersault, tuck.

A common error in executing this dive occurs during the opening. Beginners are likely to hold the legs tucked while opening the arms and trunk. The legs should initiate the opening movement and then be held in place, while the arms and head reach back for the entry.

Reverse one and one half somersault—pike. In the reach both arms remain straight as they lift directly upward. The muscles of the arms, shoulders, and body must be tense to make the legs and body lift as a unit with the arm reach. Emphasis is placed on stiffening the knees just as the ankles and toes "snap" down into the board, thrusting the legs upward. The arms hold in the upward reach as the stomach and thigh muscles contract to aid in lifting the legs toward the arms. As the legs rise upward, the hands are clasped just behind the knees. As the reverse somersault turn is completed, the diver takes a glance at the water to orient himself to his position. The body continues to turn until the diver is in a sitting position, with the legs pointing slightly upward. The leg muscles tighten, holding the legs in this position as the stomach muscles relax, allowing the body to push back away from the legs. To help in checking or stopping the body spin as the legs are straightened, the eyes are

Fig. 18-31. Flying reverse somersault, tuck.

focused on the legs momentarily. Next, the head is tilted back as the eyes seek the point of entry. The arms reach outward laterally and then close together over the head (Fig. 18-33).

Reverse one and one half somersault— layout. As the diver lands on the board in the hurdle, he sweeps the arms swifly down past the hips and lifts then upward over the head. The emphasis is on forcefully stiffening the knees, ankles, and toes as they "snap" into the board, thrusting the body upward. The arms lift upward in a fully extended position and make a continual pull backward toward the board. As the legs rise

upward, the arms make a sudden change of direction. Instead of pulling away from the legs, they push swifly to rest against the front of the thighs. This helps the legs turn faster in the reverse somersault direction. There is always a continual backward pull with the head. When the body turns to a horizontal position at the completion of one and one fourth turns, the arms sweep in reach for the water, pulling the body into a vertical entry (Fig. 18-34).

Reverse two and one half somersault— tuck. As the diver leaves the board, the arms are held about shoulder width and lifted directly overhead. The legs are extended force-

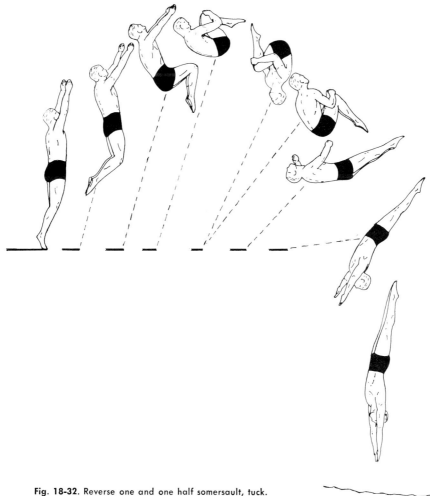

Fig. 18-32. Reverse one and one half somersault, tuck.

fully in the jump from the board, and the knees are lifted almost immediately upward toward the hands. The force from thrusting the knees upward and outward carries the diver safely away from the board. The hands move slightly forward at the peak of the lift to clasp high on the shins and quickly draw the knees tightly toward the chest.

As the diver senses the completion of two and one fourth turns, he releases his legs and tilts the head back to sight the water. Then the body snaps to a straight position, which helps to stop the rotating action. The legs kick upward at a slight angle as the arms are stretched directly for the water (Fig. 18-35).

Inward dive (cutaway)—tuck. The diver stands on the end of the board, facing inward. He jumps upward away from the board and turns a one half somersault forward to a head-first entry. In the takeoff, jump and push the legs slightly backward as the arms reach above the head and slightly forward. The hips then raise upward, and the legs draw under the body just as the arms are brought forward and downward to the shins. This contact in the tuck position is made at the peak of the dive. The head then tilts down until the eyes focus on the point of entry into the water. This causes enough rotation to put the diver's body in a head-foremost position. The legs then snap

Fig. 18-33. Reverse one and one half somersault, pike.

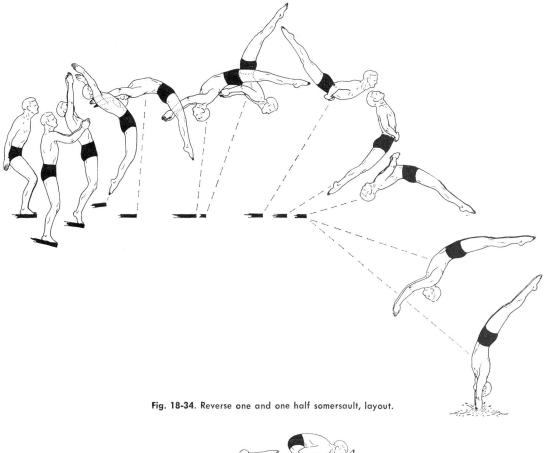

Fig. 18-34. Reverse one and one half somersault, layout.

Fig. 18-35. Reverse two and one half somersault, tuck.

Fig. 18-36. Inward dive, tuck.

Fig. 18-37. Inward dive, pike.

straight upward, and the hands slide from the shins to the hips as the body straightens. The arms then reach laterally and continue downward together for the entry (Fig. 18-36).

Inward dive—pike. While the body is poised over the end of the board, the center of weight is over the balls of the feet. During the preliminary arm movements of the takeoff, the center of weight remains in this position.

In the lift from the board, the arms raise above the head and in front of the face. Palms are facing forward and slightly depressed.

At the end of the reach, the hips flex and raise upward, the arms are brought forward and downward, and the hands touch the front of the feet at the peak. The hips lift above the head at the peak of the dive. The legs are vertical when the pike is effected. The eyes focus on the water at the peak of the dive.

The body begins to straighten as the diver drops from the peak of the dive.

As the body drops to the vertical entry, the arms reach forward, shoulder width apart, and stretch toward the bottom of the pool while the hips and legs are straightened in a well-controlled movement (Fig. 18-37).

Inward dive—layout. This dive is performed with a definite feeling of doing a forward swan dive toward the board. The emphasis, of course, is to lift the legs upward and backward to make the forward head-first rotation at a safe distance from the board. The timing of the arm swing and leg lift must 'be precise. The arms lift forward in front of the face and then move upward over the head.

While the body is poised on the end of the board, the center of weight is over the balls of the feet. In the preliminary arm movement of the takeoff, the arms press laterally downward and backward and continue forward past the hips as the knees flex, dropping the body into a crouched position. The arms continue lifting overhead with the head

directly in line with the body. The arms then are thrust downward laterally to the swan position. The downward thrust of the arms makes the lifting of the hips and legs an easy action. The knees, ankles, and toes extend down into the board and sharply "snap" rigidly upward and backward, forcing a moderate pike lift of the hips. The legs continue lifting, swiftly removing the pike, and begin to arch the body into a forward drive. It is important to keep the head erect in the takeoff and to rotate it only with the rotation of the body. One of the most common errors in this dive is bending the head downward toward the board too soon after the takeoff. It takes considerable courage to keep the head up and the eyes straight forward until the body begins to rotate into a head-foremost position. The arms remain "fixed" in this position until the diver is aiming head-first into the water. The arms quickly close overhead just above the surface of the water (Fig. 18-38).

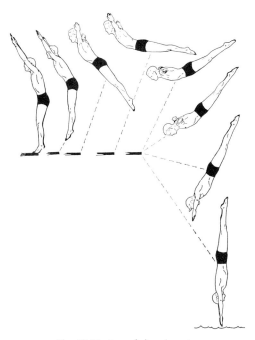

Fig. 18-38. Inward dive, layout.

Inward somersault—pike. In the takeoff, the knees and hips flex during the downward arm swing. Then simultaneously, as the arms lift up in front of the head, the legs begin pressing down onto the board. The toes, ankles, and knees extend, pushing into the board, and then the hips lift upward and back away from the board. This is followed immediately by a whip downward of the hands and the head. The head and shoulders are driven downward in chase of the lifting hips. The diver bends at the waist, grasping the legs behind the knees and keeping the legs straight. As the body rotates forward to a sitting position, the legs press down vertically, and the arms slide to the sides of the body. The head is held erect, looking at the board, and the shoulders move backward to counteract further rotation forward as the body straightens for a vertical feet-first entry (Fig. 18-39).

Inward somersault—tuck. In the takeoff the knees and hips flex during the downward arm swing. Then simultaneously as the arms lift up in front of the head, the legs begin pressing down into the board. The toes, an-

kles, and knees extend, pushing onto the board, and then the hips lift upward and back away from the board. As the hips lift upward, the arms and head drive downward in chase of the legs. The hands grasp the shins and pull the knees close to the chest. As the body spins forward to the sitting position, the legs snap directly down at the same time that the head and shoulders pull up and backward for the vertical entry (Fig. 18-40).

Inward one and one half somersault—pike. In the takeoff the knees and hips flex during the downward arm swing. Then simultaneously as the arms lift up in front of the head, the legs begin pressing down onto the board. The toes, ankles, and knees extend on the board while the hips move upward and back, followed immediately by a whip downward of the hands and the head. The hands clasp behind the knees and help to lift the hips in the direction of the spin. The emphasis is on keeping the head and shoulders erect and over the board in the takeoff until the hips begin to lift. The feeling is much like that of a forward one and

Fig. 18-39. Inward somersault, pike.

Fig. 18-40. Inward somersault, tuck.

Fig. 18-41. Inward one and one half somersault, pike.

one half pike, except that the hips and the legs push upward and back from the board. The diver "chases the legs around with the body" until the one and one half turns are completed. The water is then spotted, and the body straightens as the legs lift upward and the arms reach forward in front of the head for the vertical alignment (Fig. 18-41).

Inward one and one half somersault—tuck. In the takeoff the knees and hips flex during the downward arm swing. Then simultaneously as the arms lift up in front of the head, the legs begin pressing down onto the board. The toes, ankles, and knees extend onto the board driving the hips upward and back, with the heels lifting toward the buttocks. Immediately as the hips and legs are lifting from the board, the arms and the head whip downward, with the hands clasping the shins. It is important to keep the head and shoulders erect and over the board in the takeoff until the hips begin to lift. The feeling is much the same as for a forward one and one half somersault, tuck. The emphasis is on a continual tightening of the

tuck until the one and one half turns are complete. Upon spotting the water, the legs snap upward simultaneously overhead as the hands stretch for the water.

Common errors in executing this dive from the low board are: (1) lifting the head up during the takeoff (this causes loss of balance and control), (2) falling away from the board at the takeoff, and (3) pushing the hips away from the board instead of up above the head (the head and shoulders should cut down and under the hips) (Fig. 18-42).

Inward two and one half somersault—tuck. This dive must be started with the proper technique in the takeoff or it cannot be done. The diver must maintain good balance directly over the balls of his feet throughout the arm swing. As the arms circle past the hips and move upward, the knees and hips are flexed. The head is erect, and the eyes are focused forward at the other end of the board. Simultaneously as the legs straighten, thrusting the hips upward, the arms, in an extended position, sweep directly down and forward toward the board. The

Fig. 18-42. Inward one and one half somersault, tuck.

toes, ankles, and knees snap from the board, upward and outward, and the head and arms continue downward, "chasing" the legs. The hands grasp the shins, and the heels tuck tightly toward the buttocks as the diver begins a continual tightening of the tuck until the two and one half turns are complete. Generally the diver begins looking for the water too soon in the entry. Quite often he will reach his arms into the water first instead of simultaneously snapping his legs straight upward as the arms reach downward. The entry should be completely vertical (Fig. 18-43).

Forward dive, half twist—layout. The arms swing through the takeoff as in a swan dive, but immediately in the lift the arms begin turning the body sideward in a smoothly timed movement. The emphasis is on doing a quarter twist in the lift, with the arms held firmly at right angles to the body. The body should have very little arch. In the twist, one arm and shoulder press under the body, pointing toward the water as the other arm and shoulder turn toward the sky. The diver should have the feeling of doing a swan dive on his side. The eyes focus directly across the pool in the takeoff. As the body begins to descend head-first, the eyes are focused on the water. The twist is completed gradually as the diver nears the water. The arm extending upward is moved in a cartwheel motion laterally as it reaches downward toward the water to join with the other arm for the entry (Fig. 18-44).

Forward dive, half twist—pike. The body rises into the pike position at the peak as in the forward (jackknife) dive. When the

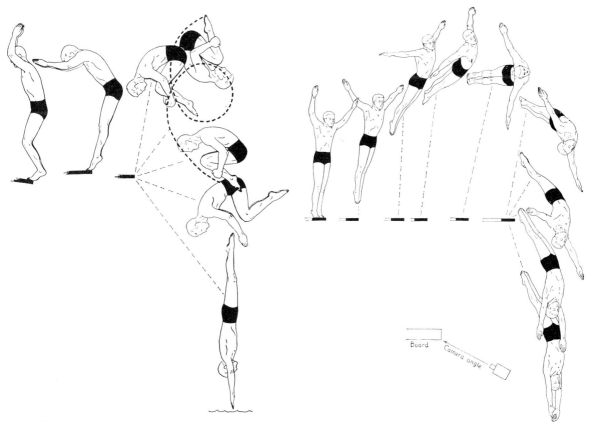

Fig. 18-43. Inward two and one half somersault, tuck.

Fig. 18-44. Forward dive, one half twist, layout.

diver is in the inverted V position as he un-pikes, the arm on the twisting side is swung around and in front of the legs as the shoulder is depressed. The opposite shoulder is raised, and the arm is borne backward. The hands steer an imaginary large wheel in the direction of the twist, and the legs bear constantly upward.

At the entry, the arms stretch toward the bottom of the pool to align the body straight for the entry (Fig. 18-45).

Forward dive, one twist—layout. The diver rises into the peak in the swan position. If the twist is toward the right, the left arm cuts in across the hip and bears downward. This movement lowers the left shoulder. The right arm is raised and centered above the head and becomes the long axis of rotation. The legs bear upward during the whole movement. A quarter twist is started, and the eyes hold a spot on the point of

entry until the twist is far enough to pull the head away. The half twist is made during the ascent to the peak, and the diver is now in a horizontal position. The twist is rapid and continual until completed.

The head is now turned sharply to the right as the right elbow drives backward and the eyes spot the water at the point of entry. The left arm is then extended toward point of entry, and the right arm joins the left in stretching toward the vertical entry. This stretching action should be emphasized in this dive because it squares the body so that the hips and shoulders are straightened at the entry.

All movements in this dive should center around the longitudinal axis of the diver. Movements of the shoulders must be loose so as to avoid any lateral action caused by strained movements of the arms.

A common error in performing this dive

Fig. 18-45. Forward dive, one half twist, pike.

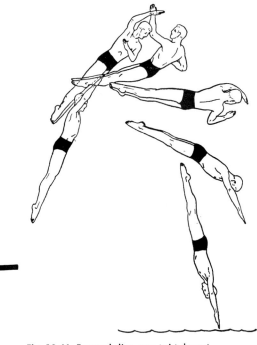

Fig. 18-46. Forward dive, one twist, layout.

is to drop a shoulder on the takeoff, causing the body to cast (Fig. 18-46).

Reverse dive (half gainer) with one half twist—layout. The lift from the takeoff is made as in the half reverse layout. As the body reaches the near-horizontal level at the peak of the dive with the arms well spread, the right arm is bent, with the elbow pulling behind the back and the arm coming to rest across the chest when the body twists to the right. The head is turned to the right, and the eyes sight the point of entry. The left shoulder is raised as the left arm is stretched upward in line with the longitudinal axis of the body. The legs bear upward throughout. These movements occur simultaneously, and there is no hesitation once they are started.

After slightly more than a one fourth turn has been made, the right arm pushes away from the chest and out to the side as the left

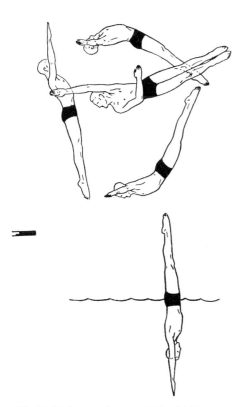

Fig. 18-47. Reverse dive, one half twist, layout.

arm also pushes out to a position straight from the shoulders. The shoulders and hips square for the vertical head-first entry by stretching the entire body and reaching for the bottom of the pool.

The arm mechanics in executing the twisting movements of this dive deviate from those described in other twisting dives. The deviation from the standard technique is used for the primary purpose of showing another standard method of arm technique in executing a twisting movement. The arm technique described in the preceding conforms to the law of action-reaction. As the arm swings straight across the chest, the body rolls toward the same side but in the opposite direction from that in which the arm is moving (Fig. 18-47).

Forward one and one half somersault, one twist—free. The diver takes off from the board as in a forward one and one half somersault in the open-pike position. As the legs begin the lift from the board, the legs move upward to straighten the body and simultaneously start the twist with both arms. In the twist one arm is brought across the front of the body while the other arm pulls behind the shoulder and over the head. The joint action initiates a fast pirouette as if the diver were standing vertically on his head in midair. The full twist is completed while the legs are still overhead. Just as the twist is being completed, the dive is "checked" by bending at the waist, pressing the hips downward and backward, and progressing toward the water head foremost. As the body is piked, the arms extend outward from the body. As the one and one half forward turns are completed, the eyes focus on the water, the body is held stationary, and the legs lift overhead to straighten into a head-first vertical position (Fig. 18-48).

Forward one and one half somersault, double twist—free. Take off from the board as in the forward one and one half somersault in the open-pike position. As the hips begin the lift from the board, the body straightens as the arms set high on the body to begin the twisting action. In twisting to the left, the right arm is started across the front of the body at the same time as the left arm pulls behind the head. Although the arms begin the initial twist while held straight, they quickly bend. The right arm bends firmly against the stomach, and the left arm bends over the head in the longitudinal axis. The fast pirouette is completed just as if the diver were standing vertically on his head in midair. As the body completes the second twist, the left arm straightens and pulls out to the side. Almost at the same time, the right arm extends laterally and the hips press downward and backward, progressing the body into a head-foremost position for the entry (Fig. 18-49).

Reverse one and one half somersault, one and one half twist—free. In the successful execution of the one and one half reverse dive, the initial start of the reverse layout must not be too arched. Throughout the takeoff of this dive, the muscles of the arms, shoulders, and body must be tense to make the body and arms lift as a unit. In making the lift from the board, the arms lift fully extended, pulling the body upward. There is tremendous emphasis on stiffening the legs as they thrust upward and outward. Hesitate from starting the twist until the legs rise to almost a horizontal position. The head should remain in a straight position with the body as the legs lift upward from the board. Then suddenly the twist is initi-

Fig. 18-48. Forward one and one half somersault, one twist, free.

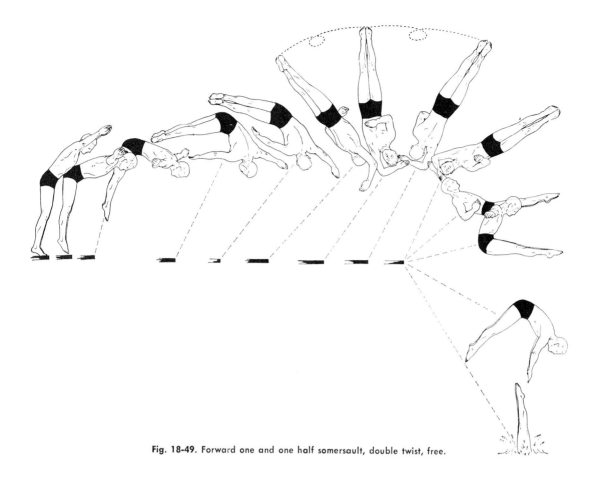

Fig. 18-49. Forward one and one half somersault, double twist, free.

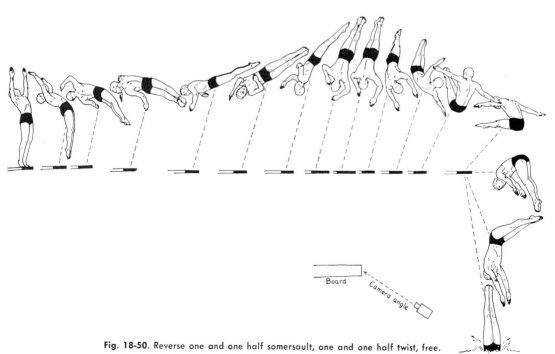

Board

Camera angle

Fig. 18-50. Reverse one and one half somersault, one and one half twist, free.

Fig. 18-51. Back one and one half somersault, one and one half twist, free.

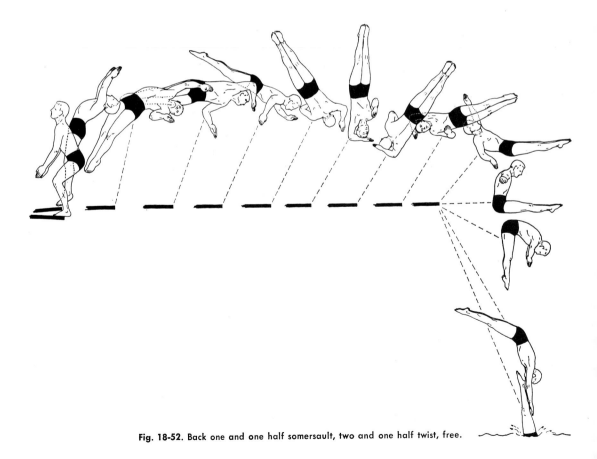

Fig. 18-52. Back one and one half somersault, two and one half twist, free.

ated, with the head, arms, and shoulders pulling backward. The twist is started with both arms simultaneously, the one elbow sharply pulling behind the shoulders as the other arm presses stiffly across and over the head and then bending firmly against the stomach. The secret to a fast pirouetting twist is to simultaneously tighten the body and snap into the twist and the arms and hips. It is important to keep the head tilted back slightly throughout the twist.

To check the body at the one and one half twist, the arm is pulled down to a lateral position to create a bend at the hips. The legs press downward and backward simultaneously as the arms press outward and downward. The chest presses down toward the legs, turning the body forward into a head-foremost position. As the one and one half forward turn is completed, the eyes spot the water, and the legs lift upward for the vertical entry (Fig. 18-50).

Back one and one half somersault, one and one half twist—free. The takeoff is begun just as it is for the back one and one half layout. Both arms lift upward above the head and at shoulder width as the diver looks skyward. There is considerable emphasis on initiating a forceful arch of the body in the thrust upward. This is done by overemphasizing the backward swing of the arms when depressing the board on the takeoff. The twist is begun immediately as the body arches upward from the board. The legs lift swiftly as the twist with the head, arms, and shoulders is begun. The twist is started by both arms moving simultaneously; the one elbow sharply jerks behind the back as the other arm sweeps across and above the head and then bends firmly down against the chest. The secret of a fast pirouetting twist is to simultaneously tighten the body, removing the arch quickly as the diver snaps into the twist with the arms. It is important to keep the head tilted back throughout the the start of the dive and the twist. The diver will have difficulty if he arches the body too far backward and downward in the takeoff instead of arching the body almost straight

up over the board. To check the twisting action at the one and one half twist, the top arm pulls down causing a bend at the hips, pressing the chest toward the legs. The arms then simultaneously push out laterally to the side. The legs push downward and backward as the somersault progresses head foremost. As the one and one half forward turn is completed, the eyes are fixed on the water, and the legs move upward to allow for a vertical entry (Fig. 18-51).

Back one and one half somersault, two and one half twist—free. Begin the takeoff and arm swing as in the back one and one half somersault, layout. Both arms lift upward at shoulder width and the head tilts back. There is considerable emphasis on initiating a forceful arch of the chest in the thrust upward. The twist is begun immediately as the body arches upward from the board. The legs lift swiftly as the twist begins with the head, arms, and shoulders. The twist is started with both arms moving simultaneously. In a twist to the left, the left arm bends as the elbow sharply jerks back while the right arm, remaining straight at first and then bending, sweeps across and above the head. Then a smooth and continuous exchange of arm positions takes place. The right arm bends down across the chest, and the left arm moves to a bent-elbow position above the head.

This latter position is held throughout the remainder of the twist. It is important to constantly pull in the direction of the twist and to keep the head tilted back. As the body turns for the completion of the two and one half twists, the change from the twisting action to the forward somersaulting progression takes place. To initiate the check in the twist, the left arm is snapped briskly downward and outward as the chest and other arm bend downward toward the legs. The hips and legs continue downward and backward as the somersault progresses head foremost. As the one and one half forward turn is completed, the eyes are fixed on the water, and the legs lift upward to allow for vertical entry (Fig. 18-52).

Chapter 19

Teaching and coaching
tower diving

INTRODUCTION

Tower diving presents one of the most thrilling and breathtaking experiences found in any sport. Diving from the high platform and floating through the air while executing certain controlled spins and gyrations before entering the water with hardly a splash never ceases to thrill the performer and spectator. Tower diving, like springboard diving, was introduced in the United States by the English at the turn of the century, and soon several springboard divers in America were trying this new sport. When tower diving was added to the 1904 Olympic Games as a new event, G. E. Sheldon won the first gold medal in diving for the United States. Since that time, the Americans have produced more diving champions from the tower than all of the other countries in the world combined. The western part of the United States has produced nearly all of the great male and female tower divers. This has been credited mainly to the longer outdoor practice time provided by ideal weather conditions along with more outdoor tower facilities than are found in any other section of the country.

The present tower diving regulations state that the diver may dive from the 10-meter platform in competition only.*

Diving from a height of 10 meters requires an abundance of courage, self-confidence, strength, body control, agility, de-sire, and coordination. A poorly executed dive from this height can result in a serious injury to the diver by his landing on the surface of the water. It is highly recommended that the diver first become somewhat proficient on the 3-meter springboard before attempting the dives from a level that is nearly three stories high.

TYPES AND CONSTRUCTION OF DIVING TOWERS

Most of the regulation towers built in this country have platforms at 5 and 10 meters. A few of these also have 7½-meter platforms. Today, the ideal tower is one with platforms at levels of 1, 3, 5, 7½, and 10 meters. The diver can learn tower diving with greater confidence and safety by first practicing the lead-up dives and desired dives on the lower platforms before trying them from the 10-meter level. The general size of the platform should be at least 22 feet long and 10 feet wide. Many modern designs are used in the construction of diving towers throughout the world, with Germany having the most modern and greatest variety.* Perhaps the most popular design in America is that with the vertical support being rectangular in shape and rising straight up or slanting toward the pool.

Diving towers are made of one or more of the following materials: cement with reinforced steel, steel tubing, steel beams,

---

*Amateur Athletic Union of the United States: Official swimming handbook, New York, 1967, Amateur Athletic Union of the United States, p. 71.

*Fabian, Dietrich: Modern swimming pools of the world, Florence, Ala., 1958, National Pool Equipment Company.

wood, or aluminum. Towers made of cement with reinforced steel seem to be the most common type, for they provide very sturdy platforms. Steel tubing and steel beams have also become quite popular in recent years. Wooden tower structures are fast becoming obsolete because they are not as safe or durable as those made of other materials. Several colleges and universities are now building indoor pools with diving towers. Many of these have been made of aluminum with steel or aluminum supports suspended from the ceiling.

The platforms are usually made with steel beam supports and surfaced with cement or wood. The surfaces are then covered with cocoa matting or some other nonskid material. Cocoa matting is most often used, for it provides a soft surface for the diver's feet and prevents him from slipping. It should be noted that, before covering the platform with cocoa matting, the matting should be soaked in water for nearly one half hour and then tacked, nailed, or tied immediately to the platform surface. This will give a smooth running surface for the divers because cocoa matting stretches when it is wet and shrinks as it dries. If the matting is not secured in this manner, it develops folds as it gets wet during use and gives the platform a bumpy running surface. A bumpy surface can easily cause the diver to trip or stumble when attempting a dive, which could result in a painful injury. Aluminum grating has been used as a surface for some new indoor platforms, and it has proved to be quite successful although it is a little rough on the feet.

Outdoor diving towers should be constructed to face north or south. This will prevent the sun from shining directly in the eyes of the diver during the early and late part of the day. The depth of the water for a 10-meter tower should be no less than 15 feet. Whenever possible, the diving towers should be built in an area that is separate from the swimming area. Most modern structures are built with separate diving wells or in pools with L or T shapes so that the diving does not interfere with the swimming.

LEARNING TO TOWER DIVE

The success of the diver in learning to tower dive depends on many different factors: the diver's personal makeup, the kind of tower and the height of the platform levels available, the background and experience of the diver, the experience and competency of the coach, the goal desired by the diver, the experienced tower divers available who can help demonstrate and encourage the learner, the temperature of the air and water, and the length of the diving season.

When first learning to tower dive, the diver should try first to make a mental and physical adjustment to the added height from which he may be diving. The beginner should realize that from 10 meters the body is traveling at approximately 32 miles an hour when it hits the water. He must recognize that the impact on the water when diving from this height is much greater than when diving from a 3-meter springboard. The diver must learn the different tower approaches and takeoffs and adjust to the lift from a solid and immobile platform. He must also discipline himself to make every effort to complete a dive that is started regardless of a faulty takeoff or poor execution of the dive in the air. Many divers have been hurt as a result of changing their minds in the middle of a dive.

Nearly every tower diver will agree that, when first learning, the difficult part of tower diving is to stand on the 10-meter platform and look down at the water and surrounding area. However, once the diver starts to learn some dives, the tower does not appear nearly so high. Whether the diver is well experienced or a beginner, it is always a challenging and thrilling experience when learning a new dive from the top platform. When executing a dive such as the forward two and one half somersault,

220 / *Swimming and diving*

the diver finds that the tower does not seem nearly as high as he first believed, for he does not spot the water at the completion of the somersaults until he is around 10 or 15 feet from the water. Actually, the time the diver is in the air when diving from the 10-meter platform is nearly the same as when diving from the 3-meter springboard, since the diver goes higher from the point of takeoff on the springboard than from the tower.

The actual execution of the dive from the 10-meter platform is basically the same as from the 3-meter springboard with the following exceptions: the takeoffs differ because there is no spring in the high platforms, the timing of the dives differs because of the differences in height, and the impact upon the surface of the water differs with height. It must also be understood that some dives that are easy to perform on the springboard are not easy to execute from the high platforms. For example, the front dive with a half twist, layout, is considered a basic dive from the 3-meter springboard, but it is a very tricky dive to execute properly from the tower. Other popular springboard dives that are rarely performed on the tower are: the front dive with a full twist; the back dive with a half twist; the back one and one half somersault, tuck or pike; the inward one and one half somersault, tuck; and the forward two and one half somersault, tuck.

The kind of dives a diver learns on the tower and how well he is able to execute these dives depend almost entirely on the diver's experience on the 3-meter springboard. For instance, a person who can successfully execute a three and one-half somersault on the springboard has little difficulty learning the same dive from the tower because he has learned the motor skills and feeling of spinning three and one half times. On the other hand, a person who has never done more than one and one half somersaults from the springboard will have great difficulty learning any forward somersault

dives beyond a one and one half somersault from the high tower.

The diver's personal makeup in reference to his courage, strength, desire, ability, and so on has a direct bearing on the diver's progress on the tower. Some divers learn tower diving very quickly because they have control of their fears and they have confidence in their abilities. This type of diver can usually take a lot of punishment when learning new dives and generally learns the dives he desires.

When learning to tower dive, most divers like to try the dive or the lead-up dive from a lower level before trying the dive from the 10-meter platform. This is almost mandatory in learning some dives. However, when the desired lower platform is not available to the diver, he either takes a chance on trying the dive without the desired build up or he postpones the learning of the dive. In the case where the tower does not extend to 10 meters, the diver can learn only those dives that can be executed from the lower platforms. It should then be concluded that the dives learned by the diver have much to do with the height of the diving towers that are available to him.

It is most important that when learning to tower dive the diver should have an experienced coach or experienced divers present, or both. The coach is usually aware of the learner's abilities and diving experience so that he can do much in directing and teaching the diver the dives within the range of his abilities. The coach can direct the proper actions in the takeoff and execution of the dive and then make corrections once the dive is attempted. If experienced divers are available, they can demonstrate the dives and do much in encouraging the learner to try them. It must be noted that persons who have not developed a sound background in tower diving should not attempt to coach or teach beginners on the tower, since their lack of knowledge could easily result in the diver being injured. Also, the beginning tower diver should not try new dives from the high platforms without a competent coach or experienced tower diver present.

It is not uncommon for an experienced 3-meter springboard diver to learn a dozen or more dives from the high platform the first day he attempts tower diving. Quite often a springboard diver will learn a full competitive list of dives on the 10-meter tower the day before or on the day of an important meet. On the other hand, many competent springboard divers have spent years learning a full list of tower dives.

It is very difficult to learn to tower dive when the weather is cold. The muscles of the diver tense up to such a degree that it is difficult for him to function properly. Cold water also provides a harder surface than warm water. Therefore, if the diver wishes to learn a new dive, he should try it when the water is relatively warm. Sometimes the need for learning certain dives for an important meet will inspire the diver to learn or try new dives from the top platform when the weather is very poor or the water is very cold, or both. Although poor weather conditions cannot be controlled, the diver can avoid uncomfortable conditions such as these by attempting only those dives he is absolutely sure he can execute safely. The welfare and safety of the diver is much more important than the learning of a new dive. The coach should not, however, let the diver use the weather or the water temperature as an excuse for not practicing.

The length of the outdoor season often has much to do with the learner. It is imperative then that the divers living in the north should carefully plan their practice sessions and try to get in as much tower diving as possible during the warm summer months.

TOWER APPROACHES AND TAKEOFFS

Because of the solid platform, the tower diver uses several approaches and takeoffs that differ from those used on the springboard. Although the diver cannot jump as

high from the platform as from the springboard, he finds the platform a much more dependable takeoff point than the often unpredictable springboard. In some instances, the diver may use the same type of approach or takeoff from the tower as he uses on the springboard. The diver often has more than one choice in the approach or takeoff when executing certain dives from the tower. The approach and takeoff most desirable is one that will give him the maximum lift and control from the tower and the one that he can perform consistently.

The rules governing the approach and takeoff from the platforms are not quite as rigid as those for the springboard, but they do require the diver to make as many smooth and natural actions as possible. It may be safe to say that, if the action on the approach and takeoff contributes to the dive's execution, then the action is permissible. The beginner should execute fundamental dives when practicing the different approaches and takeoffs from the tower. This will ensure safety to the diver and permit him to concentrate better on the desired actions. The approaches and takeoffs most commonly used when diving from the platforms are as follows.

Forward approaches and takeoffs. Forward approaches and takeoffs in tower diving include the standing takeoff, the running approach with either a one- or two-foot takeoff, and the running skip approach with a one-foot takeoff.

Standing takeoff. The diver walks to the edge of the platform and stands near the end, with the feet together and the toes on or curled over the edge. The arms are raised in front of the diver to a position shoulder width apart and at shoulder height. This stance is the same one used when standing backward on the springboard. The diver then takes off from the platform in one of the two following ways:

1. The arms drop to the sides from the stance, then lift overhead and are thrust forward and downward as the

Text continued on p. 226.

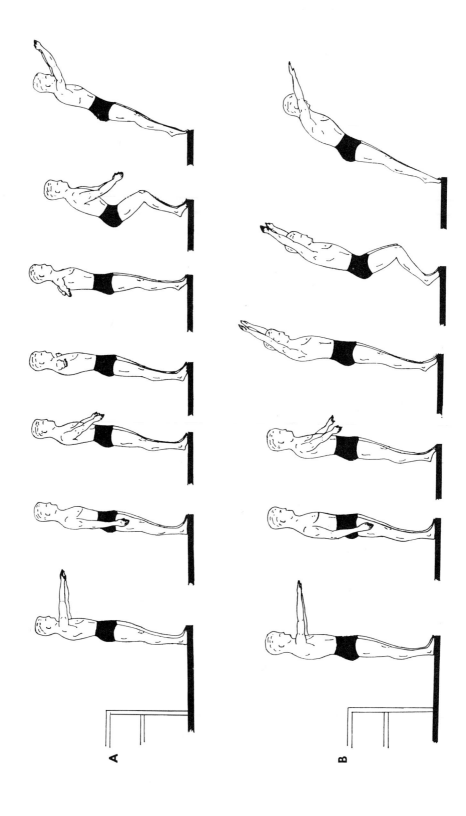

A

B

Fig. 19-1. A series of ideal form showing forward approaches and takeoffs commonly used in tower diving. **A,** Standing takeoff used for forward spinning dives. **B,** Takeoff for standing reverse dives and front dives. **C,** Running approaches with a one-foot takeoff, used when executing swan dives, reverse dives in the layout position, and front dives with a full twist in the layout position.

Continued.

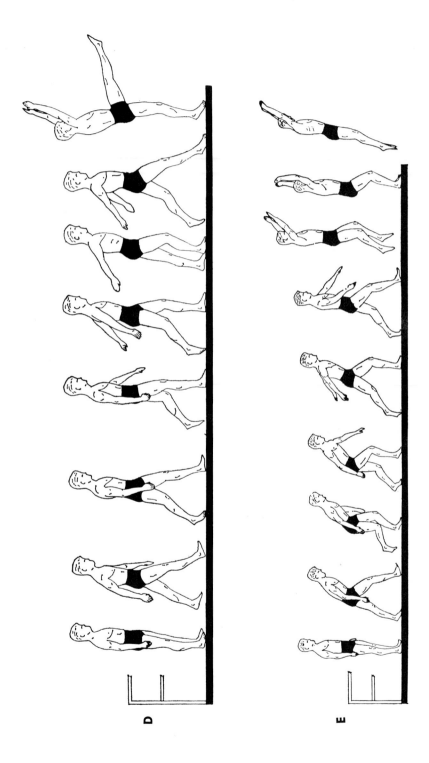

D

E

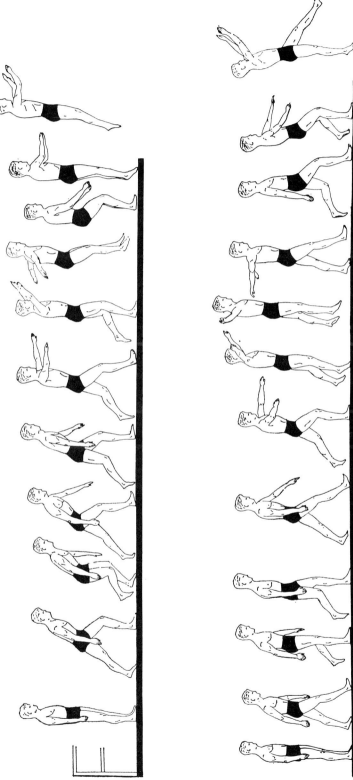

Fig. 19-1, cont'd. D, Running approach with a one-foot takeoff, used when executing reverse somersault dives and reverse twisting somersault dives. **E,** Running approach with a two-foot takeoff, used when executing reverse somersault dives, reverse twisting somersault dives, and forward twisting somersault dives. **F,** Running approach with a two-foot takeoff, similar to springboard style of approach. **G,** Running skip approach with a one-foot takeoff, used in executing reverse somersault dives, reverse twisting somersault dives, and swan dives.

hips lift upward. This action is used for standing forward spinning dives (Fig. 19-1, *A*).

2. The arms are first dropped to the sides from the stance position. There they lift upward in front of the body above shoulder height and swing behind the body, along the sides, then forward, and upward as when executing the forward takeoff from the springboard. This takeoff is used for standing reverse dives and front dives (Fig. 19-1, *B*).

Running approach with a one-foot takeoff. The diver runs easily but forcefully to the end of the platform, placing one foot near the edge as he pushes off the platform with this foot. The arms swing backward, then forward along the sides, and then upward as the diver prepares to lift from the platform. This type of takeoff is used when executing swan dives, reverse dives in the layout position, and the front dive with a full twist in layout position (Fig. 19-1, *C*). When the diver wishes to execute reverse somersaults and reverse twisting somersaults, he uses the same approach except that he walks to the end of the tower instead of running. The arm swing is also more forceful when executing the more difficult dives (Fig. 19-1, *D*).

Running approach with a two-foot takeoff. The diver takes a run toward the end of the platform. The force of the run depends on the dive that is to be performed. As he nears the end of the platform, the diver raises the arms overhead while taking a low short hop to the end of the platform where he lands on both feet simultaneously (Fig. 19-1, *E*). Another style may be used that is similar to the one used on the springboard. This is where the arms circle behind the body, along the sides, then forward, and upward as the feet land near the edge of the platform (Fig. 19-1, *F*). These two takeoffs are used when performing front dives, forward somersault dives, and forward twisting somersault dives.

Running skip approach with a one-foot takeoff. The diver walks toward the edge of the platform. As he nears the edge, the back foot is moved up to the heel of the front foot. The weight is then placed on the ball of the back foot, and the front foot takes a short step forward. The weight of the body is then placed on the front foot as the back leg swings forward and upward as when kicking a football. During this kicking action, the arms swing along the sides of the body, then forward and upward to aid in the upward lift of the body from the platform. This type of approach and takeoff is used when executing reverse somersault dives, reverse twisting somersault dives, and swandives (Fig. 19-1, *G*).

Back takeoffs. Back takeoffs include the springboard takeoff and the tower takeoff.

Springboard takeoff. The diver stands backward on the edge of the platform and uses the same movements as when taking off from the springboard. The flexion of the legs and ankles is not as deep as when springing from the springboard because the platform does not provide for any springing movement. This type of takeoff is used for all backward dives (Fig. 19-2, *A*).

Tower takeoff. Unlike the springboard backward takeoff, the arms raise overhead from the stance position and are then thrust forward and downward in front of the body as the hips lift upward. This type of takeoff is used when executing the inward dives (Fig. 19-2, *B*).

Armstand approaches and takeoffs. In all armstand dives, the head is in a position where the eyes can sight the water throughout the execution of the armstand. Some divers prefer to place the fingers, up to the first joint, over the edge of the platform when executing the armstand, whereas others prefer to place the whole hand on the surface of the platform near the edge. The armstand must be held for several seconds to exhibit control before the diver can begin the execution of a dive from this position. Once the armstand is assumed, the legs

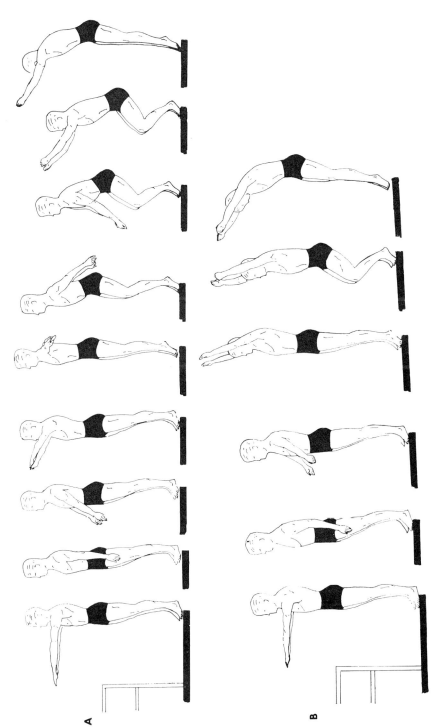

Fig. 19-2. A series of ideal form showing back takeoffs used in tower diving. **A,** Springboard takeoff, used for all backward dives. **B,** Tower takeoff, used for inward dives.

Fig. 19-3. One-leg kick-up.

Fig. 19-4. Press up in the tuck position.

Fig. 19-5. Press up in the pike position.

must be straight and together with the feet extended and the toes pointed. The back is slightly arched and the arms are straight and shoulder width apart.

One-leg kick-up. The diver kneels and assumes a "track start" position with one leg tucked in close to the chest while the other leg is extended behind the body. The hands are placed shoulder width apart on or near the end of the platform. The handstand is executed by kicking the back leg overhead as the tucked leg pushes the trunk upward. The tucked leg then extends and comes together with the other leg to form the armstand (Fig. 19-3).

Press up in the tuck position. The diver squats down near the end of the platform, with the knees together and the hands placed on or near the edge of the platform. The diver leans forward with the shoulders slightly in front of the hands. Then with the arms slightly bent, the diver pushes off with his feet and lifts the hips and tucked legs overhead. The legs extend as they lift overhead, and the arms straighten to form the armstand (Fig. 19-4).

Press up in the pike position. The diver stands near the end of the platform and bends over with the legs straight and places the hands on or near the edge of the platform. The legs are spread apart as the diver assumes the position for the handstand. When the hands are placed on the platform, the diver leans forward with the shoulders slightly in front of the hands and pushes the legs upward from the tips of his toes. The hips move slightly forward as the legs lift upward. As the straight legs lift overhead, the hips move back slightly to keep the body from falling off the platform. The arms then straighten as in doing the armstand from the tuck position (Fig. 19-5).

BASIC TOWER DIVES

A beginner on the high platform should learn certain basic dives before attempting some of the more difficult dives. The advantages of the diver learning basic dives

first are quite obvious. First of all, he can more easily adjust to the proper takeoff from the solid platform by doing dives that are relatively easy. Second, the diver can adjust more easily to the different heights and therefore reduce the chance of injury if he first learns dives that are considered basic. Many of these preliminary dives can be learned by attempting them on the 5-meter platform and then trying them on the high platform. Naturally, learning some of the basic dives on the 10-meter platform is greatly simplified if graduated platforms are available. Some of the basic tower dives are as follows:

1. Running front one and one half somersault—open or closed pike
2. Standing front dive—pike or layout
3. Back somersault—layout
4. Inward dive—pike or layout
5. Armstand, cut through—tuck
6. Flying forward one and one half somersault—pike
7. Reverse somersault—layout
8. Back dive—pike or layout
9. Standing reverse dive—pike or layout
10. Inward one and one half somersault—closed or open pike

The diver should recognize that some of these dives are more difficult to perform when attempted from the lower platforms, that is, some of these dives are actually easier to execute from the 10-meter platform than from the 5-meter level. This is especially true in the armstand dive, the flying forward one and one half somersault, and the reverse somersault.

Running front one and one half somersault—open pike. The diver makes a running approach to the end of the platform, landing near the edge on both feet, and uses one of the two actions shown in Fig. 19-1, *E* and *F*. As the diver jumps from the platform, the hips lift upward, and the body bends at the waist to form a pike position. The arms pull down laterally from overhead and move to a position level with the shoulders to form an open pike position. The downward lateral action of the arms aids in the forward rotation of the body. The diver can sight the water just as he leaves the platform, but, once the pike position is assumed, he sights his legs as he begins to somersault. Remaining in the open pike position, the diver looks for the water as he passes three quarters of a somersault. At this time, the diver begins to reach downward toward the water at an angle slightly short of vertical as his legs continue to rotate. This causes the body to straighten as it drops toward the water. The action of the somersault is controlled by the abdominal and thigh muscles along with proper timing in the reach for the water with the arms. As the diver

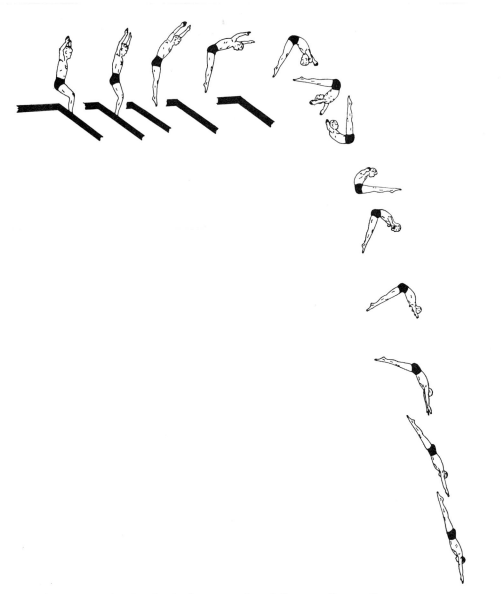

Fig. 19-6. Running front one and one half somersault, open pike.

nears the surface of the water, the arms stretch over the head in line with the body. The body straightens completely as it enters the water slightly short of a vertical position (Fig. 19-6).

Standing front dive—layout. The diver assumes a stance on the edge of the platform similar to that used when executing back-ward dives except that he stands facing the water. He then drops his arms to his sides momentarily before lifting them laterally and slightly in front of the body. As the arms near shoulder level, they circle back just behind the body and swing down past the hips. The arms bend at the elbow as they pass the hips and lift overhead. The

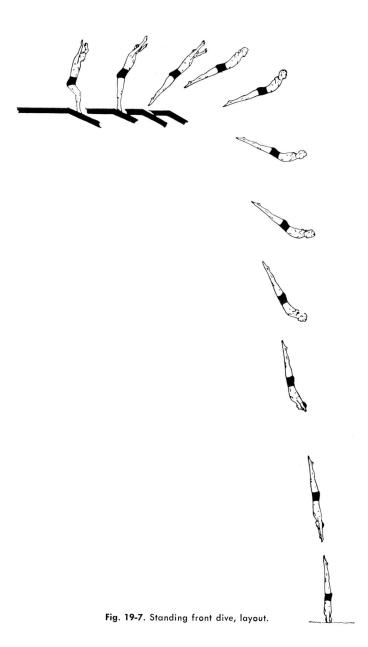

Fig. 19-7. Standing front dive, layout.

legs are coordinated with the arms as on the takeoff from the springboard, except that the legs do not bend as much at the knees and the jumping action is much faster on the platform.

As the diver jumps from the platform, the arms extend quickly and firmly to a position at right angles to the body and at shoulder level. The head remains in line with the body with the eyes looking straight ahead. The jump from the tower should not be too forceful if control of the dive is to be retained and assured. There is absolutely no movement in the body as it drops toward the water except that the eyes sight the water after the diver has dropped approximately 10 feet. Unlike the swan dive from the springboard, the legs do not lift upward after the diver leaves the platform. Instead, the body drops below the legs as the diver moves closer to the water. The body approaches a position slightly short of vertical as the diver nears the water. At this time, the arms extend directly overhead with the eyes sighting the water at the point where the body will enter. The entry is made with the hands clasped and the body stretched as much as possible (Fig. 19-7).

Back somersault—layout. The diver assumes a backward stance and then drops his arms momentarily to his sides. He then lifts the arms laterally and slightly in front of the body before circling them as shown in Fig. 19-2, *A*. The diver leans back slightly on the takeoff and then jumps up as much toward the vertical as possible. The jump is made by extending the legs and lifting the chest and head upward as the arms lift forward and upward over the head. The back arches almost immediately as the chest and head continue to lift upward, and the arms pull laterally to a swan position.

The water comes into view as the diver completes one half of the somersault. When the water is sighted, the diver can then adjust the somersault for the entry by controlling the arch in his back with the use of the stomach and thigh muscles and also by slightly changing the position of the arms. As the diver nears the water, the arms are brought down to the sides at the thighs by passing slightly in front of the body. This prevents the diver from going over on the dive, and it also eliminates most of the arch in the back. The eyes continue to sight the water almost to the time when contact is made with the water. At this last instant the head lifts to a position directly in line with the body, and the eyes sight the edge of the pool (Fig. 19-8).

Inward dive—pike. The diver drops the arms momentarily to his sides from the back stance position. The arms are then lifted laterally to a position directly over the head. With the arms remaining overhead, the diver jumps upward and slightly backward from the platform. In this action the hips drive upward, and the arms move straight down in front of the body to form a pike position. The head is lifted very slightly as the pike is made to allow the diver to sight the water and also to permit body control. The hands touch the insteps at the peak of the dive. The diver actually drops 3 or 4 feet in this position before the legs begin to swing backward and the arms start reaching for the water. In reaching downward for the water, the arms spread to a position about shoulder width to provide increased balance. The legs continue to swing back and upward during this action, and the head remains in an unstrained position with the eyes sighting the water directly below. The body straightens as the diver nears the water, with the arms extending over the head and the legs lifting upward. A breath of air is taken after the pike is made to prevent the diver from arching his back as he nears the water. The vertical entry into the water is made after the hands are clasped, and the body stretches as much as possible (Fig. 19-9).

Armstand, cut through—tuck. Once the armstand is assumed, the diver should hold the position for a short time to show that he has complete control of the armstand.

The diver begins the dive by leaning the entire body forward away from the platform. This is done by pushing the legs forward slightly, causing the body to lean. The body pivots at the shoulders as it leans over the edge of the platform. This places the arms at an angle with the body while the hands are still in contact with the platform. During the armstand and the leaning of the body, the head remains lifted slightly so that the water can be sighted throughout the entire dive. As the diver continues to lean forward, the hands push away from the platform, and the legs, which bend at the knees, pull down toward the chest. The hands grab high on the shins to form a tuck position for a brief second. The hands then release the legs, which extend toward the water, and the arms lift laterally to a swan position. A straight body position with the arms extended at right angles is maintained until the diver nearly reaches the water. At the

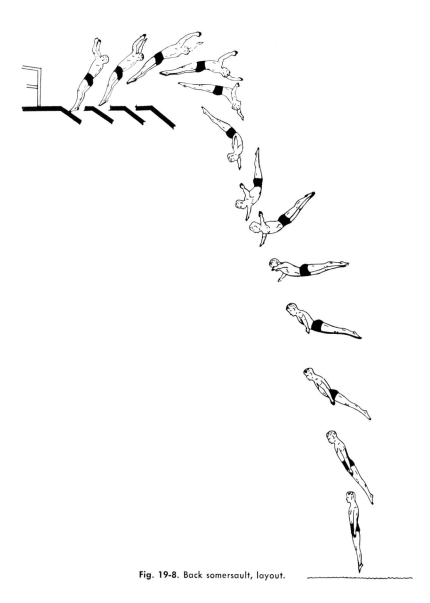

Fig. 19-8. Back somersault, layout.

last instant the arms drop slightly in front of the body to the sides for a vertical feet-first entry (Fig. 19-10).

Flying forward one and one half somer-sault—pike. The takeoff is made with the diver landing with both feet near the end of the platform and with the arms raised overhead. As the diver jumps from the plat-form, the legs push upward, the arms pull down laterally to a swan position, and the head lifts slightly to help create an arch in the back. The eyes sight the water during the flying position. This position is main-tained until the body has rotated for ap-proximately one half of a somersault. The body then changes to a pike position as it passes a vertical position. This is accom-plished by pulling the head in toward the

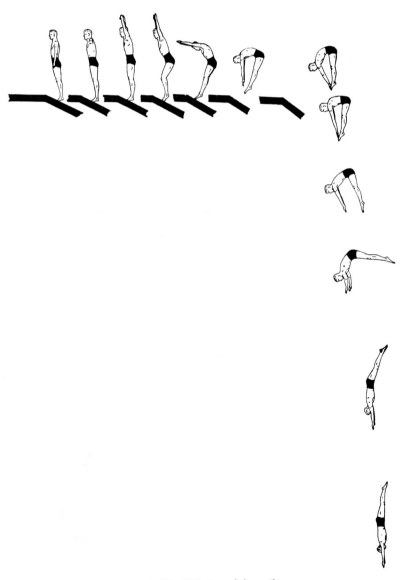

Fig. 19-9. Inward dive, pike.

chest and bending at the waist by contracting the abdominal and hip muscles. The arms remain at right angles during the change in body positions. This helps to control the speed of the somersault as the body changes position. The water can be sighted as the diver completes three quarters of a somersault. At this time, the diver begins to reach for the water as the legs continue

to rotate to a position above the head. The arms extend over the head, and the body straightens as it enters the water slightly short of vertical (Fig. 19-11).

Reverse somersault—layout. The diver leaves the platform by kicking one leg upward while lifting the arms, chest, and head. The other leg is then lifted to meet the kicking leg as the arms spread to a swan posi-

Fig. 19-10. Armstand, cut through, tuck.

tion, the head continues to pull back, and the back arches. The water is sighted as one half of a somersault is completed. The diver continues to arch the back and lift the head as the body continues to rotate. The arms are used to control the speed of the somersault as the diver nears the water. The eyes continue to sight the water in order to make the proper body adjustment for the entry. As the diver nears a complete somersault in the layout position, the arms move slightly in front of the body as they drop to the sides for a vertical feet-first entry (Fig. 19-12).

Back dive—pike. The arms circle around behind the body and then reach directly overhead with the head in line with the body as the diver jumps from the platform. The diver leans back slightly before he jumps upward in order to miss the tower.

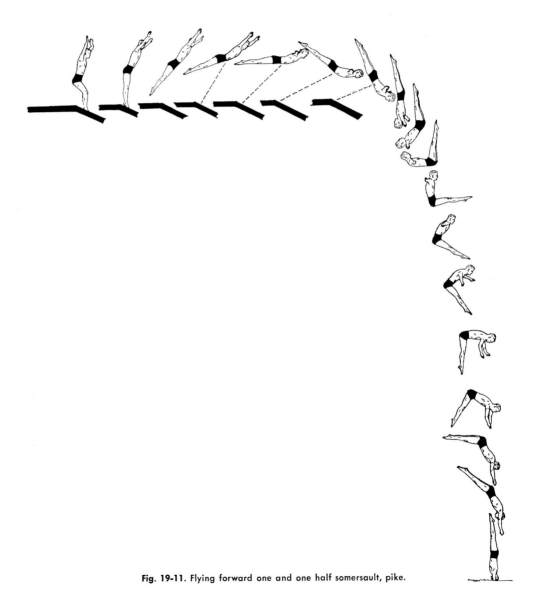

Fig. 19-11. Flying forward one and one half somersault, pike.

The legs are then lifted upward by contracting the thigh and stomach muscles. As the legs near a vertical position, the arms move forward slightly, and the hands touch the feet at the insteps. The touch is made just as the body begins to drop downward toward the water. The head is in a position that allows the diver to watch his hands touch the feet. After the touch, the arms move laterally as they extend over the head.

In the same motion, the head tilts back in search of the water, and the back arches slightly. The legs drop a little as the arms extend over the head, but this movement is compensated by the slight arch in the back, which pulls the diver around for a vertical entry (Fig. 19-13).

Standing reverse dive—pike. The arms swing forward and upward to a position directly above the head as the diver jumps

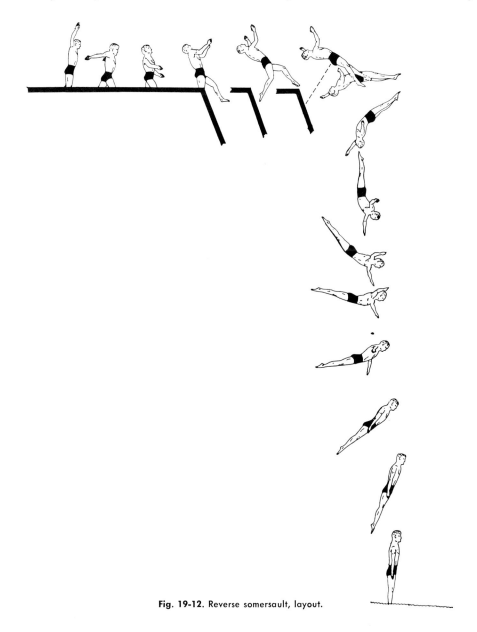

Fig. 19-12. Reverse somersault, layout.

from the platform. The head remains directly in line with the body and, as the jump is made, slightly away from the platform. The legs lift upward immediately as they leave the platform by contracting the thigh and stomach muscles along with the swing of the arms on the takeoff. As the legs move upward toward a vertical position, the arms move forward to touch the feet. The touch is made as the body begins to drop toward the water. The diver has a much better sense of direction if he watches his hands touch the feet. After the touch is made, the body begins to extend from the pike position by moving the arms laterally over the head and looking back at the water. The arms ex-

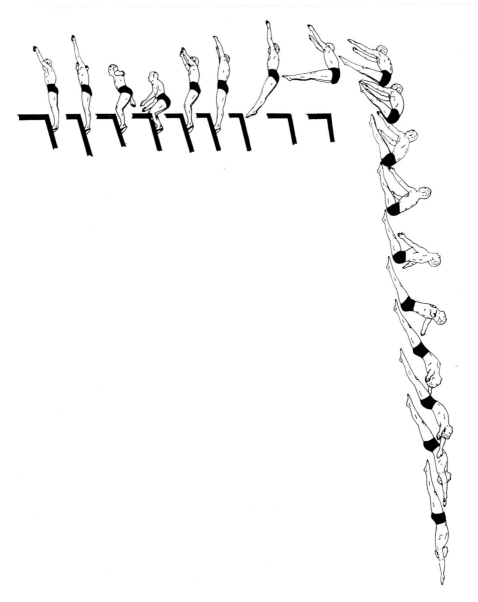

Fig. 19-13. Back dive, pike.

tend completely over the head, and the body straightens as the diver makes a vertical entry (Fig. 19-14).

Inward one and one half somersault—pike. The arms lift to a position directly over the head before the takeoff is made from the platform. In jumping from the platform, the legs extend, and the hips push upward as the arms, shoulders, and head are thrust downward. The diver begins to somersault as the body moves into a deep pike position. The arms spread to a position at right angles to the body as the pike position is started. During the somersault the eyes sight the knees, and the head remains tucked in close to the chest. The diver then

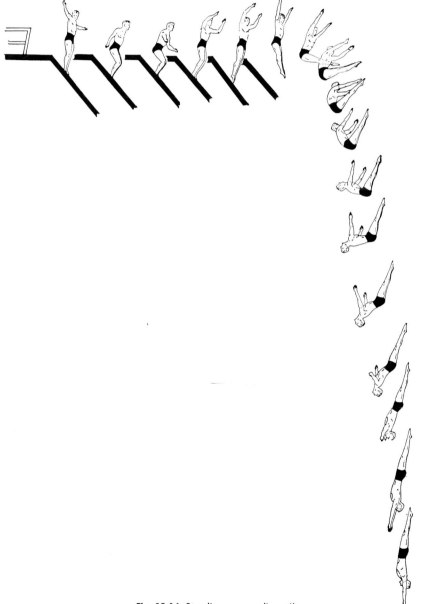

Fig. 19-14. Standing reverse dive, pike.

sights the water as he completes three quarters of a somersault. He then reaches for the water as the legs continue to lift upward, placing the body in a vertical position. Much of the somersault action is controlled when the arms are extended over the head in the reach for the water. The eyes continue to sight the water as the diver reaches for a vertical entry (Fig. 19-15).

CONDITIONING EXERCISES

Some exercises should be practiced in order to condition the diver before he begins tower diving. This applies to the experienced tower diver as well as the beginner. Hitting the water when diving from nearly 35 feet can be quite hard on the body; therefore the diver should be in very good physical condition before starting to dive from this

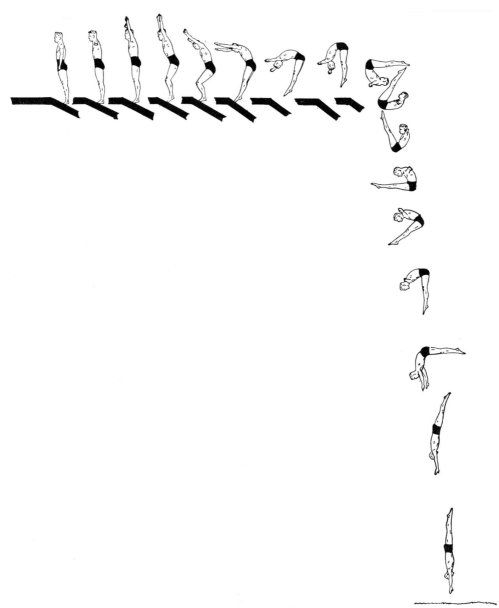

Fig. 19-15. Inward one and one half somersault, pike.

height. Generally, the muscles in the neck, the trapezius muscles, and the tricep muscles in the arms become sore during the first week or 10 days of practice. The soreness then leaves, but it sometimes reappears during the season. Much of the soreness can be prevented if the diver learns to clasp the hands together and "punch" a hole in the water as he makes the head-first entry. Some of the exercises that may prove helpful in conditioning the diver for tower diving are as follows.

Push-ups. These help condition the tricep muscles and the pectoral, or chest muscles.

Sit-ups. These condition the stomach and thigh muscles.

Leg pull-ups. Keep the knees straight while pulling the legs up. This can be done while lying on the back on the floor or while hanging from a horizontal bar. This exercise strengthens the thigh and trunk muscles.

Running in place bringing the knees up to the chest. This conditions the muscles and tendons in the small of the back and lower trunk.

Bridging. This is done with only the feet and head touching the floor with the back facing down. This exercise strengthens the neck muscles.

Although there are many other exercises that a diver may use to condition himself for tower diving, these may be considered some basic exercises that should be sufficient. These exercises should be practiced before the season and also used as warm-up exercises before each practice session begins. The diver may find some of the stretching exercises that are mentioned in the chapter on springboard diving to be helpful.

SAFETY HINTS FOR TOWER DIVING

Tower diving can be very dangerous for the beginner and experienced tower diver. Much of the danger can be eliminated, however, if certain precautions are taken. Some of these are as follows:

1. Swimmers should be kept out of the diving area while the tower is in use.
2. A diver should always check the diving area beneath the tower before executing a dive. He should also caution those on the other platform levels of his intention to dive.
3. The depth of the water should be checked, and the type and shape of the pool bottom should be explored before diving from the platforms when in a strange pool.
4. Divers should not linger in the water after the execution of a dive but should swim immediately back to the sides of the pool.
5. Diving platforms are much too dangerous for any horse play.
6. The diving platforms should be roped off with signs posted when they are not in use.
7. A diver should never practice tower diving unless another diver, qualified swimmer, or coach is present.
8. The diving area should be roped off from the swimming area when the facilities are all in the same pool. This will prevent a swimmer from accidentally swimming into a dangerous area.
9. Allow only the more experienced divers to dive from the platforms above 5 meters.
10. Do not practice tower diving just after eating. This can make a diver quite ill.

PRACTICE SESSIONS

The length of time a diver practices and the number of practice sessions he has each day during the season depends on many different factors. If the diver is going to school, working during the day, or lives in the northern part of the country, he will practice differently than the diver who has no school, does not work, or lives in a mild climate. If the diver has a coach, then the coach usually determines the length of time for each practice session and the number of sessions a day. When a coach is not available, the diver usually plans his own practice sessions, and these most often depend on when the diving tower is available. In any case the diver should practice at least 1 hour and not over 2 hours in one normal practice session. If time and conditions permit, the diver may have two practice sessions a day. When this is possible, it is recommended that he separate the practice sessions with at least 2 hours of rest. The early afternoon is usually the best time to practice when outdoors, for the sun is warm and is shining almost directly overhead, which reduces the reflection. When the weather is chilly, the diver should shorten the practice sessions or find some means of keeping warm during practice. In many cases the recreational and community pools become heavily crowded on warm afternoons so that the diver may find it to his advantage to practice in the morning or late afternoon, or both. Practicing at night is not recommended unless adequate light is available and the weather is warm.

THINGS TO REMEMBER WHEN TOWER DIVING

Below are several hints that can be helpful in making a practice session more successful when diving from the tower.

1. Warm up with some exercises, and practice some dives from the 3-meter board before diving from the tower. This will help prevent the tearing of muscles.
2. Check the water area and the other diving platforms before executing a dive.
3. Be sure to start with the more basic dives and then work toward the more difficult dives during the practice session.
4. Concentrate on the dive before making the approach to the end of the platform.
5. Do not change your mind once the dive has been started.
6. Clasp the hands together, and "punch" a hole in the water on all head-first entries.

Chapter 20

Teaching skin and scuba diving*

INTRODUCTION

The underwater world is relatively unexplored and filled with beauty beyond description. It is a world of greater depths than the highest mountain peaks and covers nearly 70% of the surface of the earth. It is inhabited by uncountable varieties of animal and plant life. It is a restless, dynamic, changing world possessing rhythm, design, movement, and power. Man is inexplicably drawn to this underwater world. He must, however, proceed with safety. This new world can be hostile and sometimes cruel. For these reasons the following information, though brief, is explicit, definite, and important for those who venture below the surface. Learn these lessons well, then enjoy the underwater world with confidence and skill.

HISTORY

The exploration of the land surface dates from the very beginning of man, and the wanderings of man over the surfaces of the world's water masses date from the beginning of recorded history; but the exploration of the underwater world is a relatively recent adventure. Though Aristotle wrote about diving devices as early as 360 B.C., and the great historian Pliny in A.D. 77 described the use of breathing tubes for underwater activity, man's real opportunity for extended underwater movement and investigation did not occur until the introduction of the self-contained underwater breathing apparatus (scuba) regulator in 1943 by Jacques-Yves Cousteau and Emile Gagnan of France.

The forerunners to modern methods of underwater exploration and sport are many. Early Greek and Roman strategists, in an effort to perfect the art of warfare, trained and equipped soldiers of strong swimming ability to approach enemy craft from below the water surface. They were supplied with air through a short length of hollow reed. Soldiers of the fifteenth and sixteenth centuries were fitted with surface-breathing bags connected to the diver by means of a hose and leather hood arrangement. These divers were held to the shallow depths, which was necessary because of their crude equipment, by weighted shoes. Benjamin Franklin, in his autobiography, described his making of hand and foot fins to facilitate faster swimming. William Forder, in the early 1800s, developed a metal helmet covering one half of the diver's body and supplied with air from the surface by means of a hand-operated bellows. In 1837, Augustus Siebe developed a full, dry diving suit with a rigid helmet. In the latter part of the 1800's the French developed a rubber diving suit and mask, supplied with air from a metal canister carried by the diver. A mechanical regulator was employed to control the flow of air. The American C. J. Lambertsen patented a successful closed circuit oxygen rebreathing unit in 1942. This unit was adopted by the

*From Armbruster, D. A.: Basic skills in sports for men and women, St. Louis, The C. V. Mosby Co.

Navy for underwater demolition teams, because with this equipment the diver's expired air did not bubble to the surface to reveal his position as he worked underwater.

In the past decade the design of the scuba has been refined and sophisticated, but the basic principle remains the same as the Cousteau-Gagnan design.

DIVING PHYSICS

As the diver goes beneath the water surface, he becomes aware of an increase in the pressure that surrounds him. This pressure has an important effect on parts of the diver's body and the air he breathes.

The air mixture compressed in a scuba tank is atmospheric air, never pure oxygen, and contains the same gas percentages (79% nitrogen, 20.93% oxygen, and 0.04% carbon dioxide). When these gases are breathed under pressure, there are several basic laws of physics that must be carefully considered.

Boyle's law states that, if temperature is constant, the volume of gas varies inversely with pressure. This simply means that when a skin diver is descending, the air in his lungs is compressed and as he surfaces it expands. This phenomenon is only important to the skin diver if he dives to exceptional depths. The scuba diver breathing air at the ambient pressure (pressure equal to the surrounding water) must realize that, if he does not exhale and breathe normally when ascending, the volume of air taken into his lungs at depth is going to expand as the pressure of the surrounding water is lessened during his ascent. This gas expansion can cause serious medical problems and might result in a fatal injury.

Henry's law states that the quantity of gas that goes into solution in any liquid is directly proportional to the partial pressure of the gas. This means that if a certain quantity of liquid is capable of absorbing one quart of gas at one atmosphere partial pressure, the same quantity of liquid would absorb two quarts of gas at two atmospheres. An understanding of gas absorption by the blood while diving is important to the diver in appreciating the need for computing a decompression dive.

We live under a constant pressure of 14.7 pounds per square inch, or one atmosphere; but when we dive beneath the surface of the ocean, we add about 0.445 pounds per square inch for every foot depth. When we reach the 33-foot depth, we have added another 14.7 pounds per square inch and are at two atmospheres absolute pressure. For each additional 33 feet we add another atmosphere of pressure. It is the effects of this pressure of water and atmosphere pressure above the water that the diver must understand and appreciate. It is this pressure that causes pain in the diver's ear as he descends, drives gas into solution, and presses his face mask against his face.

Sight and hearing are dramatically affected by the water. Because of the water's refraction and absorption of light, underwater objects appear to be about one-third closer than their actual distance and about one-fourth larger than their actual size. Sound travels much more rapidly in water than in air. When a tank is struck with a hard object such as a knife, the noise can be easily heard for quite a distance; however, it is more difficult to determine the direction from which the sound came in water than it is in the atmosphere. Communicating by voice underwater is very unsatisfactory, so divers must develop a system of hand signals that all divers in the party understand and are able to use.

SKIN DIVING

The term "skin diving" is used to describe diving activity when the diver uses mask, snorkel, and fins and holds his breath while swimming underwater. "Scuba diving" refers to underwater swimming when the diver adds to the basic skin diving items equipment designed to enable him to take his air supply beneath the surface. "Sport diving" is commonly used to include both skin and scuba diving activities.

Prerequisites

The skin and scuba diving student must first possess an advanced swimming ability and have some basic lifesaving knowledge or be the holder of a lifesaving certificate issued by the American Red Cross, YMCA, or other recognized agency. A standard first air card is also desirable.

Swimming test. The following test must not only be the minimum level of swimming competency but should be executed with a high level of skill and with relative ease.

1. Swim 300 yards using any stroke
2. Swim 50 feet underwater without swim aids.
3. Tread water or waterproof for 5 minutes.
4. Rest on back for 10 minutes with little or no movement.
5. Execute surface dives to 10 feet.

Medical examination. In addition to being a strong swimmer, the student must be in sound medical health. The physician should carefully examine for functional or structural deficiencies in the following organs:

1. Ears—average hearing and drum intact
2. Nose and throat—normal breathing
3. Sinuses—unobstructed
4. Heart and circulatory system—capable of strenuous work loads
5. Respiratory system—clear, normal, and capable of supporting heavy work
6. Eyes—20/30 or better

Chronic symptoms of nervousness, ear infections, sinus irritation, lung disease, and heart ailment should eliminate a person from this sport. No diver can be subject to fainting spells, blackouts, epilepsy, or other neurologic disorders. In addition, anyone prone to phobias, fears, and panic should be advised to find interests in other sports.

Equipment

Items essential for skin diving are the mask, snorkel, and fins (Fig. 20-1). When diving in cold water, the diver should wear a rubber wet suit. Most diving authorities insist that an inflatable safety vest be a necessary piece of equipment. Additional safety equipment should include a float with attached divers flag, such as a tire tube or paddle board, and a knife. Supplementary items of equipment are a compass, depth gauge, watch, spear gun, game and collecting bag, and photographic equipment.

Mask. The mask, sometimes called a faceplate, keeps the water from coming in contact with the surface of the eye and eliminates distortion, thereby enabling the diver's vision to be limited only by the light and clarity of the water. It also prevents water from being inhaled through the nose. The mask should fit the face with comfort and provide a watertight seal when the diver is submerged. The lens should be made of safety glass, not plastic, and secured in the mask by a metal retaining ring with a tension screw. The adjustable strap should attach on or near the front of the mask to assure a snug watertight fit. Some models have a one-way purge valve that enables the diver to clear water from the mask without chang-

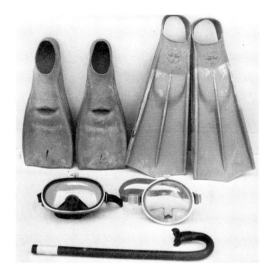

Fig. 20-1. Full-footed fins; open-heeled fins; purge-valve mask; equalizing mask; and snorkel. (From Armbruster, D. A.: Basic skills in sports for men and women, St. Louis, The C. V. Mosby Co.)

ing the swimming position. Also there are masks with molded depressions that permit the diver to close off his nostrils by pressing with the fingers, which facilitates easy clearing of the ears.

Snorkel. The snorkel is a tube that is held in the diver's mouth and extends above the surface of the water. It enables the diver to swim and breathe without lifting his head from the water. A semirigid rubber or plastic tube in the form of the letter J is the most advisable and popular among experienced divers. Those with ping-pong valves and rubber flutter valves are very dangerous and are not recommended for sport diving. A rubber mouthpiece allows the diver to maintain control of the tube and breathe with the head submerged for easy underwater viewing. The snorkel should have a soft rubber mouthpiece that is comfortable to the diver's mouth, permitting extended use without undue mouth fatigue.

Fins. Fins are mainly of two types: open heeled and full footed. Either is satisfactory, depending on the diver's preference. The purpose of the fins is to give extra power in swimming, not to increase speed. The fin should fit comfortably to allow circulation and prevent the feet from cramping but be snug enough to be secure when going through the surf. Fins of extra large design can cause undue fatigue, particularly when used by an untrained diver. Beginning divers should use a medium-size fin of medium flexibility.

Exposure dress. Wet suits made of cellular foam neoprene rubber and designed to fit snugly over the whole body are worn by almost all sport divers today. A small amount of water enters the wet suit, is quickly warmed by the diver's body, and then serves as insulation between his body and the surrounding water. These suits increase the diver's buoyancy significantly, so weights must be worn to enable him to submerge and swim with ease underwater.

Weight belt. This item deserves special attention. Commonly, lead weights attached to a web belt are used in varying amounts to overcome buoyancy. Most important is the quick-release buckle, which must be designed to operate effectively with one hand. When the diver finds himself in any questionable situation that could possibly lead to an emergency, he must be able to quickly and surely release his weight belt and allow it to fall away free and clear.

Accessory equipment. Descriptions of, and information concerning, other equipment for skin diving may be found by consulting the references at the end of the chapter. However, let it be understood that no one should dive without some type of personal float, such as an inflatable vest, in addition to a surface float. A good automobile inner tube with attached line makes a very effective and practical surface float for resting. A canvas or burlap bag tied to it serves to carry the diver's equipment.

Skin diving skills

All basic leg kicks, except breast and side stroke scissors, can and will be used while diving; however, the open, enlarged flutter kick with very loose knee action is the most common source of propelling force. Many divers alternate the dolphin kick with the flutter kick to prevent undue fatigue. A strong kick allows the diver freedom for his hands and arms to carry equipment, shoot fish, take pictures, and pick up interesting objects. Usually the arms are trailed in a comfortable position at the diver's sides when he is swimming and they are not specifically in use (Fig. 20-2). This position allows for maximum balance and relaxation. However, when swimming in turbid, murky water with poor visibility, the diver should extend both arms forward at full length to ward off undetected obstructions. When underwater, he should always swim as effortlessly as possible, conserving oxygen and thereby extending the length of "bottom time."

Diving down. When in open water, the diver should use either the tuck or pike sur-

Fig. 20-2. Skin divers in proper underwater swimming position. (From Armbruster, D. A.: Basic skills in sports for men and women, St. Louis, The C. V. Mosby Co.)

face dive to submerge. If the dive must be made through kelp or other plant life or into unfamiliar water, a feet-first dive should be executed.

Hyperventilation. Some divers extend their bottom time by means of rapid and deep breathing with exceptionally full exhalations just before submerging. No other practice in diving is more hazardous. Hyperventilation is the cause of "shallow water blackout" resulting in drowning. Instead, the diver should take two or three deep breaths and then hold a third at about two-thirds capacity just as the dive is started.

Clearing. When the diver submerges, his snorkel will be filled with water, but the air pressure in the diver's mouth prevents the water from entering the mouth and throat. Upon surfacing, the diver can blow the water in the tube out by a short forceful exhalation while keeping his face submerged.

Sometimes a small amount of water seeps into the face mask during the dive. This water should be evacuated to prevent its being inhaled through the nose. To clear

the mask, the diver should roll to one side, press the upper edge of the faceplate inward, and exhale through his nose into the mask. The water pooled in the bottom side of the mask is forced out by the air pressure. Care should be taken to release hand pressure on the mask while still blowing; otherwise water will flood into the mask through the released seal. Another method is for the diver to tilt his head back, press on top of the mask, and exhale (Fig. 20-3).

Equalizing. To provide for comfort and prevent injury, it is essential that pressure inside and outside the eardrum always be equal. When the diver descends, he must equalize the pressure on the eustachian tube side of the drum and that developed by the increasing pressure of water on the outside. Pinching the nose while blowing gently against the closed nostrils seems to work very well for most divers. Other techniques, such as swallowing and moving the jaw from side to side, should also help. The diver must never use ear plugs or place anything in the ears while diving.

Buddy diving. Never dive alone. This is

Fig. 20-3. Clearing mask—head tilted to side; head tilted back. (From Armbruster, D. A.: Basic skills in sports for men and women, St. Louis, The C. V. Mosby Co.)

the first and most important rule of safe diving. Diving and staying together takes practice between partners, but it must be done to ensure enjoyable and safe diving. You enter the water with your buddy, you dive together, and you leave the water together.

Entries. Always enter the water from as close to the surface as possible. When hunting, slip, drop, or slide feet first into the water as quietly as possible so as not to frighten game from the diving area. When the entry is from a point well above the surface, such as the side of a boat that is not equipped with a diving platform, the entry should be made with a giant stride, feet-first jump. When executing this entry, cover the face mask with one hand to prevent its being dislodged by the impact of the water. Keep other gear, such as cameras or spear gun, well away from the body. Take a giant stride well away from the takeoff point, keeping the body erect and eyes looking forward. After settling in the water, level off and make an approach swim to the diving area.

Ascending. When ascending, always extend one hand and arm overhead, looking up and turning 360 degrees around. This method should always be used to ensure the diver from coming up headfirst under another diver's tank, boat, floating object, or obstruction that could cause him serious injury.

Performance techniques. When beginning a dive, snorkel on the surface, pushing a safety float or innertube in front with the face submerged until reaching the diving location. Swim easily and relaxed, conserving energy and strength for the dive. The dive should be planned so that both buddies know the intentions of the other. A well-planned dive is the first step toward a safe dive. Surface dives should be made steep to the bottom; then, when underwater, swim slowly. Overall bottom time and total dive time can be increased by limiting the time of each single dive and by making more dives.

SCUBA DIVING

Several types and arrangements of scuba enable the diver to take his supply of air below the surface. Scuba has been the greatest advancement in man's effort to explore the underwater world. Such equipment extends diving time to over 1 hour and at depths of well over 100 feet. Scuba also frees the diver to swim with relatively complete freedom and to roam the depths at will. Though time and depths can be extended dramatically over skin diving limits, the novice scuba diver is cautioned to limit his dive time to 90% of tank capacity and to restrict depth for the first 25 or 30 dives to 33 feet. After this, the diver can move to depths of 60 or 70 feet and use up two or three tanks on a given day. Not until well after a year of regular sport diving at the depths and times just listed should the diver move into depths approaching 100 feet. These may seem to be unduly restrictive diving limits, but it is interesting to note that many amateur and recreational divers find their most interesting and enjoyable diving in around 35 feet of water. Remaining within this depth limit enables the diver to avoid a decompression dive even though he makes several dives during a 12-hour period.

Equipment

Two general classifications are recognized: the closed circuit or rebreather and the open circuit scuba. Although other equipment is sometimes used, only the open circuit scuba is used by sport divers. Open circuit scuba means that all exhaled air is exhausted into the water and none is reused. In closed circuit scuba the breathing gas is recirculated, the carbon dioxide being absorbed by granulated chemicals and the oxygen being added to a breathing bag as needed from a high pressure supply tank. Open circuit scuba uses compressed atmospheric air and never pure oxygen as in closed circuit, because 100% oxygen becomes toxic when breathed under pressure greater than 29 pounds per square inch. This pressure is reached when diving deeper than 33 feet. There are three main components of open circuit scuba: the regulator, the tank, and the valve (Fig. 20-4).

Regulator. The regulator is the heart of the scuba, since it is responsible for the delivery of the diver's air at exactly the correct

Fig. 20-4. Tank with reserve valve (J type) and harness; tank with no reserve (K type) and back-pack harness; two-hose regulator; and single-hose regulator with pressure gauge. (From Armbruster, D. A.: Basic skills in sports for men and women, St. Louis, The C. V. Mosby Co.)

pressure and whenever he inhales. For this reason the regulator is often referred to as a *demand* regulator because it permits air to flow into the diver's mouth each time he demands by his slightest inhalation. This inhalation causes a drop in the pressure on one side (dry side) of a rubber diaphragm. The water pressure on the other side (wet side) of the diaphragm is then able to push the diaphragm inward, which in turn activates a lever that opens a valve and allows air to flow through the diver's air hose. When the pressure on both sides of the diaphragm again becomes equal, the valve closes and the air flow is shut off. This pressure balance is regained when the diver discontinues inhaling.

Regulators are designed either with single or double hose. Both types are popular and have their strong points. The student should consult a detailed reference for specifications of each design.

Valves. The valve is located between the tank and the regulator. Basically, there are two types of tank valves: the constant reserve (J type) and the nonreserve (K type).

Table 20-1. Diving disorders

DISORDER	CAUSE	SYMPTOMS	TREATMENT
Drowning	Physical exhaustion; running out of air; loss of mask or mouthpiece; flooding of apparatus; entanglement	No respiration; blueness of skin	Immediate artificial respiration, preferably by mouth-to-mouth method; start at once
Air embolism	Failure to breathe normally or holding breath while ascending results in blockage of circulatory system by excessive pressure rupturing lung tissues and allowing air to enter bloodstream	Weakness; dizziness; loss of speech; paralysis of extremities; visual disturbance; staggering; bloody frothy sputum; unconsciousness; death usually within seconds after reaching surface, if not before	Recompress immediately to 74 pounds per square inch (165 feet); medical care; lower head to allow bubbles to go to feet rather than head
Decompression illness (bends or caisson disease)	Bubbles of nitrogen expand in bloodstream and tissues of body from inadequate decompression following exposure to pressure; nitrogen absorption depends on depth, time, and working rate; nitrogen more soluble in fatty tissues	Skin rash; itching; pain deep in joints, muscles, and bones; choking; visual disturbances; dizziness; convulsions; weakness in arms and legs; loss of hearing or speech; paralysis; unconsciousness; death	Recompress by Navy treatment tables; if caught in time, there are usually no serious after-effects
Nitrogen narcosis	Intoxicating effect of nitrogen when breathed under pressure; no prevention; occurs usually at about 130 feet, though reported at 30 feet	Loss of judgment and skill; feeling of greatness; slowed mental activity; fixation of ideas; similar to alcohol intoxication	Stop work; reduce pressure; effects disappear when ascending; no aftereffects
Oxygen poisoning	Using pure oxygen below 33 feet for longer than 30 minutes; does not apply to all divers, can be less, depends on CO_2 tension and work rate; not probable on compressed air until about 300 feet	Nausea; dizziness; headache; twitching of muscles around mouth and eyes; disturbance of vision (tunnel vision); numbness; unconsciousness	Surface; rest; medical care; never dive below 30 feet on pure oxygen; use only compressed air in tanks
Carbon monoxide poisoning (CO)	Contaminated air supply from internal combustion engines; improperly lubricated compressors; CO combines with blood, causing internal asphyxiation	Same as symptoms for CO_2 poisoning except lips and mouth are bright cherry red; 10% in blood causes headache and nausea; 30% causes shortness of breath; 50% causes helplessness	Surface; artificial respiration if not breathing; oxygen; medical care; may seem to be all right on bottom but lose consciousness on ascent
Apnea	Hyperventilation and extended dives in skin diving	No warning symptoms to speak of (perhaps moment of blackness before total unconsciousness)	Fresh air; artificial respiration; do not hyperventilate excessively

Table 20-1. Diving disorders—cont'd

DISORDER	CAUSE	SYMPTOMS	TREATMENT
Squeeze	Pressure differential over concerned area; middle ear and sinuses usually first place where pain felt; also teeth, face mask, suit, lung (thoracic) squeezes	Usually sharp pain caused by stretched or damaged tissues; damage can occur without pain, however	Equalize pressure on affected areas

The J-valve mechanism is preset to provide air as long as tank pressure remains above 300 pounds per square inch, but below this pressure a spring-actuated piston restricts the diver's air and breathing becomes difficult. This is a signal to the diver that he is low on air and must pull his reserve lever to open the reserve valve and allow the last 300 pounds of air to flow freely. The diver should end his dive at this time by returning to the surface station for another tank or rest period. Never continue diving when on reserve air and always check to make sure the reserve lever is in the up or loaded position before entering the water.

Never totally drain your tank of air or leave the valve open. Moisture can build up inside the tank and cause tank damage from the inside.

The nonreserve or K-type valve has no reserve feature and is simply an on-off valve control. Divers using this valve usually attach an air pressure gauge to their regulators to keep themselves constantly informed as to the air remaining in the tank. Divers can also have the J-valve structure located on the first stage of the regulator. Both arrangements are popular among good divers.

Tanks. Air cylinders for diving are available in many sizes and in single, double, and triple units. They may be constructed of high-strength steel or rust-free aluminum. The size and air pressure of the tank will generally determine the time a diver can remain submerged. However, breathing rate, water temperature, depth, and working rate are also important determinants of underwater time. The tank size usually recommended is the "standard 70." This means the tank contains 70.2 cubic feet of air when filled to 2250 pounds per square inch and will provide air for single dives within the limits of "no decompression" dives. Tanks should be hydrostated every 5 years in accordance with federal law. A yearly visual inspection by a reputable repairman is highly recommended.

Harness. A harness, often arranged in combination with a plastic form-fitting back pack, must be fitted with quick-release buckles or safety hitches and must never be put on over the weight belt. The harness must secure the scuba to the diver with comfort and allow freedom of movement in all positions, but it must also be designed to be "ditched" without hesitation or fumbling.

Scuba diving skills

Fundamentally the swimming skills employed in scuba diving are the same as those used in skin diving; however, one point of caution should be noted at this time. No one should attempt scuba diving until he is well skilled and experienced in skin diving.

Entries. When the diver enters and exits through the surf while wearing a scuba, he must remember that though he has a supply of unrestricted air he is also more vulnerable to wave action in the surf and can be easily tumbled and thrown about when attempting to come to a standing position. When exiting through the surf, the diver should remain in an extended swimming position until well up on the beach before attempting to stand, then quickly turn about and shuffle backward until clear of all surge and water action.

When entering from an elevated point, boat dock, or land, the diver should use a feet-first entry but never into unknown water. He should grasp and protect the mask with one hand as in the skin diving entry, and with the other hand hold the tank down to prevent its being forced up and striking his head. This can also be accomplished by pushing down on the waist strap.

When entering unknown water, the diver should make a feet-first drop or slide-in entry. This method also reduces the chances of frightening game from the diving area. Other methods, such as forward and backward rolls, may be used if the diver is properly trained for such entries.

Scuba drills. These drills should only be practiced with a partner and with a certified instructor observing.

1. *Submerging and swimming without a mask.* Replace and clear the mask without surfacing. (See skin diving skills for clearing.)
2. *Mouthpiece clearing.* Remove the mouthpiece underwater. Return it to the mouth, give a short sharp exhale to clear it of water, and resume breathing. Always take the first breath slowly after clearing the snorkel or mouthpiece of the regulator.
3. *Buddy breathing.* Two divers share one air supply. The diver with air passes his regulator mouthpiece to his buddy, who receives and clears the mouthpiece and takes two breaths before returning it to his buddy. The diver with the air supply always retains control of the mouthpiece. The second diver uses his hands to help swim and keep the two divers close together.
4. *Free ascent.* Practice this emergency skill to be able to function calmly in an emergency situation resulting in the complete loss of an available air supply while submerged. In this situation the diver looks up, starts his ascent with one arm extended over his head, and exhales continuously for the entire ascent. The student in the class drill of free ascent should remove his mask and then his mouthpiece before starting the free ascent. The diver's buddy and instructor, with air functioning and mask in place, must always accompany the free-ascending diver to the surface.
5. *Buoyancy testing.* This is essential because the addition of a scuba adds several pounds of negative buoyancy to the skin diver. A slight positive buoyancy is recommended for the start of a scuba dive, since most surface buoyancy is lost at 33 feet of depth. Weights should be added or subtracted to allow the diver to gradually sink after a full exhalation on the surface.
6. *Ditching and recovering.* Do this exercise involving complete mastery of equipment underwater to gain familiarization and proficiency underwater.

DIVING MEDICINE

Most diving disorders or medical problems in diving are classified as barotrauma, or a change in normal conditions caused by changing pressure. Usually it is an injury resulting from unequal pressure between a space inside the body and the outside water pressure. The cavities of the middle ear and the sinuses are most susceptible to changing pressure, but serious problems can also develop from pressure on the breathing gas. Nitrogen narcosis, oxygen toxicity, and carbon monoxide poisoning are examples of these disorders. Some of these problems and their causes, symptoms, and treatment are given in Table 20-1.

TEN BASIC RULES OF SKIN AND SCUBA DIVING

1. Be in top physical condition and have an annual medical examination.

2. Be a good swimmer.
3. Secure certified training from recognized agency.
4. Never dive alone.
5. Use safe, time-proved equipment.
6. Join a reputable diving club.
7. Be familiar with your diving area *before diving.*
8. Always use a float with surface identification, usually a diver's flag.
9. Heed all pains and strains as warning symptoms.
10. Know basic first aid.

FIVE SUPPLEMENTARY RULES OF SKIN AND SCUBA DIVING

1. Know the basic laws of diving physics and physiology.
2. Practice skin diving frequently *before* scuba diving.
3. Use only time-proved regulators and diving equipment from a reputable manufacturer.
4. Secure certified training in the use of scuba from recognized agency.
5. Never hold your breath while scuba diving.

Chapter 21

Techniques for teaching water polo

Most of the published material pertaining to water polo stresses the rules and strategy of play. A problem often encountered by physical education teachers is that of teaching an activity in which the students may have had little experience. This can become more complex if the instructor himself has had little formal experience with the activity. The instructional techniques discussed in the following pages will hopefully give teachers in such situations a guide for teaching water polo.

The methods discussed in the following pages are designed to teach a water polo course lasting 8 weeks and meeting twice a week. Programs with other meeting schedules can either expand on the ideas presented or delete them and use only those considered best.

WEEK 1—DAY 1

Upon meeting the class and introducing yourself it is wise to briefly remind the students that this is a game for advanced swimmers, and if they do not feel they have the swimming ability they should find a class more suitable. At this time any attendance and administrative policies should be mentioned so all students are clear on them. It is also a good idea, at this time, to ask the class to swim warm-up and conditioning laps during the few minutes before class begins. This will save time during the regular class and will allow the students to better keep up with the pace of the game. Other than the few announcements necessary to start the class it is best to get the students in the water and working as soon as possible. Lengthy discussions of rules and equipment should be avoided on the first day or the students will be "turned off" early. Save the rules and playing suggestions for brief periods of 2 or 3 minutes daily. Be sure to go over basic rules and strategy in early sessions and save the more advanced and technical aspects of the game for later sessions or even for an advanced class.

For an opening activity I have found the basics of passing and ball handling to work quite well. For this session start the students out in shallow water and have them practice the "dry pass." The ball should not touch the water in this type of pass. Have the students practice passing and catching with both the left and right hand. At this time the rule prohibiting the touching of the ball with both hands at the same time should be mentioned. The students should catch the ball with the fingertips, rather than with a flat hand, since this allows for a soft catch and better ball control. The second skill to be practiced on the first day is the "wet pass." In order for the player to be able to make a wet pass he must learn how to effectively pick up the ball out of the water. At this point the underwater and top of ball techniques should be introduced. Both methods require the fingers to be spread and cover as much of the ball as possible. For the underwater pick up gentle pressure should be applied to the ball to prevent any jostling and ensure a good grip. As the hand is raised it should be rotated to the starting position for the forehand or regular throw.

For the top of ball pick up a slight downward pressure should be applied to the ball using the water for leverage. Move the ball away from the body and rotate the ball in the direction of the little finger to get the hand beneath the ball. As the ball is lifted it is rotated thumb first to the throwing position. This pick up is difficult to master, since most beginners have a tendency to apply too much pressure and pop the ball out of the water, thus losing control.

After practicing these basic skills in shallow water move the class to deep water and let them experience the difference when the feet are not on the bottom. A good technique for practicing these skills is to have the class divide into groups of about eight and form a circle with about a 15-foot diameter. The class can then practice accurate passing by seeing how long they can keep the ball out of the water. Competition between groups adds to the interest.

WEEK 1—DAY 2

Class should again begin with a warm-up. After the warm-up swim take attendance and review the work of the previous day. Demonstrate again the basics of passing and picking the ball up out of the water, and ask the students if there are any questions. Begin the activity by again using the circle drill emphasizing accuracy of passing and control of the ball when catching it. After several minutes of this activity call the students to the side and divide them into groups of three for a different type of drill. This three-man drill involves the "wet pass" and practice in picking the ball out of the water. In this drill the three men swim across the width or length of the pool leading the man with the ball. For this drill the outside men should pass the ball to the center, who then passes to the other outside man. The outside men should pass the ball with their outside hand so as to give maximum protection to the ball. This should be emphasized and the students should learn to use both hands. Make sure to have the students

switch positions so all of them get a chance to play the center position.

After several minutes of these drills let the students play a game. It is important to expose them early to the real game even though they do not yet have all of the necessary skills or knowledge. An early game like this can spike interest if it is not allowed to go too long so that it becomes ragged and the players become exhausted. Get the students good and tired to show the necessity of conditioning in water polo but don't "turn them off."

WEEK 2—DAY 1

After warming up and attendance review the three-man drill and wet passing. For activity today introduce dribbling. Emphasize the head up dribble. When instructing the class on the dribble have them keep the head up and advance the ball by pushing it with the wave of water in front of the chest. Emphasize that they should not slap the ball from hand to hand or push it with the head, since this reduces the control that can be kept on the ball and also causes the swimmer to slow down while dribbling. After several minutes of drills give the class a minute or two of rest and finish class with a game. During these games at the end of class stop, the action at teachable moments and go over play situations and rules.

WEEK 2—DAY 2

Again begin with several minutes of dribbling drills and then proceed to shooting. The first shot to work on is the regular overhand shot. When working on this the student must learn how to pick the ball out of the water quickly and without losing control. The student must also get a good kick from the legs to get the throwing shoulder and elbow out of the water. This is important if the shooter is going to get anything on the ball. The rise out of the water can be practiced for several minutes before balls are used. When the balls are given to the class make sure they start about 10 to 15 feet from the goal and move back in stages from there. As the student moves back he will see the importance of a strong kick to get out of the water. These shooting drills should be done without a goalie and the class should be shown the best places to shoot—upper and lower corners. After several minutes of shooting, the drill can be enlivened by having the players swim up to the ball and pick it and shoot as fast as possible. Again end class with a short game if time permits.

WEEK 3—DAY 1

Begin the class by reviewing the fundamentals of the regular overhand shot. After this review proceed to teach the following shots which can be used in different situations around the goal and do not require the time that the regular overhand does. These shots include the push shot, sweep shot, and pop shot.

The push shot can be used when getting a rebound close in and shooting it quickly without having to straighten up and get the ball out of the water as in the overhand shot. Because this shot is literally pushed rather than thrown it can be used from only close range. This shot should be attempted from inside the 4-yard line.

The sweep shot is used when the shooter has his back to the goal and wants to get off a quick shot without turning to face the goal. This shot is executed somewhat like a hook shot in basketball, and the player should end up facing the goal when the shot is completed. An added advantage of this shot is that the ball is hidden from the goalie until the last moment of the shot.

The pop shot requires the use of both hands. It, like the push shot, should be used from close range. The swimmer uses an underwater lift to get the ball out of the water, and it is popped vertically out of the water to about eye level. The other hand comes into play at this point and snaps the ball at the goal. The strong point of this shot is the goalkeeper's tendency to react to the initial pop of the ball, this early reaction will cause the goalie's timing to be off.

After ample practice time on these shots end the class with about a 10-minute game.

WEEK 3—DAY 2

After warming up and taking attendance let the class practice the shots learned the previous day.

For activity today practice defensive tactics—grab block, lunge block, and underarm steal.

The grab block is used as a player rolls to face the goal for a shot. The defender grabs him around the waist and lunges toward the throwing arm. The grab should be a clinching type motion and the defender should go for the offensive player's arm. In teaching this maneuver show the students how to "match" arms. In this technique the defender uses the near arm to grab the opponents shooting arm. For example, if the offensive player is shooting right handed the defender should grab him around the waist with his right hand and clinch him up while lunging for the shooting arm with his left, or "matching," hand.

The lunge block is also used when the shooter is attempting to roll to pass or shoot. The defender places his right hand on the player's chest and pushes him back and down while using the player for leverage. By pushing the offensive player the defender gains extra height and has a better chance of blocking the ball with his free hand. In this maneuver the "matching" of the blocking arm is again followed. In this block the defender attempts to block the ball or cause the flight of the ball to be on a high arc so the goalie has an easy play.

The underarm steal is performed from the side of the offensive player by reaching under the arm and popping the ball into the air. When practicing this skill the defender should remain between the offensive player and his goal and close enough so that he can reach the ball when reaching for it. A common mistake for beginners is to let the offensive player get a stroke advantage and then try to reach for the ball. When this occurs the offensive player usually gains an even greater advantage.

WEEK 4—DAY 1

By this time most of the basic fundamentals of shooting, dribbling, and individual defense have been covered. The remainder of the class should be concerned mostly with refinement of these skills and development of team skills through actual playing. One specific skill that has not been discussed to this point is goalkeeping. A skill that can be worked on for goalies is the snap of the legs necessary to get the chest out of the water for blocks. The goalie and defensemen should be taught to force any shooter to the side so the goalie has a chance to cut down the shooting angle. The goalie should also be instructed to prevent as many rebounds as possible by catching the ball and getting rid of it quickly to a teammate. A good drill for the goalkeepers is to have the class spread out around the shooting area and take shots at the goal, giving the goalie only a reasonable amount of time to recover and get back to position.

Play a full-scale game the last 15 minutes of class.

WEEK 4—DAY 2

The first few minutes of class should be spent on three-on-two and three-on-one breaks. Offensively the key is to pass the ball as little as possible, making the pass to the open man when the defender moves to the man with the ball. Defensively the emphasis is on going for the man with the ball. The defenders should not back up so far as to interfere with the goalie. The defenders must be quick and try to cause a bad pass that they can intercept, or at least slow down play until teammates can catch up to the action.

After about 10 minutes of drills the class should finish with a game.

WEEKS 5, 6, AND 7

Depending on the instructor's feeling about the skill level of the class, these 3 weeks can be spent in further drills or in playing games. Each class can begin with a few minutes of various drills to correct any weaknesses noticed by the instructor, and the remainder of the class period can be spent in actual play. The actual game situation is the best teaching situation and teachable moments can be used quite effectively. The instructor can use the breaks in play following goals, fouls, out of bounds, and so on to comment on game situations. Comments made in this manner while the play is still fresh in the players' mind can add a great deal to the learning of the students. During the later weeks of the unit the instructor should look for improvement in team play and individual skills. If extra players are available they should be allowed to help officiate, since this will give them insight into the game, which they may not get from only playing. By this stage of the unit the class should be exhibiting the ability to think ahead and anticipate situations.

WEEK 8

The last week of an 8-week unit should be used for any final evaluation that needs to be done. Some evaluation of every student should have taken place by this time. This final week can be handled in several ways. One day can be spent on an official game lasting the entire class period with the class knowing they will be evaluated for performance during the game, and the other day may be spent on a written test covering the course. If an instructor feels a written test is not necessary he may use the other day for another game or for testing of individual skills. In either case, written or skill test, the test should be meaningful and cover important aspects of what has been taught, rather than "Mickey Mouse" facts or skills. Test to find out what the student knows, not what he doesn't know.

BASIC DIAGRAMS AND DESCRIPTIONS

The following pages contain diagrams and descriptions of some suggested drills that may be used in teaching a beginning water polo class.

Circle drill

An excellent drill for practicing the dry pass. Emphasize catching the ball softly with the fingers spread wide. Have all of the students practice with both left and right hands. If the class is large enough for two or more circles, competition can be easily established by having each group count the number of good passes and receptions without the ball touching the water.

A keep-away drill could also be used by having three or four defenders in the center of the circle trying to intercept the ball. Such a drill would emphasize sharp, quick passes to the open man on the part of the offense and quick reaction and hustle on the part of the defense.

Three-man passing drill

A very simple drill for practicing the wet pass. Emphasize leading the receiver, but not so much that the defense has a chance for the ball. Have all players vary positions and use both of their hands.

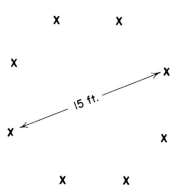

Fig. 21-1. Circle drill.

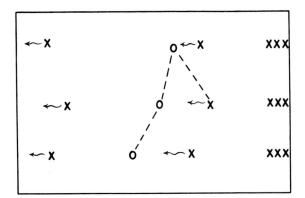

Fig. 21-2. Three-man passing drill.

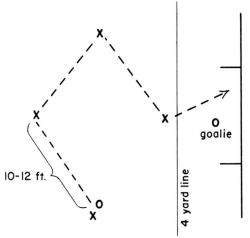

Fig. 21-3. Diamond drill.

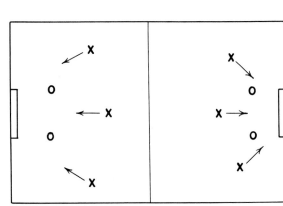

Fig. 21-4. Three-on-two drill.

Diamond drill

This is a good drill for ball handling and for practicing deflections close to the goal. The drill can be done from either direction so that all players learn to use both hands. The three lead up passes should be quick and crisp, and the player who is to deflect the shot should not catch the ball but merely change the direction of flight. The player practicing deflections should not give away the direction in which he intends to deflect the ball. He should practice varying his shots.

Three-on-two drill

This drill can be worked either from mid-pool in both directions (as shown in Fig. 21-4) or going one way. The one-way drill would provide a more realistic experience and give the participants more conditioning, but with a large class the two-way drill is probably more practical. This drill can be done with or without a goalie. Perhaps the first few attempts should be without a goalie until the students get the hang of the drill; after the students are acquainted with the procedure a goalie will add challenge to the drill.

Chapter 22

The swimming pool—
its care and maintenance

Swimming pools, both indoor and outdoor, should be constructed after thorough investigation as to length, width, and depth suitable for instruction, recreation, and competition. Usually there is a strong sentiment expressed by committees that a pool should be built for general swimming only and not for competition. Committees who have been misled by such false sentiment find out later that it is very expensive to make later changes in construction for purposes of holding competitive meets. The modern indoor and outdoor pools should be constructed to combine the several functions.

INDOOR POOL

Because of limited space and cost, sometimes the indoor pool is shortened in length or narrowed in width to distances not conducive to recognized competition. If records of any consequence were established in such odd-length pools, they would probably be rejected by a records committee. Several acceptable pool arrangements are possible. Some people favor two or even three pools in a building, one as a competitive pool and the others in separate rooms to be used for instructional or recreational purposes. Other people favor one large pool with a movable bulkhead so that any length course can be utilized. A larger pool affords greater space for instruction purposes. There are many who favor the indoor long course 50-meter pool with a bulkhead to separate the deep diving board end from the shallow swimming pool end. This latter arrangement makes diving safer and does not interfere with swimmers. This is excellent also for conditioning and training swimmers for outdoor long course meets as well as for the Olympic competition, which is always held over the long course.

Length of pool. For indoor swimming pools 75 feet is the generally accepted length in America. This is called the short-course pool. If a long-course pool is desired, 50 meters (which is approximately 55 yards) is the accepted length. A 20-yard course is no longer recommended. A world record cannot be established in such a pool, but an American record can. It has been calculated that from one half to a full second can be gained at each turn. Records for the 20-yard course are thus better than for the 25-yard course.

Width of pool. Usually the width of the swimming pool is governed by the number of lanes the space in the building can provide. Lanes should be 7 feet wide. In league or championship meets, there are six finalists, which would require six 7-foot lanes or a 42-foot width, and additional width outside lanes one and six is recommended to bring the total width to 45 feet.

Depth of pool. For adult men swimmers, 4 feet should be the minimum depth at the shallow end of the pool. The somersault turn requires this depth. For high school swimmers, 3½ feet as a minimum would possibly be satisfactory, but 4 feet as a minimum is recommended. From this depth a gradual slope should descend to the greatest depth under the springboards. The minimum depth under springboards should be 12 feet. Pool drains should never be located under the diving boards.

dine, ultraviolet, and others. Chlorine and bromine are most commonly used and are generally approved by state health departments.

Pure chlorine gas is liquefied under pressure and is available commercially in steel tanks. At room temperature it appears as a deadly green gas heavier than air. Safety precautions are to be observed in the handling and storage of chlorine tanks. The chlorine is applied to the water by means of a chlorinator. The chlorinator provides for continuous application and control of the amount of chlorine being fed into the water. It is suggested that the point of application be on the filter influent. The use of chlorine as a water disinfectant may also be accomplished by adding chemicals that release chlorine when added to the water. Calcium hypochlorite is available commercially in the form of powder, pellets, and blocks. It is a dry solid and contains 70% available chlorine by weight. When dissolved in water, a heavy precipitate of calcium carbonate is formed. If applied directly to the pool water, this precipitate would tend to make the water cloudy. The calcium hypochlorite should be dissolved in a tank of water. The precipitate is allowed to settle and clear liquid siphoned off. It is then fed to the pool by means of a hypochlorinator.

Sodium hypochlorite is a liquid chemical. In its commercial form it contains from 1% to 15% chlorine by weight. It is available in dark glass gallon jugs and 5-gallon glass carboys. Sodium hypochlorite has a tendency to deteriorate when exposed to the sun or heat. It can be applied by means of a controlled feeder or directly to the pool water by hand.

Bromine in its pure form is a dark brown liquid much heavier than water. Bromine is fed to the pool water by means of a brominator. The process consists of bubbles of water passing through the liquid bromine; absorption takes place and the resulting solution is added to the water line.

Pool managers who have used bromine claim that while it is more expensive than chlorine gas, it is safer to handle. They receive fewer complaints of skin and eye irritation and disinfectant odors. Bromine is equal to chlorine in disinfecting qualities and the bromine residual is firmer than chlorine residual.

Chlorine generators are used to produce chlorine for swimming pools. Salt is added to the pool water in the amount of 2500 milligrams per liter. Part of the recirculation water is passed through the generator and the chloride of the salt is used to produce chlorine. At the same time, a molecule of chlorine is produced, as well as a molecule of hydroxide, so that an alkali does not have to be added. Another advantage is the safety in the operation of these units.

Water testing and records

The pool manager should keep a daily record of the pool operation. The following items should be noted:

1. Number of persons using the pool per day and peak load
2. Water and air temperature
3. Chemicals used such as soda ash and alum and the amount added to the water
4. Disinfectant, the number of hours of operation, machine setting, and amount used
5. Disinfectant residual, in parts per million, at four corners of the pool
6. When filters are backwashed
7. The pH of the water
8. Water to be added
9. Hours water is being recirculated and the rate of recirculation
10. Condition of water: clear, cloudy (turbidity)
11. Dates when water samples for bacterial count are sent to health department and results on a log sheet
12. Any unusual occurrences such as motor breakdown, chlorinator breakdown, loss of electricity

The amount of disinfectant residual can

be determined by taking a small sample of the pool water and adding to it a solution of orthotolidine. If the sample contains free chlorine, it will turn yellow within a period of 3 to 6 seconds. The degree of yellow color, when compared with a set of standard colors, commonly known as a comparator or chlorine-residual testing kit, will indicate the amount of chlorine or bromine residual. The better comparators will be scaled from zero to one part per million and over in one-tenth p.p.m. steps. Most state health departments require a minimum of 0.4 residual and recommend that in outdoor pools a higher residual be maintained to take care of factors that will tend to dissipate the amount of disinfectant, such as wind, heavy usage, weather, and algae, all of which tend to lower the chlorine residual.

The existence of hypochlorous acid in pool water is commonly referred to as free chlorine residual. If the water contains ammonia and other organic materials, the chlorine may react and result in "combined chlorine" compounds, a much weaker disinfectant than hypochlorous acid. When the pool is being disinfected by "combined chlorine," it is recommended that the residual count be at a minimum of one part per million. A test sample that is slow to develop its yellow color and continues to deepen in color up to 5 minutes would indicate "combined chlorine."

Water balance

The numerical value of pH is given to indicate the acidity or alkalinity of water. Technically, pH is the logarithm of the reciprocal of the hydrogen ion concentration. The numerical scale of pH ranges from pH 1.0, a very high acid condition of the water, to pH 14.0, a very high alkaline condition. pH 7.0 is neutral, neither acid nor alkaline. Testing meters used to measure the water pH should have a minimum range of from 6.8 to 9.5. Most authorities recommend that the pH for swimming pool water be from 7.2 to 7.8 on waters that are not softened.

When chemically softened waters are used for make up, backwash, and other losses, the pH will be in the range of 8.5 to 9.5. The chlorine residual should be increased to 2 to 3 p.p.m. to compensate for the lower activity of the chlorine at this pH range. Since the chlorine is less active in this pH range, the higher chlorine residual will not be irritating to the eyes or skin.

Alum, a coagulant commonly used to aid the filtration process, may lower the pH. Chlorine gas and pure bromine also tend to lower the pH. To bring up the pH, the pool operator may use soda ash (sodium carbonate).

Filter operation

The filter should be backwashed when a predetermined head loss is reached or, if a head loss gauge is not available, when the proper rate of flow through the filter cannot be obtained. The filter should be backwashed at a prescribed rate to obtain proper expansion of the filter media. (To check the expansion and proper backwash, a device such as a garden rake can be used. When the filter is being backwashed, the rake will easily pass through the expanded sand down to the supporting bed.)

The filter should be backwashed until the backwash water becomes fairly clear. Details of the filter operation such as length in time of filter run, the rate the filter is operated, the rate at which the filter is backwashed, and the length of time of filter backwash, should be recorded.

Types of filters. Most commonly on large pools, gravity sand filtration is used. Many types of material or mixed materials may be used as filter media but the same principal of operation is applicable to all media. The rate of filtration is usually in the range of 2 gallons per minute per square foot of filter area. With proper operation of filters and correct disinfection procedure, the pool water should be clear at all times.

Pressure sand filters may be used and they may be operated at a higher filtering rate.

The disadvantages of these units are that the filter media cannot be checked for proper expansion and, when operated at higher rates, turbidity may be pushed through the filter.

The diatomite filters are commonly used on smaller pools and may be used on larger installations. There are two types of these units, that is, a pressure or vacuum type. The pressure type has the disadvantage of not being able to see if the filtering material is being displaced from the septums upon backwashing. On both types, other disadvantages are the cost and operation of the continuous feed of the filtering material and sludge disposal.

Chapter 23

How to conduct dual, championship, and summer age-group meets

The time and care spent in preparation for a swimming meet have their reward in ease and efficiency. The large number of details that require attention must be handled in an orderly manner to avoid confusing oversights. The coaches and managers owe it to the competitors, officials, and spectators to start the meet on time and provide all the information and materials to conduct the events with facility.

The use of checkoff sheets, officials' kits, and duty summaries aid in performing the several tasks. These are presented in detail in order to be of maximum benefit to the novice coach or manager.

SWIMMING MEET CHECKOFF LISTS
Things to do in preparation for swimming season

1. Arrange for competitive schedule.
2. Arrange for practice schedule, starting date, and time of daily practice periods.
3. Procure team physician and trainer.
4. Call for swimmers, divers, and student managers.
5. Announce to team members to report to equipment room for measurement for suiting.
6. Purchase personal swimming and diving equipment, such as sweat suits or bathrobes; silk, nylon, or rayon swimming trunks; lastex diving trunks; foot sandals; ear plugs; nose clips; foot dusting powder; and castor oil or mineral oil with eyedropper.

7. Procure training room equipment, such as rubbing tables, oil, alcohol, ultraviolet and infrared lamps, cold and flu shots, and vitamin tablets if recommended by team physician.
8. Secure approval of schedule by director and athletic board.
9. Secure the following training equipment:
   a. Kick boards
   b. Wheelbarrow tubes
   c. Stop watches
   d. Whistles
   e. .22 caliber gun and shells
   f. Finish curtain rope
   g. False starting check rope
   h. Clip boards and pencils
   i. Rule books: NCAA, AAU, and FINA
   j. Textbook
   k. Weight chart and scales
   l. Diving calculator
   m. Diving flash cards
   n. Judges' finish cards
   o. Timers' finish cards
   p. Wall weights and barbells
   q. Gymnasium mats
   r. Two additional springboards
10. Have coaches' own training devices, such as:
    a. Pacing machine
    b. Inner tubes and other flotation equipment
    c. Harness belt and resistance lines
    d. Rubber diving demonstrator

e. Motion picture equipment

f. Movies of swimmers and divers

11. Secure printed material for meets and training:

    a. Judges' and timers' cards

    b. Scoring forms

    c. Divers' individual score sheets

    d. Diving announcers' cards

    e. Duties of officials

    f. National record application blanks

    g. Training and conditioning rules

    h. Flexibility exercises

    i. Pool regulations

    j. Folding printed postal cards requesting official services for meets

    k. Release forms for parents of minors

    l. Printed schedules for distribution

    m. Eligibility statements for the conference or league

12. Establish eligibility and system for following athletes' scholastic progress.

13. Prepare a list and contact prospective officials.

14. Arrange for publicity such as news service and photography.

15. Prepare form for preparation of individual achievement record of potential team members for swimming guide and all-American selection.

16. Arrange for pool seating facilities such as chairs, benches, tables, bleachers, and so on.

17. Refurbish surface lane markers, diving boards and fulcrums, starting platforms, and backstroke handrail starting blocks.

18. Review home schedules of other sports for possible conflicts to make certain visiting team rooms are available.

19. Draw up contracts with scheduled teams.

Things to do one week before a meet

1. Notify visiting team coach as to date and hour of meet and to send his entries of eligible men, photos for program and publicity purposes. List hours and days pool will be available for practice.

2. Print program.

3. Mail folding postal cards to prospective officials.

4. Procure eligibility list of own team members from eligibility chairman.

5. Notify equipment manager to have all equipment ready and supply him with a list of eligible competitors for suiting-up purposes.

6. See that equipment manager makes necessary arrangements to have all equipment available for the meet.

7. Conduct time trials.

8. Make the following arrangements if meet is away from home:

    a. Arrange for hotel and transportation reservations.

    b. If transportation is by auto, insure cars by semi-school bus clause and insure each member by travelers' insurance.

    c. If special menus are required, make advance arrangements with hotels and railroad diners.

    d. Notify coach when pool is desired for practice upon arrival before meet.

    e. Pass list of team making trip, its itinerary, hotel, time of departure, arrival, and return home.

    f. Notify faculty the number of days students will be absent on trip.

    g. Have each member of team arrange with his instructors for make-up of any work, papers, or tests missed.

9. Make the following arrangements if meet is at home:

    a. Arrange for towels and dressing facilities for visiting team.

    b. Assist visiting team in obtaining transportation from depot to hotel and pool, and so on.

10. Notify referee of time of meet.

Things to do the day of the meet

1. Check officials' list of all officials who will be available from returned cards.
2. Arrange tables, chairs, and benches around pool for officials and competitors.
3. Arrange with visiting coach for his team practice.
4. Compile kits for all officials and coaches.
5. Lay out record application blanks.
6. Arrange for distribution of programs.
7. Set up and test public address system.
8. Arrange starting platforms.
9. Adjust temperature of pool to 75° F.
10. Close scum gutter drains and fill pool to scum gutter level.
11. Arrange surface lanes.
12. Set up the scoreboard.
13. Test pool lighting and ventilation.
14. Inspect bleachers for safety.
15. Check springboard and matting for possible defects.
16. Lay out catch rope and finish rope.
17. Procure 100 towels for attendants.
18. Install comb and mirror for divers.
19. Notify equipment manager to issue suits, supporters, and sweatsuits to the team, and provide him with list of members to be suited.
20. Arrange for trainers, rubbers, massage tables, and team physician.
21. Appoint custodian of equipment (stop watches, gun, clipboards, prizes, rubber bands, paper clips, and so on).
22. Appoint ticket takers and ushers with programs.
23. Obtain sharp pencils, extra 3 × 5 inch

Table 23-1. Officials' kits

OFFICIAL	NUMBER OF KITS	ITEMS
Coaches	2 or more	Clipboard and pencil; scratch paper; twelve 3 X 5 inch cards; program; list of officials; 2 individual diving score sheets; rule book
Referee (starter)	1	Program; pencil; 2 guns; 2 boxes of cartridges; whistle; rule book; list of officials showing position of judges and timers
Chief finish judge	1	Nine programs; 9 pencils; 100 judges; finish cards; 1 list of officials; 1 whistle
Chief timer	1	Five programs; 16 stop watches, checked and synchronized; 4 pencils; 50 timers' cards; 1 list of officials
Clerk of course	1	Clipboard and pencil; 1 program; 1 list of competitors; 1 list of officials; 1 whistle
Scorer	1	Clipboard; scratch paper; score sheet; 4 pencils; program; record application blanks; list of officials; rule book
Diving clerk	1	Four pencils; diving scoring table; calculator; rule book
Announcer	1	Clipboard and pencil; scratch paper; program; list of officials; information about competitors and records; whistle
Diving judges	3 or 5	Set of flash cards and program
Slap-off judges	4 or 6	Raincoat and towel; program
Inspectors of turns	4 or 6	Program; list of competitors
Scoreboard clerk	1	Program; chalk; eraser
Official scorer of meet	1	Program; score sheet
Student managers	3	Program; handy men to see that equipment is placed at proper time and see that meet runs smoothly

cards, a ream of scratch paper, rule books, and diving calculator.

24. Notify press and photographers through publicity department.

OFFICIALS' KITS

The kits listed in Table 23-1 should be made up and presented to each official upon his arrival before the meet. The kits should be collected by a manager at the end of the meet.

PREPARATIONS FOR A CHAMPIONSHIP MEET

A list of officials and duties of managers and officials is presented. These duty summaries can be copied onto cards for distribution before the meet.

Officials for championship meet*

1. One swimming referee, one starter, one assistant starter, one diving referee, one announcer, one associate announcer, and one diving announcer
2. One head judge, one assistant head judge, and two judges for each lane
3. One head timer, one assistant head timer, and four timers for each lane, one of which is designated as an alternate in the event that one of the official watches fails to function; one member to serve as takeoff judge on relays.
4. Five diving judges
5. One clerk of course and one assistant clerk of course
6. Six inspectors of turns, two storke judges
7. The following officials at the scoring table: chief recorder, record keeper verifier, card recorder, assistant recorders
8. Three computers and recorders at the diving table
9. Score board operator and assistants
10. Two false start rope attendants
11. One flip charts operator for each lane; charts indicate swimmers' time to the spectators
12. Runners to deliver finish cards to scorers' table
13. Meet physician and trainers

Duties of manager for league championship meet

1. Send circular letter to all participating coaches announcing conduct of meet arrangements as follows:
   a. Hotel accommodations and rates
   b. Dormitory housing if possible and rates
   c. Best eating accommodations
   d. Towel and locker arrangements
   e. Restate deadline for entries to be in
   f. Request publicity materials—photos, mats, records of teams and individuals
   g. Request time of arrival by auto, railroad, or bus by visiting team
   h. Notify coach to bring stop watches, white duck pants, and so on.
2. Send out entry forms for all events, receive entries, and collect entry fees.
3. Make arrangements through publicity department for program containing league, national, and world's records as well as interesting pictures of past or defending champions and entries for each event.
4. Make arrangements for adequate locker, towel, training, rubbers, and training room facilities.
5. Check with athletic manager for local schedule conflicts with date of league championships.
6. Erect adequate scoreboard for team totals.
7. Order appropriate league medals and trophies.
8. Arrange for an appropriate room for coaches' meeting.
9. Arrange for a very good public address system and an operator.
10. Arrange for a special dressing room for officials and coaches.

*See NCAA and AAU current rule changes.

11. Arrange for a lounging room for officials and coaches.
12. Notify press and radio.
13. Scratch box and notification of scratch deadline for each day's events.
    a. Assist referee and meet committee with drawing up heats, and so on.
    b. Have secretary at meeting to list heats.
    c. Have pool-bottles with numbers up to 25.
    d. Get each competitor's selected dives and order of performance from each coach.
    e. Have scratch paper and pencils available at meeting.
    f. Have duplicator and operator ready to rush through copies of heats for coaches and all officials.
    g. Pass out contestants' and officials' pass tickets to meet.
    h. Make announcements if necessary.
    i. After final selection of all officials (judges of finish, timers, slap-off judges, referee, starter, inspectors, and diving judges), have copies made for all officials and coaches.
    j. Have programs available, two for each coach and one for each of his competitors.
    k. Have original entry lists available at this meeting.
14. Check over all equipment items necessary to conduct meet and have them in readiness.
15. See that meet runs smoothly and efficiently throughout the competition.
16. Have filter operator make a final check on water temperature and see that the pool water is level with overflow gutter.
17. Have several student managers always available to remove and replace equipment whenever needed.
18. After meet have money ready to pay officials.
19. After meet make report of meet, including names of officials, competitors, and institutions, summary of the meet and split times of each event, judges of diving, scores of each dive, and the team total standing.
20. Prepare a financial report showing all guarantees, gross income of meet, receipts of expenditure, and so on.

Duties of referee

1. The referee has full jurisdiction over the meet and sees that all the rules are enforced.
2. He presides at the coaches' drawing and scratch meeting.
3. He examines each entry in the meet for eligibility.
4. He designates time of redrawing of heats and lanes after preliminary heats.
5. He assigns each official and instructs him as to his particular duty.
6. He decides all questions relating to the actual conduct of the meet. He may call on the meet committee to assist him in arriving at a decision.
7. He makes final settlement of any question or problem not covered in the rules.
8. He signals the starter that judges, timers, and inspectors are in position before each start.
9. He disqualifies competitors for any violation of the rules that he personally observes.

Duties of the starter. The starter has full control of the competitors from the time they have been assigned to their proper positions by the clerk of course until after the signal to start has been given. Before starting each heat or race, he first receives a signal from the referee that all other officials are in designated positions. He takes a position where timers can see the gun flash and competitors can hear the report. Before each heat or race he explains the following to each competitor:

1. The signal to be given to start the race
2. The distance to be covered
3. The number of laps
4. At which turn the "gun-lap" will be

given (Usually in longer races the gun warning is given two lengths before the race ends.)

5. Where the race will finish
His further duties include:

1. He makes sure he has at least three shells in his gun. (For indoors, a .22 caliber, and for outdoors, a .32 caliber.)
2. He also sees that the two officials are in place with the recall rope placed at 30 feet from starting station.
3. He has jurisdiction over false starts. (See start rule in AAU and NCAA rule books.)
4. In case the gun is improperly discharged, he calls back all competitors at once by pistol shot, and the recall rope is lowered to the surface of the water.
5. If pistol is properly discharged and any competitor or competitors have obtained an unfair advantage at the start, he recalls all competitors by pistol shot and indicates the competitor or competitors to be charged with the false start.
6. A false start is charged to any or all competitors if they leave their mark before the pistol has been fired or if a competitor is deliberately slow in taking his mark after the signal is given.
7. When a competitor is disqualified by false starts, this counts as an event for the competitor.

ELECTRONIC TIMING AND JUDGING MACHINES

There are various types of judging and timing devices on the market today. The type that utilizes the starting pistol to activate the mechanism and a touch plate in each lane to record the finish has completely eliminated human error in deciding a race. Practically all championship events use some form of electronic timing and judging mechanism. A back up, or secondary timing and judging system, is normally employed in case of mechanical failure. Skilled personnel should be selected to in-

terpret the machine results to eliminate human error in recording.

Ballot system. The ballot system is the fairest known method of selecting the official finish of a swimming race. Each of the two judges assigned to a lane has one ballot, and the official timer for that lane has another ballot, all three of equal value. The ballots for each lane are recorded and added. The swimmer having the lowest total ballot is designated as the winner of the heat. The second lowest total is second, and so on. A tie ballot remains a tie for the given place. In determining the ballot based on official time, the fastest recorded time receives a ballot of one, the second fastest a two, the third fastest a three, and so on. The ballot system is described in detail in the NCAA and AAU swimming guides.

Judges. Two lane place judges are assigned to each lane and are placed on opposite sides of the pool. Each judge determines independently where the contestant in his lanes finishes in the race and records it on the card provided for that purpose. The judge must not record a tie. Each judge must record the highest place in his lane contestant actually may have attained. For example, if a lane judge determines that the contestant in his lane has finished in a tie with another contestant for first place, he shall record a first place (1) for his lane, and the same procedure applies to similar situations involving other place positions.

A "runner" is assigned to pick up each lane judge's card immediately after each race and deliver to the scoring table.

Duties of timers. In any race the time is taken by three official timers and an alternate for each lane. They start their watches with the gun flash and stop them at the instant any part of the competitor in that lane touches the finish line. The index finger is used in starting and stopping the watch. The times registered on the three official watches for each lane are written on the card held by the head timer on the lane.

The alternate watch is never used except when one of the official timers' watches has ceased to function. If a record has been made, the watches are shown to the chief timer for inspection. The official time for that race is the one in which two or more watches agree. If all three watches disagree, the intermediate watch is the official time regardless of how much the three watches disagree. The three watches must never be averaged for the official time. If only two watches remain running at the end of a race and they disagree, the watches are averaged to the slowest one tenth of a second.

Duties of the chief timer

1. He assigns three timers and one alternate to each lane, one of these official timers to serve as head timer of that lane.
2. He supplies each head timer on each lane with cards upon which he records on its face the event, heat number, lane number, and the three official times. Throughout the race, he will also record on the back of this card the lap split times. The alternate watch is normally used for this purpose.
3. He collects all cards from all lane head timers, checks each card for errors, and then gives times to the official scorer.
4. He will designate one member of the timing team to serve as takeoff judge on relays for each lane. This judge will determine whether both feet of the second, third, and fourth contestants are still in contact with the starting mark when the preceding teammate touches the end of "the pool." He shall station himself in such a position that he can see the end of the pool and have his little finger in light contact with the little toe of the contestant. An illegal takeoff is reported to the referee and results in the disqualification of the relay team.

It will be noted that in championship races timers are placed at every lane, thus eliminating three official timers for the winner of either the heat or the final race of the qualifiers through the heats. The timers are stationed directly over their lane and can accurately judge the hand touch to the finish line, except in races that end in the open water with a pennant curtain held as a finish line. In such cases, the timers stand at the sides of the finish lines. When any part of the swimmer's body strikes the pennant curtain line or passes through this line, the timers stop their watches.

Duties of inspectors. For a six-lane pool, there should be at least one inspector for every two lanes. One or two inspectors placed opposite the finish end of the pool is entirely inadequate and unsatisfactory. It is humanly impossible to observe more than two lanes, especially if competitors happen to turn simultaneously. The inspector observes the rules of the turn and touch of all events, heats, and races and reports any infraction to the referee immediately at the end of the race. He keeps a record of the number of turns and reports which turn was violated.

Duties of clerk of course. The clerk of course should have at least two assistants and is provided with a list of the competitors with heats and lanes already drawn. He notifies each competitor to appear at the starting line and in the proper lane before the start of each race. He controls his assistants and assigns to them such duties as will assist in the prompt dispatch of the meet.

Duties of the scorer. He records the order of finish and the times of each heat in all events as given him by the head judge and head timer. He records disqualifications as given him by the referee. He keeps a running score of the meet. He also acts as clerk of the dives and records their results.

Duties of the announcer. Before the start of each event, he announces the event, the number of heats, and the method of qualifying, and at the start of each heat he announces the lane, the name of each competitor, and school or club affiliation. Immediately after the finish of each heat he announces the results as given him by the scorer. He makes any other announcements as requested by the referee or the management. He should be provided with a public address system. His enunciation should be slow, clear, and distinct.

Duties of the clerk of records. He is cognizant of all times performed in the meet. If any time might equal or break a national or world record, he should have available record application blanks. He should secure in ink the signatures of the referee, three judges, three timers, and the times of each timer opposite his signature and the certification of an engineer of the exact length of the course. The referee shall then give it final approval. This is then sent to either the NCAA or the AAU chairman of the records committees for final acceptance or rejection.

Duties of the physician. He is present throughout the championship competition and is prepared to examine any competitors requiring such service. If a competitor becomes ill after the drawing for heats is closed, he must be examined by a physician. Otherwise, if not really ill, the competitor may suffer the consequences of being disqualified from further competition and may lose all honors previously won in the championship.

Duties of the press steward. He obtains the names of all competitors in each event from the scorer and obtains the results of the heats and place winners in the final races. He keeps the press informed of the competition throughout the championships.

Duties of diving officials. The NCAA, the AAU, and the FINA rules are now identical in the rules and regulations governing the conduct of a championship diving contest. Since methods of marking and the duties of the diving referee, the judges, and the diving clerks are specifically and identically described in all three rule books of the above named organizations, no further explanation will be given here.

SUMMER AGE-GROUP SWIMMING MEET

The planning and organization for a summer age-group swimming meet is very important to ensure a smooth operation on the day of the contest. A good swimming meet demands that it start on time and finish near the time designated for it to end. For this to happen, the people conducting the meet must be well informed as to their duties. The visiting competitors, coaches, and guests have a right to expect adequate information, correct times, and all material needed to swim the events with ease.

The first procedure to follow in planning an age-group swimming meet is to form a group of persons to do the planning of the meet. This group normally consists of parents of young competitive swimmers who organize and form a local swim club. They should meet several months in advance of the contest and select a meet manager who has had some experience in the swimming world or one who will take time to study what it entails. When considering the date of the meet, it is wise to be sure there is not another meet in the area, because this will cut down on the number of entries. After this meeting the respective members must be aware of the time schedule indicating when different tasks should be done. This group must select the program of events to be contested (Table 23-2). They may consider enlisting the aid of a sponsor for the meet such as the Chamber of Commerce, the local newspaper, or a local service club.

The following committee chairmen should be selected by the meet manager:
1. Officials
2. Supplies
3. General help
4. Awards
5. Publicity
6. Clean-up
7. Food
8. Entries and programs

Officials

Every effort should be made to obtain experienced personnel to fill the key official assignments: the referee, starter, chief judge, chief timer, clerk of course, head recorder, and announcer.

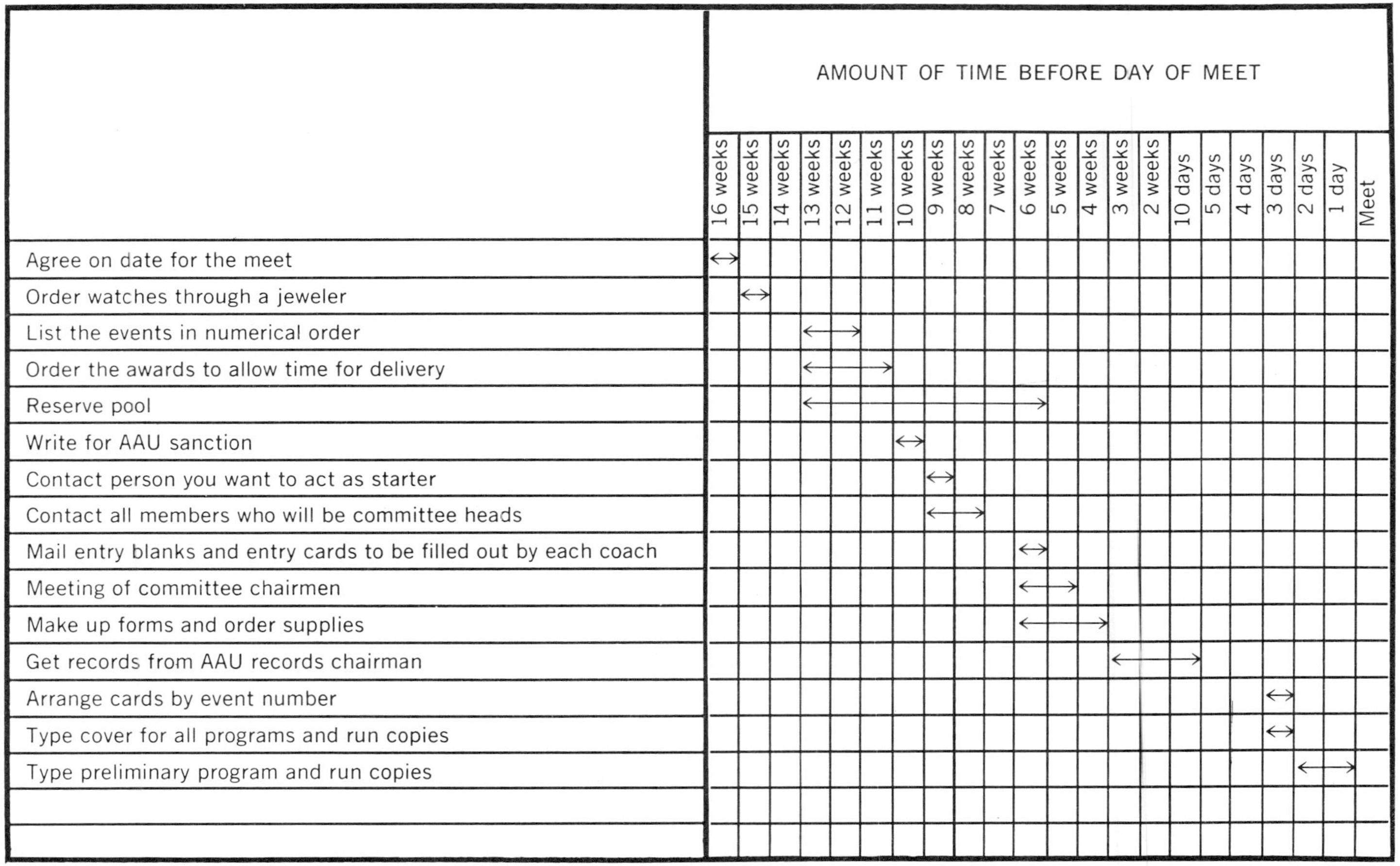

AMOUNT OF TIME BEFORE DAY OF MEET

Task	16 weeks	15 weeks	14 weeks	13 weeks	12 weeks	11 weeks	10 weeks	9 weeks	8 weeks	7 weeks	6 weeks	5 weeks	4 weeks	3 weeks	2 weeks	10 days	5 days	4 days	3 days	2 days	1 day	Meet
Agree on date for the meet	↕																					
Order watches through a jeweler		↕																				
List the events in numerical order				↕																		
Order the awards to allow time for delivery				↕																		
Reserve pool				↕																		
Write for AAU sanction							↕				↑											
Contact person you want to act as starter								↕														
Contact all members who will be committee heads									↕		↑											
Mail entry blanks and entry cards to be filled out by each coach											↕											
Meeting of committee chairmen												↕										
Make up forms and order supplies											↕		↑									
Get records from AAU records chairman														↕		↑						
Arrange cards by event number														↕								
Type cover for all programs and run copies														↕								
Type preliminary program and run copies															↕							

Fig. 23-1. A suggested time chart to assist a summer meet director.

Table 23-2. Suggested schedule of events

1. 7 and 8 100-yard medley relay
2. 9 and 10 200-yard medley relay
3. 11 and 12 200-yard medley relay
4. 13 and 14 200-yard medley relay
5. 15 and 17 200-yard medley relay
6. 7 and 8 25-yard freestyle
7. 9 and 10 50-yard freestyle
8. 11 and 12 50-yard freestyle
9. 13 and 14 50-yard freestyle
10. 15 and 17 50-yard freestyle
11. 11 and 12 200-yard individual medley relay
12. 13 and 14 200-yard individual medley relay
13. 15 and 17 200-yard individual medley relay
14. 7 and 8 25-yard butterfly
15. 9 and 10 50-yard butterfly
16. 11 and 12 50-yard butterfly
17. 13 and 14 100-yard butterfly
18. 15 and 17 100-yard butterfly
19. 11 and 12 100-yard freestyle
20. 13 and 14 100-yard freestyle
21. 15 and 17 100-yard freestyle
22. 7 and 8 25-yard backstroke
23. 9 and 10 50-yard backstroke
24. 11 and 12 50-yard backstroke
25. 13 and 14 100-yard backstroke
26. 15 and 17 100-yard backstroke
27. 7 and 8 25-yard breast stroke
28. 9 and 10 50-yard breast stroke
29. 11 and 12 50-yard breast stroke
30. 13 and 14 100-yard breast stroke
31. 15 and 17 100-yard breast stroke
32. 7 and 8 100-yard freestyle relay
33. 9 and 10 200-yard freestyle relay
34. 11 and 12 200-yard freestyle relay
35. 13 and 14 200-yard freestyle relay
36. 15 and 17 400-yard freestyle relay

The official chairman may delegate the responsibility of securing the timers to the chief timer and the judges to the chief judge. The judges and timers should be supplied with a mimeographed, detailed explanation of their duties, the time to report to the pool, and the recommended attire. Provisions should be made for relief timers and judges when a long meet is anticipated.

When there are several hundred entries in the meet, it has proved successful to provide two complete sets of officials, one set at each end of the pool. It is then possible to alternate the start of each heat at one end of the pool and then at the other, resulting in the start of a heat before the other is actually finished.

Clerk of course. The clerk of course and his assistants are responsible for lining up the contestants in their proper heats. The clerk should have one heat on the starting blocks, the next in proximity ready to move to the starting blocks, and the next several heats seated on benches ready to move forward. He must have the cooperation of the announcer who assists him by calling up the contestants at the proper times to keep the meet moving.

Head recorder. The head recorder will need several helpers and will work with the referee. He will keep track of scores and finish places of all contestants.

Announcer. The announcer will announce each event before it starts and tell the name of the contestant, lane number, and the club affiliation. He should also announce the results given him by the recorder.

Supplies

Special supplies are needed for each of the officials and their assistants, according to their individual duties, and are listed as follows:

Referee
1. A rule book that is up to date
2. A chair

Starter
1. Two guns
2. Shells
3. Bull horn
4. Assistant to fill gun

Judges
1. Benches on each side of the pool at the finish line
2. Judges' cards
3. Pencils
4. Cover to put over the judges' benches to keep the sun off

Timers
1. Chair for each timer to rest between events
2. Watch for each timer

3. Pencils
4. Clipboards for each timer or at least for official timer
5. Whistle for head timer
6. Table for head timer
7. If possible, cover for them so that they may keep out of the sun

Clerk of course

1. Table to seat three
2. Three chairs
3. Benches for three groups of contestants
4. Box with entry-time cards in order of events

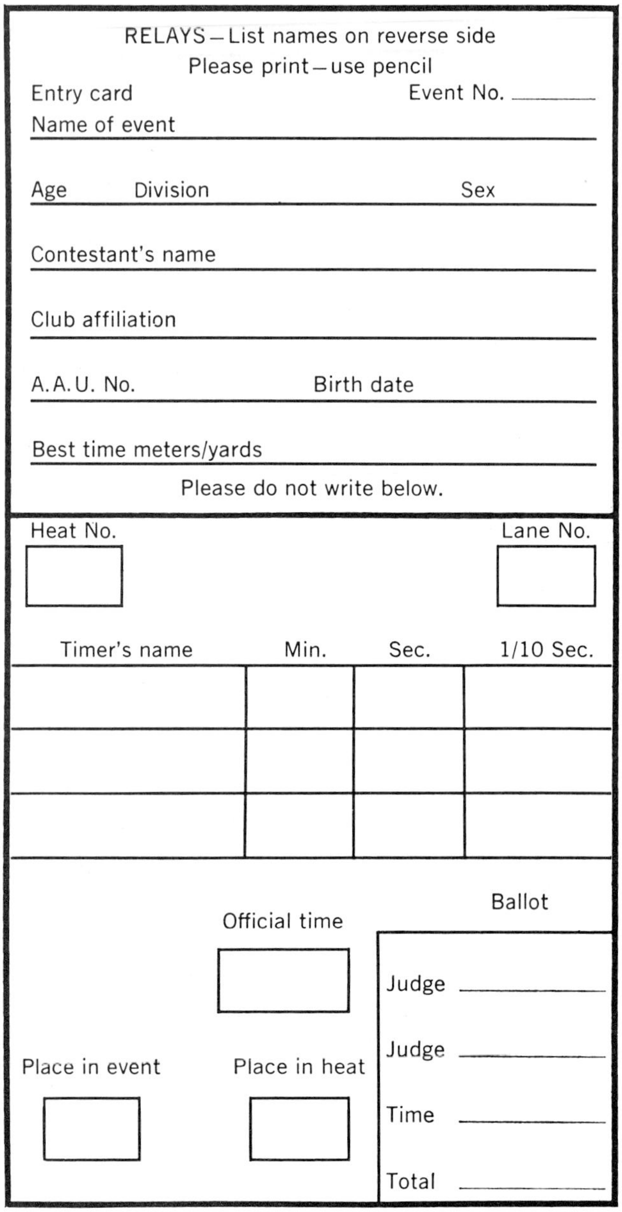

RELAYS — List names on reverse side
Please print — use pencil

Entry card   Event No. _____

Name of event _____

Age   Division _____ Sex _____

Contestant's name _____

Club affiliation _____

A.A.U. No. _____ Birth date _____

Best time meters/yards _____

Please do not write below.

Heat No.			Lane No.
Timer's name	Min.	Sec.	1/10 Sec.

Official time

Ballot

Judge _____
Judge _____
Time _____
Total _____

Place in event   Place in heat

Fig. 23-2. Suggested time card.

5. Pencils
6. Towels
7. Cover for other contestants

Recorder
1. Covers for tables
2. Two large tables
3. Twelve chairs
4. Pencils
5. Rubber bands
6. Shoe boxes to put cards in order of events
7. Tissues
8. Ash trays
9. Fly spray
10. Aspirin
11. Four typewriters
12. Stencils and correction fluid
13. Mimeograph machine and ink
14. Stapler and staples
15. Redi-forms
16. Legal-size paper for mimeograph
17. Scotch tape for runners to post results
18. Band-Aids

Announcer
1. P. A. system
2. Table (near recorder)
3. Chair

Clean-up
1. Truck
2. Garbage cans for each area of swimmers

Food for officials
1. Ice and ice chest
2. Cups and spoons
3. Coffee
4. Tea (instant)
5. Sugar and cream
6. Large coffee pot
7. Rolls, doughnuts, and sandwiches
8. Serving table
9. Chairs for workers

Miscellaneous
1. Lane markers
2. Two chairs for turn judges
3. Plenty of towels for workers
4. Bleachers for spectators
5. Tables for persons selling patches

6. Table for person disbursing officials' ribbons or pins
7. A rubber mat and a baby swim pool at gate where swimmers enter and leave the pool area.

General help

Assistant meet manager
Person to help starter fill gun
A physician engaged for the day
Runners
1. Two for timers and alternates
2. Two for judges and alternates
3. One to post results
4. One to take results to awards chairman
5. One to do general errands
6. Gatekeepers
7. Persons to hand out programs
8. Persons to sell badges

Awards

The awards chairman will order the awards at least three months in advance of the meet day. He should have an area on the deck of the pool or the office of the pool as his headquarters. The office of the pool is best because the contestants cannot get to him. He will need at least one helper to do an efficient job.

Publicity

The publicity chairman will be responsible to advertise the meet in the newspaper, on the radio and television. He may ask the press to come on the day of the meet to take pictures. He must also turn in the final results to all the news media.

Clean-up

The clean-up committee is very important. If the park and pool area are left cluttered, it will not be easy to get the facilities the next year. It is wise to have about ten persons who will keep picking up during the day. The announcer can help by asking persons not to throw waste around and to pick up before leaving. After the meet, everything should be put in a truck and the area should be left clean.

Food

A group should be selected by the chairman to have food and drink for the workers. If possible, it may be wise for a group to run a concession stand to make money for the club. The number of workers needed will be gauged by the size of operation that the chairman decides to have.

Entries and programs

The coach will send blank entry cards to the invited clubs, and these will be returned with the names, times, and affiliations of the contestants. All these entry cards have to be processed after the deadline, which is about a week before the swim meet. A force of at least ten persons will meet on the Wednesday or Thursday before the meet to put these cards in order according to the times and heats. The cards are then sent to the persons typing the programs who may be the recreation office, chamber of commerce, hired personnel, or volunteer helpers. The night or two before the event, a group will have to staple these programs together. Be sure someone is responsible for getting the programs to the meet and have someone in charge of giving them out or selling them. After the programs have been made up, the event cards (kept in order) are ready for the clerk of course. See that they get to the clerk of course in time for the scratch meeting.

Miscellaneous

Scratch meeting. This meeting is usually held within one hour before the meet. The coaches then have an opportunity to cancel out a contestant and substitute another. After the scratch meeting there can be no more changes.

Public relations. Public relations are a very important part of running an age-group swimming meet since the club or team is usually borrowing facilities. Some suggestions are as follows:

1. Send a letter to the park and recreation commission requesting the use of the pool.
2. Consult with the pool manager and tell him the layout of the meet. Ask him for extra help in the locker room on that day.
3. Meet with the manager of the concession stand to inform him about how many persons will be on hand that day and what kind of food the swimmers can eat. Ask for his cooperation.
4. Alert the park administrator and park policemen about the meet and ask them to reserve parking space for the meet manager, the ambulance (if one is to be on hand), and for several cars that may have to be used on errands.
5. Inform anyone who has anything to do with the facilities; otherwise they feel that the swimming group is trespassing.

Recorder's table

The efficiency of the recorder's table makes a great deal of difference in how fast and how well a swim meet is run. To make it possible to get all the times posted, the information to the announcer, and the places sent to the awards chairman, it is well to have plenty of help at the recorder's table. If possible, the head recorder should not do the actual scoring. He (she) should be available to answer questions from parents and coaches about times, to check on mistakes that are sometimes made by the workers, and to consult with the referee. If there is any difficulty, by being free, the recorder can pull the event, get the referee, and have this straightened out before the announcer or awards chairman gets the results. This prevents an award being given to a child who will later have to return it. All this can be done without stopping the meet.

There are many ways of setting up the scorer's table. Here is a suggested one.

There should be two large tables available for the recorder and his assistants. Seated at the first table, from left to right, in order, they should be as follows:

1. Judge and time card sorter
2. Heat ballot scorer
3. Arranger of all time cards in the event with the fastest time first
4. Announcer who will read the results directly from the cards
5. Typist who will make three copies of the first six places, listing place, name of swimmer, club or affiliation, and official time; typed copies go to the announcer, to be posted for contestants to see, and to the awards chairman.

It is wise for the front side of this table to be left empty.

At the second table, mimeographed results are made so that each coach, the records chairman, registration chairman, and AAU official may have one at the end of the meet. At this table there are two typists to cut stencils of the results of each event. One typist computes the odd number events and the other computes the even number events.

There should be a mimeograph machine on the table to run off the stencils. The finished copies of the results can then be put in piles during the meet. At the end of the meet they can be stapled together and handed out.

Index